MAO'S CRUSADE

Studies on Contemporary China

The Contemporary China Institute at the School of Oriental and African Studies (University of London) has, since its establishment in 1968, been an international centre for research and publications on twentieth-century China. *Studies on Contemporary China*, which is edited at the Institute, seeks to maintain and extend that tradition by making available the best work of scholars and China specialists throughout the world. It embraces a wide variety of subjects relating to Nationalist and Communist China, including social, political, and economic change, intellectual and cultural developments, foreign relations, and national security.

Series Editor

Dr Frank Dikötter, Director of the Contemporary China Institute

Editorial Advisory Board

Mao's Crusade

*Politics and Policy Implementation in
China's Great Leap Forward*

ALFRED L. CHAN

OXFORD

UNIVERSITY PRESS

OXFORD

UNIVERSITY PRESS

Great Clarendon Street, Oxford OX2 6DP

Oxford University Press is a department of the University of Oxford.
It furthers the University's objective of excellence in research, scholarship,
and education by publishing worldwide in

Oxford New York

Athens Auckland Bangkok Bogotá Buenos Aires Cape Town
Chennai Dar es Salaam Delhi Florence Hong Kong Istanbul Karachi
Kolkata Kuala Lumpur Madrid Melbourne Mexico City Mumbai Nairobi
Paris São Paulo Shanghai Singapore Taipei Tokyo Toronto Warsaw

with associated companies in Berlin Ibadan

Oxford is a registered trade mark of Oxford University Press
in the UK and in certain other countries

Published in the United States
by Oxford University Press Inc., New York

British Library Cataloguing in Publication Data

Data available

Library of Congress Cataloging in Publication Data

Chan, Alfred L.
Mao's crusade : politics and policy implementation in China's great leap forward /
Alfred L. Chan.
p. cm.—(Studies on contemporary China)
Includes bibliographical references and index.
1. China—Economic policy—1949–1976. 2. Guangdong Sheng (China)—Economic
policy. I. Title. II. Studies on contemporary China (Oxford, England)
HC427.9 .C476 2001   338.951'009045—dc21   00-068687

ISBN 0-19-924406-5

1 3 5 7 9 10 8 6 4 2

Typeset by Newgen Imaging Systems (P) Ltd., Chennai, India
Printed in Great Britain on acid-free paper by
Biddles Ltd.,
Guildford & King's Lynn

To My Parents

Preface

Several childhood memories from growing up in Hong Kong have left deep impressions on me. In the midst of the Great Leap Forward in 1960 I had the opportunity to visit my aunt on my first trip to a 'foreign' country—Xinhui County in Guangdong province. I remember the unfamiliar currency, and the fact that my aunt had to get up at 5 o'clock in the morning to queue up for a roast duck in order to serve her guests a superb dinner. I also remember her telling us that all window frames and even the loose screws in her sewing machine were requisitioned for the iron and steel campaign.

Back home in Hong Kong, my amah often posted parcels (wrapped in hand towels that were sewn together so that they could be reused) of food to the mainland, complaining all the time about the cost of the postage and the custom duty. Cooked rice that had been sun-dried was the staple because it weighed less. She would complain that chickens imported from China were no good, because they were all skin and bone. On the buses to school, the police would board occasionally to check for illegal migrants; several times people were led away, because the way they looked and dressed made them stand out. Indeed, at that time, I had little awareness of the fact that China was in the grip of the worst famine and devastation of the twentieth century during which millions perished.

The Great Leap Forward was a personal crusade of the flamboyant Mao Zedong, who had single-handedly cajoled, pushed, and browbeaten his colleagues, the more cautious planners, into the colossal economic and social experiment. Mao's irrationality, wishful thinking, and delusion of grandeur soon became infectious. The entire country was embarked on a massive and frenzied drive for industrialization and radical changes. Yet, as the characters in Marcel Pagnol's novels (an excerpt from the adapted screenplay is quoted below) indicate, extreme voluntarism and the misguided faith in human will-power are not unique to Mao and the Chinese. As political scientists have noted, decision-makers of both the rich and poor countries can be afflicted by the 'pathology' of decision-making—cognitive distortions, irrational consistency, 'groupthink', goal displacement, and wishful thinking. The difference is a matter of degree. Leaderships in poor countries are particularly susceptible to some kinds of grand 'transformative' visions that promise radical and rapid improvement of the livelihood of the population, given the immensity and urgency of the problems of economic backwardness and deprivation, and the need to legitimize the new regime. Yet, while misguided policies in a rich country may create costly white elephants, similar policy mistakes in poor countries may spell calamity for the entire population, because poor countries are much less able to cushion losses and spread risks. The disastrous consequences of the Great Leap Forward are a grave testimony to this fact.

A book that has taken so long to complete incurs many debts over the years, but it is a pleasure for me to acknowledge them. I am most grateful to three anonymous referees for advice and the encouragement to rethink the issues. One referee, in particular, provided detailed bibliographical guidance indispensable for the deepening of the analysis and for the completion of the book.

Research for the book has taken me to a number of libraries and the librarians' help has been invaluable. Nancy Hearst, the ever-resourceful and knowledgeable librarian at the Fairbank Center, Harvard University, provided assistance far beyond the call of duty to make my many stays at Cambridge a most pleasant experience. Jean Hung of the Universities Service Centre was always gracious and unwavering in her help. Anna U, Director of the East Asian Library, University of Toronto, has often been supportive. She also put together a grant that enabled me to purchase provincial newspapers on microfilm for my research. At the same university, the staff at the interlibrary loans department, Jane Lynch in particular, have been tireless and efficient in responding to my incessant requests for interlibrary loans. The librarians at the Hoover Institution (Stanford University), the School of Oriental and African Studies, UCLA, University of Chicago, Oriental Manuscripts Room (British Library), and the C. V. Starr East Asian Library (Columbia University), have made my sojourns there fruitful and enjoyable. I thank them all.

To my former teachers—Stuart Schram who got me interested in Mao and the Great Leap Forward, and Victor Falkenheim who inspired me in provincial politics—I owe a special debt of gratitude. I would like to thank my friends Ma Shu Yun, Kam Wing Chan, Kai Yuen Tsui, Lo Shiu Hing, Kevin Kelleher, Gregory Alexander, and Lesley Towers for their support and encouragement. Susanna Cheng and Richard Wang helped me to secure materials from China, and for this I am grateful. I am also thankful to my colleagues at Huron University College, Laura Wu, Jim Crimmins, Paul Nesbitt-Larkin, Neil Bradford, and David Blair for support and encouragement. At the University of Toronto the help from Don Schwartz, H. Gordon Skilling, the late Robert Fenn, and Michael Donnelly, are appreciated. I am thankful to Michael Frolic, David Zweig, and Michel Oksenberg for their interest at the various stages of research and writing of the book. Family friends who have shown keen interest in my project and provided companionship were Fanny Kato (and the late Nedda and Tristan Kato), and for this I am grateful.

At OUP, Rebecca Bryant ensured the expeditious processing of the manuscript, and John Callow did a splendid job of copy editing the manuscript with patience and care. Thanks are due to Don Hickerson, who applied his editorial skills and thoughtfulness to improve the flow of the presentation. Over the years, three Directors of the Contemporary China Institute have shown interest and support for the project. I would like to thank Richard Louis Edmonds and Robert Ash. Frank Dikötter, in particular, has been most supportive and expeditious in handling the manuscript.

Two fellowships from the Department of Political Science, University of Toronto, a research grant from the York University–University of Toronto Joint Centre on Modern Asia, and three travel grants from the Huron University College enabled me to complete the research. Finally, my warm appreciation goes to Michael Farewell for support, inspiration, encouragement, for reading several drafts of the book and offering many suggestions. It goes without saying that I am alone responsible for all errors in facts and interpretation in the text.

Alfred L. Chan

Toronto
November 2000

Contents

Abbreviations

APC	Agricultural Producers' Cooperative
CC	Central Committee
CCP	Chinese Communist Party
CPC	County Party Committee
FGHB	*Zhonghua Renmin Gongheguo Fagui Huibian* (A compendium of laws and regulations of the People's Republic of China)
FYP	Five-Year Plan
GLF	Great Leap Forward
GVAO	Gross Value of Agricultural Output
GVIO	Gross Value of Industrial Output
MA	Ministry of Agriculture
MM	Ministry of Metallurgy
MPC	Municipal Party Committee
NBCK	*Neibu Cankao* (Internal Reference)
NFRB	*Nanfang Ribao* (Southern Daily)
NJZWH	*Nongye Jitihua Zhongyao Wenjian Huibian* (A collection of important documents on agricultural collectivization)
NPAD	The Twelve-Year National Programme on Agricultural Development, 1956–67
NPC	National People's Congress
PPC	Provincial Party Committee
PPPC	Provincial People's Committee
RMRB	*Renmin Ribao* (People's Daily)
RMSC	*Renmin Shouce* (People's Handbook)
RWD	Rural Work Department
SC	State Council
SEC	State Economic Commission
SPC	State Planning Commission
XHBYK	*Xinhua Banyuekan* (New China Semi-Monthly)

The spring winds blows amid profuse willow wands,
  Six hundred million in this land all equal Yao and Shun,
    Crimson rains swirls in waves under our will,
      Green mountains turn to bridges at our wish.
        Gleaming mattocks fall on the Five Ridges heaven-high;
          Mighty arms move to rock the earth round the Triple River,
            We ask the God of Plague: 'Where are you bound?'
              Paper barges aflame and candle-light illuminate the sky.

Mao Zedong, *Farewell to the God of Plague* (July 1958)

JEAN: First, I'll plant some leeks, tomatoes, potatoes, chervil... That's an hour's work per day.

UGOLIN: A kitchen garden?

JEAN: Precisely. Next, I'll plan some high yield crops, vital for large-scale rabbit breeding.

UGOLIN: Large-scale? You mean big rabbits?

AIMEE: What we mean is ... hundreds of rabbits a month, if not thousands!

JEAN: No, Amiee, we'll stay within reasonable limits. Bring me my manual. You've raised rabbits, haven't you?

UGOLIN: I've got 6, and my uncle has 30.

JEAN: In spite of that ... You probably don't realize, how prolific these rodents are. Here, read this.

UGOLIN: I can read, but I don't understand numbers!

JEAN: Well, I do. It means with one pair of rabbits, a modern breeder can obtain within three years ... a monthly yield of 500 rabbits. But this expert warns that raising over 5,000 heads becomes a public health hazard. With 1,000 males and 5,000 females, a breeder would be overrun with 30,000 rabbits the first month, and 2 millions by the tenth month! A province or even a whole country could be wiped out by famine!

UGOLIN: Really?

AIMEE: Tell him about Australia!

Dialogue from the motion picture *Jean de Florette*, based on Marcel Pagnol's two novels, *The Water of the Hills: Jean de Florette* and *Manon of the Springs*, trans. W. Evan Heyningen (Berkeley: North Point Press, 1988).

1

Introduction: The Great Leap Forward (1958–1960)

During 1957 and 1958 Mao Zedong was seized by a vision that economic development in China could proceed rapidly in leaps and bounds by relying on improvisation and mass spontaneity, rather than moderately by the planned and gradual way pursued during the First Five-Year Plan (1FYP, 1953–7). Mao singlehandedly initiated the Great Leap Forward (GLF), pushing his views relentlessly, and his changing ideas and preferences shaped the momentous events of 1958 to 1960.

Although Mao's initial goal of 'overtaking Britain in fifteen years' (in total quantity of major industrial output, not per capita) was not entirely unrealistic, under political pressure the internal timetable became progressively shortened finally into only two years while numerous ambitious plans were continuously piled one onto another. Mao was confident that rapid economic development and social progress could be achieved by boosting production through mobilizing every Chinese to transform the country. By harking back to the mobilizational and guerrilla techniques of the revolutionary years, Mao thought he had discovered an original alternative to the Soviet model that China had copied during the 1FYP. Since the Leap was to be driven by the creative energies of the masses, technicians and specialists, including the Soviet experts, were sidelined. To further encourage zest in the entire population, the regime, for the first time, introduced a far-reaching administrative decentralization that challenged the centralist assumptions of the Soviet model.

As such, the GLF was a major watershed in the history of the People's Republic of China. Yet, it was both tragic and ironic that the collective euphoria, whirlwind development, and exhaustive mobilizational frenzy were largely responsible for plunging the country into an economic disaster from which it did not recover until 1965. Fully eight years were wasted in terms of economic growth and the cost of lost opportunity was enormous, considering that this major setback occurred when other Asian economies were experiencing their economic take-offs. Agricultural production plummeted for several years after 1958. The tremendous emphasis on steel production led to short-term surges in output (from 5.35m. tons in 1957 to 18.66m. tons in 1960), but then was followed by a full decade of decline. Moreover, the ubiquitous drive for steel was achieved at tremendous cost in terms of waste and sectoral imbalances. Light industry was a major casualty, resulting in acute shortages of daily necessities. Productivity, national income, and wages all declined. Budgetary deficits for the three years and the effort to cover them by printing more money led to inflationary pressure and high prices. A dramatic drop in living standards, aggravated by three years of natural calamities, led to widespread famine, starvation, demoralization, and suffering. The consequence was the most severe catastrophe of the twentieth century, as an estimated 15 to 46 million people perished during 1958–61.[1]

Politically, the GLF split the top leadership of the Chinese Communist Party (CCP), and the subsequent retrenchment from the GLF in the early 1960s was so bitterly controversial that it laid the roots of the Cultural Revolution that engulfed the country later on in the decade. In foreign relations, the Leap was among the catalysts that touched off the Sino-Soviet schism and the pull-out of Soviet assistance and experts in 1960 that made the break-up irreversible.

Such a critical, complex, and intriguing episode in Chinese political history raises important questions. Who or what was responsible for the GLF? What were the circumstances that made the GLF possible? What was the nature of Chinese politics in the late 1950s? How did the CCP whip up such a national frenzy? What was Mao's role in the campaign? Why did the GLF fail?

A pioneering study of Chinese politics before the 'Cultural Revolution' by Parris Chang has postulated that the decision-making process involved many participants, each pursuing his own vested interest, and each controlling some clout and resources. Disputes and dissension in the top leadership were common, and when the Politburo was deadlocked, the top leadership moved to the Central Committee for resolution. The bureaucracy did not always implement central directives and decisions automatically—it would block and modify central directives in order to subvert central intentions. In Chang's view, Mao was powerful, but his power was constrained and never absolute, as he was constantly being checked by colleagues who could thwart his wishes. His ability to assert himself fluctuated, and he did not always carry the day. To get his way or to overcome political constraints, he had to engage in 'politicking' and alliance building, appeal for 'outside' help, and coopt provincial leaders.[2] In retrospect, Chang has exaggerated the degree and impact of top leaders' opposition to Mao, and his analysis of 'Mao the constrained leader' and what he calls a 'pluralistic' policy-making process can no longer be adequately supported. Chang is right, however, to draw attention to the phenomenon of bureaucratic resistance (and one should add, citizen resistance) to the radical initiatives in the implementation process, but he does not sufficiently pursue it.

Among early studies of elite politics in the 1950s are Roderick MacFarquhar's two volumes on the origins of the Cultural Revolution. In the first volume, which

---

[1] For estimates of the death rate, see Basil Ashton, Kenneth Hill, Alan Piazza, and Robin Zeitz, 'Famine in China', *Population and Development Review*, 104 (December), 1984: 613–14; Jasper Becker, *Hungry Ghosts: China's Secret Famine* (London: John Murray, 1996); Dali L. Yang, *Calamity and Reform in China: State, Rural Society, and Institutional Change Since the Great Leap Famine* (Stanford: Stanford University Press, 1996), 37–8; *Zhonggong Dangshi Yanjiu*, 1997, 1–14; Thomas Bernstein, 'Stalinism, Famine, and Chinese Peasants: Grain Procurement during the Great Leap Forward', *Theory and Society* (May), 1984.

[2] Parris Chang, *Power and Policy in China*, 2nd and enlarged edn. (University Park: Pennsylvania State University Press, 1978).

focuses on the 1956 to 1957 period, MacFarquhar shares Chang's view that Mao was merely *primus inter pares* in the top leadership. In his opinion, Mao did not demand or command 'unquestioning obedience', and in the debates in the Politburo he could be defeated, ignored, and even humiliated. Other top leaders prevailed over Mao on a range of issues including the running of the economy, treatment of intellectuals, and Party rectification. In MacFarquhar's view, to overcome his 'weakness', Mao had to cultivate allies to push his cause.[3]

This picture of a Mao constantly being checked by his colleagues is no longer consistent with the findings of more recent research, but in his second volume devoted entirely to the GLF (1958–60), MacFarquhar is closer to the mark regarding Mao's role in the policy process. His evaluation changes somewhat by placing Mao in the centre of things, as the only one who could unite the leadership in launching the GLF, like a sergeant major bawling commands to his squad. And Mao's doubts about the more extreme aspects of the Leap later prompted a brief turnaround. Then again, at Lushan, he rallied the leadership to denounce and isolate Peng Dehuai solely for his critique of the Leap. The Leap was then revived, only to be abandoned again soon after. Unfortunately, this study, which was based only on documentation available in the 1980s, had of necessity to paint major events in broad strokes, missing many telling subtleties. For instance, discussion of the policy-making conferences of the Third Plenum, and at Hangzhou, Nanning, and Beidaihe, is sketchy and often tentative, and Chen Yun is said to be taking a back seat in 1958.

These trail-blazing studies offer many insights and much thoughtful analysis, but they have become seriously dated by a large outflow of new materials from China, especially during the 1990s. These new materials have cleared up riddles, exposed misconceptions, and filled in many lacunas. Many assumptions and assertions made by the above authors can no longer hold water.[4]

More recently, an influential study by David Bachman tries to explain the origins of the GLF by referring to an intense struggle between two so-called 'grand coalitions' in Chinese politics, the 'finance coalition' and the 'planning and heavy industry coalition'. The latter, which Bachman claims, favoured mobilization of heavy industry at the expense of agriculture and light industry, gained the blessing of Mao, and its institutional interests became the development strategy of the GLF. Bachman argues that Mao, who was neither interested in nor knowledgeable about economic affairs, did not invent the GLF—he simply coopted the policy package most appealing to him.[5] As such, bureaucratic interests and positions are said to be primary in Chinese policy formulation.

---

[3] *The Origins of the Cultural Revolution, i. Contradictions Among the People, 1956–1957* (London: Oxford University Press, 1974); *The Origins of the Cultural Revolution, ii. The Great Leap Forward, 1958–1960* (New York: Columbia University Press, 1983).

[4] MacFarquhar's latest contribution, *The Origins of the Cultural Revolution, iii. The Coming of the Cataclysm, 1961–1966* (Oxford: Oxford University Press, 1997), which benefits from post-Mao material, takes the story to the 1960s, and in a reconsideration of the GLF, Mao is portrayed less as a unifying sovereign and more as a suspicious Olympian Jove ready to hurl thunderbolts at his colleagues.

[5] David Bachman, *Bureaucracy, Economy, and Leadership in China: The Institutional Origins of the Great Leap Forward* (Cambridge: Cambridge University Press, 1991).

This bold and innovative reinterpretation, unfortunately, is plagued by fundamental flaws in methodology and interpretation. No evidence exists to support that these coalitions existed, or that they were engaged in life-and-death struggles with one another. The reduction of Mao to a mere referee in the bureaucratic struggle is inconsistent with the facts. Moreover, Bachman's analysis focuses on the period from September 1956 to October 1957, arguing that the economic policies of the GLF had already coalesced by the spring and summer of 1957. This leaves out completely the direct and forceful intervention by Mao from the Third Plenum (September–October 1957) onward, which in our view, is crucial for explaining the GLF. The larger context or policy environment during the 1956–7 period was *fanmaojin* (opposing rash advance), a concerted effort by planners such as Zhou Enlai, Chen Yun, Bo Yibo, Li Fuchun, and Li Xiannian, to rein in the excesses of the first leap forward of 1956. In the same period the planners also attempted to chart the future of the country by drawing up the Second Five Year Plan (2FYP), 1958–62. Inevitably, there were disagreements and even debates among the planners, and competition and conflict among the bureaucratic actors. Yet, when Mao intervened forcefully in late 1957 and in early 1958, applying closure to the discussion, and taking over running the economy from the planners, he set in motion the forces that led inexorably to the GLF. The major policy cleavage was between Mao and the planners, not among the planners themselves. A clear advantage of Bachman's analysis is to draw attention to the different shades of opinion between the planners and the bureaucratic actors in 1956–7, but he ultimately fails to demonstrate that policy formulation for the Leap was the outcome of bureaucratic rivalry and conflict.[6] In fact, in a recent study on foreign policy, Bachman concedes that Mao was the 'undisputed leader' who 'had the last word on all issues', and that the 'pattern of absolute Maoist dominance' is demonstrated by his single-handed decision to overturn the Third Five-Year Plan in favour of building the Third Front.[7]

More recent researches by Frederick Teiwes and Warren Sun, aided by new documentation, have reaffirmed convincingly the centrality of Mao's dominance in post-1949 politics. Their penetrating analyses of the Gao Gang affair, agricultural collectivization in the 1950s, and the Lin Biao affair, show that Mao's dominance of the elite decision-making process was even more extreme than previously suggested. Politics under Mao, they argue, resembled 'court politics', and Mao's authority was unrivalled and unchallenged. On issues in which he was interested,

---

[6] For detailed critiques of Bachman's book, see Frederick Teiwes and Warren Sun, *China's Road to Disaster: Mao, Central Politicians, and Provincial Leaders in the Unfolding of the Great Leap Forward, 1955–1959* (Armonk, NY: M. E. Sharpe, 1999); Alfred L. Chan, 'Leaders, Coalition Politics, and Policy Formulation in China: The Great Leap Forward Revisited', *Journal of Contemporary China*, 8 (Winter–Spring), 1995. Key archival sources readily available since the 1970s, such as the several volumes of Mao's *Mao Zedong Sixiang Wansui* (Long live Mao Zedong's Thought) n.p. 1967a, 1967b, and 1969, had already cast doubt on Bachman's thesis. Bachman's rebuttal is in, 'Chinese Bureaucratic Politics and the Origins of the Great Leap Forward', *Journal of Contemporary China*, 9 (Summer), 1995.

[7] David Bachman, 'Structure and Process in the Making of Chinese Foreign Policy', in Samuel Kim (ed.), *China and the World: Chinese Foreign Policy Faces the New Millennium* (Boulder, Colo.: Westview Press, 1998), 37, 44–5.

he exerted the dominant influence. He always got his way if he so chose, and his words had to be obeyed. Although Mao's colleagues did on occasion articulate policy preferences and represent bureaucratic interests, they were more often passive and reactive to Mao's demands, and clearly secondary in affecting policy formulation. This situation was aggravated as a result of the 'Cultural Revolution' when the imperatives of the cult of personality severely limited the policy options that could be articulated, and politics degenerated into petty squabbles and palace intrigues divorced from real policy contents.[8]

After long-standing neglect, the subject of the GLF is beginning to receive the scholarly attention it deserves, especially with an outpouring of new source materials from China.[9] Teiwes and Sun's latest volume on the GLF is a sophisticated and insightful analysis of the Leap from 1955 to 1959, with epilogues covering the period from July 1959 to 1962.[10] This most up-to-date study, fortified by new documentary research and interviews with historians and former officials in China, focuses on the central decision-making process that involved participants from both Beijing and the provinces. It explores the origins of the GLF, and attempts to explain how the 'rational' economic policies of 1956–7 yielded to the fantastic policies of the Leap. In so doing, the authors debunk the myth of the 'two-line' struggle interpretation and other misconceptions fostered both by misinterpretation of leadership conflict and misapplication of institutional analyses. During the Leap, the authors maintain, Mao was determined to exert the utmost dominance by taking personal charge of the economy, and consequently became even more intolerant of dissenting opinions. This caused a fundamental change in the clout and role of other political players. Planners who pushed *fanmaojin* in the past were either sidelined or had no choice but to go along, offering no resistance. They were replaced by zealots who catered to Mao's illusions—provincial leaders, hotheaded and sober ones alike—who were closer to Mao's heart, and exerted a certain degree of influence with him. Bureaucratic politics were muzzled, as the key concern of the ministries had become less a pursuit of bureaucratic interest than a competition to demonstrate loyalty to Mao. Teiwes and Sun present instead a picture of a dominant and unchallenged Mao, surrounded by badgered or opportunistic leaders whose only option was to closely follow (*jingen*) the leader, even into disaster. Attempts by these leaders to discreetly influence a fickle and inconsistent Mao did little to rescue a system in paralysis. They raise important questions about the sources and

---

[8] Frederick Teiwes, *Politics at Mao's Court: Gao Gang and Party Factionalism in the Early 1950s* (Armonk, NY: M. E. Sharpe, 1990); Frederick Teiwes and Warren Sun (eds.), *The Politics of Agricultural Cooperativization in China, Mao, Deng Zihui, and the 'High Tide' in 1955* (Armonk, NY: M. E. Sharpe, 1993); eid., *The Tragedy of Lin Biao: Riding the Tiger during the Cultural Revolution, 1966–1971* (London: Hurst, 1996).

[9] Jean-Luc Domenach, *The Origins of the Great Leap Forward: The Case of One Chinese Province* (Boulder, Colo.: Westview Press, 1995); Alfred L. Chan, 'The Campaign for Agricultural Development in the Great Leap Forward: A Study of Policy-making and Implementation in Liaoning', *China Quarterly*, 129 (March), 1992. Michael Schoenhals, *Saltationist Socialism: Mao Zedong and the Great Leap Forward, 1958* (Stockholm: Institutionen for Orientaliska Sprak, University of Stockholm, 1987).

[10] Teiwes and Sun, *China's Road to Disaster*.

means of Mao's power, particularly when Mao was attempting to turn things around and when he was trying to maintain the upper hand.

Teiwes and Sun's study is the most accurate and perceptual portrayal of elite politics in the period under consideration, throwing light on a whole range of issues. We share their view of a Mao-dominated political process during that time. Our aim then in this book is to further develop the themes raised by Teiwes and Sun, expanding and substantiating those for which the new materials allow for even more nuanced analysis. We will concentrate on what we call the 'High Leap' of 1958, adopting a finer focus as a means to explore the policy process of the Leap in more detail.

On the theme of central decision-making, we are interested in the nature, characteristics, and degrees of Mao's dominance, and what made him such a formidable leader. Our assumption is that Mao's dominance was derived not just from his charismatic appeal, forceful character, and unshakable confidence, but also from his strategic and tactical manœuvres over his subordinates, a fact often unexplored. Moreover, Mao's role in the policy process from the end of 1957 to the autumn of 1958 was extraordinary and even unique. During this period, Mao single-handedly switched the country onto a totally different development course, browbeat his colleagues into submission, seized the running of the economy away from the planners, and aroused every Chinese citizen into a total mobilizational frenzy. In addition to the numerous ambitious and ever-rising targets promoted by him, he ordained very restrictive timetables by which policies were to be made and implemented. These self-imposed timetables called for overtaking Britain and even the USA in a few years, for fulfilling the requirements of the Twelve-Year National Programme for Agricultural Development (NPAD) in one year, and for doubling the iron and steel output for 1958 in the four remaining months of the year, to name just a few. The urgency and pressure-cooker atmosphere thus created approximated a crisis situation, bringing tremendous stress on every Chinese. Although the strategy of the Leap was to be repeated several times in the 1960s and 1970s, it was never to reach the feverish pitch as in 1958. In this book, we are interested in how policies were made in that period of the highest duress.

Other previously ignored but important dimensions of the Mao-dominated system are the way GLF policies were implemented, the way they turned out (policy outcome), and how policy outcomes and feedback affected the calculations of the decision-makers. Mao towered over his colleagues in decision-making at the centre and controlled as well the manner by which policies were implemented. But ultimately Mao was not omnipotent, and proved unable to control the final policy outcomes, and the failure of most Leap policies is a grave testimonial to this point. Indeed, any consideration of the central decision-making process would be incomplete without referring to policy implementation; much of it was intergovernmental, involving all levels of governments and administrative units.[11] In order to fully explore the

---

[11] Dennis J. Palumbo and Donald J. Calista, *Implementation and the Policy Process: Opening Up the Black Box* (New York: Greenwood Press, 1990), 182.

policy-making process, it is necessary to link central decision-making with the work of the implementation agencies, primarily the central ministries and the provinces.

Our intention in this book is to examine central decision formulation and policy implementation as integrated parts of the policy process. This gives us a new and broader perspective on Mao and the political process, the responsibilities of various leaders, and why the Leap failed. It also allows us to comment on the relevance or irrelevance of bureaucratic and institutional politics during the High Leap. In this way, attention will go, as it should, beyond Mao's thinking and motivation to encompass the roles of other key leaders in the 'inner court', including Mao's close advisers, as well as other institutional actors among the central bureaucrats and the provincial authorities. They should all be viewed as part and parcel of the policy-making process during the GLF. All this fills an important gap in our knowledge of the Great Leap Forward and the policy process under Mao.

Politics in a Leader-dominated System

As mentioned, Mao was the dominant force in post-1949 Chinese politics because of many factors, not the least of which were his forceful personality, his charismatic appeal, and his solid self-confidence. In central decision-making, Mao's dominance was manifested by his ability to prevail over his colleagues, to subdue them, and to manipulate them, against their better judgement, into willing and even enthusiastic supporters of his vision and policies. This was particularly true when Mao felt strongly about a certain issue, and had already made up his mind before consulting his colleagues. Above all, at those times when he was being driven by a utopian vision, as during the GLF and the 'Cultural Revolution', his dominance was especially pronounced. The breadth of Mao's dominance was made crystal clear by his ability, time and again, to inspire, to arouse, and to motivate virtually the entire Chinese population from the central bureaucracy down to the grass roots.

Yet, this does not mean Mao was omnipotent, and he did not always seek to dominate everything. There were times when he decided to lie low and did not assert himself. At other times he was keen on cooperating with other leaders, and even encouraged debates, according to the avowed principles of collective leadership. Often his mind had not been made up, so he did not always pronounce the last word, or he at least allowed his colleagues the benefit of the doubt. Issues he regarded as of lesser import, he often delegated to his subordinates, and the same applied to failed policies; he often left his colleagues to pick up the pieces. At times he was even willing to yield power and official positions, although becoming resentful of his colleagues for grabbing them a little too eagerly. Even on issues he regarded as important, Mao sometimes needed advice and inspiration, and often relied on others to give his evolving ideas substance, as well as to render him support and approval. Yet, in all these cases where Mao's colleagues were allowed a certain free rein or independence, they were later to be held accountable when Mao had either made up his mind or changed it.

Therefore, Mao's exercise of his influence was variable, depending on the environment and circumstances. Other leaders on occasion disagreed with him, and were sometimes able to push forward policies contrary to his inclinations and wishes, often thinking that they were consistent with the Chairman's objectives. During the retreat from the GLF in the early 1960s, when Mao was not taking charge of day-to-day affairs, his lieutenants still checked with him on major decisions.[12] Nevertheless, once he had made up his mind, and determined to interfere, Mao usually got his way. In this respect, it would be a mistake to view his temporary indecisions and lapses as manifestations of his 'weaknesses' or the signs of a 'collective leadership'.

This brings us to another important but neglected source of Mao's dominance—the constant tactical manœuvring he employed to maintain his strength and supremacy. Mao could not always rest on his laurels as both the Lenin and Stalin of the Chinese Revolution, or take his dominance for granted. Like all politicians, he needed aggressive and ongoing tactics to secure his power, to neutralize his opponents, and to get his policies accepted. His ability to define and redefine ideology, and to set the agenda, were primary among a whole range of manœuvres that were used to assure his unassailable position. In this book, we examine more closely Mao's tactics in the context of launching and promoting the GLF.

This view of Mao as a 'supreme leader' raises another question—why did the top leaders follow him and how did they do it? The matter of 'followership' is complex— there were the true believers, the loyal subjects, the opportunists—and there were the Leninists whose primary value was unity and party discipline. Others followed because of psychological self-denial or because they were under physical duress. This range of motivations is not exhaustive, but it does suggest why Mao was so often obeyed, revered, and followed, so that in crisis after crisis, few dared to blow the whistle. The few who dared—like Deng Zihui about collectivization, Zhou Enlai about *maojin*, and Peng Dehuai about the GLF—were either destroyed politically or converted to the Maoist cause. Moreover, during the Leap, and especially in 1958, passive following was not sufficient. Mao's colleagues were expected to actively participate and to creatively apply the Chairman's policy principles. Mao might have strong ideas about the Leap, but he also needed others for active encourage- ment and support, and for fleshing out his ideas. Mao did not invent all the Leap policies, and did in fact, rely on his lieutenants for many of these policy initiatives. What were the roles and contributions of these leaders to the Leap? This seldom investigated topic will be the other major concern of this book.

The Politics of Implementation in a Mao-dominated System

To further analyse Mao's dominance, let us for analytical reasons divide the policy process into central policy formulation and policy implementation. Mao could

---

[12] MacFarquhar, *The Origins of the Cultural Revolution*, iii. 469.

prevail upon his lieutenants and inspire and move millions of Chinese citizens, yet central decisions still had to be implemented by the bureaucracy, and this was by no means automatic. Government bureaucracies, governed by their own operational preferences and vested interests, display a range of behaviour which makes control difficult, and often frustrates central wishes, initiatives and directions. Policies that profoundly affect the lives of target groups, such as workers and peasants, may often be implemented only by draconian measures, and slippages cannot be fully avoided. Typically, a good deal of the implementers' energy goes into such activities as the evasion of responsibilities, scrutiny, and blame.[13] In China, although Mao dominated decision-making and determined the manner by which policies were to be implemented, he was unable to completely control the implementation process, to command the behaviour of the peasants, workers, and cadres, or to determine the policy outcome. Consequently, most Leap policies turned out to be utter fiascos.

Implementation researches have highlighted four important factors. First, a gap often exists between the setting of policy goals and the actual policy outcome. In fact, goal modification is unavoidable when implementers are encouraged to adapt by taking into account new situations and contingencies, and to continually refine the definitions of problems and solutions. This adaptive behaviour can be detrimental to the original goals, as discretion once granted cannot be entirely controlled. Second, policies can fail because of poor problem identification, bad policy design, and vague objectives, and not due to the faults in implementation alone. Third, implementers doing their job affect all stages of the policy process— agenda setting, problem identification, formulation, implementation, feedback, and evaluation. As they engage in continuous routine problem solving, they are thereby interpreting and influencing the direction policy is going. While devising routines, taking shortcuts and making decisions, they are actually reformulating and redesigning policy. In this way, implementers shape outcomes actively, at times even more so than the original policy designers. Finally, implementation, which takes place in a bureaucratic setting, is affected by a range of self-serving behaviour, which in turn is shaped by the political, social, and economic environment. Any adequate analysis of the policy process during the GLF must take these factors into account.

There is yet no detailed study of how the GLF was implemented, but the opening of this black box will reveal that much policy was made during implementation itself. By observing this period we are able to better understand the organizational and behavioural dynamics of the Chinese policy process in general. Indeed, the general phenomena of bureaucratic competition, 'tokenism', inertia, ritualistic behaviour, 'buck-passing', and so on, has always been prevalent in Chinese politics. The Chinese people themselves, of course, discuss the subject frequently, and this

---

[13] Eugene Bardach, *The Implementation Game* (Cambridge, Mass.: MIT Press, 1977), 85 and *passim*.

itself should be a valuable source of information.[14] Indeed, the kind of bureaucratic behaviour most often chosen depends on the context of the time. What was the implementation process like when the domineering Mao chose to run the economy himself? How were policies implemented when the planners were sidelined, the planning system destroyed, and when Maoist zealots came to the fore? In 1958, the imperative of closely following the leader and the tremendous pressure exerted on the bureaucracy transformed it in important ways, so the bureaucrats had to improvise new games or strategies to lessen the pressure, to evade responsibility and to ensure their own survival.

The existence of a large amount of new information and contemporary materials such as provincial and regional newspapers makes a better understanding of the implementation process possible. In the Chinese context, the approach discussed here will enable us to examine how the intense mobilization took place, and the manner by which goals or ideals were either realized or thwarted. In our opinion, this is the key to understanding why the Leap failed.

Power and Policy Dynamics during the High Leap of 1958

To explore these issues in more depth, this book focuses on policy formulation and implementation and the vertical linkages between the centre and the provinces in policy-making in 1958. This allows us to observe, in concrete terms, the interaction between the different levels of government and party organizations, especially within the context of mobilizational campaigns. Our examination of central decision-making focuses on Mao and the other national leaders. Since agricultural and rural development and the iron and steel campaign were the two centrepieces of the Leap, we explore the roles of two central ministries—the Ministry of Agriculture (MA) and the Ministry of Metallurgy (MM)—and how they promoted and implemented the GLF campaigns. At the regional level, we focus on Guangdong province and its role in the policy process.

The choice of the central ministries has several purposes: first, by treating them as components of the centre we explore the nature of the interaction between the centre and the province in a policy-making context; second, we examine their roles as bureaucratic actors in their own right; and third, we examine them as policy implementers. The provinces, on the other hand, were the chief agents for the

---

[14] In his *Inside Bureaucracy* (Boston: Little, Brown, 1967), Anthony Downs distinguishes five types of bureaucrats—climbers, conservers, zealots, advocates, and statesmen—who are motivated by different things and who display variable behavioural patterns, see pp. 88–91. Similar analysis and categories are made by the Chinese themselves. See, for example, Zhou Enlai, 'Oppose Bureaucratism', in *Zhou Enlai Xuanji* (Beijing: Renmin chubanshe, 1984), ii. 418–22. An almost identical version is, probably erroneously, attributed to Mao. See 'Chairman Mao Discusses Twenty Manifestations of Bureaucracy', in David Milton, Nancy Milton, and Franz Schurmann, *People's China* (New York: Vintage Books, 1974), 248–51. See also Francis Rourke, *Bureaucracy, Politics, and Public Policy*, 3rd edn. (Boston: Little, Brown, 1984).

execution of central policies, and our exploration of the ways in which Guangdong province carried out these policies not only throws light on the characteristics of policy-making, but allows us to test general propositions about central–provincial relationships in China. We believe that this multi-layered analysis best reflects the various dimensions of the GLF.

Why 1958?

It is customary to treat the GLF from 1958 to 1960 as a whole, although recent research has followed a more varied time scale and avoids such rigid periodization.[15] The GLF has commonly been divided into three distinct periods, with different emphasis in policy-making in each. The first period, from the Third Plenum of September/October 1957 to November 1958, can be called the High Leap, when the most radical policies and experiments of the Leap were introduced and implemented. This was followed by a second period of retrenchment lasting about eight months from November 1958 to July 1959 during which a partial retreat from the GLF was effected. The third period, from July 1959 to January 1961, was marked by another major attempt to push forward the GLF and ended with the official termination of the GLF strategy by the centre, although the ultimate abandonment of the Leap took much longer to complete.[16]

Other studies focus more narrowly on one province,[17] and more specialized studies are now needed so that important differences and nuances are not obscured. This book will focus on the High Leap of 1958 for several reasons. First, our interest is in how and why Leap policies were formulated and implemented so there is a need to probe deeper than has previously been done, as our objective is to scrutinize events on an almost day-to-day basis. Second, Mao's dominance reached its zenith between the spring and autumn of 1958, making for an extraordinarily intense policy process.[18] The voices of moderation were stifled, and normally pragmatic leaders such as Zhou Enlai and Deng Zihui suspended their doubts and disbeliefs to follow Mao, becoming most vocal and aggressive supporters of the Leap. They were responsible for whipping up much of the Leap fervour in 1958. Yet when Mao had changed his mind, they followed him gingerly in applying retreat policies in subsequent years. This allows many analysts, especially those in China, to gloss over what happened in 1958 and focus on the later period to cite the top leaders' alleged opposition to the Leap to clear their names, thus obscuring the issues.[19] Third, 1958 was the high point of the GLF with numerous

---

[15] Teiwes and Sun, *China's Road to Disaster*, focuses on 1955 to 1959, and discusses the period from July 1959 to 1962 in two epilogues.

[16] See for example, *Dangdai Zhongguoshi Yanjiu*, 2, 1995, 28–30.

[17] Domenach, *The Origins of the Great Leap Forward*; Chan, 'Campaign for Agricultural Development'. [18] Teiwes and Sun, *China's Road to Disaster*, 178.

[19] Examples will be noted throughout this book, because even the most reputable publishers in China continue to put out hagiographies. Suffice it to note here the most egregious examples of studies of Deng

campaigns and radical innovations, but it also witnessed the retreat and abandonment of some of the original goals of the movement, when Mao began to turn around. In addition, it was also a self-contained period in terms of the yearly production cycle. Normally, policy changes were occasioned by year-end production performance reports—agricultural performance figures were known in autumn, and industrial production figures, at the end of the year. Focusing on just one year enables us to examine policy-making closely, to explore in detail the nature of policy reversals and to compare policy objectives with policy outcomes. Broadly speaking, in significant ways, especially in policy innovations, 1958 *was* the GLF; in no single year during the 1949 to 1976 period had there been an attempt at such a colossal mobilization to achieve so much in so little time. We need to treat 1958, the year of unique and extreme radicalism, as seriously as the facts suggest.

To pursue the above themes, Chapter 2 of this book will explore policy for-mulation at the centre, tracing the origins of the GLF from 1955 to 1958, paying particular attention to the manner and tactics by which Mao laid down Leap policies. Chapter 3 focuses on the Ministry of Agriculture (MA) and its role in the policy process, since the Leap began with agriculture and later extended to rural institu-tional changes. Chapter 4 is a consideration of the Ministry of Metallurgy (MM) because iron and steel production was a centrepiece of the GLF effort. We discuss in detail how a burgeoning bureaucratic organization was transformed into a Maoist agent for radicalism and mobilization. Chapter 5 discusses the implementation of agricultural and rural policies in Guangdong, and how the province was bent and shaped according to the demands of the Leap. Chapter 6 explores the imple-mentation of the industrialization policies in Guangdong, and how they were eclipsed by the mandate to enforce the iron and steel campaign. Chapter 7 will conclude with a discussion of the policy process in 1958. Our analysis will draw extensively on material made available in the post-Mao era, especially that from the 1990s, but rely equally on archival materials in order to paint as accurately as possible the various dimensions of the GLF.

Xiaoping. Most of these note his saying that everyone, including himself, was hot-headed during the Leap, but details of what he did and said are always blank. See for example, Wu Shihong and Gao Yi (eds.), *Deng Xiaoping yu Gongheguo Zhongda Lishi Shijian* (Deng Xiaoping and the major events of the Republic) (Beijing: Renmin chubanshe, 2000), 52–3; Gong Li, Zhou Jingqing, and Zhang Shu, *Deng Xiaoping zai Zhongdai Lishi Guantou* (Deng Xiaoping at critical historical junctures) (Beijing: Zhonggong zhongyang dangxiao chubanshe, 2000), 147.

2

Central Policy Formulation Under a Dominant Mao

An examination of the process of policy formulation of the Great Leap Forward in 1958 inevitably highlights Mao's predominance and the dogged but impulsive manner by which Leap policies were instigated. Driven by a grand transformative vision, he assumed direct command like a hero-emperor in personal charge of a military campaign, designing and controlling every move, and monitoring every-thing closely. The Leap was Mao's crusade; he had every incentive to see it succeed. So, in 1958, he spent close to ten months touring the country—extremely unusual in his post-1949 career—returning to Beijing only for the most important meetings or occasions. His purpose was to inspect the grass roots, garner support from regional leaders, as well as to understand and promote the GLF.[1] He also dispatched a coterie of personal aides and secretaries to act as his eyes and ears. His authority in 1958 was absolute and unrivalled, and he demanded undivided loyalty and obedience from his colleagues and subordinates. Those who questioned the Leap were brow-beaten and humiliated into impotence. The planners' feeble resistance to Mao's initiatives crumbled quickly under his relentless pressure. (The term 'planners' is used here to refer to China's top economic officials including Zhou Enlai, Chen Yun, Li Fuchun, Li Xiannian, and Bo Yibo.) They were replaced in the inner sanctum of policy formulation by zealous leaders (both central and regional) who toadied to Mao's every whim and utterance. Nevertheless, even these disciples faced risk, depending on how well they read Mao's intentions. As Mao changed position or even reversed himself, those who failed to adjust in time would also come under the chairman's wrath, e.g. Chen Boda and later, Wu Zhipu. Chinese analysts often credit Mao as the first one to initiate a turnabout by the end of 1958.[2] Under the circumstances, who else but Mao could have done so? Indeed, at many critical

---

[1] Mao's tours in 1958 are described in detail in Xiao Xinli (ed.), *Xushe Dajiang Nanbei de Mao Zedong* (Mao Zedong's inspection tours north and south of the Yangzi) (Beijing: Zhongguo shehui kexue chu-banshe, 1993); Jia Zhengqiu (ed.), *Mao Zedong Waixun Ji* (Mao Zedong's inspection tours) (Changsha: Hunan wenyi chubanshe, 1993); Zhao Zhichao, *Mao Zedong Shierci Nanxun* (Mao Zedong's twelve inspection tours to the south) (Beijing: Zhongyang wenxian chubanshe, 2000); Wu Xiaomei and Li Peng, *Mao Zedong Zouchu Hongqiang* (Mao Zedong emerges from the Red Walls) (Beijing: Zhonggong zhongyang dangxiao chubanshe, 1993).

[2] See, e.g. Bo Yibo, *Ruogan Zhongda Juece yu Shijian de Huigu* (A review of certain major policies and events) (Beijing: Zhonggong zhongyang dangxiao chubanshe, 1993), ii. 807.

junctures before then, instead of slowing down or making modifications, Mao pushed relentlessly down the road to disaster.

The GLF was born out of the First Five-Year Plan (1FYP, 1953–7) which had brought generally impressive results, particularly in industry and heavy industry. However, although collectivization was completed in a few years, agricultural production remained stagnant, as an increase in grain production barely kept up with the demands of population growth, and shortages in agricultural raw materials created bottlenecks and disproportions in the economy. Rapid industrial development was accompanied by the swelling of the urban population, putting more pressure on the urban food supply. To be sure, these problems were already recognized as early as 1956, when the Second Five-Year Plan (2FYP) was on the drawing board, and extensive discussions were reflected in the pages of the professional journals. The Soviet model, which China copied lock, stock, and barrel, came under increasingly critical light. Furthermore, at the eve of the 2FYP, there was a general desire by policy-makers to start something new, to invent and try out new approaches to existing problems. Mao shared these sentiments, but his obsession was to accelerate economic development and industrialize China rapidly. Yet, few top leaders were prepared to go to the same lengths and extremes as Mao.

More immediate events had also contributed to the sense of optimism, impatience, and imminent breakthrough that infected most Chinese leaders. 'The Hundred Flowers' and the subsequent 'Anti-Rightist Campaign' in 1956 and 1957 had tarnished the prestige of the Party, and Mao and the Party needed a breakthrough to counter the criticisms by the 'rightists'. The ongoing rectification campaign directed at the Party, which later expanded into a socialist education movement nationally, gave Mao the impression that the values and work style of the people were being transformed. In foreign affairs, China's relationship with the Soviet Union had improved. The Soviet testing of an ICBM in August, the signing of a secret Sino-Soviet defence agreement in October (which promised missile and atomic bomb technologies from 1957–61 as well as an atomic energy research institute in Beijing), and the launching of the first two Soviet Sputniks in October and November, convinced Mao that the socialist camp had surpassed the West in technical superiority.[3]

Indeed, the Leap approach did not immediately emerge full-blown in Mao's mind, as he was driven as much as by ideology as by intuition, expediency, and whim; most elements of the GLF were only gradually fleshed out in 1958. Hence the resultant development strategy was a kaleidoscope of ideas that was neither coherent nor consistent. The only constant was Mao's obsession with speed and penchant for spontaneity and periodic disorder. He was impatient with rigid rules and regulations,

---

[3] Cong Jin, *1949–1989 Nian de Zhongguo, ii. Quzhe Fazhan de Suiyue* (China 1949–1989: The years of tortuous development) (Henan: Henan renmin chubanshe, 1989), 113–14; Chu Han, *Zhongguo 1959–1961: Sannian Ziran Zaihai, Changbian Jishi* (China, 1959–1961: A detailed record of the three years of natural calamities) (Chengdu: Sichuan renmin chubanshe, 1996), 228; Liu Guoxin and Liu Xiao (eds.), *Zhonghua Renmin Gongheguo Lishi Changpian* (A detailed history of the PRC) (Nanning: Guangxi renmin chubanshe, 1994), ii. 201; Su Donghai and Fang Kongmu (eds.), *Zhonggua Renmin Gongheguo Fengyun Shilu* (A real record of the major events of the PRC). Shijiazhuang: Hebei renmin chubanshe, 1994), i. 503.

and during the GLF this was translated into a passion to dismantle the planning system copied from the Soviet Union and to resurrect methods proven effective during the revolutionary wars. Driven by a euphoric vision, Mao mistook illusion for reality, vowing to overtake Britain and the United States, in industrial production in one or two decades, and also—during 1958—periodically advancing the timetable.

The First Leap Forward, *Fanmaojin*, and Mao's Resurrection of the 'Leap' Strategy

To trace the origins of the GLF, it is necessary to examine its antecedent, the abortive first leap forward of 1956.[4] Much of the drama of the two 'Leaps' was played out between an ambitious and impatient Mao and the more cautious and responsible planners, all of them had only limited experience in running a large and complex economy. Eventually, Mao's efforts to counter the planners led to the de facto destruction of the planning system and paved the way to the Leap in 1958.

The First Leap Forward 1955–1956

After China had scored some success at the Bandung Conference (April 1955) and the Geneva Conference (April to July 1955, when a cease-fire in Indochina was agreed), the Politburo felt that an era of 'international cease-fire' had materialized, and that the 'imperial' powers were unlikely to start a world war or a war against China for another decade or so. Hence it was felt that this international relaxation of tension could afford China the breathing space to accelerate socialist construction.[5] In the summer of 1955, the State Council began to consider goals for the 2FYP and a long-range (1953–67) strategic plan. Because this plan covered two years that had already passed, it was often called the Twelve-Year Plan. The State Planning Commission (SPC) added up tentative proposals of the ministries and projected production targets for 1967 as follows: grain 300m. tons; cotton 2.8m. tons; steel 18m. tons; and coal 280m. tons.[6] The gross value of industrial and agricultural output was projected to increase 9.5 per cent in fifteen years. Yet, Mao was

---

[4] The following analysis of the 1956 Leap draws from Zhonggong Zhongyang Wenxian Yanjiushi (ed.); Jin Chongji (ed.), *Zhou Enlai Zhuan* (Beijing: Zhongyang wenxian chubanshe, 1998), iii. ch. 47; Xie Chuntao, *Dayuejin Kuanglan* (The raging waves of the GLF) (Zhengzhou: Henan renmin chubanshe, 1990), 1–29; Bo Yibo, *Ruogan Zhongda Juece yu Shijian de Huigu* (A review of certain major policies and events) (Beijing: Zhonggong zhongyang dangxiao chubanshe, 1993 and 1997), i. 521–61; Lin Yunhui, Fan Shouxin, Zhang Gong, *1949–1989 Niande Zhongguo, i. Kaige Xingjinde Shiqi* (China 1949–1989, i. The period of triumphant advance) (Henan: Henan renmin chubanshe, 1989), ch. 11; Cong Jin, *Quzhe Fazhan*, ch. 1; Ceng Yingwang, *Zhongguo de Zong Guanjia Zhou Enlai* (China's chief steward Zhou Enlai) (Beijing: zhonggong dangshi chubanshe, 1996), 449–66, and *Unpublished Chinese Documents on Opposing Rash Advance and the Great Leap Forward* nos. 1–6 (n.p.: *c.*1992), 1–32.

[5] Bo Yibo, *Huigu*, i. 408, 485–7, 525.

[6] The actual outputs for grain, cotton, steel, and coal in 1967 were 218m., 2.4m., 10m., and 206m. tons. *Zhongguo Tongji Nianjian* (Statistical Yearbook of China) (Beijing: Guojia tontjiju, 1983), 162–3, 244–5.

dissatisfied with these optimistic projections. In particular, he was displeased with the outcome of the 1955 plan. Because capital investment was trimmed halfway during the year by the planners worried about an overheated economy, there was a year-end surplus of 1.8bn. *yuan* and large amounts of leftover raw materials, such as steel, iron, coal, and cement. The Soviet Union was asked to absorb these surpluses, but once the contracts were signed, China had to renege because the campaign for the criticism of 'rightist conservatism' had stimulated demands for inputs, turning surpluses into shortages.[7] The Chinese side was embarrassed not only by the cancelled contracts, but also by China's apparent reliance on the Soviet Union to solve its problems. Repeated self-criticisms by Premier Zhou Enlai failed to placate Mao.

In the second half of 1955, Mao also wanted to accelerate collectivization, and repeatedly criticized those who favoured a slower tempo, such as Deng Zihui, as 'women with bound feet'. Soon, he concluded that the perceived timidness of his colleagues—'rightist conservatism'—was the main obstacle to economic and socialist development. In the two prefaces to the book *Socialist Upsurge in China's Countryside* edited and annotated by him (published in September and December 1955, respectively), he lashed out at the *fanmaojin* (opposing rash advance) of 1953 and 1955, blaming those who refused to attempt tasks he thought could be achieved with some exertion. Hence, Mao decided that the current task was to accelerate and expand production, and to 'endlessly' criticize rightist conservatism (in agriculture, industry, transportation, science, culture and education, and health). He prophesied that agricultural production, as well as development in industry and communications, would increase scores of fold in the future. In particular, Mao predicted that grain production in 1967 would double or triple the record achieved before 1949, to 450 to 500m. tons.[8]

Mao used the publication of this book to reveal his position not because inner party channels of communication were blocked, or opposition was insurmountable, but because he characteristically wanted to bypass the central bureaucratic channels and appeal directly to and educate the public, and to set up an 'opposite'. If the planners had not read his intentions, he certainly was not going to tell them precisely what to do. In contrast, Mao had also found that regional and local authorities were more sensitive to his radical initiatives, so he attempted to exploit what he thought were 'creative tensions' between the two groups to get his way. Snubbing the planners, he met with provincial party secretaries at Hangzhou and Tianjin in November and drafted a document called 'Seventeen Articles On Agriculture' as a countermeasure. Subsequently, Mao oversaw its expansion into the *National Programme for Agricultural Development, 1956–1967* (draft) (NPAD, commonly

---

[7] Bo Yibo, *Huigu*, i. 523; Mao Zedong, *Maozhu Weikan Gao, 'Mao Zedong Sixiang Wansui' Beiji Ji Qita* (Unofficial published works of Mao Zedong: Additional volumes of 'Long Live Mao Zedong's Thought' and other secret speeches of Mao) (Oakton, Virginia: Center for Chinese Research Materials, 1990), xiii. 190.

[8] Mao Zedong, *Mao Zedong Xuanji* (Selected works of Mao Zedong) (Beijing: Renmin chubanshe, 1977), v. 218–24, 252; Bo Yibo, *Huigu*, i. 524–6; Su Donghai and Fang Kongmu, *Fengyun Shulu*, 383.

called the Forty Articles) in January 1956. Apart from a few ambitious and controversial items, the NPAD was essentially a checklist of commonsense things to be accomplished in the next twelve years.[9] For instance, Article 1 called for the acceleration of collectivization by turning 85 per cent of all rural households into lower agricultural producers' cooperatives (APCs) in 1956 (up from the 60 per cent achieved in 1955). However, the more controversial Article 2 called on the 'more mature' lower APCs to 'promote' themselves into advanced APCs in order not to obstruct the development of the productive forces.[10] Areas already with some advanced APCs were told to complete the transformation of all collectives into advanced APCs by 1957. This was an ambitious timetable, but eventually zealous implementation by the lower cadres quickly turned more than 90 per cent of all rural households into advanced APCs by the end of 1956, exceeding all expectations. Mao felt vindicated, although the hasty amalgamation created many organizational and management problems, which led to widespread peasant demands for withdrawal and splitting of the APCs.[11]

Article 6 set projected grain output/*mu* for 1967 as follows: for the areas north of the Huang He, Qingling and Bailong Jiang, the goal was 400 *jin*; for the areas north of the Huai He, 500 *jin*; and the areas south of the Huang He, Qinling, and Bailong Jiang, 800 *jin*. These targets were often called the '4, 5, and 8' and they compared with the 1955 output/*mu* of 150, 208, and 400 *jin*, respectively. This projection would see grain and cotton output reaching a cumulative height of 500m. and 5m. tons, respectively, in 1967, greatly exceeding the State Council's projections. As previously observed, these goals were wildly overambitious, as in reality, China did not produce 456m. tons of grain until 1993, and 4.63m. tons of cotton until 1983. Even the more conservative State Council figures were off the mark.[12]

Another ambitious item was the introduction of 6 million double-shared and double-wheeled ploughs and other agricultural machinery nationwide (Article 11). The articles on water conservancy, increased fertilizer application, redesign of farm tools, intensive farming, multiple cropping, reclamation of land, etc., were methods aimed at raising output. Other articles included the introduction or improvement of social welfare, animal husbandry, soil quality, reserve grain, agricultural research, rural transportation, broadcasting and telephone networks, and so on. Less controversial articles dealt with the issues of allowing rich peasants to join the APCs, the treatment of counter-revolutionaries, the building of reserve grain, establishment

---

[9] *Zhonghua Renmin Gongheguo Fagui Huibian* (A compendium of laws and regulations of the People's Republic of China) (Beijing: Falu chubanshe, 1981 and 1982) (hereafter *FGHB*), iii. 1–23.

[10] In the lower APCs, with an average of 20–30 households, the peasants pooled their land, draught animals, and farm tools, and remuneration was calculated on the basis of their work and the land and capital they had contributed. Land was still privately owned. However, in the advanced APCs, with an average of 200–300 households, private owership of land was abolished, and remuneration was calculated entirely on work contributed.

[11] Liu Guoxin and Liu Xiao, *Lishi Changpian*, i. 177; Bo Yibo, *Huigu*, ii. 729.

[12] Xie Chuntao, *Dayuejin*, 4; Bo's estimates were 532m. and 6m. tons, *Huigu*, ii. 524. *Zhongguo Tongji Nianjian 1994* (Statistical Yearbook of China 1994) (Beijing: Chinese Statistical Publishing House, 1994), 345–6.

of HEP stations in each *xiang*, self-sufficiency in fertilizers by the APCs, soil improvement, reclamation of land, afforestation, improvement of living conditions, and the removal of illiteracy. On paper these provisions look innocuous enough as a long-term agenda for rural development, and the snubbed planners were unwilling to antagonize the Chairman even more. For instance, Zhou Enlai and Chen Yun supported the NPAD, and Zhou welcomed it as a spur for agricultural development, and defended it against concerns that it might place too much burden on the peasants.[13] Furthermore, Zhou argued that the NPAD could promote development in other economic sectors, so that industrialization could be achieved with less than the three five-year plans previously assumed. He was also mindful of the fact that the Party Centre had decided in 1943 to give Mao the 'final decision power' on major issues. Although Hu Qiaomu pointed out recently that this final say referred to the power of the Chairman in dealing with day-to-day affairs in the Secretariat, not decision in the Politburo,[14] this finer point was overlooked at that time. Moreover, when the Politburo finally passed the NPAD on 23 January 1956, the targets for 1967 (500m. tons of grain and 5m. tons of cotton) were eradicated as a concession. But when Liao Luyan introduced it two days later at the Supreme State Conference using Mao's copies, the targets were reinstalled.[15] Although little information is available about this episode, the possibility that this was a ploy used by Mao to trick the Politburo cannot be ruled out. In any case, once the NPAD was published, it spurred the release of spontaneous and sometimes irresponsible energies to attempt everything at once in a hurry, inspiring copycats in *other* sectors such as industry and transport. Many other ministries began to revise their plans and to raise their targets.[16] In this way the NPAD was the catalyst that sparked off the 1956 Leap, affecting not just the agricultural sector.

Bowing to Mao's initiative, the planners coined the slogan of *duohao kuaisheng* (more, better, faster, and more economical). At a briefing conference by the industrial ministries, Zhou and Bo said that industrial work must follow the principle of 'more, faster, and better', and Li Fuchun concurred by adding the words 'more economical'. Mao was pleased with this adage, so the words *duohao kuaisheng* became a formal slogan when it was introduced in an *RMRB* editorial on New Year 1956.

The NPAD, the slogans of *duohao kuaisheng* and of 'accomplishing the 1FYP ahead of schedule', the criticism of rightist conservatism, and the grain target of 500m. tons for 1967, touched off the first 'leap forward'. Many units began to set up

[13] Zhonggong Zhongyang Wenxian Yanjiushi, *Zhou Enlai Jingji Wenxuan* (Selected works on economics by Zhou Enlai) (Beijing: Zhongyang wenxian chubanshe, 1993), 244; Bo Yibo, *Huigu*, i. 530–1; *Zong Guanjia*, 452; Li Rui, *Dayuejin Qinliji* (A record of my personal experience of the GLF) (Shanghai: Shanghai yuandong chubanshe, 1996), 204. *Dangde Wenxian*, 1988, no. 2: 9–10.

[14] Li Haiwen (ed.), *Zhou Enlai Yanjiu Shuping* (Discourse on research on Zhou Enlai) (Beijing: Zhongyang wenxian chubanshe, 1997), 420–1; Hu Qiaomu, *Hu Qiaomu Huiyi Mao Zedong* (Hu Qiaomu's reminiscences of Mao Zedong) (Beijing: Renmin chubanshe, 1994), 273.

[15] *Zhou Enlai Zhuan*, iii. 1218 n. 1; *Unpublished Chinese Documents*, 5.

[16] Peng Gangzi and Wu Jinming, *Zhonghua Renmin Gongheguo Nongye Fanzhen Shi* (A history of agricultural development in the PRC) (Changsha: Hunan renmin chubanshe, 1998), 74.

equally overambitious targets and expand their scales of production accordingly. The hands of the planners were forced. Hence, in drafting the 1956 plan, they were obliged to raise the gross value of industrial and agricultural output by 15.9 per cent, so that production of steel, grain, and cotton was to be 61, 9.25, and 18.3 per cent higher than 1955. On 14 January, the SPC revised the major targets for 1962, the last year of the 2FYP, by basically substituting them with targets originally set for 1967, so that grain output would be 320m. tons, cotton 3.5m. tons, steel 12m. tons. For 1967, the grain target was raised to 500m. tons, cotton 5m. tons, coal 330m. tons, and steel 24m. tons. Mao was finally satisfied with these projections, but wanted even more steel—15m. tons for 1962 and 30m. tons for 1967. These hikes required the retroactive addition of hundreds of construction projects, and similar proportionate increases were set for the second and third FYPs. Furthermore, a Party Centre directive of 4 October 1955, urged all ministries and localities to surpass the control figures set up by the SPC as much as possible.[17] Consequently, many units pledged to fulfil the 15-year Strategic Plan and the NPAD in five or even three years. To honour these pledges, the provinces and ministries in turn demanded a total capital investment of 15.3 and even 20bn. *yuan* in 1956, although the originally planned figure was only 11.27bn. *yuan*, and revenue was projected to be 9.29bn. *yuan*. The planners were alarmed, but in contrast, Mao was so pleased with this stampede that he bragged that China's speed of development could exceed that of the Soviet Union.[18]

Such a large scale of construction required funds and raw materials that were unavailable, creating all sorts of bottlenecks and work stoppages. For instance, excessive loans to agriculture, handicraft, and other enterprises and efforts to alleviate the tight money supply required dipping into the reserves and printing more money, which aggravated inflationary pressures.[19] Wages for the 1.4 million extra work force recruited was another financial burden. Furthermore, the NPAD called for the manufacture of 6 million double-wheeled and double-shared ploughs in 3–5 years, as it was hoped that a massive injection of these ploughs would lay the foundation toward agricultural mechanization. Yet these ploughs were too heavy and cumbersome for the draught animals and especially unsuitable for terraced or paddy fields in south China. Subsequently, huge unsold stockpiles and returns forced Mao to admit (in October 1957) that the 6 million target was 'subjectivism', and mention of the ploughs was dropped from the revised draft of the NPAD.[20]

Meanwhile, the burden of damage control fell on the shoulders of the planners, particularly Zhou and Chen. Zhou called for the quelling of *maojin* (rash advance), the restoration of planning and comprehensive balance (especially concerning raw

---

[17] Su Donghai and Fang Kongmu, *Fengyun Shulu*, 367; Lin Yunhui *et al.*, *Kaige Xingjin de Shiqi*, pp. 619 ff.

[18] Bo Yibo, *Huigu*, i. 526–7, 542; Cong Yingwang, *Zong Guanjia*, 451–2.

[19] Xie Chuntao, *Dayuejin*, 5; Lin Yunhui *et al.*, *Kaige Xingjin de Shiqi*, 621–4.

[20] Mao Zedong, *Mao Zedong Sixiang Wansui* (Long live Mao Zedong's Thought!) (n.p. 1969), 142; Zhonggong Zhongyang Wenxian Yanjiushi (ed.), *Zhou Enlai Nianpu, 1949–1976* (Chronicles of Zhou Enlai, 1949–1976) (Beijing: Zhongyang wenxian chubanshe, 1997), i. 601.

materials), but the planners' chief weapon was the cutting of capital investment for 1956 from 17 to 14.7bn. *yuan* in February. In June, this was further trimmed to 14bn. *yuan*.[21] Yet, at a Politburo meeting in April, Mao pushed for the retroactive raising of capital investment, but few could support the idea. Zhou tried hard to plead his case, but Mao persisted and promptly adjourned the meeting. Afterwards, Zhou approached Mao personally, saying that he could not in good conscience support the retroactive increase. Mao reportedly was greatly offended, and left Beijing a few days later, leaving everyone in the lurch.[22] In any case, the later cut was coordinated by an *RMRB* editorial published on 20 June calling for opposition to *both* conservatism and rashness, citing the abortive campaign to eliminate illiteracy and the double-wheeled and double-shared ploughs as examples of *maojin*. When the draft of this editorial was submitted to Mao for approval, his response was ambiguous; he inscribed only three words '*bukanle*' which could mean either disapproval or approval.[23] The fact that his subordinates published it showed that they assumed that the Chairman did not object to it. Mao was more ambivalent about *fanmaojin* in 1956; he favoured a leap, but was also willing to let the planners have a say, admitting the problems it brought on several occasions. Moreover, his attention was distracted by de-Stalinization in the Soviet Union and the upheavals in Poland and Hungary. In the summer of 1956 when the planners began to draft the 2FYP in a spirit of restraint, Mao accepted many of the proposed targets.[24]

Soviet opinion conveyed in August/September also lent support to the planners' restraint. All these enabled the enshrinement of the principles of 'opposing conservatism and *maojin*', 'steady advance based on comprehensive balance in economic construction' (the planners' mantras) at the Eighth Party Congress (12–27 September). The critique of *maojin* was mentioned in reports made by Liu, Zhou, and Bo, and in the Resolution on the Political Report. On the draft for the 2FYP, Zhou struck out the words *duohao kuaisheng*, and the slogan disappeared officially for more than a year.[25] Then the planners applied the other weapon, the lowering of the targets for grain, cotton, and steel for the 2FYP originally submitted by the SPC. All this could not have been done without the implicit or explicit approval of Mao, and the leaders understood that there was a consensus on the subject.

[21] Bo Yibo, *Huigu*, i. 535; *Dangde Wenxian*, 1988, no. 2, 6–8; 1990, no. 2, 6.

[22] *Zhou Enlai Zhuan*, iii. 1227; Li Ping, *Kaiguo Zongli*, 356; Xie Chuntao, *Dayuejin*, 10; *Unpublished Chinese Documents*, 10–11; Li Haiwen, *Zhou Enlai Yanjiu Shuping*, 422; Yin Jiamin, *Gongheguo Fengyun zhong de Mao Zedong yu Zhou Enlai* (Mao Zedong and Zhou Enlai in the stormy years of the Republic) (Beijing: Zhonggong zhongyang dangxiao chubanshe, 1999), 206–7.

[23] In 1958, Mao made clear his hostility to this editorial, but in June 1956, he was more ambivalent or undecided, as these words can convey different meanings ranging from approval ('It's fine. There's no need for me to read it'.) to rejection, and even boycott ('I won't read it'). It would be wrong to accept at face value Mao's later comments.

[24] See the speeches delivered by the top leaders at the Eighth Party Congress (September 1956), many of them were critical of the problem of *maojin*. Mao personally read and approved these speeches. See *Renmin Shouce* (People's Handbook), 1957, 15, 25, 39, 74–5; Mao Zedong, *Jianguo Yilai Mao Zedong Wengao* (The manuscripts of Mao Zedong after the founding of the state) (Beijing: Zhongyang wenxian chubanshe, 1987 to 1998), vi. 136–200, *passim*. For more details, see *Zhou Enlai Zhuan*, iii. 1234–9.

[25] *RMSC* (1957), 15, 25, 39, 74–5; Lin Yunhui *et al.*, *Kaige Xingjin de Shiqi*, 632.

Yet after the Congress, when the 1957 plan was on the drawing board, planners again had to wrestle with the tide unleashed by the Leap impulses, as the projected capital investment submitted by the ministries and provinces for 1957 totalled up to 24.3bn. *yuan*, far exceeding the 14bn. *yuan* invested in 1956. Furthermore, despite the planners' efforts, 1956 ended with 2 to 3bn. *yuan* in the red.

At the Second Plenum (November 1956), Mao seemed to have come around to the viewpoints of the planners by admitting the inappropriate use of 2–3bn. *yuan* in 1956, the need to compress the 1957 plan, and the recognition of contraints of funds and raw materials.[26] Thus emboldened, Zhou spoke arrogantly and matter-of-factedly about the 'laughable' mistakes associated with *maojin*. According to him, things should be cooled down on all fronts, lest the tension and waste generated should disrupt the economy and create social unrest on the scale of that which had happened in Eastern Europe. Grain production and farm acreage should only be increased slowly, and the desire for 30m. tons of steel for the 3FYP was unrealistic. Unworkable targets made during the Eighth Party Congress and contained in the NPAD should be trimmed. For instance, the NPAD specified that more than 10m. *mu* of land be reclaimed every year for 12 years, but the 500m. *yuan* per annum required was clearly out of the question. Zhou would never have attacked these pet projects of Mao in such abandon if Mao had not signalled his approval, if only temporarily. Mao probably realized the need to slow things down for 1957, although he was much easier on the mistakes of *maojin* than Zhou and cautioned that the enthusiasm of the cadres and the masses should not be dampened. In 1958, his retroactive hostility toward the decisions of this Plenum as the most concentrated expression of *fanmaojin* did not erase the fact that he was much more conciliatory at the time.[27] Anyhow, before Zhou left for a visit to Pakistan in January 1957, he instructed Chen to slash the budget within 10bn. *yuan*. When Chen telephoned Bo, Bo misheard the figure to be 11bn. *yuan*, so that figure stuck.[28]

By January 1957, however, Mao's position had hardened, blaming *fanmaojin* for the encouragement of 'rightist' tendencies.[29] Now that Mao's position was made clear, Zhou had to backtrack. His report to the Fourth Session of the First National People's Congress (June/July 1957) was tight-lipped about the mistakes caused by *maojin*. To cover himself, Zhou about-faced and rebuffed the view that in 1956 there was an 'all-round *maojin*'. Instead, he claimed that the adoption of the *yuejin* (leap forward) method in 1956 had enabled a surge in the economic performance. This first ever use of the words *yuejin* won Mao's praise.[30]

---

[26] *Mao Wengao*, vi 244–6. See also *Mao Xuanji*, v. 313–18; *Mao Weikan*, xiA. 112–14; Mao Zedong, *Mao Zedong Wenji* (Collected works of Mao Zedong) (Beijing: Renmin chubanshe, 1999); vii. 159–61.

[27] *Zhou Enlai Jingji Wenxuan*, 338–45; cf. Shi Zhongquan, *Zhou Enlai de Zhuoyue Fengxian* (Zhou Enlai's outstanding contributions) (Beijing: Zhonggong Zhongyang dangxiao chubanshe, 1993), 324–5, 334; Li Rui, *Li Rui Wenji, ii. Mao Zedong de Wannian Beiju* (Collected Works of Li Rui, ii. The tragedy of Mao Zedong's last years) (Haikou: Nanfang chubanshe, 1999), 84–5.

[28] See n. 22; Bo Yibo, *Huigu*, i. 554–5; Li Ping, *Kaiguo Zongli*, 359; Ceng Yingwang, *Zong Guanjia*, 458. [29] *Mao Weikan*, xiA. 118–25.

[30] Cong Jin, *Quzhe Fazhan*, 101 n. 1, 108; *Mao Wengao*, vii. 254.

In the second half of 1957, once the disturbances in Eastern Europe had been settled and the Anti-Rightist campaign concluded, Mao's full attention was drawn back to the economy.[31] Although the 1957 plan was completed with some successes—the budget was balanced with a small surplus, and the total value of industrial and agricultural product was up 10 per cent—Mao concluded that 1957 was not as good as 1956. Industrial production was up only 10 per cent from the year before, far from the 30 per cent increase achieved in 1956. The agricultural plan had not reached the targeted increase of 4.9 per cent and grain production rose marginally to 185m. tons, or 2.5 per cent over that of 1956, barely sufficient to match the population increase. This was a slump, and *fanmaojin* was chiefly responsible as it had dampened the enthusiasm of the masses, he concluded. Furthermore, the rightists' criticism of his 'delusion of grandeur' (*haoda xigong*) seemed to have echoed those who found *maojin* distasteful. Privately, Mao was also toying with the possibility of developing the economy faster and better than the Soviet Union.[32]

The Third Plenum (20 September–9 October)

By the Third Plenum in the autumn of 1957, Mao was determined to revive the 'leap forward' strategy of development by overturning the more cautious approach pursued by the planners, and therefore the conference became a curtain-raiser for the process that led inexorably to the GLF. However, Mao did not dominate the conference proceedings as much as he did subsequent events, cooperating with other top leaders on certain agreed-upon issues, and divergent opinions were still being expressed. Yet, he was assertive and manipulative, springing surprises which caught his colleagues off guard.

The Plenum met to consider the two issues of the rectification campaign and rural problems. It had been expanded according to Mao's wishes to include first secretaries of provincial, district, and county party committees, as Mao could always count on the regional leaders for support of more radical policies.[33] Deng Xiaoping reported on the rectification campaign, Chen Yun on administrative reform and the problem of raising agricultural production, and Zhou Enlai on labour wages and insurance.[34]

The Plenum was the first to be convened after the Anti-Rightist Campaign. Mao's thinking had changed in important ways since the summer of 1957. Criticism by the 'rightists' had convinced Mao that conservatism was the major ideological enemy, and that the CCP should adopt more radical economic policies to draw the line between itself and the 'rightists'. More particularly Mao attributed the stagnation in agricultural production to rightist inertia. In September/October, the prognosis for

---

[31] Bo Yibo, *Huigu*, ii. 635.

[32] Cong Jin, *Quzhe Fazhan*, 101–2. A more official estimate in *Zhongguo Tongji Nianjian* (1983) puts the 1957 grain production at 195m. tons, or 1.2 per cent over the 1956 production of 192.75m. tons, see p. 158.

[33] *Mao Wengao*, vi. 554–5; Bo Yibo, *Huigu*, ii. 624.

[34] *Renmin Ribao* (People's Daily), 10 October 1957.

agricultural production was not good—there were severe shortages in grain and cotton. Even with the substantial grain increase of 1956, it was necessary to dip into the grain reserve, and it seemed that 1957 was no exception. Overall, the annual increases in grain since 1949 (estimated at a yearly rate of between 12 and 15m. tons by 1957) were too small to support population growth. If this trend was to continue, per capita consumption might be reduced even further during the 2FYP.[35] Therefore, Mao felt vindicated that he was right in pushing the first Leap of 1956, and that the retreat in 1957 was wrong or at least ineffectual. In his view, the planners had botched their chance, so he was ready to revive the Leap strategy of rural mobilization and development.

To legitimize this initiative, Mao first resorted to a wholesale redefinition of ideology, whatever his real beliefs. The day before the Plenum, he abruptly dropped a bombshell when talking with central leaders, asserting categorically that the principal contradiction during the entire transition period was the struggle between the proletariat and the capitalists, between socialism and capitalism, and by extension, between individualism and collectivism.[36] This was a unilateral revision of the resolution of the Eighth Party Congress which had declared that the contradiction between the proletariat and capitalists had basically been resolved.[37] Many delegates were perplexed, and a heated debate ensued, although many were quick to jump on Mao's side.[38] On 7 October, Mao repeated his new views on contradiction to the team leaders in his concluding speech to the conference. Once this speech was transmitted and discussed, no more objections were raised.[39] The Plenum acceded to his wishes, although no formal declaration was made. Mao's notion that the principal contradiction was still the struggle between the proletariat and the capitalists and between socialism and capitalism was influenced by the events in Eastern Europe and the Anti-Rightist Campaign. Consequently, if intense struggle was still the norm, then the solution was more radical policy and accelerated collectivization.[40] If capitalism was the chief danger, and if Mao was the defender of the socialist transition, then struggle would be more uncompromising. After the Plenum, an additional group of people were retroactively labelled 'rightists'.[41]

[35] Chen Yun, *Chen Yun Wenxuan* (Selected Works of Chen Yun) (Beijing: Renmin chubanshe, 1995) iii (1956–85), 78, 387, n. 39; *Mao Weikan*, xiA. 194.

[36] For Mao, all societies are rife with contradictions (some more fundamental and others more secondary) that are interconnected with one another. Once the principal contradiction (or, fundamental problem) has been identified and resolved, other secondary contradictions will also disappear. Indeed, Mao's definitions of the principal contradiction varied greatly over time and were seldom consistent; they could refer to disparate things such as class struggle, rightist opposition, *fanmaojin*, inadequate quantities of steel, and so on. [37] *RMSC*, 1957, 55.

[38] Ma Qibin, *et al.* (eds.), *Zhongguo Gongchandang Zhizheng Sishinian, 1949–1989* (The CCP's 40 years' rule, 1949–1989) (Beijing: Zhonggong dangshi ziliao chubanshe, 1989; Zhonggong dangshi chubanshe, rev., enlarged edn. 1991), 132–3.

[39] Bo Yibo, *Huigu*, ii. 624–9; text is in *Wansui* (1969), 122–6. See also, *Mao Weikan*, xiA. 196–9; Cong Jin, *Quzhe Fazhan*, 79–82. [40] *Mao Xuanji*, v. 475; Bo Yibo, *Huigu*, ii. 629.

[41] Xing Chongzhi, Jiang Shunxue, Liao Gailong, and Zhao Xuemin (eds.), *Mao Zedong Yanjiu Shidian* (A dictionary of events for the research of Mao Zedong) (Shijiazhuang: Hebei renmin chubanshe, 1992), 357.

In the following months, it became clear that Mao increasingly read ideological and class implications into policy differences. As if this were insufficient, Mao's discourse on the issue of red and expert claimed that both were necessary, although politics was primary, and that some cadres were more white, grey, or pink, than red (ideologically motivated). Only those who were blazing red were leftists, he said.[42] This was another obvious dig at those he regarded as insufficiently committed ideologically, particularly the planners who did not always toe Mao's line. Mao had not only thrown down the gauntlet, he had won the first round.

Mao's discourse on ideology inevitably affected the policy choices dealing with agricultural stagnation. Although all agreed that agriculture development should be accelerated, there was no consensus regarding how this should be accomplished. On this issue, Chen Yun was clearly out of joint with the Chairman. While Mao was advocating the revival of the mobilization strategy of the 1956 Leap to accelerate development, Chen, in his speech of 24 September, was still promoting gradual improvement by producing more chemical fertilizer and artificial fibre, by water conservancy, and by the boosting of agricultural investment (from 7 per cent of total capital investment to 12, or even 20 per cent). During the first leap forward, Chen maintained, the targets were too high, exceeding the country's capability; decisions were made too quickly, and the expectation that *duohao kuaisheng* could be achieved all at once was unrealistic.[43] On the other hand, Zhou's speech delivered on 26 October focused on the problems involved with the unplanned increase in urban population, hikes in the labour wage bill, and cost increases for insurance, welfare, and subsidies—caused in part by the 1956 leap. He recommended the creation of employment by sending surplus urban population to the countryside for rural activities, but did not mention the NPAD.[44]

Mao's complaint aside, the NPAD had never died completely—a programme sponsored by the Chairman simply could not be consigned to oblivion and the leaders continued to pay lip service to it. Liu Shaoqi called it the 'long-term plan for rural construction' in April 1957 while talking to students at Changsha.[45] In February, Liao Luyan told a conference for agricultural labourer models that output/ *mu* specified in the NPAD would be achieved. At the same conference, Deng Zihui praised the NPAD,[46] and at the NPC in June/July, Bo praised it as well.[47] By the summer of 1957, Mao apparently regarded the revival of the NPAD as the best hope in combating the agricultural bottleneck, so on 21 August, the Party Centre issued the revised draft of the NPAD, touting it as a guiding programme of struggle which would accelerate agricultural production, industrialization and the improvement

[42] *Mao Xuanji*, v. 471–2.

[43] Chen Yun, *Chen Yun Wenxuan*. iii. 76–86. Since the view contained in this section of Chen's speech was inconsistent with that of Mao's, it was not published until recently.

[44] *Zhou Enlai Jingji Wenxuan*, 374–92; Ceng Yingwang, *Zong Guanjia*, 394–9.

[45] Liu Shaoqi, *Liu Shaoqi Xuanji* (Selected Works of Liu Shaoqi) (Beijing: Renmin chubanshe, 1985), ii. 286.   [46] *RMRB*, February 19 and 22 1957.   [47] *RMSC*, 1958, 225.

of the standard of living.[48] With Mao's prodding, the Conference duly passed the revised draft of the NPAD. The revised draft differed only slightly from the original draft, but the context had changed. For instance, Article 1, the major bone of contention in 1956 because it called for acceleration of collectivization, had become obsolete; it was replaced by a non-controversial call to consolidate advanced APCs during the 2FYP *or* beyond.[49] The 5–7 year time limit specified in the draft for the elimination of the four pests, illiteracy, and urban unemployment was extended to 12 years. Article 6 added a paragraph on the promotion of the chemical fertilizer industry, reflecting Chen Yun's idea that the fastest way to raise agricultural production was by a rapid increase in chemical fertilizer.[50] Chen's idea that land reclamation was not the way to raise production might have resulted in cancellation of Article 19 on the subject, so it became just a subsection in Article 4 of the new version. Other articles were merely a checklist of things to be done in the next twelve years, such as the development of animal husbandry and seed selection, soil improvement, and afforestation, as well as protection of women and children, and development of rural broadcasting, transportation, and commercial networks, etc. At the end of 1957, the NPAD, for the most part, was no longer the lightning rod as it had been in 1956. The most controversial provision of the revised draft was the continuance of the '4, 5, 8' targets, which still pledged to fulfil the grossly unrealistic goals of 532m. tons of grain and 6m. tons of cotton by 1967.

At one point, Mao warned that those who did not support the NPAD were akin to 'promoters of retrogression', just like the rightists.[51] As some localities had already mapped out plans according to the NPAD, Mao charged everyone else to make plans accordingly. He also reaffirmed the goal of 20m. tons of steel to be achieved in 15 years.[52] Indicative of Mao's supreme confidence in China's ability to raise yields was his musing that since some counties had already produced one thousand *jin/mu*, intensive cultivation might in the future enable 1 *mu* (as opposed to 3 *mu*) of land to produce enough food for one person. In 1958, this idea would inform his initiatives on the 'three-three system', deep ploughing, close planting, and the like.[53] The revived NPAD, the mobilization approach to development, and the high targets adopted were a direct rebuke to the planners. Even though the planners tried to accommodate Mao's advancing targets they were always kept behind.

---

[48] Zhonggong Zhongyang Wenxian Yanjiushi, *Zhou Enlai Nianpu 1949–1976* (Chronicles of Zhou Enlai) (Beijing: Zhongyang wenxian chubanshe, 1997), ii. 70; *Zhonghua Renmin Gongheguo Jingji Guanli Dashiji*. (A Chronology of major events in the economic management of the PRC) (Beijing: Zhongguo jingji chubanshe, 1986), 100; Liu Guoxin and Liu Xiao, *Lishi Changpian*, 197, erroneously puts the date as 21 July. [49] *FGHB*, vi. 40. [50] *Chen Yun Wenxuan*, iii. 80–3.

[51] *Mao Weikan*, xiA. 199; Bo Yibo, *Huigu*, ii. 636. The edited and polished version in Mao, *Xuanji*, v. 466, 474–5 omits the figures.

[52] Ibid. 474. See also Renmin Ribao She Guonei Ziliao Zu and Zhongguo Gongye Jingji Xiehui Tiaoyan Zu (eds.), *Zhonghua Renmin Gongheguo Gongye Dashiji, 1949–1990* (A chronology of major events in the industrial sector in the PRC, 1949–1990) (Changsha: Hunan chubanshe, 1992), 14.

[53] Mao, *Xuanji*, v. 469.

However, on the issue of economic decentralization, the first-ever attempt to reform the country's economic system, Mao and the planners were more in tune with one another, at least for the time being. Even as early as the 1FYP, many Chinese had begun to question the rigidity of the highly centralized Soviet model, and many provinces had complained to Mao in 1955.[54] In his Ten Great Relationships speech of 1956, Mao laid down the need for decentralization and charged the planners to examine the matter. Chen Yun and the other planners viewed decentralization more in the context of strengthening planning, coordination, and balance, and ensuring that changes were not too disruptive. In January 1957, a five-man group led by Chen Yun was entrusted with the task of reforming the administrative system. It decided that some powers of enterprise management and finance, and some taxes and enterprise profit retention should be decentralized to the localities, but that coordination and balancing should be strengthened simultaneously.[55] In August, Bo's recommendations on reform of the planning system, accepted by the five-man group, stressed 'big plan, small freedoms'.[56] Chen Yun's speech at the Third Plenum also underscored the further strengthening of balance and the interests of the whole, especially after decentralization. Without balance based on the whole, he maintained, the economy was not really a planned one.[57] Subsequently, three decrees on industrial, commercial, and fiscal decentralization, masterminded by Chen Yun, were issued in November 1957.[58]

Briefly, these orderly changes designed to encourage the initiative of localities and enterprises were to be accomplished in the following ways. All the 'large-scale mines, metallurgical enterprises, chemical industrial enterprises, important coal and coke bases, large hydroelectric networks, hydro-stations, petroleum refineries, large-scale and precision machineries, electrical and precision machinery factories, war (military) industries and other industries with sophisticated technology' remained under the jurisdiction of the central ministries, using the dual rule formula—this meant that ministerial supervision from Beijing was primary, although local authorities were also urged to apply 'leadership and supervision' over those enterprises located within their geographical jurisdictions. All other enterprises formerly run directly by the ministries were transferred to local authorities. In addition, it was stipulated that profits of these *xiafang* (sent downwards) enterprises were to be divided between the local authorities and the central ministries at a 2 : 8 ratio, effective for three years, and that profits of the largest enterprises mentioned above were to be retained by the central ministries alone.[59] The power of local authorities in resource allocation and personnel management was expanded, and the number of mandatory targets was reduced.[60] In turn, enterprises would retain some of their profits, and the cautious planners also ensured that funds for capital

[54] Bo Yibo, *Huigu*, ii. 782–3.   [55] Ibid. 791–5; *Chen Yun Wenxuan*, iii. 75–7.
[56] Bo Yibo, *Huigu*, ii. 793–4; *Zhonghua Renmin Gongheguo Guomin Jingji he Shehui Fazhan Jihua Dashi Jiyao, 1949–1985* (A summary of major events in the national economic and social development planning of the PRC, 1949–1985) (Beijing: Hongqi chubanshe, 1987), 108–9.
[57] Chen Yun, *Wenxuan*, iii. 75–7.   [58] Ibid. 87–104; *FGHB*, vi. 391–7, 355–7; vii. 331–2.
[59] *RMRB*, 25 June 1958; *FGHB*, vii. 331–2.   [60] *FGHB*, vi. 391–7, 355–7; vii. 331–2.

construction for provinces and enterprises were still to be allocated directly by the centre. Local authorities wishing to use their funds for capital construction were required to obtain permission from the ministries. A ceiling of 3 to 3.6bn. *yuan* was placed on new fiscal revenue for the provinces. If their revenue exceeded this, readjustment would be made after one year.[61]

These were far-reaching reforms of the highly centralized system, but minor compared to Mao's future schemes of 1958 which were to totally subvert the intentions of the planners, Chen's in particular. To be sure, both Mao and the planners felt the need for decentralization, but the planners' vision also soon fell victim to Mao's hostility toward *fanmaojin*. If the planners were too restrained, Mao threw caution to the winds. In particular, Mao's disagreement with Chen on *maojin* prompted him to go so far as to discard comprehensive balance altogether. In an important way, Mao's dialectical thinking led him to treat Chen and the planners as his opposite, and in his endeavour to prove them wrong, he would go so far as to take policy positions directly contradictory to theirs.

On the last day, Mao surprised everyone by dropping another bombshell by directly attacking *fanmaojin* for the first time since December 1955.[62] According to him, there was a production high tide in 1955, but 1956 came to grief (*chiqui*) because rightist deviation and slackness conspired to create a lost opportunity. Three things that had been abandoned then—the slogan of *duohuo kuaisheng*, the NPAD, and the 'committee for the promotion of progress'[63]—Mao proposed to revive. Moreover, he claimed, the real problems with 1956 were the overspending of 3bn. *yuan* and the manufacturing of six million sets of double-shared and double-wheeled ploughs, and this could have been dealt with easily, without requiring the scrapping of the leap forward of 1956 and the retreat in 1957. The principle of a communist party was to advance, Mao maintained, not to retreat.[64]

After the Plenum the GLF gathered momentum when on 26 October the *RMRB* published the revised draft of the NPAD. Mao, in the name of the Party Centre, issued a directive urging party committees at all levels to organize a nationwide discussion of the NPAD by spending seven to ten evenings on how to implement it.[65] In December, impressed by reports in the *Anhui Ribao* on the campaign for hygiene and the elimination of the four pests (as required by the NPAD), he instructed Hu Qiaomu to reprint them in the *RMRB* and write editorials to laud them. Then he instructed the Party Centre and the State Council to issue a joint directive to make this mobilization campaign national.[66]

---

[61] *Chen Yun Wenxuan*, iii. 76–7, 100, 103.   [62] *Mao Weikan*, xiA. 215.

[63] No information exists to ascertain whether this was merely the kind of metaphor Mao often indulged in or whether it was really a committee. According to Shi Zhongquan, it was an organization set up to promote agricultural development headed by Chen Yun, *Zhuoyue Fengxian*, 329, n. 2.

[64] Bo Yibo, *Huigu*, ii. 636.

[65] *Mao Wengao*, vi. 610–11; Ho Ping (ed.), *Mao Zedong Dacidian*, (A dictionary of Mao Zedong) (Beijing: Zhongguo guoji guangbo chubanshe, 1992), 179; Gu Longsheng (ed.), *Mao Zedong Jingji Nianpu* (Chronicle of Mao Zedong and the economy) (Beijing: Zhonggong zhongyang dangxiao chubanshe, 1993), 405.   [66] *Mao Wengao*, vi. 666–8. Text of the directive is in *FGHB*, vii. 453–9.

To coordinate Mao's offensive, the *RMRB* published a barrage of articles to laud the NPAD and the 1956 Leap, to criticize the past opponents to *maojin*, and to promote a high-tide in agricultural production in four editorials on 26, 27 October, 13 November, and 12 December. The battle against *fanmaojin* escalated progressively. Between 1955 and 1957, Mao had often complained that the *RMRB* had not coordinated fully the propaganda of the Party Centre. So in June 1957, he coopted Wu Lengxi by hand-picking him as chief editor of the *RMRB* and director of the New China News Agency to ensure that they would become his personal mouthpiece. Subsequently, these organizations became Mao's most powerful weapons and vociferous promoters of Leap policies, as *RMRB* editorials were more influential than Central Committee directives.[67]

As the meaning of the Leap unfolded gradually, the 27 October editorial used the words 'leap forward' publicly for the first time when it praised the NPAD, criticized 'rightist conservatism', and urged the localities to make plans according to the requirements of the NPAD, as well as to constantly struggle against conservative tendencies and 'evil winds'. The 13 November editorial, personally approved by Mao, publicized the critique of *fanmaojin* for the first time. It accused those who were afflicted by 'rightist conservatism' for behaving like 'slow-crawling snails' oblivious to the necessities for a great leap forward, and regarded the NPAD and the correct 'leap forward' to be *maojin*. Mao was pleased with the term 'leap forward', and in May 1958 suggested jokingly that the inventor of the term be given a doctorate degree.[68] A 12 December *RMRB* editorial penned by Mao's secretary, Hu Qiaomu, and revised by Mao, lauded the 'leap forward' of 1956 and the principle of *duohao kuaishang*. It blasted those who had the temerity to suggest that the NPAD and the 1956 plan were *maojin*, and that they did not work. It was imprudent of them to suggest that they would rather commit the mistake of conservatism than *maojin*. It demanded criticism of *fanmaojin*, and on this basis, the drawing up of more advanced 1958 targets.[69] Hu also wrote a New Year editorial that trumpeted the GLF. This propaganda campaign was Mao's unnamed yet open repudiation of the planners, especially Chen Yun, and they knew it.[70]

---

[67] The *RMRB* had earned Mao's confidence, and this explains why he took the unusual step of placing Wu's name at the head of a list of leaders, ahead of Zhou Enlai and Liu Shaoqi, in the note announcing the Nanning Conference. Mao was signalling his commendation of a comparatively minor official whom he felt had been more responsive to his cues than the planners, in the same way he lauded Ke Qingshi later on. Wu is either being evasive or incorrect when he claims in a recent memoir that few understood the significance of the incident at the time, and that he thought Mao was after him for the *fanmaojin* editorial of 20 June 1956, a piece for which he was not responsible. See Wu Lengxi, *Yi Mao Zhuxi: Wo Qinahen Jinglide Ruoghan Zhongda Lishi Shijian Pianduan* (Remembering Chairman Mao: Fragments of certain historical events which I personally experienced) (Beijing: Xinhua chubanshe, 1995), *passim.* and 41–9; Renmin Ribao Baoshi Bianjizu (ed.), *Renmin Ribao Huiyilu* (Recollections about the People's Daily) (Beijing: Renmin ribao chubanshe, 1988), 1–4.

[68] *Mao Wengao*, vii. 254; Cong Jin, *Quzhe Fazhan*, 108. Then someone said that Zhou was the first one to use the term 'leap forward'. Ibid. 101, n. 1.

[69] Xie, *Dayuejin*, 26–7; Cao Junjie, *Zhongguo Erqiao* (China's two Qiaos) (Nanjing: Jiangsu renmin chubanshe, 1996), 86–7.

[70] Sun Yeli and Xiong Lianghua (eds.), *Fengyun zhong de Chen Yun*, 133–4.

Mao's offensive found an unexpected boost from the Soviets. After the Third Plenum, Mao led a Chinese delegation to attend the Moscow Conference from 2 to 21 November. Although the Chinese disputed with the Soviets on the issues of peaceful coexistence and the struggle against 'reactionary forces', Mao was convinced that 'the East wind prevailed over the West wind'.[71] At the same conference, held during the celebration of the fortieth anniversary of the Russian Revolution, Khrushchev broached his own grandiose economic drive aimed at overtaking the United States in fifteen years. Internally it was decided that the Soviet Union would 'enter communism' in twelve years from 1959. Mao, thus inspired, was not to be left behind by such a challenge to the capitalist camp. On 18 November he followed suit with the slogan of 'Overtake Britain in fifteen years' (in total output of key industrial products, not in per capita terms).[72] Furthermore, at the Twenty-first Party Congress (February 1959), Khrushchev openly announced that the Soviet Union had entered the state of 'full-scale commencement in building communism'.

Mao's new offensive and his criticism of *fanmaojin* on the last day of the Third Plenum caught the planners off guard. For instance, on 1 October, the State Council announced the approved control figures and targets for 1958 submitted by the SEC— the gross value of industrial output (GVIO) for 1958 and grain production were up slightly, but capital investment, gross value of agricultural output (GVAO), and cotton production were set below the 1957 level. Even after the Third Plenum, the resurrection of the NPAD and Mao's open commitment of 'overtaking Britain', the planners were still slow to jump into action. At the National Planning Conference (28 November–12 December) targets for the new 1958 plan were set slightly higher for capital investment, GVIO, GVAO, steel, coal and cotton, but the grain target was set 2m. tons lower than the figures set in October, and GVAO was set lower than that accomplished in 1957. This was hardly what Mao had expected. From Moscow he sent a letter of warning, but to no avail.[73] Mao's repeated prodding and disappointment would later turn into fury.

Upon his return to China, Mao tightened his grip by convening several conferences on how to accelerate production and by issuing a directive on the 2FYP that was duly transmitted by the SPC on 4 December. In it, Mao reminded the planners to implement the principle of *duohao kuaisheng* and to strive hard to accelerate production and capital investment. The production high tides of 1956, he reiterated, were basically correct (despite defects), and to overtake Britain in fifteen years those

[71] Su Donghai and Fang Kongmu (eds.), *Fengyun Shulu*, 509–10.
[72] *Mao Wengao*, vi. 635. It was estimated that British production of 21m. tons of steel in 1957 could rise to 36m. tons, whereas China could produce 40 to 45m. tons, by 1972. Cong Jin *Quzhe Fazhan*, 107.
[73] *Mao Weikan*, xiB. 8. Other accounts claim that Mao telephoned from Moscow, criticizing *fanmaojin*, urging the term should never be mentioned again, as it was necessary to be 'rash' *(mao)* to build socialism. Xiao Donglian, Xie Chuntao, Zhu Di, and Qiao Jining, *Qiusuo Zhongguo: 'Wenge' Qian Shinian Shi* (China's quest: A history of the decade before the 'Cultural Revolution') (Beijing: Hongqi chubanshe, 1999), i. 276; Yang Mingwei, *Zouchu Kunjing: Zhou Enlai zai 1960–1965* (Escape from dire straits: Zhou Enlai in 1960–1965) (Beijing: Zhongyang wenxian chubanshe, 2000), 17; Yang Shengqun and Tian Songnian (eds.), *Gongheguo Zhongda Juece de Lailong Qumai* (The origins and development of the PRC's major policies) (Nanjing: Jiangsu renmin chubanshe, 1995), 260.

in charge of industry must also draft 40 articles like the NPAD as targets for struggle. He argued for the setting up of priorities, but in the same breath, added a long list of priorities that included coal, petroleum, metallurgy, chemical industry, agricultural machinery, atomic energy, aerospace, wireless, and precision machinery industries.[74]

While Mao was still trying to impress upon the planners to see things his way, Ke Qingshi, First Party Secretary of Shanghai, was quick to jump on the bandwagon, vouching for Mao's views on *fanmaojin* and his revision of ideological principles. In two reports, one made on 13 November to the Zhejiang Four-Level Cadre Conference and another on 25 December to the Party Congress at Shanghai, Ke elaborated at length on Mao's new theory of 'the principal contradiction'. The rapid development on all fronts in Shanghai was normal, not *maojin*, he said, and he agreed with Mao that rightist conservatism was causing trouble, and that all must insist on the *duohao kuaisheng* principle. 'Revolutionary enthusiasm' must be maintained and the NPAD must be completed ahead of schedule. These reports pleased Mao, as selections from them were reprinted in *RMRB* a month later, and he praised them repeatedly at the Nanning Conference in January 1958. Ke was way ahead of the central leaders, Mao maintained, so everyone must learn from him. This prompted Tao Zhu and others to pledge that they would surpass Ke.[75]

On 31 December 1957, Mao decided to take matters into his own hands by issuing another directive on economic planning to be transmitted by the SPC. He now demanded that industry, transport, commerce, handicraft industry, post-secondary institutions, etc. draw up plans like the NPAD, and decentralization was to extend to culture, education, and health. The directive conceded that during the 1956 leap, too many things were attempted, but it should not be called *maojin* because to oppose *maojin* would lead to laxity, and because the current task was to promote progress. Planning departments were enjoined to consult the Party Centre regularly on drafting of the 2FYP so that it would not be presented with a fait accompli. Increasingly after the Third Plenum and throughout the GLF, Mao continually equated himself with the Party Centre. Ultimately, he broached a new idea that cooperative regions comprising several provinces should be established to encourage coordination, so that the central ministries could be relieved of their functions.[76] As was made clear later, this was Mao's strategy to further dismantle the central planning system by devolving power to the local authorities who were more supportive of this vision.

Other top leaders who rallied round Mao's initiatives at this time were Liu Shaoqi and Li Fuchun. Their vehicle was the Conference of the All-China Federation of Trade Unions, (2–12 December) during which Liu formally transmitted Mao's slogan of overtaking Britain in the production of steel and other industrial products. Both praised the *duohuo kuaisheng* principle and the NPAD. Li, in particular, was

[74] Xing Chongzhi *et al.*, *Mao Zedong Yanjiu Shidian*, 358. Ma Qibin *et al.*, *Zizheng Sishinian*, 135.
[75] Li Rui, *Dayuejin*, 47–57, 73; Bo Yibo, *Huigu*, ii. 639.
[76] *Jingji he Shehui Fazhan Jihua Dashi*, 113.

the first planner to reverse himself. Either he was swept along by euphoria, or he realized that the Chairman's wishes could not be resisted, or both. At the conference he asserted the need and the possibility to surpass Britain, and attacked those 'erroneous' ideas that underestimated China's ability to develop at high speed and to strive to realize its potential. Pledging to overturn the targets for the 2FYP set at the Eighth Party Congress, he estimated that China could produce 40m. tons of steel in 1972, thereby surpassing the projected British production in the same year. Production of other industrial products, such as coal, machinery, cement, and chemical fertilizer, he maintained, would also exceed British output by then.[77]

Nevertheless, the revised targets for the 2FYP revealed by Li were still the ones designed by the planners; they only slightly exceeded those decided by the Eighth Party Congress.[78] Grain estimate was actually down 10m. tons. The most dramatic increase was chemical fertilizer, from 3m. tons to 7m. tons, reflecting Chen Yun's preferences. The NPAD called for the reclamation of land, the raising of hogs for manure, and the development of chemical fertilizer. Chen rejected the first and qualified the second in favour of the last. Although Li broke ranks with the other planners, there was no time to raise the targets. So Li pledged that the production targets were not finalized, and that further adjustments in steel production were in the works. Indeed, at this time, astronomical increases in production targets were still not the norm.[79] Liu and Li's timely support kept them in Mao's good books and spared them the humiliations that befell other top leaders later. The easy-going Li, in particular, was the only planner not obliged to make any self-criticism in 1958, despite his role in *fanmaojin*, as he and his wife were close family friends of Mao (all three of them hailed from Hunan), and Li was always more attuned to Mao's wishes.[80]

Another national leader who sensed the change in the political wind was Liao Luyan, the Minister of Agriculture. He was thrust into the limelight in January 1956 when chosen to introduce the NPAD at the Supreme State Conference. As the NPAD was sidelined by *fanmaojin*, he drifted along with the trend and for this he was severely reprimanded by Mao in early 1958. Meanwhile, he trimmed his sails accordingly. When chairing the National Agricultural Conference (9–24 December) to promote the NPAD and to map out plans for 1958 and 2FYP, he urged the localities to find ways to realize the NPAD and to promote the high tide in production in 1958. Liao backed Mao's claim that 'a rush of wind' in 1956/7 had blown away the *duohao kuaisheng*, weakened the '4,5,8' goals, destroyed motivation, and led to losses in 1957. To have a GLF in agriculture, it was necessary to 'battle hard for 10 years to fulfil the NPAD', and since according to him 'the next ten years are

---

[77] *RMRB*, December 3 and 8 1957; Gu Shiming, Li Guangui, and Sun Jianping, *Li Fuchun Jingji Sixiang Yanjiu* (Research on Li Funchun's economic thought) (Xining: Qinghai renmin chubanshe, 1992), 76, 114–15.

[78] The targets were: steel 12m. tons, coal 230m. tons, electricity 44bn. watts, chemical fertilizer 70m. tons, cement 12.5m. tons, grain 240m. tons, cotton 2.15m. tons, hogs 220m. heads.

[79] *RMRB*, 8 December 1957; *FGHB*, iii. 6–8.

[80] Teiwes and Sun, *China's Road to Disaster*, 49–51; Xiao Donglian *et al.*, *Qiusuo Zhongguo*, ii. 1106.

dependent on the first three, and the first three years on the first', all must make hay while the sun shone in 1958.[81]

Mao's initiatives also fell on more receptive ears among the provincial leaders. From November to December, some of them criticized rightist conservatism at their party congresses, and organized 'high tides' in industrial and agricultural production. Millions were mobilized to build water conservancy projects, to raise pigs, and to accumulate manure in order to kick off the GLF. In particular, the campaign to eliminate the 'four pests' inaugurated according to the NPAD in Hangzhou and Shanghai pleased Mao, who then urged it to be turned into a national movement.[82] As the localities competed to raise targets, slogans such as 'hard struggle for three years, basically transform the country', 'realize the NPAD in five to seven years' began to be heard.[83] In this atmosphere, the *RMRB*'s New Year editorial went one step further and coined the slogan 'surpass the USA in 20 to 30 years'.[84]

Hangzhou Conference (3–4 January 1958)

Mao made his point, but still found the atmosphere in Beijing stifling. He bore a grudge against *fanmaojin* in 1956, felt vindicated by what he thought was the lacklustre economic performance of 1957, and considered that 'rightist conservatism' was obstructing another emerging leap. As Shanghai and Zhejiang enthusiastically supported his initiatives, in stark contrast to the planners, he travelled to East China on 31 December (excusing himself from the meeting of the standing committee of the Politburo to discuss the 1958 plan and the 2FYP) to flesh out his ambitious programmes. On the same day the SPC transmitted another directive by Mao that urged the following: the areas of industry, transportation, agriculture, commerce, handicraft, post-secondary education, cultivation of urban-peasant intellectuals, science, and urban planning, should draw up long-term plans like the NPAD; the provinces should band together to form economic regions; the upsurge in 1956 was not *maojin*, and opposing *maojin* would dampen things; and as soon as the contours of the 2FYP was drawn up it should be submitted to the Party Centre so that there would not be a fait accompli.[85] When Mao felt that the central planners had not given what he wanted, he shunned them, and increasingly turned to the ministries and regional authorities for inspiration for his radical initiatives, and to marshal their support to bring additional pressure to bear on the planners.[86]

While the planners failed or were unwilling to divine Mao's intentions, he found a soulmate in the Ministry of Metallurgy, and heaped on it lavish praise on at least

---

[81] *RMRB*, 10 and 28 December 1957; *RMSC*, 1958, 516; *Mao Weikan*, xiB. 10. During the Leap and perhaps in other periods, Mao's negative comments on someone or something, even made in an off-hand manner, could be construed to be criticisms, and were taken seriously by all.
[82] *Mao Wengao*, vii. 4–5.   [83] Xie Chuntao, *Dayuejin*, 29; Cong Jin, *Quzhe Fazhan*, 109
[84] Xie Chuntao, *Dayuejin*, 23–5; *RMRB*, 1 January 1958.
[85] *Jingji he Shehui Fazhan Jihua Dashi*, 113.
[86] Bo Yibo, *Huigu*, ii. 636–7; Shi Zhongquan, *Zhuoyue Fengxian*, 328.

three different occasions. The second of the two reports submitted by the MM, which Mao commended, was distributed to the Conference. These two reports catered to Mao's vision. The first discussed the race in the production of non-ferrous metals among nations, and projected that after 1962, nine provinces would be able to produce non-ferrous metals, and that in the future, more than twenty provinces, not just the MM, would cooperate to produce non-ferrous metals.

The second report, which focused on the attack on dogmatism, opened with the claim that the metallurgical industries and industry in general would develop so fast that China could overtake Britain in just ten years, and the US in twenty. The application of the 'red and expert' principle had changed attitudes, enabling the MM to economize. For instance, from a purely technical standpoint, an ore-dressing factory required 46m. *yuan* to build, but only 22m. *yuan* when the perspective of thrift was applied. The report went on to argue that political campaigns actually promote, not inhibit, production. The use of *dazibao* (big character posters) encouraged the raising of targets to 0.5m. tons of steel, 0.45m. tons of pig iron, the raising of standard of production, and the solving of nagging problems such as wages and welfare. The report then criticized the Soviet experience for its reliance on central ministries (not the localities), the one-man management method, the emphasis on the large (not the small and medium sized), the 'tedious' balancing method, the reliance on material incentives and the wearisome rules and regulations.

Finally, the *coup de maître*—the MM projected that steel production could reach 15m. tons during the 2FYP and it would strive to produce 20m. tons by 1962, 40m. tons by 1967, 70m. tons by 1972, and 100m. tons by 1977. This was music to Mao's ears, so he enjoined other ministries to learn from the MM in overcoming the tendencies towards dogmatism, empiricism, 'departmentalism', conservatism, and the neglect of politics, and being red in favour of expert.[87]

Two other ministers who pandered to Mao's whims were also commended. Peng Tao, Minister of Chemical Industries, pledged to raise production to catch up with Britain in five to ten years by building thousands of chemical fertilizer factories and to follow Mao's proposal to allow the provinces to build 110,000 kilometres of railways by 1972 (up from 80,000 in 1958). Others present, such as Henan's Wu Zhipu and Chen Zhenren, vice-director of the Central Rural Work Department, gave extravagant reports that pleased Mao. In contrast, Mao's anger with the planners, particularly Chen and Zhou, intensified.

This formed the background when Mao travelled to his beloved second home, Hangzhou, for a work conference, to discuss methods of leadership in economic construction. The provincial authorities were eager to say what Mao wanted to hear, and he in turn was impressed by the 'patriotic' campaign to eliminate the 'four pests'

---

[87] Li Rui, *Dayuejin*, 234–7; Sun Yeli and Xiong Lianghua, *Fengyun zhong de Chen Yun*, 156. Dogmatism was taken to mean the uncritical copying of foreign (read, Soviet) experience without reference to the real situation in China. Empiricism referred to the alleged tendency of the cadres to view things from the perspective of their past experience, without realizing that with the change in the productive forces and relations, things that were impossible in the past could now be accomplished. And 'departmentalism' meant the protection of the interests of bureaucratic turfs.

in Shanghai, Hubei's experimental plots, and by claims that the large-scale water conservancy campaigns in Anhui in one winter had exceeded the total work amount of the previous seven years. These displays of mass enthusiasm, he felt, had fully vindicated the need to criticize rightist conservatism. As he told the Conference, 'It feels very good criticizing rightist conservatism. The more criticism the merrier'.[88] In contrast, he lost his temper at one point and blasted several other leaders, chastising Zhou Enlai and Bo Yibo by name.[89] The Chairman had registered his strongest displeasure.

New departures required new measures. At this meeting, Mao also began to draft a new document entitled 'Seventeen Articles', which, when later expanded into the 'Sixty Articles on Work Method', would become his most important personal manifesto for a new and alternative developmental strategy that refuted the planners and their methods. At this stage, however, the Seventeen Articles was a fairly innocuous hotchpotch of things such as water supply and fertilizer application to be 'done well'. Other more specific articles urged everyone to combat waste and to introduce experimental plots. The more ambitious Article 9 called on the country to launch 'patriotic' campaigns to eliminate the 'four pests'. This campaign was inspired by the ones conducted in Shanghai and Hangzhou, and Mao was so impressed that he issued a directive in the name of the Party Centre that ordered its immediate adoption nationally.[90] Article 6 said it was desirable for those who were red (ideologically motivated) to become experts as well, because the approaching technical revolution would require many experts, and politicians should also learn professional skills. Article 16 on permanent revolution said that one revolution should follow another in close succession, as collectivization had followed land reform, and as the New Democracy could not be consolidated too far because it had to be demolished. Mao soon latched onto this idea to demand radical and continuous change. Article 11 ordered the provinces to promote industry to ensure that the GVIO in the provinces exceeded their GVAO during the 2FYP, although Mao observed that a national balance must be maintained. Finally, Article 17 observed that imbalance was both a social law and a law of the universe, because enterprises, workshops, and individuals produced at variable speed. The important point was to have comparison and competition.[91] At this stage, this notion of imbalance referred only to the performance of individual enterprises and groups, but soon Mao would elevate it into a philosophical principle governing national economic planning in order to repudiate the modi operandi of the planners.

---

[88] *Mao Weikan*, xiB. 1. For Mao and Hangzhou, see Yang Qingwang (ed.), *Mao Zedong Zhidian Jianshan* (Mao Zedong commands and appreciates the country) (Beijing: Zhongyang wenxian chubanshe, 2000), ii. 1416–34.

[89] *Zhou Enlai Zhuan*, iii. 1365. Yin Jiamin, *Mao Zedong yu Zhou Enlai*, 213. In Chinese communist practice, *dianming* (named) criticism was often much more serious than *budianming* (unnamed) criticism. In other instances, unnamed criticism—the practice of referring to alleged culprits as 'so-and-so', or with lables such as 'sham Marxists', 'tide-watchers'—were used when the party had not reached a verdict, or when Mao wished to keep some reserve.   [90] *Mao Wengao*, vii. 4–5.

[91] *Mao Weikan*, xiB. 2–5.

Finally, Mao instructed that documents like the NPAD be drafted for industry, science, culture, and education, and restated his idea of dividing the country into cooperative regions each containing several provinces.[92] In 1958, these cooperative regions, led by zealous provincial leaders, were Mao's closest allies in advancing Leap policies.

The Climax of *Fanmaojin* and the Nanning Conference (11–22 January): Mao Turns the Table

After Hangzhou, Mao travelled to Nanning to continue his campaign of building support for his initiatives and to flesh out the Leap policies. Shunning the planners, Mao intended to convene a work conference with only the first secretaries of the nine provinces and two municipalities. Only when Zhou reminded him that the Fifth Session of the First National People's Congress was slated to meet in February to discuss the 1958 plan, that he allowed Chen Yun, Li Fuchun, Li Xiannian, and Bo Yibo to attend. Eventually Mao's handpicked list included twenty-seven central and regional leaders (including himself) but only twenty-five attended. Chen absented himself because of illness, which might have been political, knowing that he would bear the brunt of Mao's wrath. Absent as well was Pan Fusheng, Henan's first secretary, who was also under a political cloud.

The planners were scheduled to report on the 1958 plan and budget,[93] but when Mao encountered them he could scarcely control his anger. On the first evening of the conference, a testy Mao lambasted the State Council and the central ministries and commissions for their alleged failures to consult him and for their resistance to carrying out his wishes, directing his barbs specifically against *fanmaojin*. According to Mao, *fanmaojin* had thrown cold water on the Chinese people. If temporary and secondary problems were viewed in context (as 'one finger out of ten'), then the slogan of *duohao kuaisheng*, the NPAD, and the 'committee for the promotion of progress', would not have been overturned. *Fanmaojin* served as an excuse for the rightist attack. He then urged that the term *fanmaojin* never be mentioned again, and raised the ante by warning that it was a *political* issue, and that those who opposed *maojin* were only 50 metres from being rightist.

By contrast, Mao heaped lavish praise on Ke Qingshi. Truth, he said, emerged from Shanghai and the localities, not from Beijing.[94] Then he chided the central leaders for lacking vision and for not using their brains. Producing Ke's report to the

---

[92] Ibid. 1. As early as the end of February, the North China Economic Cooperative Conference was held during which Tan discoursed on his favourite subject of water conservancy. *Neibu Cankao* (Internal Reference) (hereafter, *NBCK*), 4 March 1958, 3–9.

[93] *Mao Wengao*, vii. 11; Liao Gailong, Zhao Baoxu, and Du Qinglin (eds.), *Dangdai Zhongguo Zhengzhi Dashidian, 1949–1990* (A dictionary of major events in contemporary Chinese politics, 1949–1990) (Changchun: Jilin wenshi chubanshe, 1991), 597; *Dangshi Tongxun*, 1987, xii. 31.

[94] Li Rui, *Dajuejin*, 56.

Shanghai Municipal Party Congress, he pointedly defied Zhou, 'You are the premier..., can you produce a document like this one?' Zhou had to say 'No'. Mao then drew the line in the sand, saying 'Aren't you opposed to *maojin*? I'm opposed to *fanmaojin*'.[95] This outburst struck fear among the planners, so after every meeting they met until the small hours, scrambling to discuss how to offer self-criticisms.[96] Sensing that Mao was annoyed with Chen, Ke scored further points with the Chairman by attacking the absent Chen for his alleged iron-fisted control, and for his rejection of Shanghai's request for a large coal-gas project.[97] Others who basked in the limelight were the leaders of Anhui, who claimed that the province had introduced water conservancy in one year to areas exceeding the total accomplished in the previous eight, at a much lower cost. Hubei was also commended because it promised to accomplish ten years' plan in six.[98]

Among the twenty-two documents distributed at the conference, the sections on *fanmaojin* contained in Li Xiannian's report to the Third Session of First National People's Congress, Zhou's speech at the Second Plenum, and the *RMRB* editorial of 20 June 1957, were singled out as erroneous material to be criticized.[99] Mao now took the editorial as a personal attack on him, and underlining the offending passages, he inscribed the words 'vulgar dialectics', 'vulgar Marxism', and 'this is directed pointedly at me', in the margins. In another critique of the *RMRB*, Mao also ordered the censure of all the news and propaganda about *fanmaojin* since June 1956.[100]

Such vehement broadsides by Mao pushed his shaken colleagues into a corner. When Bo was slated to report on the implementation of the 1957 plan and the draft 1958 plan on 15 January, there was no time to manœuvre. In order not to add fire to Mao's wrath and be labelled a rightist, he seized on an expedient suggestion to set up two sets of plans, one for the state, and another one with higher targets, for the enterprises. Two sets of plans were not Bo's original idea;[101] however, as Mao had already mentioned it in his 12 January speech, Bo was forced to play along.[102] This did not placate Mao entirely, as he accused Bo of being a 'middle-of-the-roader', if not 'rightist-leaning'.[103]

Other anxious leaders were at a loss about what to do to calm Mao's outburst. According to Liu's divination, Mao's targets were to be the top economic decision-makers, that is, Zhou, Chen, the two Li's, and Bo, who were at the forefront of *fanmaojin*. However, on the night of 17 January, Mao toned things down a little by meeting with Li Fuchun, Li Xiannian, and Bo, and assured them that his criticism was directed principally at Chen. On the night of 19 January, Zhou, hoping to diffuse the tension, offered his self-criticism to Mao personally, admitting that *fanmaojin* was an error in principle and a manifestation of rightist conservatism, and

[95] Bo Yibo, *Huigu*, ii. 639.
[96] *Zhou Enlai Zhuan*, iii. 1367–8.
[97] Li Rui, *Dajuejin*, 15, 57.
[98] *Mao Weikan*, xiB, 7; Li Rui, *Dayuejin*, 73.
[99] Cong Jin, *Quzhe Fazhan*, 111.
[100] *Mao Wengao*, vii. 32–36; *Mao Weikan*, ix. 160.
[101] Cong Jin, *Quzhe Fazhan*, 118.
[102] *Wansui* (1969), 153.
[103] Bo Yibo, *Huigu*, ii. 638, 682.

accepted main responsibility for the alleged errors.[104] At this time, Mao was considering replacing Zhou with Ke as the premier. Zhou sensed this but feared that if he offered his resignation then, it would be interpreted as a sign of stubborn resistance to Mao. Only at a Politburo meeting in June did he feel it appropriate to raise the issue of whether he was still the suitable person to be premier, but received the endorsement of the Politburo, and presumably Mao. After Nanning, Zhou kept his opinions to himself,[105] or more accurately, hung more gingerly on Mao's every word. In the end, the planners were obliged to raise the targets for the 1958 plan previously mooted according to the spirit of *fanmaojin* at the National Planing conference.[106]

The Sixty Articles

This then was the background to the brainstorming that transformed the Seventeen Articles into the Sixty Articles on Work Methods under the editorship of Mao. His claim that he had been struggling for such a document for the previous eight years was exaggerated,[107] but it was without doubt his manifesto for a new development strategy that repudiated the planners, whom Mao thought had lost their bearings and who had to have their world-view reoriented. Hence Mao told Liu that the discussions were a form of internal rectification of the Party Centre.[108] The invocation of the term rectification conjured up images that everyone would be corrected through criticism and self-criticism and the study of Mao's thought. In other words, Mao was asserting his ideological supremacy, and no dissent would be tolerated.

Like its predecessor, the Sixty Articles is a hotchpotch of ideas culled from reports, discussions, speeches by Mao, and impromptu ideas expressed at the Nanning Conference. It encompassed not just work methods, but also work goals, theoretical principles, and a catalogue of other things. The most important new item, Article 9, ordered the central government to set up two sets of plans. Fulfilment of the targets of the first plan was mandatory, and a second set of plans, containing even higher targets, was expected to be fulfilled with additional exertion. Furthermore, provincial governments were ordered to set up two sets of plans—their first set, which must be fulfilled, was an integral part of the Centre's second set and the basis for interprovincial appraisal and comparison (*pingbi*). Their second set of plans, however, contained even higher targets that were also expected to be attained.

---

[104] Ibid. 638; Li Rui, *Dayuejin*, 72; The text of Zhou's self-criticism is in Shi Zhongquan, *Zhuoyue Fengxian*, 330–2.

[105] Li Peng, *Kaiguo Zongli*, 362–3; Jiang Mingwu *et al.*, *Zhou Enlai de Licheng* (Beijing: Jiefang wenyi chubanshe, 1996), 122; Sun Yeli and Xiong Lianghua, *Jingji Fengyun zhong de Chen Yun*, 141. Another source claims that Zhou did try to exert some minor influence. For instance, the budgetary report for 1958 claimed that China would overtake Britain within fifteen years, but Zhou revised it to say 'fifteen years or a little more time'. Yang Shengqun and Tian Songnian, *Zhongda Juece de Lailong Qumai*, 261.

[106] Xie Chuntao, *Dayuejin*, 32; Liao Gailong *et al.*, *Zhengzhi Dashidian*, 597; the best figures are in *Jingji he Shehui Fazhan Jihua Dashi*, 116–17.　　　　　　　　　　　　　[107] *Mao Weikan*, xiB. 7.

[108] *Mao Wengao*, vii. 83.

This pattern would be duplicated down the administrative ladder, so that the aggregate targets for a whole range of products would become progressively more inflated as they were transmitted downwards. By the time a target reached the grass roots it would have five or six sets of plans.[109] Article 22 expanded the meaning of imbalance by saying that it was constant and absolute, whereas balance was temporary and relative, and that the conversion from balance to imbalance represented a qualitative change. When applied to the economy by Mao, this philosophical principle meant that even though balance was normal, the conversion from balance to imbalance represented certain progress as well.[110] These two articles were highly significant because, literally with the stroke of his pen, a spiteful Mao had explicitly refuted the planners and their modi operandi built up over the previous eight years.[111] In effect, Mao wanted to whiplash the economy from balance to imbalance in order to achieve maximum growth. His obsession with speed and rapid social transformation had triumphed over the careful planning and balancing of the planners. No longer were plans devised with reference to past records and present capabilities, but with goals like overtaking Britain and the USA. For instance, since Britain was expected to produce 40m. tons of steel in 1972, so China should produce 45m. tons by then. This goal would in turn determine the yearly production of steel, and *all* other economic targets.[112] In any case, these teleological economic plans were soon rendered meaningless, even those with the avowed goal of surpassing Britain, as between 1958 and 1960, every sector and unit was urged to race ahead at super speed, doubling, tripling, or further multiplying production targets at will as if the sky was the limit. In this context, the draft economic plan and budget for 1958 proposed by Bo and Li, and presented to the Fifth Session of the National People's Congress in February, with targets even higher than those proposed in October—subsequently called 'the first set of plans'— was a dead letter.

Articles 12 and 13, inspired by Anhui's proposal of 'transforming itself in three years', put forward the slogan 'struggle hard for three years, and basically transform large parts of the country', and Article 12 stipulated that the NPAD should be achieved in six to eight years. Liu Shaoqi's personal contribution, Article 23, enjoined the revision or abolition of all governmental rules and regulations that hindered the enthusiasm of the masses or the productive forces.[113] In 1958, this was carte blanche for the breakdown of the standard operating procedures of all government organizations and enterprises.[114] Mao's notion of 'one finger versus ten

---

[109] *Mao Wengao*, vii. 48; Bo Yibo, *Huigu*, ii. 682.   [110] *Mao Weikan*, xiB. 2–3; *Mao Wengao*, vii. 54.

[111] Li Rui's description of an event illustrates this point. Tian Jiaying told Li Rui that at one of the meetings between Mao and Tan Zhenlin to discuss economic and other affairs in 1958, an irate Mao suddenly slammed his hand on the table (a Chinese expression of anger), and snapped, 'Only Chen Yun can manage the economy! You *don't* think I can do it?' in Li Rui, *Lushan Huiyi Shilu* (A true record of the Lushan Conference), 3rd rev. edn. (Zhengzhou: Henan renmin chubanshe, 2000); *Lushan Huiyi*, 13.

[112] Cong Jin, *Quzhe Fazhan*, 119.

[113] *Mao Wengao*, vii. 46, 49, 54–5. Zhonggong Zhongyang Wenxian Yanjiushi (ed.), *Liu Shaoqi Nianpu, 1898–1969* (Chronicles of Liu Shaoqii, 1898–1969) (Beijing: Zhongyang wenxian chubanshe, 1996), ii. 413–14.   [114] *Mao Weikan*, xiB. 29.

fingers' (part versus the whole; and mistakes in work should not be over-emphasized) was enshrined as Article 34.

In Article 21 Mao elaborated on ideas mentioned at Hangzhou and redefined the current task through his idea of permanent revolution, which stated that revolutions should continue in rapid succession. Since 1949, land reform had been followed by the three major socialist transformations—agricultural collectivization, the sociali-zation of private enterprises and handicraft industries completed in 1956, and the socialist revolution on the political and ideological front which would be basically concluded by 1 July. The current task, according to Mao's new definition, was to be a technical revolution that would facilitate the goal of overtaking Britain in fifteen years or a little longer. Hence, he urged the Party to move its focus of attention to the 'technical revolution'.[115] Other more mundane articles urged the studying of science and technology (Article 39), philosophy and political economy (Article 40), history and law (Article 41), and literature (Article 42). Article 51 called for the launching of a 'patriotic hygiene' campaign to eliminate the 'four pests'. On 12 February, the Party Centre and the State Council, in carrying out Mao's wish, issued a directive on the launching of such a campaign.[116] Finally, Article 60 related Mao's desire (probably genuine) to step down as State Chairman so that he could eschew most ceremonial and administrative duties and focus on Party decision-making and the-oretical matters. Despite this, his instinct to control had plunged himself into all sorts of policy and administrative details during the GLF.[117]

Another key decision made by Mao was to form large cooperatives comprising several advanced APCs. Since 1955, Mao had been obsessed with creating large collectives that he thought would benefit by economies of scale and thereby vigorously promote production and mechanization. According to him, by 1955, he had already advocated the creation of 15,000 to 25,000 large collectives with 5,000 to 6,000 households each, encompassing 20,000 to 30,000 people.[118] Yet the peasant revolt against the advanced APCs beginning in the autumn of 1956 led central leaders to make concessions by shrinking the size of the collectives, and designating the production team (with around 20 households each) as the basic production unit. This downsizing, it was decided, would remain unchanged for ten years.[119] Mao had occasionally given his nod to such retreat policies, but by 1958, he was determined to shun the advice of the planners and to follow his instinct. Moreover, the problems encountered by the large-scale irrigation and water conservancy campaigns introduced in the winter of 1957/8 led many localities to

[115] This contradicted his view that the principal contradiction was between the proletariat and the capitalists made in September/October 1957 and shows how his ideological definition shifted according to his priorities. *Mao Wengao*, vii. 51–2.

[116] *FGHB*, vii. 453–9; Liu Guoxin and Liu Xiao, *Lishi Changpian*, 207.

[117] Gao Zhi and Zhang Nieer (eds.), *Jiyao Mishu de Sinian* (The remembrances of the confidential secretaries) (Beijing: Zhonggong zhongyang dangxiao chubanshe, 1993), 155–56; Wu Xiaomei and Liu Peng, *Zouchang Hongqiang*, 15. Mao was probably appalled by the recent succession struggles in the Soviet Union, and wanted to set himself apart from Stalin. McFarquhar, *Origins*, ii. 32. Ye Yongli, *Mao Zedong yu Liu Shaoqi* (Mao Zedong and Liu Shaoqi) (n.p.: Yuanfang chubanshe, 2000), 314–15.

[118] *Mao Weikan*, xiii. 144.   [119] Bo Yibo, *Huigu*, ii. 729.

amalgamate the APCs, prompting Mao to reopen the issue. After being informed that Guangxi had amalgamated the collectives, Mao said, 'they can create federated governments so that one large cooperative can contain [several] cooperatives'. Subsequently, Mao's opinion on amalgamation of the collectives was passed by the Chengdu Conference in March and the Politburo on 8 April.[120] Continued improvization along the same line would ultimately lead to his decision to form the communes in the summer.

Nanning showed that Mao's hostility toward the planning establishment was so intense that he was bent on demolishing it. His heavy-handed censure of *fanmaojin* and his prohibition of the mention of the term imposed a closure on the discussion of *maojin*, and opened a floodgate of irresponsible energies in the years to come. The conference was a turning point because a supremely confident Mao would no longer tolerate even limited dissenting views of his colleagues as he did before 1957, or be contented to be part of a collective leadership in economic matters.[121] One source said that after Nanning Mao seldom attended Politburo meetings, although he would set the agenda for them, and then let the Politburo members report to him the decisions for his approval. If these decisions were not to his liking, the Politburo had to discuss them again, or simply act according to Mao's preference.[122] On the other hand, he met constantly with like-minded or compliant leaders to push his cause. Wu Lengxi, for instance, obliged by drafting several weighty editorials to promote Mao's new ideas.[123] Consequently, Mao elevated himself above the Politburo, and would completely ignore the bickering of the planners, setting the nation's goals by himself. In this manner he told the Supreme State Conference in January that China should produce 40m. tons of steel, 500m. tons of coal, and 40m. watts of electricity by 1972, and that the NPAD could be accomplished in eight years.[124] He was determined to become the supreme commander of the Leap.

Decentralization Is Accelerated

As the momentum of the GLF gathered, Mao began to consider expanding the scope of decentralization to encourage new initiatives, since he had found the provinces to be his most trusted allies. At the Hangzhou and Nanning conferences, Mao had favoured the granting of even more economic power to the provinces, hoping to coopt them for his attack on *fanmaojin*, to neutralize the planners, and to free them from the comprehensive balance of the central plan.[125] At Nanning he

---

[120] Bo Yibo, *Huigu*, ii. 729; Cong Jin, *Quzhe Fazhan*, 143.
[121] Frederick Teiwes, *Politics and Purges in China*. 2nd edn. (Boulder, Colo.: Westview) p. li; Teiwes and Sun, *Agricultural Cooperativization*, 17.
[122] *Unpublished Chinese Documents*, 195. We counted 29 Politburo meetings from the conclusion of the Nanning conference to the end of 1958, many of which were chaired by Liu Shaoqi and Zhou Enlai. See *Zhou Enlai Nianpu*, ii. 121–99.   [123] Wu Lengxi, *Yi Mao Zhuxi*, 59; *RMRB*, 28 February 1958.
[124] *Wansui* (1969), 155.   [125] Ibid. 146–7. *Mao Weikan*, xiB. 3. *Mao Wengao*, vii. 17.

had already planned to hold four meetings a year with the five provinces in East China to promote the Leap and to harness their enthusiasm.[126] Soon this idea was expanded. On 6 February, in acceding to Mao's wish, the Party Centre decided to divide the country into seven Cooperative Regions (North-East, North China, East China, South China, Central China, South-West, and North-West) to promote *duohao kuaisheng* and fulfilment of the new economic plans. These regions were told to convene regular conferences to exchange information and mutual support, to resolve problems, and to serve as the units for 'appraisal-through-comparison' (*pingbi*).[127]

At a Spring Festival (18 February) reception, Mao went one step further by declaring that the centre's monopoly on power had constrained the productive forces. The centre should not run too many things, he said, whereas the provinces should run most economic affairs because they were better at it and could be trusted. Therefore, industry, agriculture, finance, commerce, culture, and education should *all* be decentralized. All provinces should open iron mines, small iron and steel mills, chemical fertilizer factories, machinery factories, etc. if they had the raw materials. Even special districts, counties, and towns, could run their own industries so that the enthusiasm of more units could be mobilized.

On the issue of the damming of the Three Gorges, a huge water conservancy project advocated by Lin Yishan, the Director of the Changjiang Water Conservation Committee, and by the Ministry of Water Conservancy, which would have dynamized the NPAD and the GLF, Mao was more sober. He accepted the dissenting opinion from Li Rui of the Ministry of Electrical Industry after listening to presentations from both sides. Nevertheless, when Mao was informed that there was rivalry between the two ministries, he ordered an instant merger of the two, showing his intolerance for any bureaucratic wrangling.[128]

The political fallout of Mao's intervention was immediate. The Fifth Session of the First NPC (1–11 February) approved the 1958 budget and the economic plan submitted by Li Xiannian and Bo Yibo, which included higher targets than those set in the months before. Moreover, it was pointed out that these figures were *only* the centre's first set of plans, and that all ministries and localities should work out a second set of plans accordingly.[129] This prompted the delegates from the ministries and provinces to compete in pledging Leaps in sectors as diverse as water transport, food processing, commerce, science, and so on. Henan vowed to be 'water conservation(ized)' in 1959, and to realize the '4, 5, 8' targets in 1962. Hebei pledged to complete a ten-year plan in just five years.[130] In their reports, Li and Bo gave obligatory apologies for their roles in *fanmaojin*, and Premier Zhou was relieved of

---

[126] *Mao Weikan*, xiB. 10.   [127] *Jingji Guanli Dashiji*, 104.

[128] Li Rui, *Dayuejin*, 1–29. Wu Xiaomei and Liu Peng, *Zouchu Hongqiang*, 22–9.

[129] Xie Chuntao, *Dayuejin*, 35; *Jingji he Shehui Fazhan Jihua Dashiji*, 117.

[130] *Unpublished Chinese Documents*, 272. The Chinese word *hua* (-ize) is a suffix used widely during the GLF. When attached to nouns or adjectives, it turns them into verbs such as 'modernize' and 'industrialize'. When these verbs are put in the past participle form, it means the completion of the process, such as industrialized, modernized, and water-conservation(ized).

his concurrent position as Foreign Minister.[131] In addition, as early as December 1957, the official journals of the SPC and the State Statistical Bureau, *Jihua Jingji* (Planned Economy) and *Tongji Gongzuo* (Statistical Work), were suspended, to be replaced by a single journal, *Jihua yu Tongji* (Planning and Statistics). The planning system was totally devastated.

Expanded Politburo Meeting (Beijing, 13–23 February)

Meanwhile, Mao's broadside against the top leaders at Nanning sent shock waves all the way to Beijing. On returning to the capital he convened an expanded Politburo meeting to transmit the spirit of the Nanning conference, to discuss the Sixty Articles, and to continue the criticism of *fanmaojin*. Mao was now able to confront Chen, who had been absent from Nanning and Hangzhou, directly. At a 18 February (Spring Festival in 1958) Politburo meeting, called ostensibly to discuss adopting the Sixty Articles, Mao in fact presented them as a fait accompli because he specified that the discussion was to take the form of rectification (*zhengfeng*) at the centre. As mentioned, his invocation of the term 'rectification' was a particularly lethal weapon because it conjured up rituals such as criticism and self-criticism to unify thinking under Mao's thought.[132] Indeed, he accused his colleagues again of not being too much different from the rightists, and claimed that *fanmaojin* was not real Marxism. 'I don't approve of calling *fanmaojin* Marxist', he said, 'I approve calling *maojin* Marxist. This *maojin* is good; it enables the peasants to run more water conservancy (projects)!' Henceforth, the conference decided that the slogan *fanmaojin* would be forbidden.[133] When it was Chen's turn to talk, an irritated Mao interjected repeatedly and chastised the State Council for stonewalling his efforts to have input into the 1FYP and yearly economic plans, although he was obliged to sign them.[134]

At the end, though still bitter, Mao held out an olive branch. To soothe the frayed nerves of his colleagues, he said,

I had to fire a cannon at Nanning. It was only a small blast, but it made many comrades nervous. Comrade Xiannian could not sleep at night without taking sleeping pills. Why should you be so nervous? In future [I] still have to rely on you people to do things, no others will do.

---

[131] *RMRB*, 12 and 13 February 1958; *Zhou Enlai Zhuan*, iii. 1370. This might be another symbolic humiliation of the Premier, because Zhou continued to take charge of China's foreign policy until his death in 1976. The view contained in *Bainianchao*, 5, 1999, 29, that Mao dismissed Zhou because he was discontented with Zhou's 'peaceful coexistence' policy requires more proof.

[132] *Zheng* is an ominous word in Chinese communist parlance that means to fix, punish, or make someone suffer. So *aizheng* means to suffer criticism or attack. It follows that the word rectification (*zhengfeng*) implied punishment and suffering. The mere mention of these words, despite Mao's protestation to the contrary, raised the spectre that it was within his power to make people suffer.

[133] Liu Guoxin and Liu Xiao, *Lishi Changpian*, 207.

[134] Bo Yibo, *Huigu*, ii. 650; Sun Yeli and Xiong Lianghua, *Fengyun Zhong de Chen Yun*, 138; *Mao Wengao*, vii. 83.

Despite this reassurance, Chen, Li Xiannian, and Bo still felt obliged to give self-criticisms, and accept responsibilities for the alleged errors of *fanmaojin*.[135] They were humiliated and immobilized.

During the conference, Mao sponsored another initiative by penning an *RMRB* editorial (18 February) lauding the ongoing anti-waste and anti-conservatism campaign in the enterprises and government organs. As in the Sixty Articles, Mao called on every unit, factory, cooperative, school, armed forces unit, and so on, to 'struggle' against waste once a year, using the method of 'airing of views, rectification, and reform'. Eventually, on 3 March, the Party Centre launched a formal 'two-anti' (*shangfan*) campaign against waste, bureaucratism, 'lethargy', evil influence (*xieqi*), and conservatism (or the 'five winds') nationally for two to three months. This directive claimed that once the campaign was 'firmly grasped', then the same amount of manpower, funds, and supplies 'would enable [the people] to accomplish results several dozen percent or even several folds more than the original plan, given the same financial and manpower resources'. This marked Mao's direct appeal to the country to mobilize and disarm the 'conservatives' to give the country a free hand.[136] Consequently, many ministries and provinces felt obliged to revise their production plans once again.[137]

The Great Leap Forward Takes Shape: The Chengdu Conference (8–26 March)

With all the key planners in the dock, the floodgates holding back impulsiveness were overrun. Furthermore, to mobilize for wider support and to generate more publicity for the GLF, an exhilarated Mao brought his campaign to another regional centre, Chengdu, as only a few leaders from the central and south provinces and only a few ministries were present at Nanning.[138] This work conference of the expanded Politburo was attended by 39 participants, including Politburo members, ministers of the Ministries of Metallurgy, Railways, and Chemical Engineering, the directors of the Cooperative Regions, and some provincial first secretaries. It met sometimes in Plenum and sometimes in three small groups. Mao's speeches were delivered to the entire Plenum, although he kept tabs on the discussions of the small groups by his secretaries' briefings.[139] The conference discussed and passed 37 documents on the second set of plans for 1958 for local industries, the amalgamation of small APCs, and the socialist transformation of the remaining private enterprises, individual handicraftsmen, and small pedlars.

Two out of the six speeches Mao gave at this work conference referred to *fanmaojin*. On the first day of the conference, Mao set the tone by repeating that

---

[135] Bo Yibo, *Huigu*, ii: 639–40, 644–45, 650. The text of Chen's self-criticism is in Sun Yeli and Xiong Lianghua, *Fengyun Zhong de Chen Yun*, 137 and 145.

[136] *RMRB*, 4 March 1958; *Mao Weikan*, xiB. 22–3; Bo Yibo, *Huigu*, ii. 796.

[137] *Unpublished Chinese Documents*, 274.

[138] Li Rui, *Dayuejin*, 256–7; Wu Lengxi, *Yi Mao Zhuxi*, 60–5.   [139] Ibid. 160–1.

fanmaojin was an error in principle, although he also tried to tone things down, and declared that he would not *zheng* (fix) anyone. Referring to his broadside against *fanmaojin* he said,

One work method is the Marxist adventurism, and the other is anti-Marxist *fanmaojin*. Which method should we choose? . . . I think we should take the *maojin* route.[140]

At Nanning [we] raised this question, and many comrades were nervous, but things are better now. My objective in clarifying the matter is to enable us to achieve a common language, to do things well . . . I absolutely did not want to make life difficult for any of my colleagues.[141]

He further underscored that the slogan of *fanmaojin* should be shelved in favour of anti-rightist conservatism.[142] In his opinion, the *fanmaojin* of 1956 was inconsistent with either materialism or dialectics, and the provincial secretaries were not consulted before it was implemented. The State Council, in adopting the *fanmaojin* policy, had alienated many ministries, because the later were divided—although the ministries of finance and commerce demurred, the industrial ministries were in favour of doing things in a big way.[143]

In another shrewd manipulation of the definition of ideology, Mao now linked *fanmaojin* directly to the rightist attack of 1957. Both, Mao reasoned, stemmed from the failure to appreciate the enthusiasm of the peasants after collectivization. Therefore, he ordered the reprint of part of the preface he wrote for the 1955 book, *Socialist Upsurge In China's Countryside*, and distributed it with his explanation, . . . 'We did not anticipate that such a great storm would burst upon the world in 1956, nor did we anticipate that a campaign of *fanmaojin* would occur in the same year in our country, a campaign that dampened the enthusiasm of the masses. Both events gave considerable ammunition to the rightists in mounting their wild attacks'.[144]

On 18 March, Chen Boda elaborated at length on Mao's ideas from theoretical and historical perspectives, while Mao contributed with many interjections. In this lengthy 'duet', the two maintained that China had entered the stage where 'one day equals twenty years', and that the economy could develop at high speed. Disagreement over the speed of development had been the key policy divergence in the period of socialist construction, and speed was also seen as the key issue in the competition with the imperialists. Chen and Mao claimed that the cult of personality was necessary to establish the authority of the 'helmsman' who navigated the oceans, and a correct cult of personality was required to sustain unity. Finally, both claimed that the Nanning and Chengdu conferences were really rectification conferences for the centre and provinces to 'unify thinking and action' in order to remove obstacles to the development of the productive forces.[145]

Finally, Mao referred to the 'two divergent opinions on speed' by equating the disagreement between him and Deng Zihui on collectivization with the dispute

---

[140] *Mao Weikan*, xiB. 25.   [141] Ibid. 26. *Mao Wengao*, vii. 108.
[142] Bo Yibo, *Huigu*, ii. 640, 644.   [143] Ibid. 640; *Mao Weikan*, xiB. 36.
[144] *Mao Xuanji*, v. 226.   [145] Li Rui, *Dayuejin*, 195–207; Bo Yibo, *Huigu*, ii. 661.

between him and the *fanmaojin* 'faction'. The implication that Mao's correct policies were opposed by incorrect ones, was clear for everyone to see.[146] Mao raised the stakes further by declaring that the divergent opinions in the CCP should best be viewed as a form of class struggle. Referring to the provincial purges in 1957, Mao said that 'anti-Party cliques' existed in eight provinces, and 'rightist' activities in others. During the class struggle, those 'capitalists' hiding within the Party would surely be exposed. The line was drawn in the sand. Chen earned Mao's trust in the inner circle. When Mao proposed to start *Hongqi* (Red Flag), a new theoretical journal for the Central Committee, undoubtedly to tighten his ideological grip, Chen was entrusted with the editorship. Chen obliged, despite his early reluctance.[147] In the second half of 1958, the authoritative articles in this journal were Mao's weapons to promote the various aspects of the GLF, but when Mao reversed himself in November, Chen became the scapegoat and fell from grace temporarily.

As the GLF methods swerved from the established path, Mao viewed the Soviet model in an increasingly critical light. Indiscriminate copying of the Soviet Union, especially in industry and planning, he announced, was a kind of 'superstition' (*mixin*, literally blind faith) or dogmatism that was extremely harmful. Hence the need was to break out of the existing mould to 'liberate' one's thinking and to unleash the creativity of the masses.[148] Soon, the code word 'superstition' as used by Mao was broadened to include reliance on Soviet experience, Marxist classics, views of the academics and experts, and existing rules and regulations.[149]

This view of superstition was inconsistent with his position as a 'supreme leader', but Mao was confident that he alone stood for the truth, and sought to make his position supreme by raising the issue of the cult of personality. There were correct and incorrect cults of personality, he argued, and it was necessary to idolize the leader if he stood for the truth.[150] This affirmation of the cult of personality was an open renunciation of the Soviet policy of de-Stalinization and the resolutions laid down by the CCP's Eighth Party Congress. It also established Mao's position as the 'correct' and paramount decision-maker during the Leap. With this new discourse Mao elevated himself formally above the Party and would no longer be bound by its resolutions. Accordingly, sycophants were quick to embrace these viewpoints. For instance, Tao Zhu gushed, '[We must] have blind faith [*mixin*] in the Chairman', and Ke chimed in, 'We have to trust the Chairman to the degree of blind faith, we should obey the Chairman to the extent of total abandon (*mangmu*)'.[151] These adulations received the expressed appreciation from the Chairman.

On the other hand, Liu's timely support of Mao's GLF initiatives spared him open humiliations despite his role in the offending editorial, although he, too, was obliged to criticize himself, and accepted Mao's views on high-speed development.

---

[146] *RMRB*, 27 May 1958; see also *Unpublished Chinese Documents*, 288–9.
[147] *Mao Weikan*, xiB. 33.   [148] Ibid. 26–7.
[149] Li Rui, *Dayuejin*, 258.   [150] *Mao Weikan*, xiB. 28.
[151] Cong Jin, *Quzhe Fazhan*, 117; Xie Chuntao, *Dayuejin*, 40.

Subsequently, he also championed Mao's view of the cult of personality and consistently deferred to Mao from then on.[152] As he announced to the delegates:

The chairman is much wiser than we are. In every respect—thinking, perspective, foresight, and method—we are way behind. Our task is to learn from him seriously. We can say we can do this. This is not beyond our reach . . . Of course, certain aspects of the Chairman, like his breadth of historical knowledge, his revolutionary experiences, and his strong memory, are difficult to surpass.[153]

Mao's triumph over his colleagues was complete. The delegates were either pushing for more investigation of the responsibility for *fanmaojin* or offering more self-criticisms on why they had failed to appreciate Mao's new ideas. Others had no choice but to toe the line. In a speech on foreign affairs and *fanmaojin* delivered on 19 March, Zhou Enlai, too, saw fit to insert a few paragraphs of self-criticism, saying that he had lacked faith in matters of principles, and that he had not understood that economic construction could follow the *duohao kuaisheng*.[154] On 21 March, Chen Yun offered a lengthy self-criticism on his role in *fanmaojin*, citing his excessive fear of the deficit and his failure to supply information to Mao and the Politburo, and vowing to make amends with concrete measures.[155] At the end of the conference, even Mao indicated that he did not want to hear any more self-criticism or talk about investigations of responsibility, although he also implied that offenders should prove themselves with actions, as words were cheap.[156]

In contrast, two persons singled out for praise were Wang Heshou and Wu Zhipu. In their extravagant reports about how to implement GLF policies, the former pledged to accelerate production to catch up with Britain and the USA, strive to produce 20m. tons of steel in 1962, 40m. in 1967, and 70m. in 1972, to save on investment, and to mobilize the masses in order to break down 'dogmatism'. Wu, on the other hand, pledged to rely on mass mobilization to mechanize irrigation and water conservancy in two years, agriculture in five years, and the fulfilment of the NPAD in 1958 or 1959 in Henan. He claimed that Henan would try to manufacture cement and pig iron by the indigenous method, and that illiteracy could be wiped out in 50 to 80 days in each APC.[157] Conferences like these gave the ministries and provinces excellent opportunities to ingratiate themselves with Mao either out of opportunism or faith in the Chairman, or both. Those caught without an extravagant report lost their chances.

[152] Zhonggong Zhongyang Wenxian Yanjiushi, Jin Chongji, and Huang Zheng (eds.), *Liu Shaoqi Zhuan* (A biography of Liu Shaoqi) (Beijing: Zhongyang wenxian chubanshe, 1998), ii. 828–32; Huang Zheng (ed.), *Gongheguo Zhuxi Li Shaoqi* (Liu Shaoqi, Chairman of the Republic) (Beijing: Zhonggong dangshi chubanshe, 1998), 1194–5; Zhang Wenhe and Li Yifan, *Zoujin Liu Shaoqi* (Getting close to Liu Shaoqi) (Beijing: Zhongyang wenxian chubanshe, 1998), 336; Yang Shengqun and Tian Songnian, *Zongda Juece*, 262; Zhang Taozhi. *Zhonghua Renmin Gongheguo Yanyi* (A historical novel of the PRC) (Beijing: Zuojia chubanshe, 1996), ii. 540.   [153] Li Rui, *Dayuejin*, 224.
[154] Ibid. 224–5; Shi Zhongquan, *Zhuoyue Fengxian*, 332–3; *Unpublished Chinese Documents*, 286–7.
[155] Ibid. 221–5.
[156] *Mao Weikan*, xiB. 36; Yang Shengqun and Tian Songnian, *Zhongda Juece*, 262.
[157] Li Rui, *Dayuejin*, 234 ff.

This was the case with Ke Qingshi, the star at Nanning, who received a cold reception at Chengdu because he did not have an article prepared. To make good, he asked Li Rui to pen an article on how to have a GLF in education and culture, turn everyone into university graduates, and build universities everywhere. Because the ideas were insubstantial, Li grudgingly wrote down one or two thousand words, but the article was not chosen to be duplicated for distribution at the conference, so Ke blamed Li for it. From then on, he always brought along Zhang Chunqiao to all central conferences.[158]

Riding the wave of triumph, Mao formally proposed the gradual amalgamation of the smaller APCs into larger ones and a directive to this effect was promulgated in March, leading to a movement to build large collectives in the first half of 1958.[159] The conference also decided to combine the previously mooted slogans and turn them into a General Line for development that said 'Summon up fully one's enthusiasm, and strive upstream, to build socialism by using more, faster, better, and more economical results'.[160] A second set of accounts for the 1958 economic plan and budget, with targets much higher than those made public in February, submitted by the party committees of the SEC and the Ministry of Finance, was passed by the conference. The GVIO was raised from 74.7 to 90.4bn. *yuan*; the GVAO from 68.8 to 75.4bn. *yuan*; grain from 196 to 215.8m. tons; and steel production from 6.25 to 7m. tons.[161]

In any case, these targets or 'control figures', high as they were, were subsequently raised again in the Party Congress in May, and despite the number crunching, they no longer bore any relation to reality and became meaningless in themselves. They were only significant as reminders to raise production dramatically and as indicators of loyalty to Mao's cause. For instance, right after Chengdu, the SEC sent six vice-directors to the Cooperative Regions to explain the centre's second set of plans, which would become the provinces' first set of plans. The second set of plans of the provinces, in turn, were anywhere from 40 to 50 per cent, or even two or three times, higher than the provinces' first plans. At the county level and lower levels, the aggregates were even higher, making a mockery of the planning system.[162]

In theoretical matters, Mao proposed a new theory of two exploiting classes and painted a more dangerous picture of socialist transition. The first class included the

---

[158] Ibid. 215.

[159] Zhonghua Renmin Gongheguo Guojia Nongye Weiyuanhui Bangongting, *Nongye Jitihua Zhongyao Wenjian Huibian* (A collection of important documents on agricultural collectivization, ii. 1958–1981) (Beijing: Zhonggong dangshi ziliao chubanshe, 1981), 15 (hereafter, *NJZWH*); Chen Jiyuan, Chen Jiaji, and Yang Xun. *Zhongguo Nongcun Jingji Bianqian, 1949–1989* (The economic changes in China's countryside) (Taiyuan: Shanxi jingji chubanshe, 1993), 300; *Mao Weikan*, xiB. 42, 46.

[160] Bo Yibo, *Huigu*, ii. 662–3.

[161] The GVIO accomplished in 1957 was 6.8bn. *yuan*; the GVAO was 64.9bn. *yuan*. Grain output in 1957 was 185m. tons, and steel production was 5.24m. tons. For details of the second set of plans, see *Zhonggong Dangshi Jiaoxue Cankao Ziliao* (CCP history teaching reference materials) (n.p.: Zhongguo renmin jiefangjun guofang daxue dangshi dangjian zhenggong jiaoyanshi, 1986), xxii. 414–21.

[162] *Jingji Guanli Dashiji*, 110.

imperialist, feudal remnants of the bureaucratic bourgeoisie, those among the landlords, rich peasants, counter-revolutionaries, bad elements who had not been reformed, and rightists. The second comprised most of the national bourgeoisie, the democratic parties, and capitalist intellectuals. According to Mao, both were anti-socialist, and the former should be treated as enemies of the people.[163] This was a conscious effort to overturn the evaluations of the Eighth Party Congress, which resolved that the classes in the first category had basically been destroyed, that the contradiction between the people and the bourgeoisie was basically resolved, and that the socialist system had already been established.[164] One may also add that with the state controlling the means of production and the completion of collect-ivization by 1956/57, classes in the orthodox Marxist sense no longer existed. Despite his actual views on class configuration, especially after the Anti-Rightist Campaign, Mao's redefinition was intended, at least partially, to underscore the hostility of the enemies so that the Party would rally under his leadership. The equation of 'rightists' with 'enemies' must certainly have struck fear into those who might be labelled rightist.

Decentralization is Rushed

As mentioned, Mao's desire to reform the superstructure led him to consider a more extreme version of decentralization than the one envisaged by Chen's regulations of the past November.[165] He shared with the planners the virtues of decontrol, but sought to weaken the central bureaucracy and enhance the role of the provinces because he felt that they were more receptive to his Leap initiatives, particularly the promotion of local industries.

At Chengdu, Guangdong claimed that financial and industrial decentralization there had already proven advantageous—provincial investment was raised from the centrally approved 119 to 226m. *yuan*, although the original figure was almost the amount invested during the entire 1FYP. The bulk of this increase, according to Guangdong officials, would come from savings from the 'anti-waste' and econo-mizing efforts of the enterprises. Hence, they urged the centre to keep the financial arrangement unchanged for five years and to approve its five-year investment plan. They also claimed that those enterprises located in the provinces were still dom-inated by the central ministries, making it impossible for provinces to get involved, resulting in duplication and waste. Hence, they proposed that enterprises whose production was closely related to the regional economy be assigned to localities. Further decentralization, they claimed, could promote local initiatives. This was exactly what Mao wanted to hear, and therefore he instructed speedy consideration and implementation.[166] A regulation duly passed by the conference stated that when

---

[163] *Mao Weikan*, xiB. 39: Xie Chuntao, *Dayuejin*, 40; *Mao Wengao*, vii. 119.

[164] *RMSC*, 1957, 55.

[165] 'The more drastic the better' was his view on decentralization at that time, Mao reminisced in June 1959. Gu Longsheng, *Mao Zedong Jingji Nianpu*, 472.

[166] *Mao Wengao*, vii. 127–8; *Nanfang Ribao* (Southern Daily) (hereafter, *NFRB*), 30 January 1958.

the provinces wanted to build above-norm[167] enterprises, they could take charge of the design and budgeting, if they submitted a brief plan to the centre for approval. The provinces were allowed to approve other above-norm construction projects producing goods not requiring national balance or coordination, provided that they submitted this on file to the relevant ministries.[168]

After the Chengdu Conference, and in compliance with Mao's wish, the CC and SC quickly promulgated another decree on 11 April 1958, to accelerate and expand the list of enterprises to be decentralized. Only those enterprises that were most important and special were to be retained.[169] Local authorities were allowed to share the profit of certain ministry-managed enterprises located in their areas of jurisdiction. They were also given the power to make adjustments affecting even enterprises remaining under the management of central ministries in matters such as production planning and cooperation, material transfer, and allocation of manpower, if they fulfilled central plans. For other ministry-managed raw material industrial enterprises, the portion of profit exceeding the state plan quota was to be divided between the ministry and local authorities.[170]

Only seven weeks later, another decree (2 June) ordered that as many enterprises as possible should be decentralized, and as quickly as possible, and that all transfers had to be completed in a *fortnight*.[171] This showed Mao's impatience in shaking the enterprises free of all central ministry controls. Subsequently, with undue haste, 80 per cent (or about 8,800 in number) of all the enterprises belonging to the industrial ministries were transferred to the local authorities by mid-June.[172] At the end of the year, the percentage had gone up to 87 per cent.[173] Nevertheless, some provinces, supposedly the beneficiaries of decentralization, found these changes too overwhelming; for instance, Yunnan, Guizhou and Ningxia pleaded that they were unable to handle some new coal mines, so their management was reverted to the Ministry of Coal Industry.[174]

In the end, 885 out of 1,165 enterprises directly managed by the ministries were handed down to the provincial governments. This included all the enterprises previously managed by the Ministry of Textile, 96 per cent of all the units of the Ministry of Light Industry, 91 per cent of the Ministry of Chemical Industry; 81 percent of the Ministry of Machinery (civilian use); 77.7 per cent of the Ministry

---

[167] The 'norm' for capital investment for heavy industrial projects ranged from 5 to 10 million *yuan*, and from 3 to 5 million *yuan* for light industrial projects. Before 1957, all 'above-norm' projects and enterprises were controlled by the central agencies such as the SPC, SEC, or the ministries. Robert Bowie and John Fairbank, *Communist China 1955–59: Policy Documents with Analysis* (Cambridge, Mass.: Harvard University Press, 1962), 423; Audrey Donnithorne, *China's Economic System* (London: Allen & Unwin, 1967), 473–4.   [168] *Jingji he Shehui Fazhan Jihua Dashi*, 118.

[169] *FGHB*, vi. 392; vii. 331.

[170] Ibid. vi. 392; vii. 331–2. See also *Beijing Review* (hereafter, *BR*), 1958, 19: 6.

[171] Bo Yibo, *Huigu*, ii. 798. Zhonghua Renmin Gongheguo Dadian Pianweihui (ed.). *Zhonghua Renmin Gongheguo Dadian* (A major dictionary of the PRC) (Beijing: Zhongguo jingji chubanshe, 1994), 547–8.   [172] *RMRB*, 25 June 1958.

[173] Liu Guoguang and Wang Ruisun, *Zhongguo De Jingji Tizhi Gaige* (The reform of China's economic system) (Beijing: Renmin chubanshe, 1982), 5.   [174] *RMRB*, 25 June 1958.

of Metallurgy, and more than 66 per cent of enterprises in all other ministries.[175] Henceforth, the central economic planning and management system shrank dramatically in 1958, and the provinces used their new powers to compete in building enterprises and start construction projects according to the demands of the Leap, resulting in grossly expanded investment. Moreover, the number of central ministries was reduced from 41 in 1957 to 33 in 1958, and to 30 in 1959, so that many party and government personnel were sent downward to lower levels to participate in labour or in administration. At the end of 1959, there were only 39 central ministries and commissions, or 60 central organs (if the staff organs, secretariat, attached to the State Council, were included) compared to 48 and 81, respectively, in 1956.[176]

Mao was convinced that these draconian decentralization measures would spur production and industrialization, with the provinces taking the lead. At Chengdu he had slapped a new task onto the provinces; they were required to raise their GVIO to exceed their GVIO in five or seven years, exceeding the previous demand of five to ten years. Another central directive demanded that they launch a campaign to redesign farm tools, in order to realize mechanization and semi-mechanization in five to seven years.[177] Yet, Mao was not totally oblivious to the danger of ever-raising targets. Just as the country was gearing up for the GLF, he expressed concern about overzealousness, exaggeration, and impractically high targets, and counselled his subordinates to tone it down. Nevertheless, on the whole, he still thought these transgressions harmless and wanted to push ahead.[178]

The Chengdu Conference gave the GLF a tremendous push. In early April, Deng Xiaoping, Li Fuchun, and Bo duly transmitted the spirit of the Conference to other national leaders. Immediately after Chengdu, Mao travelled by train and arrived at Wuhan on 28 March for more briefings and rest. As Wu Zhipu and Zhou Xiaozhou were absent from Chengdu, Mao wanted to fill them in with details of the two exploiting classes and smashing superstitions, etc.[179]

Mao continued to promote his cause, not unaware of the extravagant claims, but more concerned to prove himself right in the end. He summoned provincial secretaries from South Central and East China to a briefing meeting at Hankou (1–6 April), to listen to Wu Zipu's (Henan) and Zeng Xisheng's (Anhui) plan for 'battle hard for three years'. Again he poured scorn on *fanmaojin*, disputed the claim that 1957 was more practical than 1956, and called for criticism of the 'safe and reliable' faction. In a country as vast as China, Mao reasoned, the emphasis on the 'safe and reliable' would only lead to calamity, and one way to deal with conservatives was to launch new slogans and create new tasks from time to time. Accordingly, he approved the 'leap forward' plans submitted by the provinces. However, when

---

[175] Bo Yibo, *Huigu*, ii. 798; *Jingji he Shehui Fazhan Jihua Dashi*, 120–21.

[176] Su Shangyao and Han Wenwei, *Zhongguo Renmin Gongheguo Zhongyang Zhengfu Jigou* (The government structure of the PRC) (Beijing: Jingji kexue chubanshe, 1993), 7–9.

[177] Xie Chuntao, *Dayuejin*, 41; *NJZWH*, ii. 17–18.

[178] *Mao Weikan*, xiB. 26, 30, 38. Cases of cadre exaggeration and coercion were already reported in *NBCK*, 7 March 1958, 3–4.   [179] Li Rui, *Dayuejin*, 262.

Henan boasted that it would accomplish the provisions in the NPAD in just *one* year, and Anhui projected too many large-scale water conservancy campaigns, Mao told them to tone down and leave some leeway. He realized that the current propaganda stressed 'more' and 'faster' at the expense of 'better' and 'more economically'. Therefore, he called for realism in the current high tide of production, so that work could be combined with rest. The *RMRB* was told to stop making propaganda of 'ize' (*hua*)[180] lightly, because he was suspicious about claims by some places that they could be 'water conservation(ized)' in three years. On the other hand, Mao also indicated that if a bumper harvest did not materialize, or if the leap were to come to naught, the 'tide-watchers' would feel vindicated, and then there would be another *fanmaojin*.[181] Here he was presenting his subordinates with a double-edged sword— he urged for more caution, but at the same time, applied more pressure and hinted that no let-down was admissible.

Mao's next task was to ensure that leap policies would be enshrined in the coming Party Congress. On 13 April, he left Wuhan for Guangzhou, to which he had summoned the heads of the industrial ministries (including the ministries of metallurgy, chemical industries, railways, hydroelectric power, and geology) to report to him directly on how to overtake Britain in fifteen years. Meanwhile, Mao told the top leaders that, contrary to previous estimates, China could catch up with the capitalist countries in agriculture and industry even sooner—Britain in ten years, and the USA in twenty, although the slogan on catching up with Britain in fifteen years would still be kept.[182] His method was to reverse the past experience of relying on the centre, by relying instead on a combination of large, medium, and small modes of production, so that half of the responsibilities would be assigned to the localities. At the secret Guangzhou meeting (26–9 April) he also posed the new question of whether the USA could be surpassed in the same period. Those who told Mao what he wanted to hear garnered praise from him. For instance, a most extravagant report submitted by Liu Lanbo, deputy minister of the Ministry of Water Conservancy and Electricity, claimed that development of electric power was slow in the past because the planning ministries mechanically applied the principle of balance. Therefore, from then on he would urge seizing the initiative, relying on a combination of big, medium, and small hydroelectric stations. Particular emphasis would be put on the medium and small ones, and since they were run by the local authorities, half of the responsibilities of the ministry would have been devolved to the provinces.

[180] The Chinese word *hua* is a suffix used widely during the GLF. When attached to nouns or adjectives, it turns them into verbs such as 'modernize' and 'industrialize'. When these verbs are put in the past participle form, it means the completion of the process, such as 'industrialized', 'modernized', and 'water-conservationized'.

[181] *Mao Weikan*, xiB. 53–54; Bo, *Huigu*, ii. 641; Cong Jin, *Quzhe Fazhan*, 113; Xie Chuntao, *Dayuejin*, 44; Wu Xiaomei and Liu Peng, *Zouchu Hongqiang*, 80; Jia Zhengqiu, *Mao Zedong Waixun Ji*, 451–2; Wu Lengxi, *Yi Mao Zhuxi*, 66–8.

[182] *Mao Wengao*, vii. 177, 185–8; *Dangde Wenxian*, 1994, 4: 77. Before Mao's disclosure, Liu Shaoqi had already told the ambassador of the German Democratic Republic that because of the Leap, the economic targets, which were far too low, had to be revised, and that catching up with Britain required only ten, not fifteen, years. *Liu Shaoqi Nianpu*, 421.

Liu Lanbo further claimed that during the 2FYP, production could be accelerated so that Britain could be surpassed in ten years. The entire country would be electrified by mobilizing the masses to run hydroelectric factories. Since most of the water conservancy projects would generate electricity, the minister broached the slogan 'all people run electricity', which began the GLF convention of 'all people run this and that'. Mao praised the report for having put 'politics in command' (*zhengzhi tongshuai*) and suggested other ministries should imitate this and that of the MM to present at the forthcoming Party Congress. On the other hand, Liu Jingfan, deputy minister of the Ministry of Geology, who failed to read the Chairman's intentions, was rebuked by an irate Mao for not getting to the point.[183] Overall, buoyed by the fervour, Mao now urged the conference to consider the prospect of surpassing the USA in fifteen years by redefining the priorities.[184]

On 23 April, he sent a letter to all provincial secretaries urging them to shift their attention to industry, transport, finance, education and culture, and military affairs, because agriculture had received sufficient attention in the past winter. They were also urged to make projections about the value of industrial product in their areas by 1962 by using the *yixu daishi*[185] method, and bring these suggestions to the Party Congress.[186]

The Great Leap Forward is Officially Launched: The Second Session of the Eighth Party Congress (5 to 23 May)

After much fermentation, the Second Session of the Eighth Party Congress (5–23 May 1958) was convened to formalize and legitimize the decisions made in the previous months, to inform the Party, and to gear the Party up for the total mobilization. It approved the so-called 'General Line for Socialist Construction' and the slogan of 'exerting the utmost efforts, and pressing ahead consistently to achieve greater, faster, better, and more economical results'. Liu Shaoqi delivered the Work Report on behalf of the Party Centre, and made the concluding statements regarding *fanmaojin*. Tan Zhenlin presented the second revised draft of the NPAD.

The combined report (*huizong*) on the second sets of accounts for the 2FYP submitted by the SPC and the Central Financial and Economic Group contained two targets for each item—for instance, the steel target for 1962 was set at 25 and 30m. tons.

---

[183] Li Rui, *Dayuejin*, 272.

[184] *Mao Wengao*, vii. 185–8; Li Rui, *Dayuejin*, 269–76; *Dangde Wenxian*, 1994, 4: 77. It is more than ironic that, forty years later, Li Rui, a severe critic of the GLF, deputy minister of the minister and Mao's secretary, still regards the talks about the GLF in HEP as 'realistic'.

[185] This means the use of the insubstantial (probability and possibility) or ideology to guide practical work. A method often promoted by Mao during the GLF is *wuxu*, which means to give preference to principles and ideology, or to make projections and set goals according to the requirements of the current Party line. In reality it means to hypothesize boldly, or simply to brag. During the GLF, the frequent use of this method often led to boasting and exaggeration. The opposite of *wuxu* is *wushi*, which means to deal with matters in a concrete and realistic manner.

[186] *Mao Wengao*, vii. 183–4; Bo Yibao, *Huigu*, ii. 692–3.

Li Fuchun's shining moment came when he explained these revised targets. According to him, China could develop at an ultra speed unprecedented in the world, because of the crises in the USA and the superiority of the socialist system. Therefore, he proposed to raise the targets for the 2FYP by basing them on the goal of overtaking Britain in major industrial outputs in seven years, and the USA in fifteen years. In this way, it would take China only twenty years to accomplish what had taken the capitalist countries one to two centuries to achieve.[187] Moreover, he added, the boost in grain production in 1958 would exceed the total increase of the past five years. But the hyperbole did not stop there. Wang Heshou one-upped Li by claiming that steel production would reach 12m. tons in 1959, 30m. tons in 1962, 70m. tons in 1967, and 120m. tons in 1972, therefore enabling China to surpass Britain in five years, and catch up with the USA in fifteen.[188] On 7 May Mao mused that steel production for 1962 would probably be 30–40m. tons; and in 1966, 51m. tons. Other industrial ministries followed suit with equally extravagant pledges.[189]

By this time, the planners had to make a 180-degree turnaround to placate Mao. As Mao tended to propose ever more ambitious targets, they had to be more extravagant just to catch up. This was the strategy embraced by Li Fuchun, who claimed that the unprecedented high speed of development in China was made possible by the unstoppable revolutionary enthusiasm of the masses, by their competition and exertion.

Tan presented the second revised draft of the NPAD by citing the history of the document and indulging in the obligatory carping at *fanmaojin*. Yet, ironically, formal approval of the NPAD also signalled its demise, since the '4, 5, and 8' targets were claimed to have been fulfilled or soon to be fulfilled, the significance of its formal introduction was symbolic—it vindicated Mao. After June 1958, the document was gradually forgotten, being overtaken by more radical slogans-cum-policies.

On 7 May, Mao pitched in by talking about surpassing the steel production of the Soviet Union. Since the Soviet Union produced 51m. tons in 1957, he argued that it was possible for China to produce that much by 1965. On 18 May, Mao explicitly approved Li Fuchun's opinion, and pronounced the new goal of catching up with Britain in *seven* years, and the USA in fifteen to seventeen years.[190] He now viewed catching up mostly in terms of industrial production and among these steel production was the determinant.[191]

Mao endorsed reports by the various ministries on how to implement the spirit of the Chengdu Conference and how to surpass Britain and the United States even

---

[187] Gu Shiming *et al.*, *Li Fuchun Jingji Sixiang*, 114–15. (Li ultimately threw in his lot with Mao's Leap strategy and he was given the opportunity to present a detailed statement of it in the journal *Hoping he Shehuizhuyi Wenti* (The problems of peace and socialism), 1 (Sept.) 1958, 12–19. Details are in Xie Chuntao, *Dayuejin*, 50; Liao Gailong *et al.*, *Zhengzhi Dacidian*, 601; Li Rui, *Dayuejin*, 309–12.

[188] Bo Yibo, *Huigu*, ii. 695; Gu Shiming *et al.*, *Li Fuchun Jingji Sixiang*, 114–15. In 1958, the Chinese assumed that the British steel production in 1957 was 20m. tons, rising to 33m. tons in 1967, 40m. tons in 1972. The US steel production of 102m. tons in 1958 was assumed to be relatively constant. Cong Jin, *Quzhe Fazhan*, 107, 119; Bo Yibo, *Huigu*, ii. 691–4.   [189] Li Rui, *Dayuejin*, 303 ff.

[190] Bo Yibo, *Huigu*, ii. 695–6; *Mao Wengao*, vii. 236.

[191] Xie Chuntao, *Dayuejin*, 56.

sooner, in about five and fifteen years, respectively.[192] Liu's allegiance to Mao was absolute. His incantatory political report, delivered on 5 May, was a total and unconditional vindication and adulation of Mao. It formally enumerated and endorsed item by item the main ideas articulated by him since 1956, including the two exploiting classes, the principal contradiction between the proletariat and the bourgeoisie, and between the socialist and capitalist roads, the criticism of *fanmaojin*, the desirability of high speed development, the need of a cult of personality, and so on.[193] In particular, Liu quoted Marx's saying of 'One day equals twenty years' to underline that the speed of construction was the key issue, and that labour efficiency should be greatly improved to surpass Britain and other capitalist countries in the shortest time possible.

On past disagreement about the tempo of economic development, Liu's report dichotomized between Mao's 'correct' method of 'better and faster' and an erroneous method he called 'slower and not so well'. Apart from repudiating the planners, Liu also tried to suppress all dissent, and to pre-empt criticism in the future. Hence Liu parroted Mao's call for vigilance against the 'tide-watchers' and the 'autumn harvest account settlers', and the exposition of the 'wind directions' (the notion that the East wind had prevailed over the West wind). All 'party committees, organizations, military units, factories, and cooperatives' were ordered to plant 'red flags' and to pull out the 'white flags', that is, to weed out all laggards and detractors of the GLF at every level.[194] After the Congress, the assignment of red or white flags to all units (including enterprises, government organizations, schools, provinces, and so on) based on aspirations and performance turned into a national political campaign. Those who were most fanatic were accorded the red flag status and those most sober, the white flag. Tremendous pressure was exerted on white flag designates to move up, fuelling exaggerations.

Under these circumstances, small group discussions of Liu's report on 6 and 7 May were mostly ritualistic. Moreover, some of the delegates suggested that Liu's summation on *fanmaojin* was too lenient, and that the mistakes of *fanmaojin* must be struggled against thoroughly because it was an error in principle. Some wondered aloud if central leaders really respected Mao's opinions, as the Eighth Party Congress omitted the mention of *duohao kuaisheng*, and the 2FYP was too conservative. Others maintained that it was necessary to smash superstition, but the faith in Mao was not blind faith, and the past practice of studying mainly the works of Marx, Engels, Lenin, and Stalin at the expense of Mao's writings must be corrected. Since Mao really developed Marxism, the term 'Maoism' should be created, although others demurred. On the issue of speed, some delegates argued that rightist conservatism had not yet been resolved. Mao's view of the two

---

[192] Xie Chuntao, *Dayuejin*, 49–50.   [193] *RMRB*, 27 May 1958.

[194] Ibid.; Mao Zedong, *Wansui* (1969), 194, 200, 204, 211–12, 220; Xie Chuntao, *Dayuejin*, 50–1. The raising of the spectre of 'tide-watchers' and 'account-settlers' were more general means to warn against any dissent or any future opposition to the Leap. I do not think Liu and Mao had any particular persons in mind, as MacFarquhar alleges in *Origins*, ii. 56–8.

exploiting classes was accepted with no objection. Cooler heads, however, wondered if China could surpass the capitalist countries in agricultural production and yield/unit in the allotted time, and suggested the reports should leave some leeway. The claim of creating 35m. *mu* of arable land in 7 months and afforestation of 29m. *mu* in 4 months should be trimmed.[195] Mao weighed in as well. On 13 and 24 May, he inserted a few more corrections in Liu's speech before it was officially published in the *RMRB* on 27 May. While some of these changes were stylistic, other more substantial revisions stated that everyone should champion the slogans of the 'promoters of progress' not those of the 'promoters of retrogression', and that the 'autumn-account settlers', who would never learn, would lose in the end. Mao also declared that development in 1956 was a 'leap forward', 1957 was a year of 'conservatism', and 1958 was 'GLF'. Metaphorically, this high, low, and even higher tides were compared to a saddle.[196]

Exuding hope, confidence and aspirations of breakthroughs, Mao delivered five major speeches to the Congress, repeating familiar themes such as the need to be creative by smashing the blind faith in experts and the Soviet Union. He dwelt at length on examples of how the young regularly surpassed the old, students surpassed teachers, and amateurs surpassed the experts, only if they 'dared' to think, to speak, and to act. Everyone, not just experts, could run industry. All major scientific and technological inventions were invented by the oppressed and by those who had little education. Hence the layman leading the expert was a general law. This suggestion that amateurs superseded experts was soon transformed into a general GLF principle and was applied to every economic sector, including industry. The Maoist ideal of combining the red and the expert ultimately weighed in favour of the red, who were often Party members, or members of masses with revolutionary enthusiasm. He was so impressed by reports of close planting and deep ploughing in Changge County, Henan, that he urged everyone to copy the practice. Finally, Mao claimed China would develop much faster than the Soviet Union, the slogan *duohao kuaisheng* was more judicious and China would enter communism sooner than the Soviet Union.[197]

Extensive small group discussion after each speech of Mao focused on how to apply and elaborate on the main themes. For instance, the Jinsha County party secretary said that he used to fear both experts and foreigners, because they seemed to know so much. They disapproved of the mass campaign to mine phosphorus but he now realized that it was right for the masses to do so. Hunan's delegation said that the Chairman's talk on superstition was extremely meaningful—it was perfectly possible to catch up with Britain in seven years and with the USA in eight years. The problem was whether they had the guts, since the Chairman had pointed the way. The Shandong delegation claimed that the red thread that ran through Mao's talks was dialectics, and that this had inspired and educated them so that their thinking was liberated. The First Ministry of Machinery promptly compiled a collection of

[195] Xing Chongzhi *et al.*, Mao Zedong Yanjiu Shidian, 242; Li Rui, *Dayuejin*, 284–7; see also *Unpublished Chinese Documents*, 77–80.   [196] *Mao Wengao*, vii. 221–6.
[197] *Mao Weikan*, xiB. 55–71.

biographies of inventors to substantiate Mao's claim that most scientific inventors were non-experts, not well educated, and had low social status.[198]

Delegates to the Congress, particularly local officials, vied with one another about how to implement *duohao kuaisheng* and the general line, and how to promote the GLF. Zealots from Central and South China, in particular, were the most extravagant. Li Jingquan of Sichuan lauded the 'correct' *duohao kuaisheng* principle of 1956 and reproached those who doubted it and the NPAD. Sichuan would strive to achieve the NPAD in three to five years, making the province self-sufficient in clothing. Tao Zhu of Guangdong, after the usual carping about those who opposed *maojin* in 1956, criticized some in the Party for worshipping foreigners, their books, and their experience. They did not study Mao's work hard enough. Mao, he said, taught him not to fear Marx, because everyone could become Marx. Henan's Wu Zhipu claimed that rightist conservatism was the major danger confronting the Party. Hubei's Wang Renzhong dwelt on the experimental plots which originated in Hongan County and how they had changed social attitudes. Ke, whose article was not selected at Chengdu, now made sure that his speech, penned by Zhang Chunqiao, was a winner. He spoke on his vision of the cultural revolution and the future society after China had surpassed Britain and where everyone could understand 'Das Capital', advanced mathematics, astronomy, geology, etc. Cities would turn into huge parks, and villages would turn into small cities dotted with factories and clean streets. China's athletes would win many medals at international competitions.[199]

Lu Dingyi's speech, however, was a direct transmission of Mao and Liu's views of a future society with many communist communes, each with its own industry, agriculture, universities, schools, hospitals, scientific research institutes, shops, transportation facilities, day centres, police, and public mess halls. This dream of utopia, Lu asserted, would not only be realized, but also surpassed. These ideas, when fleshed out more three months later, would inform Mao's decision to form the people's communes.

In this atmosphere, the Party Centre approved another 1958 plan by the SEC that contained higher targets than the second plan submitted on 7 March. In this plan, the GVIO was raised from 90.4 to 91.5bn. *yuan*; the GVAO from 75.4 to 79.3bn. *yuan*; grain from 215.8 to 219.85m. tons; and steel production from 7 to 7.11m. tons.[200]

In any case, these rituals of lauding Mao's ideas were matched by equally extravagant rituals of self-criticisms—those who had criticized the 1956 leap and had orchestrated the 1957 economic retrenchment, including Zhou Enlai, Chen Yun, Bo Yibo, Li Xiannian, were humiliated again as they were obliged to criticize themselves publicly.[201] Their lengthy and exaggerated catalogue of *mea culpa* conceded

---

[198] Li Rui, *Dayuejin*, 297 ff.   [199] Ibid. 317 ff.

[200] *Jingji Guanli Dashiji*, 110; *Jingji he Shehui Fazhan Jihua Dashi*, 119.

[201] For the texts of these self-criticisms, see Cong Jin, *Quzhe Fazhan*, 123–31. Zhou's fear and agony in preparing the self-criticism is captured in the memoir by his former secretary, Fan Ruoyu, in Wen Jin, *Zhongguo Zuohuo* (China's leftist disasters) (n.p.: Zhaohua chubanshe, 1993), ii. 291 ff.; Bo Yibo, *Huigu*, 651. One account claims that Zhou took over 10 days (and 7 behind closed doors) to prepare for the self-criticism. Yang Shengqun and Tian Songnian, *Zhongda Juece*, 263.

point by point the main ideas and complaints made by Mao since the Third Plenum. For instance, all confessed that they had exaggerated the problems of the 1956 leap, not realizing that they were problems of 'one finger out of ten'. Their misplaced concern with balance and stability had led to a conservative plan in 1957, and dampened the enthusiasm of the masses. *Fanmaojin* was an error in principle and all of them were responsible, and thanks to the teachings of Mao, they realized their mistakes. Zhou also conceded Mao's complaint at Nanning that the planners had failed to consult the Party Centre (that is, Mao) regularly and often overwhelmed it with huge amounts of data and information, making it unable to make accurate analyses.

These self-criticisms delivered to the Congress were no surprise to Mao, as he had cleared them beforehand. Some more serious self-incriminatory remarks in Zhou's version were edited out by the Standing Committee of the Politburo and the Secretariat (and presumably Mao).[202] In contrast, Chen's version was revised by Mao the night before, and, adding insult to injury, Mao put these words in Chen's mouth: 'We must always keep the Party Centre and the Party Committees at all levels informed about finance and economic conditions, and must correct the erroneous method of providing little or no information about financial and economic conditions, and then overwhelming them like "torrential rain".' After being so thoroughly humiliated, the planners had no choice but to recant. All reservations about the GLF were stifled. One account claims that after the trauma at the Congress, planners like Zhou and Chen reversed their position from *fanmaojin* to the support of the GLF, and although the self-criticisms were involuntary, they did reflect some changes in their thinking.[203] This contains an element of truth. One should not underestimate the power of the Leninist discipline of party unity and team effort, self-denial, and obedience to a Chairman who had been proven correct frequently in the past. As can be seen later, both Zhou and Chen supported and promoted certain GLF policies in 1958, with Zhou more enthusiastic than Chen. Passive resistance or inaction, on Chen's part, often assumed by some analysts to show Chen's opposition to the GLF, was impossible, as we shall see later. With top leaders of the stature of Zhou and Chen humiliated, it became impossible for anyone of a lesser rank to speak out, given the hierarchical structure of Chinese Leninism. Neither, however, would they feel obliged to bear responsibility.[204]

Then, on 17 May, Mao praised Zhou to reassure him.[205] By 20 May, he was ready to let the sleeping dog lie, saying that *fanmaojin* had been clarified, and a new unity had been struck. This unity would be solidified in the future by more criticism and self-criticism. So, although the original outline of Mao's talk to be delivered on the last day of the Congress contained another diatribe against the opponents of *maojin*, Mao decided to leave it out, in the interest of restraint. The deleted

---

[202] Li Ping, *Kaiguo Zongli*, 362.   [203] Chen Jiyuan *et al.*, *Jingji Bianqian*, 288–90.
[204] Quan Yanchi and Huang Linuo, *Tian Dao: Zhou Hui yu Lushan Huiyi* (Heaven's way: Zhou Hui and the Lushan Conference) (Guangzhou: Guangdong Luyou chubanshe, 1997), 127. A recent effort to show Chen's 'huge' efforts to mitigate the losses incurred during the Leap, especially in 1958, is unconvincing. See *Dangde Wenxian*, 1998, 3: 21, see also, 3–20.   [205] *Wansui* (1969), 201.

passage said:

The preface to the Socialist High Tide in China's Countryside, the committee for the promotion of progress, the NPAD, the Ten Great Relations, [the slogan of] *duohao kuaisheng*,
were all passed by the central conferences. Some cadres agreed to them and not one person
was opposed. Yet in just one month or five months, they were contesting, were disagreeing,
and were suspicious. They did not take the legal procedure and try to change things at similar
meetings, but instead engaged in opposition activities and advocated *fanmaojin*... This
exploded at the Second Plenum of the Eighth Party Congress.[206]

In any case, his point had been made, and forcefully. Even then, Zhou felt obliged to
appease Mao more. On the night of 26 May he wrote Mao a letter that said,

My concern then was to protect socialism, and to attack the Rightists. [I] started with the
achievements in construction, and affirmed that construction in 1956 was a leap forward
development, and abandoned the estimate that 1956 construction was a mistake of adventurism. Yet, at that time, I did not realize that *fanmaojin* was a mistake in principle.[207]

The Congress enshrined all the ideas contained in the Sixty Articles, e.g. the
abolition of rules and regulations, experimental plots, 'big blooming contending, big
debate', etc., but few new decisions were made. It was mainly a public summation of
the initiatives made in the previous few months so that the entire Party would be
informed of the new changes and be warned about the consequences of not fully
toeing Mao's line. As Mao's ideas became predominant and the only legitimate
ones, dissenting opinions were totally stifled. Mao claimed that the Party was unified, although he also warned the members of the CC that they should preserve
this unity, for nothing good would come if they attempted to split the Party.[208]
Hence the deliberations, and even the self-criticisms, assumed a ritualistic quality.
The planners had criticized themselves so often before in front of Mao that the
repeated performances were more for the consumption of Party delegates. In any
case, this was the kind of 'unity' Mao desired. Yet their combined effect was to
foster recklessness and *xiazhihui*—a Chinese concept meaning the giving of arbitrary, confused, and impractical orders.

At the Fifth Plenum held immediately after the Congress (25 May), the most vocal
supporters of the Leap were duly rewarded. Ke Qingshi, Li Jingquan, and Tan
Zhanlin were elevated into the Politburo whereas Li Fuchun and Li Xiannian were
recruited into the Secretariat. Li Xiannian emerged unscathed from the criticism of
him at the Nanning Conference and in the second half of 1959 became a staunch
supporter of most GLF policies.[209] The Plenum also announced the publication of
Hongqi, a 'revolutionary and critical' journal combining theory and practice with
Chen Boda as the chief editor, although preparation for this was underway before.
The first issue was published on 1 June, and during the GLF, the journal was
monopolized by Mao and the Maoists to promote Leap policies.

---

[206] Bo Yibo, *Huigu*, ii. 642–3.   [207] Ibid. 646.
[208] *Mao Weikan*, xiB. 64.   [209] *RMRB* 26 May 1958.

Collective Euphoria and Leap Fever

The Congress whipped up a frenzy and euphoria spread as the GLF unfolded nationally. As the timetable of catching up with Britain kept advancing, the 26–30 May Enlarged Politburo Meeting raised the steel target for 1958 to 8 or 8.5m. tons (this became the third set of accounts) and the target for 1962 was set at 40m. tons.[210] In other words, Mao's projections made on 7 May were duly made official. This set the tone for exhilarated reports from the regions which further bolstered Mao's confidence. Since the central statistical system, the last vestige of the planning system, was destroyed by decentralization,[211] Mao did not have to hear what he did not want to.

The Second Five-Year Plan

In June, Mao instructed Deng Xiaoping to work out the layout of the 2FYP according to the principles of *duohao kuaisheng*,[212] implicitly overturning the targets set at the Eighth Party Congress of September, 1956. The MM led the way and reported on 7 June that the projected production of steel for 1958 was 8.2m. tons, and that its planned steel target for 1962 was 60m. tons, double the amount decided at the Party Congress in May.[213] On June 12, in its report to the Party Centre, the Party Committee of the SEC claimed that the Leap targets of the local metallurgical industries had already exceeded the second account of the 2FYP, and that the steel output for 1959 would double that of the accomplished target of 1958.[214]

As decentralization was implemented with torrential speed, the planners were sidelined, and the ministries were stripped of many of their responsibilities, the major functions for coordinating production, supply, and sales were supposed to be performed by the Cooperative Regions. Yet, starting in June, these Cooperative Regions clamoured to promote radical Leap policies, so central demands escalated correspondingly. On 1 June, a Party Centre decision, reflecting Mao's preference, ordered the strengthening of the Cooperative Regions and encouraged their 'enthusiasm' by giving the Regions organizational shape. Henceforth, the Cooperative Regions would set up their own coordinating committees and economic planning offices as their leadership core. They were charged with the *new* responsibility of building a large industrial backbone and economic centres so that they could quickly become relatively self-sufficient and self-contained industrial systems.[215] Although formally these Cooperative Regions were answerable to the SPC and the

---

[210] Bo Yibo, *Huigu*, ii. 696; Xie Chuntao, *Dayuejin*, 56.

[211] Choh-ming Li, *The Statistical System of Communist China* (Berkeley: University of California Press, 1962), 73–108. For details of how statistical work was ordered to 'battle hard' for three years to revolutionize itself to serve 'politics', see Wang Yifu, *Xin Zhongguo Tongji Shigao* (Draft history of New China's statistics) (Beijing: Zhongguo tongji chubanshe, 1986), 105–18.

[212] *Mao Wengao*, vii. 264.   [213] Bo Yibo, *Huigu*, ii. 696; *Mao Wengao*, vii. 267, 279.

[214] Bo Yibo, *Huigu*, ii. 697.

[215] *Jingji he Shehui Fazhan Jihua Dashi*, 120; Bo Yibo, *Huigu*, ii. 798–80; *Xin Jianshe* (New Construction), 10, 1958, 45–51, 57.

SEC, in 1958, guided by their exuberant directors, they were unaccountable to anyone except Mao.

Meanwhile, Mao tried half-heartedly to bring the planners back into the fold. On 10 June he decided to establish small groups on finance and economics, law and politics, foreign affairs, science, culture and education, answerable to the Politburo and the Secretariat. Chen Yun was assigned to lead the Finance and Economic Small Group. Under the circumstances, however, Chen had little impact in stemming the adventurist tide, and indeed, he was obliged to rubber-stamp many unworkable policies.[216]

After the Congress, Mao retained the seven directors of the Cooperative Regions and the first secretaries of the provinces for a pep talk, most likely on the subject of accelerating industrial and agricultural production.[217] Ke Qingshi, the newly-minted Politburo member and new director of the East China Cooperative Region, responded with relish. At a meeting of the East China planning conference at the end of May, prompted by planners and ministers (Li Fuchun, Wang Heshou, Zhao Erlu, and Lu Zheng Cao) who descended on Shanghai, Ke bragged that the five provinces in East China alone could produce 6 to 7m. tons of steel in 1958, and 8m. in 1959. This set off a chain of hyperboles, as other Cooperative Regions followed suit with their own bravados. All this fed Mao's fancy of doubling the 1957 production in 1958.[218]

This also galvanized zealots like Li Fuchun, who, like Mao, increasingly viewed economic development in terms of steel production.[219] On 16 June, after reviewing the targets submitted by the ministries, the SPC, SEC, and the MOF reported to the Central Finance and Economic Small Group, and on this basis, Li presented to the Party Centre the new and more extravagant 'Main Points for the 2FYP'. This estimated that it would take less than three years to overtake Britain in iron, steel, and other major industrial production, and that the NPAD could be achieved in three years.[220] Therefore the goal of the 2FYP was to fulfil the NPAD ahead of schedule, and to build up a comprehensive industrial system so that China could catch up or surpass Britain in just five years, and the USA in ten years. By 1962, the North China, North-East, East China, and Central China Cooperative Regions would all have developed comprehensive industrial systems and the South-West, North-West, and South China Cooperative Regions would have 'basically' comprehensive industrial systems. Other production targets for 1962 were arranged teleologically

---

[216] *Mao Wengao*, vii. 268–9. Mao wrote the policy document authorizing the formation of these small groups, and then told Deng Xiaoping to have it discussed and passed at the Politburo. See also, Bo Yibo, *Huigu*, ii. 799–80. Sun Yeli and Xiong Lianghua, *Jingji Fengyun Zhong de Chun Yun*, 148. The other members of the Finance and Economic Group were Li Fuchun, Bo Yibo, and Tan Zhenlin.

[217] *Mao Wengao*, vii. 255.

[218] Bo Yibo, *Huigu*, ii. 701; Liu Suinian and Wu Qungan (eds.), *Dayuejin he Tiaozheng Shiqide Guomin Jingji, 1958–1965* (The national economy during the GLF and the adjustment period, 1958–1965) (Harbin: Heilongjiang renmin chubanshe, 1984), 23–4; Xie Chuntao, *Dayuejin*, 56; Cong Jin, *Quzhe Fazhan*, 138.

[219] Guo Shiming *et al.*, *Li Fuchun Jingji Sixiang*, 50, 74–80; *RMRB*, 26 September 1958.

[220] Bo Yibo, *Huigu*, ii. 697; Cong Jin, *Quzhe Fazhan*, 134–6.

by presuming that steel production could reach 60m. tons in 1962, and that steel and machinery would spur production on other fronts. Li's other fantastic projections predicted that steel production would reach 100m. tons in 1967, investment during the 2FYP would be 300bn. *yuan*, and annual growth rates for industry and agriculture would be 45 and 21 per cent, respectively. Since 1959 was the crucial year, it must have a greater leap than 1958–steel output must strive for 20–25m. tons to surpass Britain and Japan, and grain production must reach 300m. tons. As Li was having his field day, other planners were emboldened to play the game. Li Xiannian chimed in with a financial report that predicted that revenue for 2FYP would be 400bn. *yuan* and expenditure 434bn. *yuan*, and more than 70 per cent of this would be channelled into capital investment. His assumption was that the GVIO could increase 44.2 per cent yearly.[221]

Bo Yibo, not to be outdone, submitted the report 'Surpass Britain in *Two* [emphasis mine] Years' on behalf of the party committee of the SEC to the Politburo on 17 June. It claimed that in 1958, grain production would increase 30 per cent to 235m. tons, cotton 30–50 per cent to 2.2 to 2.5m. tons, and the GVIO, 50+ per cent. GVIO would rise more than 50 percent to 110bn. *yuan*, and capital investment would double to 24bn. *yuan*. Steel production would reach 10m. tons, and coal 210m. tons. In 1959, grain production would reach 300m. tons, cotton 3m. tons. The GVIO would be raised from 167 to 178bn. yuan. Steel production would soar to 25m. tons, and capital investment would soar to 45bn. *yuan*. According to Bo, the 13,000 blast furnaces and 200 converters built in 1958 alone had boosted the capacity for smelting iron and steel to 20m. and 10m. tons. These were extravagant and irresponsible claims, yet some at the meeting found them too low.[222] Mao had not yet had his final say.

Based on these reports the three planners submitted a totally fantastic 2FYP.[223] Bo might have some reservations about the projected steel target, but since he had offered self-criticism at the Party Congress, he was not in a position to resist the trend. Indeed, these reports won Mao's highest praise–he called them excellent documents that 'opened people's eyes', making clear that this kind of number crunching was what he wanted.[224]

Armed with these estimates, Mao called for a meeting of all members of the Standing Committee of the Politburo and others (on 18 June) at the swimming pool at Zhongnanhai and put his personal stamp of approval on the high steel targets. Bo recalled how he bent again under the tremendous pressure applied by Mao:

In June/July of 1958 Chairman Mao said to me, 'Now in agriculture we have found a way, and this is grasping grain as the key link, and comprehensive development. My idea is to use agriculture to pressure industry; since the problem of agriculture is resolved, what are you

---

[221] Ibid. 136–7.
[222] Bo Yibo, *Huigu*, ii. 698; Ma Qibin *et al.*, *Zhizheng Sishinian*, 146–7; Sun Yeli and Xiong Lianghua, *Jingji Fengyun zhong de Chen Yun*, 148; Cong Jin, *Quzhe Fazhan*, 137–8.
[223] For an outline of this 2FYP, see *Jingji Guanli Dashiji*, 112–13.
[224] *Mao Wengao*, vii. 273–6, 278.

going to do with industry?' The Chairman's intention was for us to flesh out the slogans of surpassing Britain's top annual production record of 22 million tons of steel. Without really thinking about it, I replied, 'That would mean in industry, grasp steel as the key link to spur on everything'. The Chairman said 'Good! Very good! Let's do it this way'. Therefore this slogan was broached. Today I offer a self-criticism, this slogan was wrong and I was responsible.[225]

Bo might have coined the slogan 'steel as the key link' and it spurred on the iron and steel campaign later in 1958, but the notion that a huge amount of steel was the key for economic leaps was already entrenched in Mao's mind. Now that Mao had impressed upon his colleagues the centrality of steel, he took care to consider the linkages between steel, the machinery industry, the electrical industry, and railway transport. Once all these were developed, he said, then everything would be speeded up. The *RMRB* picked up the message, and published an article entitled 'steel as the key link' on 1 July.[226]

Exhilarated by the earnestness of the planners, Mao began to view the progressive hiking of the 1958 steel target by the MM to 6m., 7m., and then 9m. tons as a sign of tardiness, because he was increasingly inclined to simply double (*fanfan)*[227] the 1957 output. Mao's taste for steel was insatiable, but his other calculation was to use steel to pressure or galvanize all other sectors, especially the reluctant bureaucracy, so that there would be a GLF on *all* fronts.[228] Once his mind was made up, on 19 June, Mao slapped at Bo, 'Make it snappy! Let's just double it! Why dilly-dally? Let's make it 11 million tons'.

When commenting on Bo's report, Mao said, 'It will not take fifteen or even seven years to surpass Britain; all that is required is two to three years. It is possible to do it in 2 years. The main thing is steel. As long as we reach 25m. tons in steel production in 1959, we would have overtaken Britain'. Therefore, at another swimming pool meeting on the same day, Mao told the central leaders to double the 1958 steel output to 10.7m. tons, although the internal target was 11m. tons. The die was cast. Almost instantly, on 20 June, new steel quotas were assigned to the production units.[229] On the other hand, the harried Wang did not know when to stop. In a further report submitted to Mao and the Party Centre on 21 June, he boasted that steel production for 1959 and 1962 could reach 30m. and 80–90m. tons, respectively, trumping even Mao's highest fancies so far. In any case, Mao took this seriously and circulated the report widely to all cooperative regions, provinces, CC members, and all party committees of the state organizations. In December, he admitted he had approved of producing 30m. tons of steel in 1959, and even entertained the idea of having 100–120m. tons for 1962.[230] Again on 21 June, Mao told the Military Affairs Commission that he was fully confident that China could

---

[225] Cong Jin, *Quzhe Fazhan*, 155; Bo Yibo, *Huigu*, ii. 698.   [226] Ibid. 699.

[227] *Fanfan* is a mahjong term. Depending on the strength of the winner's suit, others will have to pay double, triple, quadruple, and so on. Mao's adoption of this terminology is reflective of the gambler mentality he was in at that time.   [228] Li Rui, *Lushan Huiyi*, 36.

[229] *Dangshi Jiliao*, xlvii. 218; Cong Jin, *Quzhe Fazhan*, 138; Yang Shengqun and Tian Songnian, *Zhongda Juece*, 218, 282.   [230] *Mao Wengao*, vii. 281–2; *Wansui* (1969), 264.

surpass Britain in three years, and the USA in ten.[231] Although the planners were hotheaded, Mao continued to push for more. Illustrative of Mao's pressure tactics was his conversation with Wang. He queried Wang on whether the steel target could be doubled, and if not, why. Wang had no choice but to concur.[232] Once the decision was made, the planners had no choice but to propagate it. For instance, Zhou Enlai toured Guangzhou and Shanghai in late June to late July to promote the various aspects of the GLF, and to ascertain that steel production in 1958 and 1959 should reach the targets designed.[233]

The MM's obsession with quantity at the expense of everything else inevitably led to limited variety and shoddy quality of steel, which brought it into conflict with the First Ministry of Machine Industry. Yet these bureaucratic differences were totally suppressed. No evidence existed that the First Ministry had complained to Mao about its predicament; in fact, like other ministries, its reports submitted to Mao in June pleased the Chairman, who promptly distributed them to the MAC conference. When the political climate changed at the beginning of the Lushan Conference in 1959, minister Zhao Erlu was said to have shipped boxes of sub-standard pig iron to the conference to show his grievances, but changed his mind when the tide turned again.[234]

Leap Fever in Agriculture

In agriculture, Mao's penchant for the grandiose also set off a chain reaction of exaggeration. On 11 June, the MA presented its 2FYP by raising targets for grain and cotton to 425 and 4m. tons, respectively, by 1962, so that per capita grain would reach 2,000 *jin*.[235] On 22 June, Mao endorsed this plan, and was so pleased with it that he retitled the report 'The Future of Agriculture is Extremely Bright'. This fed his fancy that once production of grain, steel, and machinery were abundant, all the rest would follow. On 19 June, the agricultural conference of the East China Agricultural Cooperation Region vowed to produce grain at more than 1000 kg per capita in three to five years, and even the low-yield North-West Cooperative Region pledged in July to raise per capita grain to 550 kg in 1958, 1,000 kg in 1959, and 1,500 kg in 1962 (actual per capital grain in 1958 was 203 kg). No sooner had these pledges been made when they were escalated into *actual* claims. In June Henan Weixing APC led the pack by claiming that it had achieved wheat yield/mu of 1,765 kg, and Chuo Tou APC, Hebei, claimed 2,551 kg. In early July, even the State Statistic Bureau put forward the principle of statistics in the service of politics, and encouraged all to compete and outdo each another in hyperbole. Hence, Henan's Heping APC claimed it had harvested 3,660 kg/*mu* of wheat; in August Hubei's Maxihe Xiang claimed early rice had reached 18,450 kg/*mu*, Hongqi

[231] *Mao Weikan*, xiB. 75–6; Liu Guoxin and Liu Xiao, *Lishi Changpian*, ii. 35.
[232] Bo Yibo, *Huigu*, ii. 700.   [233] Shi Zhongquan, *Zhuoyue Fengxian*, 348–9.
[234] *Mao Wengao*, vii. 291; Li Rui, *Lushan Huiyi*, 40, 82, 84, 107.
[235] Ma Qibin *et al.*, *Shizheng Sishinian*, 146–7; *Mao Wengao*, vii. 280.

People's Commune claimed rice of more than 650,000 kg/*mu*. The praise heaped upon these models by the media and the Party further fuelled the exaggerations.[236]

Furthermore, on 23 July, when the MA added up the grain estimates from the provinces for 1958, it came to a staggering 500m. tons, 69 per cent over the 1957 output of 298m. tons. Even Mao found these figures incredible, so the figures made public were trimmed to 300–350m. tons. Yet the media continued to trumpet the 'satellites' and 'shocking miracles'. An *RMRB* editorial (23 July) proclaimed the bankruptcy of the view that agricultural production could increase only a few per-cent or dozens of percent. It claimed that China had become second in world pro-duction of wheat, surpassing the USA, and could produce as much grain as it wished.[237] Other leaders also chimed in. Vice-premier and Minister of Foreign Affairs Chen Yi claimed he had witnessed in Guangdong yields/*mu* of 500,000 kg of yams, 300,000 kg of sugar cane, and 25,000 kg of rice. Tao Zhu boasted that yield/*mu* in Guangdong would reach 2,000 to 5,000 kg/*mu*. Even astrophysicist Qian Xuesen, China's father of rocket technology, weighed in with an article praising the reported high yields, and claimed that if plants could utilize only 30 per cent of the solar energy, then wheat output per *mu* could reach as much as 40,000 *jin*.[238] Zhou inspected a plot of wheat said to have harvested 10,000 *jin*/*mu* by using electric lights and fans to promote growth and to circulate the air. Most present at this event realized that wheat from many *mu* had been gathered together to show off, but Zhou said nothing. Propaganda themes in the press matched these exaggerations with slogans such as 'the bigger the gall one has, the greater the amount [of crops] the earth will yield', and 'we can produce as much grain as we will it'.[239] Soon the view that within a few years, China would produce sufficient food to feed everyone on earth gained currency, and Mao seemed to agree.[240] On 3 August, the Party Centre issued a directive on controlling claims of extraordinary high yields, but to no avail.[241] In fact, Mao continued to fan the fire of exaggeration by not challenging the fantastic claims reported to him on his tours, but instead expressing delight and encouragement.[242] He was swayed by the propaganda, and probably considered the exaggerations harmless, as long as real growth and enthusiasm were maintained.

As these extravagant claims continued to flood the press, the prevalent concern was how to dispose of such huge quantities of grain. When asked by Mao, the party secretary at Xushui county, Hebei, was vague about what would be done with this super harvest, so Mao could only suggest that perhaps everyone in China would eat five meals a day. In the craze for dramatic high yields, many localities also pushed through foolhardy policies of deep ploughing and close planting—the fields were ploughed to a depth of 45–90 cm and plants were packed tightly together—that were both futile and counterproductive.

---

[236] *NJZWH*, ii. 207. A series of tables on claims on high-yield records are in Xie Chuntao, *Dayuejin*, 59–65.
[237] See also *RMRB*, 3 August 1958.
[238] *Zhongguo Qingnian Bao* (Chinese Youth Newspaper), 16 June 1958.
[239] *RMRB*, 3 August and 26 September 1958; Xie Chuntao, *Dayuejin*, 59–67; Li Ping, *Kaiguo Zongli*, 365; Ma Qibin *et al.*, *Shizheng Sishinian*, 148–9.   [240] Bo Yibo, *Huigu*, ii. 767; *Mao Weikan*, ii. 302.
[241] Chu Han, *Sannian Ziran Zaihai*, 106.   [242] Chen Jiyuan *et al.*, *Jingji Bianqian*, 294–5.

Decentralization in the summer of 1958

As the mania for dramatic yields snowballed, production targets of industrial enterprises increased several fold, so they had to enlarge their labour pool to meet the challenge. Hence the Ministry of Labour decided that it would abandon its previously tight control over the recruitment of new workers, and delegated the power of labour recruitment and readjustment to the provinces. Henceforth, the recruitment plan in 1958 would no longer require its approval. Although the ministry said that urban workers (particularly women), not rural residents, should be recruited, new workers came primarily from the countryside. Subsequently, it was estimated that 10 million more workers were recruited in 1958 alone, forcing the Party Centre to call for an immediate halt in January 1959.[243]

The dazzling speed with which enterprises were decentralized created chaos and confusion on the industrial front, but the Coordinating Regions were ineffective in dealing with the situation. Enterprises hitherto under the vertical chain of command by the ministries were now put under horizontal supervision by the provinces. Previous contractual relations and supply sources were disrupted, enterprises were scrambling for whatever raw materials they could get, and shortages were in turn leading to work stoppages and delays in shipment. Some raided the state-owned enterprises for equipment and supplies. Because of the uncertainty, enterprises were reluctant to sign new contracts. This free-for-all situation was compounded by ever-rising production targets, large-scale recruitment of workers, and proliferation of construction projects, making mockery of the planned economy. Moreover, the immense iron and steel campaign further complicated matters.[244]

Mao added fuel to the confusion. In June he came up with the snap idea of urging the Cooperative Regions to form independent industrial systems,[245] but in August, when inspecting Tianjin, he raised the stakes by calling upon all the *provinces* to do the same. This oral directive immediately turned into a rallying point for the provinces, leading to a national drive for industrial and construction projects. Soon, even non-industrial provinces like Gansu felt obliged to brag that it had created hundreds of thousands of factories and mines, and Neimenggu claimed that it had built 1,267 new factories and mines. Overall, the provinces understood that they had to run all sorts of industries at once, and must become self-sufficient and self-reliant. This aggravated the existing problems of hoarding and supply coordination.[246]

The Formation of the Communes from June to August

Collectivization was a controversial issue among the Chinese leadership from 1955 to 1957, and although by 1957 more than 90 per cent of peasant households had

---

[243] *Jingji Guanli Dashiji*, 113, 120. This changed the policy prohibiting migration to the cities operative since 1956. [244] Bo Yibo, *Huigu*, ii. 800–1.
[245] These were supposed to be self-sufficient entities with their own industrial systems and raw materials supplies. [246] *Mao Wengao*, vii. 318; Xie Chuntao, *Dayuejin*, 57–8.

joined advanced APCs (each averaging 200–300 households), they were far from being consolidated, being plagued by numerous management, labour organization, remuneration, and incentive problems. However, the large-scale water irrigation campaigns undertaken in the winter of 1957/8 affected huge areas and required manpower and capital beyond the capability of individual advanced APCs. This prompted Mao to entertain the idea of creating even larger agricultural units. At Nanning, Mao endorsed reports about the amalgamation of the APCs in Guangxi. Subsequently, a document on the amalgamation of the APCs reflecting his view was passed at Chengdu on 22 March, and the Politburo approved it on 8 April.[247] At that time, amalgamation was left to the discretion of the provinces, which responded enthusiastically. Guangdong and Liaoning were the pace-setters; Liaoning began mergers in March and by late May 9,297 advanced APCs were merged into 1,551 larger cooperatives, averaging 1,855 households each. Henan, Hebei, Jiangsu, and Zhejiang followed suit.[248] The relative smooth manner by which amalgamation was implemented in early 1958 contrasted starkly with the resistance and stormy debate during collectivization between 1955 and 1957, partly because the division of the harvest was not yet involved, and Mao's virulent attack on *fanmaojin* precluded any dissent.

These larger APCs were still agricultural and economic units, not communes that were both political and economic entities that encompassed the functions of industry, agriculture, commerce, education, and the militia. Nevertheless, Mao's suggestion made at Nanning for localities to find out how long it would take for their GVIO to exceed their GVAO was fleshed out by an SPC document passed by the Chengdu conference. This document first broached the subject of asking the APCs to run local industries. Subsequently, these collective industries, together with large-scale irrigation and water works, and the high tide in agricultural production, created shortages of labour, which was alleviated in part by the formation of public mess halls and nurseries, foreshadowing the communes. Some localities also began to build 'agricultural universities' to popularize new agricultural techniques.[249] Further-more, before the communes were formally declared, Mao was toying with utopian ideas. At Chengdu, Mao referred approvingly to Kang Youwei's *Datongshu* (The Book of Great Harmony) and the eventual abolition of the family.[250] Returning to Beijing from the secret Guangzhou Conference, where Mao was briefed about preparations for the coming Party Congress, Liu Shaoqi, Zhou Enlai, Lu Dingyi, and Deng Liqun were musing about utopian socialism and how to promote communism by introducing such things as day-care centres, collectivism, and collectivized livelihood. At the stopover at Zhengzhou, Liu instructed Wu Zhipu, Henan

---

[247] *NJZWH*, ii. 15.

[248] Chan, 'Campaign for Agricultural Development', 61–2; Bo Yibo, *Huigu*, ii. 730.

[249] Ibid. 731.

[250] Ibid. 772–6. *Mao Weikan*, xiB. 33. The ideas of Kang's book *Datongshu* (The Book of Universal Commonwealth) were mainly Confucian, and Kang's ideal state of *datong* was a selfless society where everyone would care for each other.

party chief, to experiment with these ideas. Wu took this tip-off seriously, turning Henan into a bell-wether of communization later on. Liu even charged Deng to edit a book on utopian socialism. At the Party Congress, Lu's speech, which was a relay of his conversation with Mao and Liu, claimed that utopia could soon be realized:[251]

'When Chairman Mao and comrade Shaoqi talked about the state of affairs in the next few decades, they said, at that time there will be many communist communes in the countryside of our country. Each commune will have its own agriculture, university, hospital, scientific research institutes, shops and service trades, communications, nurseries and public mess halls, clubs, and civilian police to maintain law and order. Many rural communes will surround the cities, making for even larger communist communes. The notion of utopia mentioned by our predecessors will be realized and surpassed. Our educational principles and other educational affairs will also develop according to this goal'.[252]

In the same vein, Mao told Chen Boda that the combination of the *xiang* (the lowest unit of government administration) and the APC would be the mainspring of communism because it would take charge of everything, including industry, agriculture, commerce, education, and the military.[253] After the Party Congress, various localities began to test run communist communes.[254] On 14 June, Liu's speech on the socialization of domestic labour called for the large-scale establishment of public mess halls, nurseries, and homes for the elderly. In a 30 June conversation with the editor of *Beijing Ribao* (Beijing Daily), he claimed that communism could be achieved in thirty to forty years, so it was necessary to start experimenting with the grass-roots organization of communist society.[255]

On the other hand, after returning to Beijing from Guangzhou, Lu immediately organized the Central Propaganda Department to edit the book entitled 'Marx, Engels, Lenin, and Stalin on Communism'. Engels' comment on the future communist society which referred twice to the communes as the grass-roots communist organization was the first quotation collected. According to Bo, this book influenced Mao's decision to create the communes, as he repeatedly recommended it at the Beidaihe Conference.[256]

In June, some amalgamated APCs began to call themselves communes. The *xiang* party secretary of Chengnan, after hearing a speech by the party secretary of the Provincial Party Committee (PPC) that called for each county to run a rudimentary communist *xiang* or APC, mobilized the four APCs to apply to become the Red Flag Communist Commune. In the same month, the Qianyang commune in Liaoning, with 13,000 households and a population of 72,000, was formed by the merger of five APCs so that the Andong County Party Committee (CPC) could experiment with the transfer of the collective ownership to all-people ownership.[257]

In late June and early July, at the agricultural cooperative conference, Tan Zhenlin referred to the Chayashan Sputnik APC in Henan as a communist commune for the

[251] Bo Yibo, ii. 731–2, 773–4; Ye Yongli, *Mao Zedong yu Liu Shaoqi*, 306–308.
[252] Bo Yibo, *Huigu*, ii. 732–3.　　[253] Ibid. 734.　　[254] *Dangshi Ziliao*, xlvii. 212.
[255] Bo Yibo, *Huigu*, ii. 734.　　[256] Ibid. 736.　　[257] Ibid. 735.

first time because of its bumper harvest and its fundamental changes in management and scale of operations had undergone fundamental changes. Therefore he ordered that 10 to 15 per cent of all APCs in East China should make the transition to something more advanced, like state farms or communes with around 10,000 households. After the conference Tan also summoned cadres from the Chayashan Sputnik commune to report to him at Zhengzhou, and lectured them on ways of running communes.[258]

A turning point came when Mao instructed the Henan leaders to cooperate with Chen Boda and the *Hongqi* journal to create a charter for the Chayashan commune, which Mao received 'as if he had come across some treasures'.[259] After revisions by Mao, the charter was circulated to the provinces and counties for discussion and reference, and Mao instructed his subordinates to brag (*chui*) about it and communism.[260]

Simultaneously, *Hongqi*, the newly created theoretical journal under the editorship of Chen Boda, became Mao's most powerful instrument to popularize his ideas and to promote the large communes. In June, the first issue carried an instruction written by Mao on 15 April entitled 'Introducing a Cooperative'. It said that the communist spirit and political consciousness of the people were developing rapidly, showing that the economic, political, thought, technical, and cultural revolutions were racing ahead.[261] A 8 July *RMRB* article praised practices in places like Hunan and Fujian forming public mess halls as new steps towards collective production. This provided a powerful signal for many localities to form communes.

In July, two articles by Chen Boda published in *Hongqi* further trumpeted the idea of the communes. The first article, 'Brand New Society, Brand New People', claimed that the APCs had created hundreds of thousands of industries and mines, and praised Xuguang APC for being a people's commune combining industry and agriculture and for the unprecedented development of the productive forces.[262] The second article, 'Under the Banner of Mao Zedong', conveyed Mao's vision of the communes which by combining industry, agriculture, commerce, education, and military, would develop gradually to become the basic social unit. At a time when the economy and culture were developing at lightning speed, Chen argued, the transition to communism would not be far off.[263]

These strong central signals galvanized the localities, and the two earliest communes in Henan, Xinxiang's Qiliying and Suiping's Chayashan, soon became national models to be emulated. In July, a mass campaign to build communes began in Henan. On 4 and 5, August an exuberant Mao inspected Xushui and Anguo counties to promote the communes, and had nothing but praise for their labour

---

[258] Bo Yibo, *Huigu*, ii. 737.

[259] Ibid. 738; *Mao Weikan*, xiB. 197. Full text in *Hongqi* (Red Flag), 1958 7: 16–22. See also, Han Taihua, *Gongheguo Zhilu: Tansuo yu Daijia* (The path of the republic: The search and the price) (Beijing: Beijing chubanshe, 1999), 67–9.

[260] Bo Yibo, *Huigu*, ii. 738; *Mao Wengao*, vii. 345; *Mao Weikan*, ii. 305.

[261] *Mao Wengao*, vii. 177.   [262] *Hongqi*, 1958, 3: 9–11; Bo Yibo, *Huigu*, ii. 736–7.

[263] *Hongqi*, 1959, 4: 8–9; Bo Yibo, *Huigu*, ii. 738; *Mao Wengao*, vii. 317–18.

organization along military lines and collectivized living. At Baoding he told the secretary of the District Party Committee that large communes with 8,000 members were also fine, and the communes should combine industry, agriculture, commerce, education, and the militia. The principle of 'everyone a soldier'—which meant that all able-bodied males would be organized into the militia—should be applied and weapons should be distributed to the militia. On 6 August, Chen Zhengren, vice-director of the Rural Work Department, went to Xushui to transmit the central instruction to establish test points for communism, and within a few days, the 248 APCs in the county were amalgamated into seven large communes with an average of 9,000 households and 45,000 members each. These communes began to introduce a free-supply system, to issue guns and rifles to the militia, and to militarize labour organization. At this stage, the large collectives were given different names, such as communist communes, large cooperatives, or collective farms. Nevertheless, on 6 August, when Mao inspected the Henan Qiliying commune formed only two days before, he said that 'People's Commune' was probably a good name, as it combined industry, agriculture, commerce, education, military, production management, and livelihood *with* political power. The masses could pick a name they liked as a prefix to the word commune.[264]

Again on 9 August, when cadres at Shandong told Mao that they were creating large farms, Mao replied that it was better to form people's communes. The name stuck. When on 13 August, *RMRB* published Mao's endorsement of the communes, a mass fervour to set up the communes set in. Henan was the bell-wether and by the 22 August, it claimed that 38,473 APCs were merged into 1,172 communes, with an average of 7,200 households each.[265]

In all, the genesis of the communes could be traced to certain practical needs arising from the Leap, combined with the connivance of the subordinates, and above all, Mao's vision and utopianism, his penchant for the big, all-purpose collectives. Although Mao disclaimed the right of invention at the Lushan Conference in 1959, he nevertheless was the motivating force behind the communes.

The Plunge: The Expanded Politburo Conference at Beidaihe (17–30 August)

The Beidaihe Conference found the Chairman in his most exuberant and san-guine mood, and his dominance over policy formulation was complete. This was reflected by the decisions made, most notably the final versions of the 1959 plan, the 2FYP, and the 40 documents produced.[266] Yet, he also realized that steel

---

[264] *RMRB*, 23 August 1958; Bo Yibo, *Huigu*, ii. 739–40; Cong Jin, *Quzhe Fazhan*, 158–9; Wu Xiaomei and Li Peng, *Zouchou Hongqiang*, 133 ff.

[265] *NJZWH*, ii. 89; Xie Chuntao, *Dayuejin*, 72.

[266] List of documents in *Mao Wengao*, vii. 363–4. All the documents were personally examined and corrected by him before he gave them the final stamp of approval. *Mao Wengao*, vii. 345–47, 351, 356–61, 367–69.

production, the centrepiece of the GLF, was in trouble, unless herculean measures were adopted.

On the agenda he sent out about the conference on 1 August, Mao jotted down 17 items, setting the parameters of discussion.[267] Underlying his buoyancy was his conviction that an extraordinary harvest in 1958 had raised agricultural production by leaps and bounds. Even when allowances were made for exaggerations, he thought, grain output had reached 325–50m. tons, so every Chinese could have 500 kg. Hence the grain problem was said to have been resolved once and for all. Furthermore, Mao expected that per capita grain production would rise even further—to 750 kg in 1959, and 1,000 kg in 1960, the 'saturation' point. Further increases, such as 1,500 kg per person, he feared, would 'make things difficult'. He was so confident about the super harvest that his chief concern was how to store the excess grain; subsequently, a resolution on storage specifics was published.[268]

Another of Mao's obsessions, the steel target for 1958, was a different matter. When Khrushchev visited China from 31 July to 3 August, an excited Mao revealed to him the 1958 and 1959 steel targets of 10.7 and 25–30m. tons. Khrushchev was sceptical, although he diplomatically said that the Chinese could accomplish them. Yet, Khrushchev's lack of interest in this was taken by Mao to be a vote of no-confidence, even a snub. Similarly, when Chen Yun asked Ivan Arkhipov, chief adviser of the Soviet experts, whether he thought China's 1959 steel target could be fulfilled, Arkhipov tried to be tactful, but ultimately was negative. When Bo Yibo gave Arkhipov the official line that the targets were achievable because the Chinese had the mass line and the indigenous method, the latter replied that the indigenous method was essentially useless. When this conversation was relayed, the Chinese side felt insulted and was indignant.[269] Henceforth, the Chinese were eager to prove the Soviets wrong as a matter of national pride. For Mao, the GLF in steel production was his initiative against *fanmaojin* and therefore a political question, so he was ready to take extraordinary measures at Beidaihe.[270] Throughout August, he kept harping the importance of steel.[271]

Yet, although the Beidaihe decisions marked the climax of the GLF, it was clear that the iron and steel campaign had stalled. The wild enthusiasm of Mao and his colleagues contrasted sharply with the actual performance. The steel target was doubled unofficially in June by Mao, but production had been disappointing. July was an unsatisfactory month, producing only 0.7m. tons, making for a total of only 3.8m. tons for the year, leaving the bulk to be accomplished in the four remaining months of 1958.[272] Both iron and steel were in short supply and many producers preferred to hoard them in exchange for other resources to satisfy the spiralling targets. Others were scurrying around searching for them. Representatives from one APC, which drove to Angang demanding iron and steel, would not budge until

---

[267] *Mao Wengao*, vii. 343–4.   [268] *Dangshi Ziliao*, xlvii. 231.
[269] Sun Yeli and Xiong Lianghua, *Jingji Fengyun zhong de Chen Yun*, 151; Bo Yibo, *Huigu*, ii. 704.
[270] *Dangshi Yanjiu*, ii. 62.   [271] Bo Yibo, *Huigu*, ii. 705; *Dangshi Jiliao*, xlvii. 214.
[272] Bo Yibo, *Huigu*, ii. 702–3; *Dangshi Yanjiu*, ii. 62.

demands were met.[273] By mid-August, the danger of plan non-fulfilment was obvious, prompting Mao to convene the Beidaihe Conference. It was also apparent that the smelting capacity was insufficient for the task. Furthermore, coking coal, pig iron, and electricity, were all in short supply, and the transportation system was hopelessly overwhelmed.[274]

Mao sensed that the target could probably not be fulfilled, but determined that everyone should risk everything (*pinming*, literally to risk one's life) on a gamble. On 16 August, the day before the Conference, he had decided on several emergency measures—a mass movement, Party secretaries taking charge, and all-party and all-people smelting steel, to this end. This meant that party leaders at all administrative levels were to take personal charge of the iron and steel campaign, 'as they would on a battle field'. He also declared that the task of leadership should be shifted from agriculture to industry, and the provincial first secretaries were ordered to focus on nothing but industrial work, particularly iron and steel.[275] One aim of the Conference, therefore, was less to announce the doubling of targets than to find ways to revive the sagging iron and steel campaign. Mao's opening speech stressed his anxiety that the 10.7m. tons of steel might be unrealizable, although he still hoped for 30m. tons in 1959, 50m. tons in 1960, and 80m. tons by 1962, so that China could then overtake the USA.[276] Discussions during the first few days of the conference identified the following problems—small blast furnaces were unreliable, the peasants lacked skill at smelting iron and steel, and raw materials and equipment for iron and steel smelting were either unavailable or were wrestled away by other pursuits outside the economic plan. Nevertheless Mao was determined to push ahead with herculean measures.

After hearing the reports, Mao telephoned Chen Yun with the following eight-point command. First, the SEC would henceforth switch its function to direct supervision of day-to-day production, and yield its formal duties of drafting yearly plans to the SPC. Second, control of the distribution of raw materials and equipment (especially rolled steel) must be tightened, so that all necessary resources could be diverted to iron and steel production. Third, production and installation of smelting equipment must be improved. Fourth, all machinery factories must use all steel at their disposal for the manufacture of machinery and equipment for iron and steel smelting. Fifth, all provincial party committees were required to 'grasp' steel as their most important task. Sixth, Mao slapped an additional 0.5m. tons of steel on the MM, boosting the target for 1958 to 11.5m. tons, just to be on the safe side. Seventh, the strictest discipline was to be applied to the drive for steel, and not a ton less was acceptable. If plans were not fulfilled, six degrees of punishment ranging from warning, dismissal, to the withdrawal of party membership would be applied. Mao also made clear that steel was his personal initiative and if it failed, he would have to

---

[273] *Mao Weikan*, ii. 300, 302.

[274] Xie Chuntao, *Dayuejin*, 85–86; *Dayuejin yu Tiao Zheng*, 29–30; *Dangshi Jiliao*, xlvii. 214.

[275] Xie Chuntao, *Dayuejin*, 74; *Dangshi Ziliao*, xlvii. 215; *Mao Weikan*, ii. 295.

[276] Ibid. 295; *Dangshi Jiliao*, xlvii. 218.

make a self-criticism. Therefore, no one should let him down. Finally, Mao ordered that all provincial secretaries in charge of industry be summoned to Beidaihe for a Conference for Industrial Secretaries (25–31 August), to be held concurrently with the Beidaihe Conference to apply maximun pressure for the completion of the 1958 steel target. On 21 August, Chen Yun duly transmitted these orders to the expanded Politburo conference, and mentioned Arkhipov's slight, to the anger of those present.[277]

Chen, who is regarded by analysts as being inactive during this time because of his disagreement with Mao on the Leap,[278] in fact was charged with implementing many of Mao's misdirected policies, including the iron and steel campaign. Even after he was disgraced, Mao had not left him alone. In fact, if he succeeded, he could redeem himself, but if he failed, Mao could shift the blame on him. Either way, the Chairman held all the cards. Having made a scathing self-criticism at the Party Congress, he had no choice but to swim with the tide. When the Conference for Industrial Secretaries met to discuss how to fulfil the 1958 targets, Chen gave a couple of speeches exhorting the party committees to mobilize mass campaigns using indigenous furnaces, because modern furnaces were insufficient to produce the year's quota of steel.

Although the Party Centre was at fault in altering the targets so close to year's end, the industrial secretaries criticized themselves one after the other. In addition, Bo also urged an emergency mobilization. On the 30 August, he led the industrial secretaries and party secretaries of the major steel mills to see Mao, who queried them individually on whether the 10.5m. tons of steel was possible. One by one these secretaries pledged passionately to fulfil the targets, and Wang Heshou gave his personal assurances. Mao, however, realizing that it was an uphill battle, recited verses from a Chinese poem to express his sentiment, 'The sun at dusk is absolutely glorious, except that it is too close to the evening'.[279]

Like everyone else, Bo offered his pledge, despite his reservations, but also proposed the publication of the steel target in the communique. His calculation was that since the target had already been disclosed to some foreign sources, and Mao was adamant that even a ton less was unacceptable, to reveal the target could generate more pressure on everyone, leaving no room to retreat or to shirk responsibility. Forty years later, Bo accepted responsibility for this, citing his 'lack of integrity' as the motive. In any case, even if Bo had not advocated this policy, others would have done so to heed Mao's intentions.

---

[277] Xie Chuntao, *Dayuejin*, 73–4; Sun Yeli and Xiong Lianghua, *Jingji Fengyun zhong de Chen Yun*, 153–4; *Mao Weikan*, ii. 303; *Dangshi Ziliao*, xlvii. 218; Li Rui. *Li Rui Wenji, ii. Mao Zedong de Wannian Beiju* (Selected Works of Li Rui, ii. The tragedy of Mao Zedong's last years) (Haikou: Nanfang chubanshe, 1999), 120–2.

[278] Roderick MacFarquhar, *Origins*, ii. 163. Also, the view held by Nicholas Lardy and Kenneth Lieberthal that Chen was 'pushed off centre stage' by Mao and that his 'influence in economic affairs diminished' needs to be qualified. See their *Chen Yun's Strategy for China's Economic Development* (Armonk, NY: M. E. Sharpe, 1983), pp. xii, xxii.

[279] Bo Yibo, *Huigu*, ii. 705; Li Rui, *Wenji*, ii. 140; Sun Yeli and Xiong Lianghua, *Jingji Fengyun zhong de Chen Yun*, 154.

The more cautious Chen, on the other hand, met with the heads of the MM, demanding more detailed accounts, but was ultimately 'convinced', and counselled Mao that the 10.7m. tons were possible.[280] Mao's ability to prevail over his subordinates, and to make them act against their own wishes and better judgement was extraordinary.[281] In any case, most of them realized that it was a lost cause to manufacture 6m. tons in the remaining months of 1958, but since the Chairman's wish could not be resisted, the ensuing campaign was a lavish and reckless spectacle to accomplish a mission impossible, as we shall see in Chapter 3.[282]

Eventually, even more extraordinary measures were adopted by the Beidaihe Conference and the Conference for Industrial Secretaries to force the accomplishment of the steel targets. First, the provincial first secretaries were ordered to take charge of the iron and steel campaign, now designated their top priority. On 25 September, the Party Centre went one step further by ordering party secretaries from the provinces, districts, counties, and *xiang* to take personal command at the iron and steel sites. Second, it was decided at the Conference for Industrial Secretaries that all raw materials, including pig iron, coal, electricity, and transport, must first satisfy the needs of the metallurgy industry before other departments could lay claim to them. A monthly table of quotas for iron and steel production was set up, and even provinces with virtually no iron and steel capability, such as Guangxi, were assigned compulsory quotas.[283] After the Beidaihe Conference, the Party Centre and the Secretariat convened four telephone conferences to press for iron and steel. For instance, on 4 September, Tan Zhenlin and Peng Zhen conveyed Mao's wishes that one ton less was regarded as a failure and inadmissible. Indeed, even Premier Zhou was heavily involved. On 14 September, alarmed by the slow progress of production in September, he called for an emergency meeting to urge extraordinary measures to complete the monthly plan.[284]

On 17 and 23 September, the Ministry of Transport and the Party Centre issued emergency instructions ordering all available means of transport from all organizations, including schools and the army, to be made available for iron and steel production alone. This was dubbed the All People Run Transport Campaign, and subsequently these 'all-people-run-campaigns' were extended to the production of coal and electricity, geological prospecting, and so on, all in the service of steel.[285] Li Fuchun, on the other hand, urged the 30,000 staff and workers at Angang to further 'liberate their thinking, smash superstitions, develop the subjective initiative', and to 'run wild' (*danao*) the technical revolution in order to accomplish the quota of 4.5m. tons of steel. Claiming to represent everyone at Anshan, he pledged to the Party Centre and Mao that Angang's quota would be realized.[286]

---

[280] Ibid. 157.   [281] Bo Yibo, *Huigu*, ii. 702–3, 706–7.
[282] Xie Chuntao, *Dayuejin*, 76–7; *Dangshi Ziliao*, xlvii. 226.
[283] Xie Chuntao, *Dayuejin*, 86–90.
[284] Cong Jin, *Quzhe Fazhan*, 160; *Mao Wengao*, vii. 421; *Zhou Enlai Nianpu*, ii. 169–70.
[285] Xie Chuntao, *Dayuejin*, 86–90.   [286] *RMRB*, 26 September 1958.

Between 10 and 29 September, Mao left the business of the capital to his colleagues and toured the provinces along the Yangzi. Upon his return, he contributed a news report to the *RMRB* demanding that all industrial enterprises run large-scale mass movements to smelt steel, and criticized those who allegedly dismissed these activities as 'unorthodox', 'rural work style', and 'guerrilla habits'.[287] This injunction set off another mobilization campaign that kept the enterprises reeling.

Economic 'Planning' for the Future

Mao's dominance and his buoyancy were also reflected in economic plans. When the 1959 plan and the 2FYP, which had been submitted by the SPC and SEC and repeatedly discussed by the Cooperative Regions and the Politburo, were presented at Beidaihe, Mao, Liu Shaoqi and others ordered further increases. In particular, Mao gave the planners another dressing-down by castigating the reports for lacking in style, logic, enthusiasm, and theoretical sophistication, and ordered the reports to be rewritten repeatedly until they became more acceptable to him. Mao faulted the author(s) of the report for not being particularly competent in industrial work, and more importantly, for not understanding dialectics and the principal contradiction. Finally, Mao urged them to draft a forty article plan (*à la* NPAD) for industry in order to catch up with the USA in *five* years, and surpassing it in *seven*.[288]

Since 'steel as the key link' was now regarded as the principal contradiction, any failure to mention it in the document, perhaps even any inability to anticipate Mao's desires, would have incurred Mao's displeasure. However, Mao's definition of the principal contradiction was to evolve over time, as we shall see below. Ultimately, the Politburo specified that targets for steel production should reach 27 to 30m. tons in 1959, 50m. tons by 1960, and 80 to 100m. tons in 1962. Grain production should reach 400 to 500m. tons by 1959, and 750m. tons in 1962. In turn, the steel and grain targets were used as reference points to set all other production targets for 1959 and the 2FYP.[289] When commenting on the 1959 plan presented by the SPC and the SEC, Li Fuchun called for a hard battle for three years to complete the building of socialism during the 2FYP and to realize socialist industrialization. If China could produce 80 to 100m. tons of steel in 1962 as projected by Mao, perhaps in certain respects China could make the transition to communism by introducing policies such as free rice, free clothing, free urban housing, and so on.[290] In the end, capital investment for the 1959 plan was raised from 48 to 50.12bn. *yuan* (excluding the funds raised by the localities and enterprises themselves), revenue from 70 to 72.25bn. *yuan*, and electricity from 52 to 58 billion watts. The successful fulfilment of the 1959 plan would have meant that production of iron and steel and several other major industrial products would surpass that of Britain in just *two* years, and this was the message Mao conveyed to the Supreme State Conference in 5–8

[287] *Mao Wengao*, vii. 429–31.   [288] Ibid. 367–9.
[289] Bo Yibo, *Huigu*, ii. 707; *Jingji he Shehui Fazhan Jihua Dashi*, 123.
[290] Gu Shiming, *et al.*, *Li Fuchun Jingji Sixiang*, 116.

September. This conference found Mao at his most extravagant. Since he was convinced that grain output in 1958 had more than doubled, he thought that China should, in about fifteen years, produce 300 (or even 700)m. tons of steel and 1,750m. tons of grain. Dismissing difficulties in industry as a kind of blind faith, he now declared a new definition of the principal contradiction that he faulted his colleagues for failing to see: grain and steel were the two most important things—with steel all kinds of machinery could be manufactured. Using military metaphors, Mao said that the 'three marshals' were grain, steel, and machinery, and the two 'forward eche-lons' (*xianxing*) were railway transport and electricity. Once these three marshals have assumed command (*shengzhang*), then victory is within grasp.[291] This new definition of the principal contradiction was less a profound observation than cir-cular reasoning. In other words, Mao was saying that steel, grain, and machinery were decisive in overtaking the capitalist countries (in the production of these three items), and railway transport and electricity were the prerequisites. As late as early October, Mao still exuded confidence when discussing the 1958 steel target with delegates from Eastern European countries. He said that there were many 'fools' in the world, including himself and his colleagues, who were ignorant of the principle of 'steel as the key link'. Now he realized that once steel was grasped, other sectors could follow. He then took credit for the decision to double the 1957 steel target.[292]

To ensure the fulfilment of these extremely ambitious targets and to prepare for 1960, 70 per cent of the revenue of 1959 would be earmarked for capital investment. Similarly, the inflated targets for the 2FYP were hoped to be realized by three years of 'hard struggle' (*kuzhan*) and two years of maximum exertion. Such measures were regarded as necessary to turn China into a socialist country with modern industry, agriculture, science, and culture, in order to facilitate the transition to communism.[293] Yet Mao, who had a penchant for spontaneity, could not ignore the confusion and acute problems on the industrial front, but his half-hearted support for re-establishing some planning priorities and coordination came to nothing. For instance, several regulations were issued during the August Beidaihe Conference to address these problems. The first regulation, issued by the Party Centre, emphasized the orderly organization of economic cooperation by the signing and strict obser-vation of existing contracts. It forbade the unilateral termination of contracts.[294] The second, issued by the CC and the State Council, called for the orderly allocation of goods and material to ensure balance, and designated the centre as the allocator of key raw materials and equipment, albeit with consultation with the provinces. The SPC and the SEC were empowered to make adjustments during implementation.[295] The third, issued by the State Council on strengthening the planning system, attempted to demarcate responsibility between the centre and the provinces by more clearly stressing comprehensive balance. It called for all economic and cultural projects to be included in the state plan and restated the obvious—the centre was

---

[291] *Mao Wengao*, vii. 388–9.   [292] Shi Zhongquan, *Zhuoyue Fengxian*, 348, n. 1.
[293] *Dangshi Ziliao*, xlvii. 228.   [294] Ibid. 229–30.
[295] *FGHB*, vii. 100–1; *Jingji Guanli Dashiji*, 115.

responsible for making yearly, long-term plans, and economic outlays for the entire country. The centre controlled the key targets, and the Cooperative Regions were to adjust their plans on production, training, and labour supply using comprehensive balance. These regulations bore the unmistakable imprint of the planners, especially Chen Yun, and the mention of the term comprehensive balance was significant, especially in the face of Mao's view that imbalance was the universal law. Yet, these regulations could not have been promulgated without Mao's blessing or at least his nod.[296]

In any case, these regulations were so ambiguous and were implemented so haphazardly (given the circumstances of improvisation and cavalier treatment of rules and regulations) that they had virtually no impact in stemming the tide of recklessness, and most were not formally promulgated for another month. In fact, they were no match for slogans such as: 'One day is equivalent to 20 years', 'fear only the limitation of your vision, never your capability to achieve', and 'the more guts you have, the more the earth will produce', which called for even more exaggeration. A similar fate befell the regulation halting recruitment of new workers.[297] In any case, another regulation (published 28 August), which allowed the provinces to approve above-norm construction projects, cancelled out the above regulations.[298] So it was ironic that in September, Chen was named the head of the Party's Capital Construction Committee, and in October, the director of the State Capital Construction Commission under the State Council. Under the circumstances, he was unable to resist the trend.[299]

Mao's Utopianism and the Official Decision to form the People's Communes

On the issue of communes, Mao was no less dominant, masterminding the idea and using his predilection and manipulation to turn communization into a colossal national movement. Mao's utopianism and constant advocacy throughout 1958 made the scattered ideas of the commune congeal, his tactical intervention was responsible for its hasty introduction, and the political pressure generated by *fan-maojin* made dissent impossible.

The central circular (1 August) drafted by Mao announcing the Beidaihe Conference had seventeen items on the agenda, including one on cooperativization, but none dealing with the communes.[300] However, just before the meeting, Mao instructed those in charge of agriculture and forestry (*nonglin kou*) to draft a document entitled 'Opinion on the Formation of the People's Communes in the

[296] *FGHB*, viii. 96–9, 100–1; *Jingji Guanli Dashiji*, 115.
[297] Bo Yibo, *Huigu*, ii. 801.
[298] *FGHB*, vii. 102–3; *Jingji he Shehui Fazhan Jihua Dashi*, 124.
[299] Sun Yeli and Xiong Lianghua, *Jingji Fengyun zhong de Chen Yun*, 160 ff.
[300] *Mao Wengao*, vii. 343.

Rural Areas' and distribute it with the draft regulations of the Chayashan commune on the *first day* of the conference. There he praised it as one of the best documents.[301] The astounded Politburo had no choice but to go along, and no dissenting opinion was expressed. Since a tidal wave of communization was already a fait accompli in some provinces, the conference was then forced to draft and pass a formal document on the communes.

Mao underestimated the difficulties in forming communes because he thought the most formidable part of collectivization, the transition from lower to advanced APCs, which involved the abolition of private property, was already history.[302] In various speeches to the Politburo and the heads of the Cooperative Regions, he discoursed on the communes and issued instructions like a commander-in-chief, but his vision was highly speculative, and was to clarify only gradually. For instance, in his most ebullient mood, Mao envisaged communes as huge agricultural units the size of smaller cities, each with roads big enough to double as airport runways.[303] Huge communes, like the Xiuwu commune in Henan with 29,000 households and 130,000 members, were desirable because they were powerful and easy to run. Their economies were supposed to be easy to incorporate into the state plan, since Mao had hoped that agricultural products could be directly requisitioned from the peasants, much like the requisitioning of industrial products, without going through a sale mechanism. The communes could also liberate women, abolish patriarchy, and raise labour efficiency, he thought.[304]

Mao also approved Xushui's method of the three-'ize' (militarize, combatize, and disciplinize) and the division of communes into regiments, companies, and brigades. These were to be production armies, organized and deployed like military units, capable of raising production, and improving people's livelihood, as well as providing spare time for rest and study. He reckoned it to be a kind of 'military democracy'.

At Beidaihe, Mao articulated a radical vision of rural transformation in part because he was nostalgic about the practices of the pre-1949 revolutionary struggles, such as the free supply system. In his mind, wages were a 'bourgeois right' whereas the supply system and living communally were a communist work style—the antithesis of the capitalist work style—so he toyed with the idea of replacing wages with free supply.[305] Citing past experience, he rejected the claim that a free supply system would foster laziness.[306] He also raised the issue of 'eat rice without pay' by relating it to the story of Zhang Ling, the head of a religious sect, and his followers, who were entitled to eat free after having contributing 5 *dou* (or decalitre) of rice. Zhang Ling's career was continued by his son Zhang Xin and grandson Zhang Lu. After praising 'subjective initiative', Mao even stated baldly that some aspects of utopian socialism should be practised.[307] Finally, Mao wanted to abolish the 'capitalist remnants' such as private plots, and private raising of livestock, to replace

---

[301] Bo Yibo, *Huigu*, ii. 741.   [302] Ibid. 777.   [303] *Mao Weikan*, xiii. 144.
[304] Ibid. 133, 145.   [305] Ibid. ii. 304.   [306] Bo Yibo, *Huigu*, ii. 772.
[307] *Mao Weikan*, ii. 300, 304–5, 317.

them with mess halls, nurseries, sewing teams, and the wage system.[308] This unorthodox advocacy is a testimonial to Mao's extreme optimism, considering his past and bitter experience with doctrinal disputes within the CCP and within the Soviet Union.[309]

During the Beidaihe Conference, the delegates visited Xushui, and from then on, it became a Mecca for many foreign and domestic delegations, many regarding it as the Party Centre's model for communization.[310] Consequently, acting on Mao's proposal, the Beidaihe Conference issued a Resolution formally announcing the formation of communes (29 August). The Resolution showed certain restraints, especially in the context of Mao's fantasies—no doubt even Mao had to be careful with a document dealing with the widely disparate conditions of the country—but Mao's utopianism still seeped through, making for a very ambiguous document. For instance, the Resolution ordered the merger of the APCs into larger collectives and communes step by step with 'no compulsory or rash steps' or any adverse effect on production, but it also said that it was better to accomplish it in one stroke (*yiqi he cheng*). The prescribed method of merger, and mass mobilization combined with blooming, contending, and debating, was a prescription for excess, given the context of the time. The Resolution said that the ideal was to have one *xiang* comprising one commune with around 2,000 households, although smaller communes with less than 2,000 households and large ones with 6–7,000 households were also fine. However, huge communes with more than 20,000 households should neither be advocated nor opposed, so the sanctioned range—2,000 to 20,000 households—was enormous. The original system of management and production of the APCs could remain unchanged although they could elect an administrative committee for unified planning and management, a process known as 'changing the upper structure while keeping the lower structure unchanged'. Even the size, the speed, and the methods of merger were to be decided according to local conditions. Mergers could take place in the autumn or following spring, although joint plans for post-autumn capital construction in agriculture and preparatory work for the next year was to be done.

The resolution anticipated disputes because different APCs had different economic backgrounds, assets and liabilities, but advised against the squaring of accounts. Cadres must use the spirit of communism to educate the masses not to be concerned with trifles. Things such as private plots should not be dealt with in a hurry. Fruit trees could remain private, and shares and foundation funds could be dealt with some years later. Yet, it also said that private plots might be managed collectively. Mao was cautious enough to insert a passage of about 400 words that said that the transfer of private ownership to all-people ownership should not be effected immediately—it could take three to six years or longer. The communes were still socialist, so the principle of 'from each according to his ability, and to each according to his labour' still applied. Only after many years, when social product had increased, and communist consciousness and morality heightened; when education became universal; when gaps between workers and peasants, town and

---

[308] *Mao Weikan*, ii. 314.   [309] Ibid. 295–321.   [310] Bo Yibo, *Huigu*, ii. 750–1.

country, mental and manual labour had disappeared; when bourgeois rights were eliminated; and when state functions were limited to external defence and no internal role, then the stage of communism could be realized. It was better to stick to collective ownership to avoid unnecessary trouble in making the transition, Mao maintained, but also said that the system of ownership already contained certain elements of all-people ownership.[311]

The Resolution went on to say that the system of distribution was not to be changed to avoid adverse effects on production, and that the original system of payment according to work day could be retained. If conditions permitted, a wage system could be introduced. Nevertheless, at the end, the Resolution said that the commune was the best organization to make the transition to communism and become the basic unit of a future communist society. Although the present stage was to build socialism, the people should actively prepare for the transition to communism, as the attainment of communism was no longer a remote event.

Overall, the Resolution was extremely ambiguous because it reflected Mao's own struggle between utopian aspirations and the need to be realistic. Consequently, it issued mixed signals, but in the highly charged atmosphere of that time, it was natural for subordinates to ignore the cautious finer points in favour of more radical measures. For instance, on 11 September, the *RMRB* published the CCP directive on the launching of a socialist and communist education campaign in the winter and spring of 1958–9. The gist of the campaign was to propagandize the communes and the Leap, and to work out even more advanced targets by using the method of 'pulling white flags, and planting red flags'.[312] In any case, the Resolution was not the final word on the communes because fantastic propaganda and pronouncements in other sources from September onwards greatly exacerbated a radicalism that led directly to the phenomenon called the 'communist wind'. Furthermore, even before the Resolution on the communes was finally published on 10 September in *RMRB*, *Hongqi* published an editorial on 1 September entitled 'Welcome the High tide of Communization' with the charter of the Weixing commune that articulated a more radical version of the commune. The later stated baldly that all savings belonging to the APCs should be pooled into the commune without compensation, and that the communes would take responsibility for all debts incurred by the former APCs. Peasants who joined the communes must surrender private plots, houses, livestock, and woods to the communes so that the remnants of the 'individual economy' could be destroyed. The free food supply system would also be introduced. This contrasted with the provisions in the Beidaihe resolution, which said that the differences between APCs should be recognized, that levelling should be avoided, and that resolution of ownership issues of private plots, and fruit trees should be postponed to

---

[311] *Mao Wengao*, vii. 360.

[312] *FGHB*, vii. 5–8. 'Pulling white flags and planting red flags' meant more than the identification of the laggards and the advanced to fuel competition. 'Pulling white flags' also meant the removal and punishment of cadres and citizens remotely suspected of resisting the GLF. For instance, in Zhenyuan county, Gansu, 870 rural cadres were dismissed and more than 1,000 'class enemies' were arrested by October 1958 to implement this slogan-cum-policy. *Bainianchao*, 4, 1999, 50–1.

the future.[313] On 4 September an *RMRB* editorial praised the Weixing model and cited it as a model for emulation. Although it said that not all communes could match this advanced model, most communes in this early stage copied this prototype.[314]

Soon the free food system caught on, goaded by the catchy slogan, 'eat rice without pay'. In mid-September some central leaders drafted a document that specified that food should be free in the communes, and the wages of the members should be deposited with the communes without interest. Their needs would be met by purchases by the communes, or members could use their deposits as exchange for goods. These cash-free transactions would then reduce the scope of currency circulation and eventually abolish capitalism.[315]

The High Tide for the Formation of the Communes and the 'Communist Wind'[316]

These various initiatives unleashed a colossal movement for the formation of communes and subsequently, many new radical features, not mentioned in the Beidaihe resolution, were improvised. With lightning speed, at the end of September, or less than one month after the publication of the resolution, 90.4 per cent of all rural households were merged into 23,397 communes. Indeed, such haste meant that organizational problems were swept under the carpet. While communes varied greatly in size and features, the average had 4,797 households, 60,000 *mu*, and 10,000 labourers. They were much larger than the APCs, which had an average 170 households, 2,000 *mu*, and 350 labourers. For instance, the Weixing commune merged 27 APCs with 9, 369 households. The Surpass Britain commune merged 68 APCs with 20,457 households. In addition, there were also 94 huge communes comprising an entire county and other federations of communes at the county level.[317]

The assets of all APCs, including land, livestock, farm tools, private plots, orchards, and public properties were turned over to the communes for unified management. The state also decentralized to the communes local branches of the Ministries of Grain, Commerce, Finance, Banking, and Supply, as well as marketing and credit co-ops.[318]

Before communization, the *xiang* was the lowest level of political power and APCs were the grass-roots economic organization but communization combined administrative and economic functions by merging the *xiang* into the communes. The *xiang* chief became the commune chief, the *xiang* People's Congress became the Commune People's Congress, and the *xiang* People's Committee became the Commune Executive Committee.[319] Therefore, communes were not just economic

---

[313] *FGHB*, viii. 3.   [314] Bo Yibo, *Huigu*, ii. 748; *Hongqi*, 1958, 7: 16–17.
[315] Bo Yibo, *Huigu*, ii. 753.   [316] This term was not used by Mao until February 1959. Ibid. 756.
[317] *NJZWH*, ii. 84; *RMRB* 1 October 1958; Xie Chuntao, *Dayuejin*, 102.
[318] Bo Yibo, *Huigu*, ii. 748.
[319] Ibid. By the end of August, Henan had claimed that its cities and towns had formed 509 *urban* communes which had canteens, nurseries, household-work mutual teams, and so on. *NBCK*, 16 September 1958, 7–16.

units, they were also administrative and governmental units in charge of industry, agriculture, commerce, education, and the military. These changes could have tightened the government's direct control over the grass roots.

Most commune organization followed the three-tiered structure of Chayashan commune—commune, production brigade (*guanli qu*), and production team. The commune was empowered to impose centralized control over all government and production activities, including assignment of labour, transfer of resources, and distribution of production. In turn, it assumed the chief responsibility of providing for its members. The production brigade managed production and part of the economic accounting, pooling all gains into the communes. Production teams functioned as mere sub-units of the production organization.[320] Yet, demarcation of responsibilities between these administrative levels never became clear, given the confusion of the period.

The new distribution system, introduced in late 1958, was to be a combination of both wages and free supply. There were many versions of free supply, often accounting for as much as 50–80 per cent of the members' income. One version provided only grain staples, while another provided full meals (grain and non-staples like meat and vegetables), and a third supplied both food and clothing. Some communes included 7 or 10 guarantees of such things as meals, clothing, housing, education, wedding and funeral expenses, heating coal, haircuts, retirement, movies, and so on. Some supplied comprehensive coverage of all living expenses. Overall, grain, no longer being distributed, was assigned to canteens, and commune members were given meal coupons. The most common practice was free meals ('eat rice without pay').

A more extreme case was the large Xushui commune that comprised an entire county. In September, it abolished all wages and the principle of remuneration according to labour in favour of comprehensive provision of meals, housing, clothing, health, and *all* daily necessities. These entitlements were universal, regardless of the work contributed. This distribution system was touted as a major step towards the communist principle of 'from each according to his ability, to each according to his need'.[321]

Initial peasant reaction to the communes were not entirely negative. It ranged from genuine enthusiasm, passive resistance, muted opposition to open defiance. Decades later many still remembered fondly their experience during communization, especially the free food.[322] Yet, the generous provisions could not be sustained. After the autumn of 1958, many communes, unable to honour the meal coupons, were only able to supply the lowest standard of food. Little or no wages were distributed, and most communes were unable to honour the guarantees of other daily necessities. Consequently, the incentive to work plummeted.[323]

---

[320] Xie Chuntao, *Dayuejin*, 101–3.   [321] Bo Yibo, *Huigu*, ii. 751.

[322] For instance, see Helen Siu, *Agents and Victims in South China* (New Haven: Yale University Press, 1989), 176–7; William Hinton, *Shenfan: The Continuing Revolution in a Chinese Village* (New York: Random House, 1983), 204–32.   [323] Bo Yibo, ii. 750, 760.

The policy of 'three-ize'—militarize organization, combatize action, collectivize livelihood—prescribed that labour and production be organized along military lines in the communes, so that members could be mobilized easily for the various campaigns. Members, both men and women, were organized into battalions and companies so that work resembled military manœuvres—they would march to work every morning in squads, beating drums and waving flags. Private houses were confiscated to turn into dormitories, and males, females, and the elderly were segregated in separate dwellings.[324] At the end of September, Shanxi claimed that it had created a labour army of 4.29 million. Gansu, Sichuan, Guangxi, and Yunnan all claimed that they had formed labour field armies (*yezhan*) to engage in campaigns for iron and steel, water conservancy, agricultural production, road building, and transportation. Labour use and efficiency was said to have gone up 20–30 per cent. 'Collectivize livelihood' meant the creation of mess halls, nurseries, and old-people's homes. Figures from 11 provinces claimed that 1.45 million mess halls and 1.26 million day-cares, as well as grain-processing, sewing, and laundry groups had greatly advanced the cause of women. More than twenty million women were said to have been liberated from household work to agricultural and industrial production.[325]

Yet the 'labour armies' were in fact *corvee* labour for such activities as the iron and steel campaign and water conservancy, often carried out far away from the homes of the peasants conscripted. Many cadres equated 'militarization' with orders and domination, and penalties, including physical abuses and withholding of food, were meted out for slight disobedience.[326] Setting up of the various welfare facilities such as mess halls, nurseries, and old-people's homes required the commandeering of people's houses, food, furniture, kitchen utensils and other personal belongings. The building of new residential areas also led to large-scale demolition of houses in some places.[327] These made a mockery of the provision in the Resolution that houses and means of livelihood should remain in private hands.

Buoyed by extravagant propaganda and continuous political pressures, the communes competed with one another to report extraordinary claims of super harvests that were hardly credible. Yet, under the circumstances, for leaders and peasants alike, the suspension of their disbelief had become the only appropriate thing to do. For instance, when Bo Yibo visited Xushui with delegates from the Beidaihe Conference, he already realized that the demonstrations of extraordinary yields in the cotton fields were fake.[328] Yet it was inopportune to point out these deceptions, lest it would be construed by the Maoists as inhibiting the enthusiasm of the masses. When top leaders did nothing to question the exaggerations, the subordinates were emboldened to play the game.

---

[324] Sun Yeli and Xiong Lianghua, *Jingji Fengyun zhong de Chen Yun*, 159. For a report of the militarization of the *Weixing* Commune, see *NBCK*, 17 October 1958, 15–21; Sulamith Potter and Jack Potter, *China's Peasants* (Cambridge: Cambridge University Press, 1990), 69; Helen Siu, *Agents and Victims*, 170.   [325] *RMRB*, 1 October 1958; Xie Chuntao, *Dayuejin*, 106.
[326] *NBCK*, 11 December 1958, 11.   [327] Bo Yibo, *Huigu*, ii. 761–2.   [328] Ibid. 751.

The 'Communist Wind' or Free-for-All[329]

Since the Resolution said that communism was not a distant future, many communes were quick to announce the transition from collective ownership to 'all-people ownership'. Many localities planned to realize communism by specific dates. For instance, Xushui claimed it would do it by 1963, and Shandong's Fan county one-upped the competition by picking 1960. Meanwhile, Fan county's report painted an extravagant picture (in seven and eight-character verses) to describe the future communist society. For instance, it claimed that it would set up an industrial network in one year and achieve industrialization and electrification in two years, so that smoke stacks would appear like a forest. It would manufacture tractors and motor vehicles, and radios would become commonplace. Yields of 10 to 15,000 kg/*mu* would create huge abundances in food for enjoyment at any time. This impressed Mao, who compared the report to a poem, and said that it was feasible. Exuberant claims like these emboldened Mao to estimate that China could enter communism before the Soviet Union.[330]

Mao's view in turn encouraged many units to plan for the transition to communism, and the attitude of the Party Centre was to allow them. For instance, Shouzhang county commune and Fan county commune planned to make the transition to communism by 1960. In Paomaxiang, when the party secretary announced that November would mark the beginning of communism, people immediately took to the streets to loot the stores and grab whatever belonged to other people or to cooperatives, because the literal translation of the word communism in Chinese meant 'the ism of common property'.[331]

This truncated view of communism led to another controversial and disruptive feature of communization—the phenomenon of 'one, equalize; two, transfer; three, recovery of funds'. The former two together were often called *ping duei*, or levelling and transfer. Equalization meant the levelling of property and assets among the former APCs in the communes, while transfer meant requisition and removal of such property and assets. Recovery of funds referred to attempts by banks and credit agencies, fearing the confusion surrounding communization and driven by the need to fund GLF projects, to retrieve loans to the APCs.[332] For many, these amounted to the expropriation of the APCs, especially the better-off ones, and this created 'fierce struggles' between the communes and production teams over manpower and property.[333]

Ping duei was a disruptive feature of the communes, aggravated by the numerous attempts to falsify breakthroughs and accomplishments. Moreover, other administrative units also joined the fray. For instance, although the model regulations of Chayashan designated production brigades units to manage production and units of

---

[329] The following, unless otherwise stated, draws from Mao's speeches made at the Second Zhengzhou Conference (27 February–5 March 1959) on the 'communist wind'. *Mao Weikan*, xiB. 163–81; *Mao Wengao*, viii. 65–75; *Wansui* (1967), 48–9.

[330] Text in *Mao Wengao*, vii. 494–7.   [331] Bo Yibo, *Huigu*, ii. 754.

[332] *NJZWH*, 141–2.   [333] *Mao Weikan*, xiB. 163, 183.

accounting, it also said that the communes would be responsible for all gains and losses. In effect, this turned the communes into accounting units as well, which meant that all properties, including land, livestock, trees, large farm tools, fruit trees, vegetables, and all agricultural products, whether harvested or not, belonged to the communes. The communes then had the power to move land and property around. They commandeered labour and materials from production brigades for building offices and guest houses, for running their own businesses, and for equalizing property among production brigades. For instance, in 1959, Chayashan commune claimed to have created 'satellites' of some 10,000 hog farms and 10,000 chicken farms from scratch, but in reality these animals were commandeered from the peasants by force, striking fear and anxiety among the peasantry.[334] Misappropriation was also severe between production brigades and production teams, as the former also commandeered assets from the latter at will and without compensation. Once an order was issued production teams had to put down their work and help other teams. Even money paid to the production teams for their products was confiscated to support the poorer teams.

The merger of government administration and commune management enabled the commune to use administrative orders to enforce its decisions and to make requisitions, aggravating problems of 'the communist wind' and 'commandism'; those who disobeyed orders could be deprived of the right to eat.[335] Under these circumstances, even the counties joined in. The transition from collective ownership to all-people ownership implied that the state could requisition and redistribute labour, resources, and funds from the communes at will and without compensation. Therefore, some counties tried to reallocate funds, land, and resources within the county as a whole. As the various big projects such as iron and steel, small industries, water conservancy, purchase of agricultural machinery, repairs to roads, small railways, etc., demanded large amounts of raw materials, counties requisitioned whatever they needed freely without compensation.[336] Furthermore, to fund the industrial, iron and steel campaigns, banks retrieved loans they had made to the peasants, regardless of when they were due.[337]

Soon this 'communist wind' spread to special district and provincial levels as well. At the beginning large items such as land, housing, funds, and grain, were seized, but then even smaller amounts were seized. As the saying went, 'money was grabbed, materials were transferred, houses were demolished, grain was snatched'. It was estimated nationally that, in this free-for-all situation, about 2 to 3bn. *yuan* were appropriated from the APCs for these purposes. In 1959, because of the shortage of supplementary food, various government organizations, armies, factories, and schools appropriated land, seeds, tools, animals, fertilizer, and labour in

---

[334] Bo Yibo, *Huigu*, ii. 759. In another case that happened in Sichuan, after the District authorities had decided to gather hogs from several *xiang* and APCs to create a 'hog satellite', most of the hogs died of diseases, lack of food, and generally poor management. *NBCK*, 3 December 1958, 24.

[335] Bo Yibo, *Huigu*, ii. 762.   [336] Ibid. 757.

[337] Xie Chuntao, *Dayuejin*, 110; Bo Yibo, *Huigu*, ii. 757.

the countryside freely for their own production, but hauled away the produce, contributing neither to the agricultural tax nor the public grain (*gongliang*). Other units exploited the confusion to enrich themselves. For instance, a propaganda unit in Henan appropriated fifty-four hogs and two stockmen from Chayashan commune. In 1961, it was estimated that a national total of 25bn. *yuan*, or an average of 49 *yuan* per rural inhabitant, was siphoned off during the GLF years. This was a tremendous amount, considering that the average annual consumption of the peasants was only 68 *yuan* in 1961.[338]

In resisting the extensive *ping duei*, peasants in the production brigades and teams set up sentry, concealed grain, and divided the harvest, tools, and animals among themselves, consuming as much as they could. Collective property became fair game for all. Trees were felled, and tea plants were denuded. In areas most affected, there were large-scale outflows of labour, sabotage, slaughter of livestock, and destruction of farm tools. As the peasants lost all incentive to work, farm work was done sloppily, and large tracts of land were left barren. Production plummeted after autumn harvest, leading to unusual nationwide shortages of grain, oil, pork, and vegetables, and eventually to widespread malnutrition.[339]

This mêlée was aggravated not only by the literal translation of the word 'communism', but also by the phrase 'to each according to his needs' (*gequ suoxu*) which in Chinese literally meant 'everyone takes what he needs'. Some thought 'all-people ownership' meant everything was free. In the spirit of communism, all debts were either written off or repaid by public funds, and everything was up for grabs. The distinction between private and public property broke down—crops could be harvested by anyone, grain could be requisitioned without compensation, and even personal belongings could be claimed by anyone. It was open season for anyone who wished to fish in these troubled waters.[340]

The state's high procurement of grain aggravated matters—the state's requisition quota rose in direct proportion to the high estimates of 410m. tons of grain in 1958. In fact, total grain procurement was raised from 48m. tons in 1957 to 58.75m. tons in 1958, or a 22.4 per cent hike, although the actual grain output for 1958 was only just above 200m. tons, or 2.5 per cent over the production of 1957. Since the summer harvest was totally consumed under the initial stage of communization, autumn procurement spread uncertainty, fear, and resentment. This was exacerbated by the first *emergency* Party Centre and State Council directive issued since the GLF ordering the use of the surprise attack method (*tuji*) to procure grain.[341] Nevertheless, grain procurement was carried out slowly, the reserves were down, and many localities appealed to the centre for grain.[342] In 1959, forced requisition took on the character of a war against the peasantry.

---

[338] Ibid. 763–5; *NJZWH*, 142 ff, 182.   [339] Bo Yibo, *Huigu*, ii. 765; *Mao Weikan*, xiB. 179.
[340] Bo Yibo, *Huigu*, ii. 765; *NJZWH*, ii. 85, 89, 142–3; *NBCK*, 11 December 1958, 5 ff; *Mao Weikan*, xiB. 168.
[341] Xie Chuntao, *Dayuejin*, 110; Cong Jin, *Quzhe Fazhan*, 161; *FGHB*, viii. 169–71; Chu Han, *Sannian Ziran Zaihai*, p. 108.   [342] *Gongheguo Dadian*, 549.

By October/November, internal news reached Mao showing that an unprecedented wave of typhoid, dysentery, and gastro-enteritis, caused by the unhygienic canteens, lack of rest, hot food, and heat in the communes, had affected twenty-one counties and municipalities in Hebei.[343] One report also showed that 30 per cent of residents of one old-people's home in Henan had died, and the rest had fled.[344] Coercion, as well as verbal and physical abuse of commune members were so severe that many ran away. Furthermore, false reporting was universal. In Hubei, an investigation of one commune that claimed it had produced an unbelievable 69,000 *jin* of wheat in one experimental plot revealed that local cadres had forced the commune members to gather wheat from 10 *mu* at one spot. Mao was also aware that the peasants were hard-pressed by the numerous work tasks, and the cadres, who feared the label of 'rightist leaning', were compelled to fulfil overtly high targets, and were therefore indifferent to the well-being of the masses. A report from Yunnan that reached Mao in November described serious deaths by oedema, diarrhoea, and measles in the spring/summer of 1958 as a result of cadre coercion. Mao cautioned against making mistakes in these areas again, and referred to it often.[345] In Beijing and Shanghai, fear about the establishment of urban communes, the abolition of money, and the confiscation of property led to bank runs and panic buying.[346]

Bo Yibo was right to observe that Mao was extremely anxious from mid-October to December. He had high hopes for the GLF, but was not blind to the problems. He worked non-stop, tightly supervising every move and attempting to maintain control. He convened conferences, discussed matters, inspected the localities, and charged subordinates to inspect further.[347] Essentially, the GLF was Mao's enterprise; he had every incentive to see it succeed. Ultimately, Mao's faith in the communes was unwavering, and without benefit of hindsight, he was relatively unfazed by the problems. In fact, the possibility that the communes could be short-cuts to communism still excited him.

Between 13 and 17 October, Mao inspected the Hebei and Tianjin areas (where he was briefed by Xushui leaders) to discuss the problems of iron and steel production and the communes with regional leaders. By late October, after he was briefed on a discussion by the North and North-East Nine Province Agricultural Cooperative Conference, he realized for the first time the gravity of the problems confronting the communes. Goaded by the slogan 'grain as the key link' and pressed by the need to supply grain free, many communes had abandoned economic or cash crops in favour of grain and potatoes. Communization created the impression that self-sufficiency was a goal in itself, and that trade and exchange was to be avoided. For all these reasons the communes were unable to earn sufficient cash to pay out as wages, and free supplies became the bulk of the remuneration. Consequently, families with more able-bodied labourers felt that they were short-changed.

---

[343] *Mao Wengao*, vii. 530–1.   [344] *Mao Weikan*, xiii. 206.
[345] *Mao Wengao*, vii. 584–6, 594–5; 614–15. See also, *NBCK*, 11 December 1958, 5–6, 9–10.
[346] Bo Yibo, *Huigu*, ii. 809; *NBCK*, 4 November 1958, 3–5.   [347] Bo Yibo, *Huigu*, ii. 817–18.

Soon, even the families with few able-bodied labourers, presumably the bene-ficiaries of free supplies, did not feel particularly privileged because of the deteri-orating quality of the supplies. Except for a brief period at the beginning of communization, the communes were only able to provide the bare basic minimum of grain with no meat, vegetables, oil, or salt. The massive slaughter of animals and the concealment of grain by the peasants themselves aggravated the problem. Most mess halls were unsheltered, their locations far from homes and inconvenient, and food was often cold. Other amenities such as child-care and old-people's homes were also poorly run and therefore unpopular. China simply did not have the material wherewithal to run such ambitious social programmes. Mao was also aware of the coercion and abuse perpetrated by the cadres in the name of 'militarization of command', and the numerous projects not only put severe strain on the labour supply, it also deprived the peasants of rest. At this stage, Mao's immediate solution was to issue instructions to cool things down for the first time during the Leap. Mao declared that exchange was eternal, and that the scope of free supplies should be reduced, perhaps to equal that of wages. The principle of remuneration according to labour, and some wage differentials should be allowed. Since a worker at Angang could generate production value of 18,000 *yuan* and an average peasant only 700 *yuan*, there was not much that could be extracted. So in the communes, the transition to all-people ownership could wait perhaps twelve or more years, not the three to five years (or longer) predicted at Beidaihe.[348] On the other hand, his long-term solution, transmitted as instructions by Chen Zhengren, were even more intensive farming by shrinking the size of farmland by the introduction of deep ploughing, fertilizer application, and irrigation (as embodied in the 'three-three' system),[349] and the redesign of farm tools. He approved a recommendation made by the Cooperative Regions to turn one-tenth of all farmland into high-yield fields capable of producing 5,000 to 10,000 *jin/mu*. Mao mused that chemical fertilizer might be dispensed with, because the Leap was achieved by relying on organic and indigenous fertilizer—this was another dig at Chen Yun.

At the same time, as Mao began to sense danger, he dispatched three inspec-tion teams to different communes in Henan to gather information for him. On 17 October, he dispatched Liu Zihou to Xushui, and two days later, he sent Chen Boda, Zhang Chunqiao, Hu Sheng, and Li Youjiu on a special plane to inspect the Weixing commune, so that they could report to him at Zhengzhou. On 26 October, he dispatched Wu Lengxi and Tian Jiaying to Shouwu and Qiliying communes. Indicative of his utopian aspirations was his instruction to Chen to take the book '*Marx, Engels, Lenin, and Stalin on Communism*' to read during his tour. Chen was a leading theoretician and Zhang had just attracted Mao's attention, so Mao wanted them to judge if these communist principles could be

---

[348] *Mao Weikan*, xiii. 229–30.
[349] The existing cultivated land would shrink to one-third of its original area, whereas the other two-thirds would be reserved for fallowing, parks, and afforestation.

applied.[350] Simultaneously, he also consulted with Zhou Enlai, Chen Yun, Peng Zhen, Chen Yi, Li Fuchun, Bo Yibo, and Wang Heshou. On 31 October, Mao took a special train south, stopping frequently to inspect and to listen to reports from regional leaders on the communes and the iron and steel campaign.[351] Mao's conversations with local officials at Shijiazhuang, Handan in Hebei, and Xinxiang, Henan, show that he observed first-hand problems such as cadre coercion and the communes' inability to pay wages. Yet, he still believed that a huge bumper harvest had brought an inexhaustible supply of grain, and urged the continued promotion of the iron and steel campaign, the 'three-three' system, deep ploughing, the mess halls, and the nurseries.[352]

However, the situation at Xushui, a model commune, must have dampened Mao's expectations. The report by the Intelligence Unit of the Central Staff Office (dated 18 October) to Mao about Xushui confirmed the widespread use of summary methods, coercion, and false reporting there. Because of the innumerable tasks assigned to the county, grain estimates had been exaggerated. As private plots had been abolished, the members no longer raised poultry, and soon no eggs or poultry were available. Although the county bragged about turning itself into a 'cultured' county by September 1958, there were in fact many illiterates. When in Hebei at the end of October, Mao was told by Lin Tie and Liu Zihou that even Xushui had used brutal methods to deal with its members (i.e. had used debates to harass dissidents), and that the supply of rice was insecure.[353]

Second Thoughts: The Zhengzhou Work Conference (2–10 November) and Rural Problems

Mao arrived at Zhengzhou in a mixed mood of optimism and wariness. It was now two months after Beidaihe, and the problems in the communes had to be fixed. He picked Zhengzhou for the conference because Henan was the bell-wether of the commune movement, and the problems surrounding the communes there were most representative. While Mao wanted to press the Leap ahead and secure the Leap approach for the future, he could no longer dismiss the negative news reports made by his personal aides as 'one finger out of ten'. Ultimately he decided to cool things down and to approve some adjustments in the communes, but in general, still wanted to forge ahead. Equally important

---

[350] Zhonggong Zhongyang Dangshi Yanjiushi Keyanju (ed.), *Mao Zedong de Zuji* (The footprints of Mao Zedong) (Beijing: Zhonggong dangshi chubanshe, 1993), 482–3; *Mao Wengao*, vii. 463–5; Mianhuai Mao Zedong editorial group. *Mianhuai Mao Zedong* (Cherish the memory of Mao Zedong) (Beijing: Zhongyang wenxian chubanshe, 1993), 250–3; Ye Yonglie. *Zhang Chunqiao Zhuan* (Biography of Zhang Chunqiao) (Beijing: Zuojia chubanshe, 1993), 97.

[351] Bo Yibo, *Huigu*, ii. 807–8.

[352] *Mao Weikan*, ix. 167–81; see also Xie Chuntao, *Dayuejin*, 115.

[353] *Mao Wengao*, vii. 522–4; Bo Yibo, *Huigu*, ii. 760–1. For a first-hand account of the Xushui phenomenon in 1958, see *Bainianchao*, 7, 1999, 53–59.

at that time, Mao was wrestling to clarify the issues for himself, and his ambivalence was to be reflected in the various speeches he gave.[354]

The proceedings of the nine-day conference took place as follows:

2 November	The conference opened in Mao's special train with only the first secretaries of Shanxi, Gansu, Shaanxi, Henan, and Hebei in attendance. Mao listened to reports and delivered an important speech.
3 November	The conference was expanded with the arrival of the provincial first secretaries of Shangdong, Anhui, Hunan, and Hubei.
4 and 5 November	Mao presided over the meetings and listened to reports by small groups. Mao declared that the delegates should refer to Stalin's *Economic Problems of Socialism in the USSR* when discussing the problems and the nature of the communes.
6 November	With the arrival of central leaders, Mao reorganized the discussion groups in the meeting, and put Deng Xiaoping in charge of the discussion of the commune problems. As the delegation expanded, the conference moved from the train to a larger venue.
7 and 8 November	Deng chaired the meeting and discussed the commune problems one by one and produced the document 'Notes on the Zhengzhou Conference'. Meanwhile, Mao continued with the study of Stalin's *Economic Problems of Socialism in the USSR* and revising the New Forty Articles, and retitling it 'Forty Article Outline on Building Socialism (1958–1972)'.
9 and 10 November	Mao led the delegates to study Stalin's theories and the problems in the communes, and criticized the New Forty Articles for avoiding the issue of commodity production.
10 November	Mao revised 'Notes on the Zhengzhou Conference' and retitled it 'Zhengzhou Conference Resolution on Certain Problems Regarding the People's Communes'.

The Communes

Since the communes were Mao's brainchild, he also took personal charge of applying the remedies. At the beginning of the Conference (2–5 November) his original intention was to stay on his special train, listen to reports from his inspection teams, and to consult only with provincial leaders on the issues surrounding communization. This would prepare him for the Politburo meeting preceding the Sixth Plenum. However, the bad news contained in the reports convinced him of the need to be more circumspect. Furthermore, he felt that a new comprehensive document on the communes was needed to 'unify' thinking and end the confusion of the previous months. Ironically, while Mao was beginning

[354] Available Mao speeches made at the Zhengzhou Conference are in *Mao Weikan*, xiii. 173–95; xiB. 110–122.

to cool things down, his allies, unaware of his new intentions, were still forging ahead. On 3 November, the two hotheads of the leap, Wu Zhipu and Zeng Xisheng, still in an ebullient mode, proposed a new and more radical Forty Articles, as the NPAD had become obsolete. Mao supported the idea, and divided the delegates into four groups—industry; agriculture; education, science, and culture; and commerce—to draft the new Forty Articles. On 4 November, Wu reported that two topics had been discussed: the Forty Articles Outline on the Development of the People's Communes (1958–1967) and the Outline on Building of Communism in China in Ten Years. To hold things back, Mao struck out the word 'communism' and replaced it with 'socialism' and expanded the lead time to fifteen years, so the document that emerged became the 'Forty Articles Outline on Building Socialism in Fifteen Years' (1958–1972).[355] Eventually, the drafts by Wu and others were revised by Mao many times, who excised elements he regarded as 'leftist'. For instance, in discussing the new Forty Articles, Mao said that expectations had to be dashed, and the speedy transition to communism should be downplayed.

One thing clearest in Mao's mind was the need to resume and expand commodity production and exchange, so on the first day of the conference, he set the tone by declaring that communes should not strive for self-sufficiency, and that besides production for their own consumption, they must also produce commercial goods in order to be able to exchange other desired goods and to earn money to disburse as wages.[356] Mao realized that many cadres, fearing the stigma that commodity production and exchange equated capitalism, continued to suppress it in favour of administrative allocation. So he now took pains to emphasize the importance of commodity production and trade in both the 'primary' and the 'construction' stages of socialism, and cited Lenin and Stalin to that effect.[357]

In this context, Mao was quick to disown both the idea of abolishing commodity exchange and its proponents altogether. The hapless Chen Boda, whom Mao dispatched to inspect Weixing commune, was summoned to Zhengzhou to report his findings. Before he had a chance to speak, he was sternly rebuked by Mao, who accused him of being one of the 'so-called' Marxist economists who were totally inadequate when it came to practical matters. They had 'too much Marxism', and confused the issues, Mao maintained. In a letter dated 9 November that was sent to the party committees of the centre, provinces, districts, and counties, Mao turned the unnamed critique of Chen into a bit of a national event. At the end of the Conference, Mao banished Chen to Guangdong to 'learn from Tao Zhu', because, as Mao said, he had not learned Marxism-Leninism.[358] This sudden repudiation of Chen, the country's leading theoretician and Mao's own mouthpiece on the Leap and the communes, created a convenient scapegoat for

---

[355] Duan and Kong, in *Mao Zedong de Zuji*, 484–5; *Mao Wengao*, vii. 508.

[356] *Mao Weikan*, ix. 181, 184; For example, ibid. xiii. 181, 191; Xie Chuntao, *Dayuejin*, 116–17.

[357] *Mao Weikangao*, xiii. 193.

[358] Ibid. 187, 195; *Mao Wengao*, vii. 510. Another account claims that Chen did report on his ideas of replacing money with 'labour coupons'. *Mianhuai*, ii. 340.

the practical and theoretical confusions surrounding the communes, so that Mao's infallibility could be preserved. Instantly, Chen was turned into a pariah, and people avoided him like the plague.[359] Chen later rose again, but was finally purged with connection to the Lin Biao affair, for nothing more significant than the minor infraction he had committed here. In Mao's court, absolute loyalty to Mao was the bare minimum expected by the Chairman, but it did not guarantee security of tenure. Even minor lapses, when affected by other factors, such as Mao's personal whims, perceptions, or subjective likes and dislikes, could have fatal consequences.

In stark contrast to Chen's predicament was the case of Zhang Chunqiao. Operating under the frenzied atmosphere of building communes and taking his cue from Mao's passing reference to the abolition of bourgeois rights, Zhang wrote an article developing the idea, and urging the abolition of the wage system in favour of the free supply system.[360] Mao had endorsed most, if not all, of Zhang's ideas, but now that Mao had decided to backtrack, he declared that only some elements of bourgeois rights, like strict hierarchy and reliance on qualifications, should be abolished. Other bourgeois rights, such as an 'appropriate' wage system, some necessary wage differentials, and remuneration according to labour, should be preserved.[361] Zhang, for some unknown reason, escaped serious reprimand. In any case, Mao's critique of the two, disparate though it was, issued a clear signal of his willingness for a policy change. Mao also felt that the pervasive bragging and fabrication had to be dealt with seriously, although his previous position had been to accept all claims at face value in order not to dampen enthusiasm. Now he declared, grain output for 1958 was 370m. tons, not the 450m. tons previously claimed.

Mao was particularly disheartened to find that the model Xushui turned out to be a hoax. The Intelligence Unit of the Central Staff Office reported (on 18 October) that production tasks there were so overwhelming that false reporting was rampant, and that the cadres had terrorized commune members by tying up and beating them. After the abolition of private plots and the introduction of mess halls, poultry was no longer being kept.[362] Mao was also informed that Xushui had gathered up hogs to show off, and that its iron and steel figures were mostly fake. At the end of October, Mao again dispatched Hebei's governor, Liu Zihou to Xushui to investigate whether that county would be able to make the transition to communism. Yet, upon their return, the work team told Mao that Xushui simply lacked the material wherewithal to make the transition. There were many shortages, and people there ate in open-air canteens that served sub-standard food, and grumbled about the barrack style of

[359] Nan Guang (ed.), *Mao Zedong he Ta de Sida Mishu* (Mao Zedong and his four major secretaries) (Guiyang: Guizhou minzu chubanshe, 1993), 235; Chen's own version of the event, which states that Mao had misunderstood him, is in Ye Yonglie, *Mao Zedong de Mishu Men* (Mao Zedong's Secretaries) (Shanghai: Shanghai renmin chubanshe, 1994), 176 ff. See also, Ye Yonglie, *Chen Boda Zhuan* (Biography of Chen Boda) new edn. (Beijing: Renmin Ribao chubanshe, 1999), 333–5. Chen's own version of the event is in Chen Boda, *Chen Boda Yigao: Yuzhong Zizhu ji Gita* (The posthumous manuscripts of Chen Boda: His account written in prison) (Hong Kong: Cosmos Books, 1998), 72–3.
[360] *RMRB*, 13 October 1958; *Mao Wengao*, vii. 447–8; *Mao Weikan*, xiB. 84.
[361] Ibid. 181–2. [362] *Mao Wengao*, vii. 522–4.

living which divded men and women into separate quarters.[363] In November, the commune raised 5.5m. *yuan* to pay its members, and in December, had to divert 7m. *yuan* from the circulating funds of the commercial departments. But soon, all sources were exhausted, and the commune could no longer support itself.[364] Mao now observed that huge communes comprising one county such as Xushui were too big and unwieldy. In his words, these mammoth communes could breed *Qinshihuang* (dictators) and criticized Xushui as an 'independent kingdom'. Soon after this, huge communes comprising an entire county were divided up, reversing the 'bigger the better' trend.[365] He instructed that from then on the Xushui model should not be advertised, and told the *RMRB* to tone down its propaganda.

Yet Mao continued to be ambiguous and contradictory—in the face of severe problems, he still cherished several ideals of the commune. For instance, on 3 November, he raised the issue of 'eating rice without pay' by referring again to the story of Zhang Lu.[366] And on 6 November, he found new light in another rosy report conveyed by the Propaganda Department which claimed that Fan county in Shandong planned to make the transition to communism by 1960. This report rhapsodized a utopian future of a modern county that would be thoroughly electrified and industrialized. Since agricultural output would reach 20 or 30,000 *jin/mu*, there would be abundant food supplies, universal health care, and education, and everything would be free. Distribution would be assigned to each according to his needs, and things would be 'better than in heaven'. Mao was won over by this vision, praising the report as both meaningful and poetic, and as likely to be achieved. If three years were not quite sufficient for building communism, an extension could be sought. Again, he dispatched Chen Boda, Zhang Chunqiao, and Li Youjiu to observe Fan county, presumably to explore its communist potential. The report was reprinted as an official document for the Sixth Plenum.[367]

Mao's new hope was soon dashed. On 9 November, he announced that the Fan county claims were so fantastic that they should be investigated.[368] The next day, Mao fell back on the Xushui model. In a comment on a report on Xushui he tried to balance the achievements and shortcomings, and not to repudiate it outright.[369] A few days later, Mao was again aroused by the 'mass' debate in Fan county regarding whether one county alone could realize communism by applying the principle of 'to each according to his need'.[370] On the issue of urban communes, Mao ultimately affirmed it. By 1 October, Henan, riding the wave of communization, claimed that it had already created 482 urban communes. Other cities followed the example. This, and the fear of the abolition of money, led to bank runs and hoarding of luxury and other goods in Shanghai. On 5 November, Ke Qingshi reported on the chaotic

---

[363] *Mao Zhuxi Zoubian Zuguo Dadi* (Chairman Mao travels all over the country) (Taiyuan: Shanxi renmin chubanshe, 1993), 236–40.
[364] Bo Yibo, *Huigu*, ii. 750–1.   [365] *Mao Weikan*, xiii. 179; Bo Yibo, *Huigu*, ii. 749.
[366] Ibid. 775.   [367] *Mao Wengao*, vii. 494–97; *Mao Weikan*, xiii. 176. Bo Yibo, *Huigu*, ii. 754.
[368] *Mao Weikan*, xiii. 186; Bo Yibo, *Huigu*, ii. 810.
[369] *Mao Wengao*, vii. 522–4.   [370] Ibid. 535–6.

situation in Shanghai. Although Mao had reservations about the urban commune, he decided to push ahead.[371]

As Mao continued to wrestle with the commune ideal and to clarify the issues, he turned to theoretical matters. He did this by drawing inspirations from Stalin's *Economic Problems of Socialism in the Soviet Union*, which addressed issues of commodity exchange, transition from socialism to communism, and from collective ownership to the all-people ownership. Mao was critical of some of Stalin's ideas, such as his alleged neglect of matters in the superstructure and his distrust of the peasantry, but the first three chapters of *Economic Problems* supported Mao's current view that in socialism, commodity production and exchange, and the law of value should be preserved. One might also add that Stalin's argument that the five-year plans in the Soviet Union might not have conformed with the law of balanced and proportional development lent certain support to Mao in his contention with the planners.[372] As economic plans in China drawn up in the past had caused their share of turbulence, Mao argued, future plans should be mooted by the Party, not just by the SPC and the SEC, and involve everyone.[373] Although he was ready to apply the brakes, he was not ready to admit that the planners had been right.

Ironically, while at the beginning of the Leap Mao had urged the smashing of blind faith in bookish learning, spurring creativity, breaking of rules, and independence from the Soviet way, he now urged the return to the sacred texts (or as he said 'restoring "blind faith"') and to Soviet orthodoxy. He realized that he had swerved too far, and made a kind of self-criticism by bowing to the Stalinist canon. At the Conference, Mao led the delegates through Stalin's *Economic Problems* paragraph by paragraph, and jotted down detailed comments in the margins.[374] On 9 November, he sent a letter to all cadres at the county level and above asking them to discuss this book paragraph by paragraph and the book on communism by Marx and Engels to clear up 'a large mess of confused thought'.[375] Mao realized that he had erred, but everyone had to be corrected. Directly after the Conference, Mao instructed Liu, Zhou, and Deng to study the New Forty Articles, the 15-year plan, and Stalin's *Economic Problems*. So between 14 and 19 November, Liu, Zhou, and Deng duly led the Politburo and Secretariat members to study these documents.[376]

After much study and pondering, Mao's major conclusion was that there should be two distinct transitions, one from socialism to communism, and the other, from the principle of 'to each according to his labour' to the principle of 'to each according to his needs', and that a line should be drawn between collective ownership and all-people ownership. In other words, Mao claimed that China was still in the stage of socialism, and that the principles of collective ownership and remuneration according to labour still applied. Although the free supply system signified a partial dismantlement of the socialist principle of remuneration according to

[371] Bo Yibo, *Huigu*, ii. 755–6, 809.
[372] Bruce Franklin (ed.), *The Essential Stalin: Major Theoretical Writings, 1905–1952* (New York: Doubleday, 1972), 445 ff.   [373] *Mao Weikan*, xiB. 124.   [374] Ibid. 123–8; xiii. 225–8.
[375] Xie Chuntao, *Dayuejin*, 116–17.   [376] *Mao Wengao*, vii. 525–6; Bo Yibo, *Huigu*, ii. 812.

labour and a partial fulfilment of the principle of 'to each according to his needs', it did not follow that full communism had been achieved. Ownership by the whole people meant that the state could requisition and redistribute all funds, goods, and property from production units such as communes and factories freely and without compensation. But if the communes were not fully industrialized, and agriculture was not operated like factories, then there would be no material abundance for this kind of unified requisition. Citing Stalin, he said that the idea to expropriate the rural small producers could only come from 'half-baked Marxists'.[377] At Beidaihe, Mao estimated that the transition from socialism to communism could be made in three to six years, but now he reckoned that this time span was too short; that was why he lengthened the time period in the New Forty Articles to fifteen years.[378] So, in effect, Mao was telling everyone to slow things down, although still aspiring to the principles of remuneration by need and all-people ownership.

Mao's directive, issued on the last day of the conference (10 November), specified that the document was to be transmitted, after being rubber-stamped by the Politburo at Zhengzhou (although not all Politburo members were present), to various provincial authorities for instant implementation.[379] Two days later, Mao decided to take the document to the Politburo conference at Wuchang for more discussion, in case there was more input, although this was not to prevent provincial leaders from discussing and implementing policies contained in the document.

Rural Planning

In any case, the New Forty Articles, drafted under the radical spirit of autumn 1958, was another mobilizational programme like the *NPAD*. It included many extreme policies such as nationwide implementation of the 'three-three' system, deep ploughing (from 30 cm to 213 cm [*sic*]; this was more like mining than ploughing!), application of deep ploughing to forestry management, mess halls, nurseries, and the 'everyone a soldier' campaign started in 1958. On the other hand, it also called for guarantees of sufficient food and rest for commune members, restoring commodity production, and combining revolutionary enthusiasm with realism and practicability, which reflected that a certain learning had taken place.[380] Yet, privately Mao still hoped that after 1972 China could make the transition to communism.[381] Although the document was revised by Mao and ultimately no decision on its formal promulgation was made, these radical policies were implemented anyway.

Since the New Forty Articles covered planning for the next three five-year plans, Mao decided to expand the arena of discussion by summoning central leaders like Liu, Deng, and the directors of the Four Cooperative Regions to Zhengzhou, raising the total number of participants to 31. Perhaps he also realized the gravity of the situation, and could no longer exclude the central leaders from the deliberations.

---

[377] *Mao Weikan*, xiii. 173–4, 192; Xie Chuntao, *Dayuejin*, 116; Bruce Franklin, *Essential Stalin*, 454.
[378] *Mao Zedong de Zuji*, 487.   [379] *Mao Wengao*, vii. 520.
[380] The incomplete document is ibid. 503–9.   [381] *Mao Weikan*, xiii. 173.

On 6 November, Mao placed Deng Xiaoping in charge of a discussion of commune problems, the criteria for the successful building of socialism, transition to communism, and the transition from collective ownership to all-people ownership by all people. Deng chaired the meetings of the following two days which discussed the problems one by one, and he produced the document 'Notes on the Zhengzhou Conference'. On 10 November, Mao revised this document and retitled it 'Zhengzhou Resolution on Certain Problems Regarding the People's Communes'. In it, Mao tried to define the criteria for the successful building of socialism, new policies for the communes and urban communes, work methods, and so on. As a policy document it was vague and general—the subtler theoretical part on socialism and the meaning of socialism and on comprehensive all-people ownership would be bound to confuse the grass-roots cadres. The document urged trying out of the urban communes earnestly, although the process in big cities should be slow. It mentioned the responsibility system and the granting of power and incentives to the production brigades and teams, without elaboration. So two days after the Zhengzhou Conference, Mao expressed dissatisfaction with it, and a brand new draft was sketched at the Wuchang Conference and the Sixth Plenum.[382] Meanwhile, Mao continued to study Stalin's *Economic Problems*. On the last two days of the conference, Mao and the delegates studied Stalin's book, and Mao discoursed on Stalin's theories and the problems in the communes, criticizing the New Forty Articles for avoiding the issue of commodity production.

Industrial Policy

At this point, Mao seemed to be less alarmed by the many problems on the industrial front than he was with the implications of rural problems and communization, which were potentially more explosive. The focus at Zhengzhou was on the communes, and there was little room for anything else. He did affirm the need to try out urban communes, however. In any case, the goal of overtaking Britain in fifteen years had acquired such a political and symbolic significance—it was China's challenge to the world—that no let down was tolerated.

In fact, the National Planning Conference concluded on 30 October by deciding to follow the Beidaihe targets for 1959, vowing to realize 30m. tons of steel. It even raised the coal target from 380 to 540m. tons, electricity from 52,000m. to 64,000m. volts, and new railway lines from 10,000 to 12,000 km.[383] In early November, localities and ministries had reported to the Secretariat serious problems of the breakdown of coordination and dislocation of production. High steel targets had created widespread shortages in coal, electricity, and ore, and deprived other industries of their raw materials. The transportation system, in particular, was overwhelmed by huge amounts of raw materials to be shipped.[384] As Mao

[382] *Mao Wengao*, vii. 513–21, 575. [383] *Jingji he Shehui Fazhan Jihua Dashi*, 126.
[384] Xie Chuntao, *Dayuejin*, 86, 128.

noted, the Shijiazhuang Pharmaceutical Factory almost suspended production when much of its staff was dragged away for deep ploughing and for the iron and steel campaign. Iron and steel production turned out to be costly, wasteful, and money-losing, as the indigenous method consumed more than five times as much coal as the modern plants.[385]

In spite of this, in industrial work, Mao reaffirmed the developmental strategy of 'steel as the key link, the three marshals, and the two advanced units'.[386] This led to a *wuxu* discussion about how to surpass production in Britain in *per capita* terms, not just in total production. Since it was projected that in 1972, on average every Briton would have 500 kg of steel, China would require 400m. tons (assuming the Chinese population would be 800 million by then) to catch up with Britain. Zealot Wang Renzhong then proposed that steel production should reach 400m. tons in ten years. Indeed, the Chinese probably realized this braggadocio had gone too far, as a weary Zeng Xisheng pointed out that this meant that Anhui's share alone would be 30m. tons![387]

Returning to the situation in 1958, Mao was not unaware that steel production up to October was only 7.2m. tons, almost 4m. tons short of the 1958 target, and that the exhausted peasantry had neglected agriculture in their attempt to smelt steel. The MM finally mustered enough courage to report to Mao, albeit in the usual manner of stressing the positive, that much of the 10.7m. tons of steel would be 'indigenous steel' incapable of being rolled into useful steel products. The key-point iron and steel mills were unable to fulfil their plans, so rolled steel would be short. The quality of pig iron was poor, and the 'steel' smelted by the indigenous method produced small lumps, not large ingots that could be rolled.[388] On 3 November, Mao finally admitted that the obsession with steel might not be a good thing, and that the peasants should be allowed sufficient food and rest. On 5 November, he proposed to strike the iron and steel target of 400m. tons out of the 10-year plan, 'not to surpass the USA, just Britain'. Consequently, the three other major targets contained in the New Forty Articles on machinery, coal, and electricity, were omitted as well.[389]

Even Chen Yun, whom analysts assumed was inactive, toed the line carefully, no matter his private thoughts. In his 17 November report (for the Party Committee of the State Capital Construction Commission) to Mao on the key current tasks for capital construction, he urged that industrial layout should be appropriately dispersed, so that small and medium-sized industrial enterprises should predominate. This would ensure an early start to production and the transfer of technology and experience. Hence, he recommended that the provinces should disperse industries and shrink the scale of the enterprises. Construction of large projects which could not be reduced in size should be postponed. Some priorities must be set for capital

---

[385] *Mao Weikan*, xiii. 180, 191.

[386] Ibid. 173, 185, 190; Su Donghai and Fang Kongmu, *Fengyun Shilu*, 578.

[387] *Dangshi Ziliao*, 1997, lxi. 60; Bo Yibo, *Huigu*, ii. 708–9; see also *Mao Weikan*, ix. 184.

[388] *Mao Wengao*, vii. 474–6.

[389] Bo Yibo, *Huigu*, ii. 808, 813; Duan and Kong, *Mao Zedong de Zuji*, 490; Su Donghai and Fang Kongmu, *Fengyun Shilu*, 578–9.

construction, but according to the principle of 'steel as the key link', this meant that the highest priority was to equip iron and steel enterprises and other support industries such as transport and communication to realize the goal of 30m. tons of steel for 1959. In industrial design, the modern and indigenous methods must be combined. The ministries were urged to re-examine and revise the design of construction projects accordingly. Chen urged that the creativity of the masses should be encouraged to create groups of new enterprises and construction projects as soon as possible and at lower cost. The ministries were urged to manufacture complete sets of equipment and the necessary accessories so that provinces could be reassured of supplies. In capital construction, party leadership should be strengthened and mass movement promoted.[390] This complete endorsement of the GLF and total reversal of Chen's preferences was approved by Mao. This shows that even the most independent mind in the Chinese leadership and the sole person who could resist Mao had to conform.

Zhengzhou was a sort of transition. After rushing headlong into the Leap, Mao was forced to stop and rethink the situation, although he did not doubt the general direction it was heading. He was now prepared to curb excesses and therefore signalled his approval for change, albeit hesitantly. The New Forty Articles presented at the Conference, which were very much a product of the ballyhoo, now received Mao's criticism, although in the end, the Conference was inconclusive in that no formal decisions were issued, it paved the way for the temporary and tactical retreat sanctioned a month later. Overall, the conduct of the Conference amply demonstrated Mao's predominance. Chinese historians like to credit Mao as the first to rectify leftist mistakes at Zhengzhou, but in the context of his stubborn dominance, who else but he could have formally authorized a mild turnaround. Indeed, as his position shifted haltingly towards the side of caution, those among his subordinates who failed to read his new intentions and who continued to propound radical policies incurred not only the Chairman's wrath, but also became Mao's scapegoats.

The Reckoning: The Enlarged Politburo Meeting, Wuchang 21–27 November 1958, and the Sixth Plenum, 28 November–10 December

Between 11 and 20 November, Mao inspected Henan and Hubei, speaking to local officials daily. On 15 November he arrived at Wuchang and spent the next few days conferring with more central and local officials.[391] An *RMRB* (25 November) report carried Khrushchev's report to the Twentieth Party Congress which stated that the Soviet Union would use the coming fifteen years to build the material and technical basis for the transition to communism. This prompted Mao to rethink the Beidaihe

---

[390] *Mao Wengao*, vii. 549–50.   [391] Bo Yibo, *Huigu*, ii. 812.

assumption of using only three to six years to realize communism.[392] Bad news, too, shook Mao's confidence, and he began to fear that he might have committed the mistake of impetuosity. The iron and steel campaign involving 60 millon participants and the policy of subordinating everything to it had created tense situations in every area—the transportation system was clogged, there were general shortages everywhere, especially in electricity and machinery parts, and both agricultural and industrial products could not be shipped to their destinations. In the big cities, the supply of pork and grain was exhausted, affecting exports.[393] Light industry was a casualty not only because it was deprived of raw materials, but also because many of its enterprises had been converted to steel-smelting and related activities. What was worse, at most 8.5m. tons out of the projected production of 11m. tons of steel were of good quality. A report from Hebei said that the breakneck pace of work, unhygienic mess halls, and the lack of food and rest had caused an unprecedented spread of typhoid, dysentry, and gastro-enteritis, affecting twenty-one counties. Indeed, all of these represented only the tip of the iceberg,[394] and as early as February 1959, Mao talked about 5 million people suffering from oedema.[395]

Mao now wanted to tone things down, and rein in the bravado previously encouraged by him. 'In smashing blind faith', he said 'take care not to demolish scientific truths as well'.[396] Between 21 and 27 November, Mao convened an enlarged Politburo conference to flesh out the ideas articulated at Zhengzhou, to prepare for the Sixth Plenum, and to draw up the 1959 plan. The conference also had to deal with the problems of the communes, the communist wind, bragging, and high targets. Here, Mao turned the corner by admitting his faults. His implicit self-criticism soon turned explicit. A more thorny issue was the year-end appraisal of the GLF and what production figures to make public, since the statistical system had been destroyed, and reports from lower levels were wildly exaggerated.[397] On the very first day of the conference, Mao set the tone by telling the delegates that anxiety had prevented him from sleeping and that it was time to 'compress the air' and to lower the unrealistic targets. A troubled Mao came close to conceding the virtues of planned and proportionate development by saying one ton of steel required so many tons of other materials and raw materials, and so on, although he defended as a kind of proportion the GLF strategy of simultaneous development, combining indigenous and modern methods, and simultaneous use of small, medium, and large scales of production. Dropping his past disdain of central government documents, he praised the twelve reports submitted by the ministries for incorporating the vocabulary of the Leap and perhaps very high targets, just the way he had desired in the past. Yet, in a dramatic turnaround, Mao now told them to tone

---

[392] *Dangshi Ziliao*, 1997, lxi. 56.

[393] Bo Yibo, *Huigu*, ii. 814; Xie Chuntao, *Dayuejin*, 96–7.

[394] *Mao Wengao*, vii. 530–1; *Dangshi Ziliao*, 1997, lxi. 55.

[395] Gu Longsheng, *Mao Zedong Jingji Nianpu*, 445–6.   [396] *Mao Weikan*, xiB. 138.

[397] *Zhengzhi Daishidian*, 611; Jin Zhao, *Lushan Michuan* (A secret history of Lushan) (Beijing: Zhongguo dangan chubanshe, 1995), 457.

things down. Was 400m. tons of steel really possible? He mused. 'Targets should be more realistic'. 'Strings pulled too tight will snap', he added.[398] Repeatedly, he stressed that China would never make the transition to communism before the Soviet Union.[399] In his first implicit self-criticism since the Leap, amidst Politburo colleagues he had browbeaten into submission, he said that in contrast to the cautious Soviets, many Chinese, including himself, were 'harum-scarums'. He even conceded the need for planned and proportionate development, although he maintained that no one had yet known the laws of development.[400] On 21 November, Mao told Wu Lengxi to tone down the propaganda of the New China News Agency and the *RMRB* and stop reporting the extravagant claims in the fields at face value.[401]

During the conference, reports finally bubbled to the surface showed that the communes were in disarray. Many nurseries and old-people's homes were on the verge of collapse.[402] Deaths by various diseases caused by overwork and cadre callousness were occurring in Guangxi at the time of the conference. Mao now admitted that he and the Party Centre had pushed far too hard. In turn, he claimed cadres at the lower levels had no choice but to pressure their subordinates, oblivious to their suffering; to do otherwise would have left them open to charges of 'rightism'. Henceforth, Mao reckoned, the work burden must be lightened.[403]

Other reports that reached Mao showed that misrepresentation was universal. For instance, one commune borrowed hogs from other places to show off to the inspectors and returned them afterwards. In the rural areas, cadre coercion and abuse was met with equally determined resistance, or at most, ritualistic compliance. For instance, a *xiafang* (sent downwards) cadre from Zhongnanhai reported that a collective ordered its members to uproot 300 *mu* of maize to make way for sweet potatoes (to raise yield/*mu*) though maize was already as tall as human beings. The peasants complied, although they cut only 30 *mu*. Another reported that a certain county ordered toiling around-the-clock and forbade sleep. The peasants coped by having children act as sentries; when the cadres arrived, they got up to work, but once the cadres left, they went back to sleep again. In other places, the peasants turned on the lights at the work sites at night, while they were asleep at home.[404] One report submitted by Hubei party secretary Wang Renzhong said that a commune in Siu County boasted that it had created a record of 60,000 *jin/mu* of wheat, but in reality the cadres had forced the peasants to uproot the crops from ten other *mu* and gathered them in one spot. Mao authorized this report to be distributed at the Plenum.[405]

---

[398] *Mao Weikan*, xiii. 196, 207–8; xiB. 133.

[399] People like Liu Shaoqi and Peng Zhen argued that once the peasants had reached a consumption level of 150–200 *yuan*, the transition from collective ownership to all-people ownership should be effected. Otherwise, when the income of the peasants exceeded that of the workers, as in Romania, the transition would become more difficult. Mao toyed with this idea, but ultimately rejected it. *Mao Weikan*, xiB. 131–9; *Dangshi Jiliao*, 1997 lxi. 56–7; Cong Jin, *Quzhe Fazhan*, 168, n. 1, 245.

[400] *Mao Weikan*, xiB. 128–31.   [401] Mao, *Wenji*, vii. 443–4.   [402] *Mao Weikan*, xiii. 206.

[403] Ibid. 203.

[404] Ibid. 214. Mao also realized that some cadres had terrorized the peasants. Ibid. xiB. 158; *Wansui* (1969), 275.   [405] *Mao Wengao*, vii. 614–15.

Mao therefore concluded that the communes had to be rectified for another four months. To restore work incentives, he conceded that some 'bourgeois rights', such as wage differentials and ranks, should still be maintained. If the communes did not succeed, he warned, China would go under (*wangguo*). He also redefined communism by adding five more preconditions: abundant material goods, communist consciousness, cultural and educational development, the elimination of the three big differences, and the elimination of the state. Mao redrafted and expanded the Resolution on the communes by incorporating these discussions.[406]

Mao began to call into question the targets set at Beidaihe and admitted that the doubling of the 1957 steel output in 1958 was risky. The Beidaihe document on the communes, influenced by Henan, was defective, because it assumed that it would only take three to four years in North China (or five to six years in South China) to make the transition to all-people ownership.[407]

Another worrisome issue was the steel target for 1959, as Mao realized that the 27–30m. tons set at Beidaihe was out of the question, so he sought advice from the planners. Li Fuchun favoured 25m. tons, Zhao Er Lu favoured 16m. tons, and Bo Yibo suggested internal and open targets of 18 and 16m. tons, respectively. After much anguish, Mao took the middle course and settled on 18m. tons (with a second set of accounts at 22m. tons) somewhat apologetically, and said that he would be satisfied with 15m. tons of good steel.[408] As steel remained the standard by which all other targets were made, targets of the other ministries were to be trimmed accordingly. Overall, Mao wanted the lowering of sights, and he put it dramatically, 'Right now I am opposed to *maojin*. In the past, others contested my *maojin*, now I am opposing their *maojin*'.[409] Anyone who has an appreciation of Chinese culture would understand that the planners' figures were more intended to save the Chairman's face by providing him with a way out, and a knowing Mao played along, shifting the blame on some imaginary hotheads. To drive home his point, Mao added that if all the current tasks such as water conservancy, iron and steel, coal, copper, tin, aluminium, transport, processing and chemical industries were pursued, then at least 10 per cent, or even half China's population, could die.[410]

In this context, Mao 'refused' to believe that grain output for 1958 was an incredible 450m. tons, although he settled on 370m. tons, double the 1957 output. In fact, the 1958 output was closer to 200m. tons, only 4.95m. tons more than the 1957 production. Moreover, although some parts of China had achieved bumper harvests, others had encountered climate adversities.[411] Apparently, he was not ready to come completely down to earth, and still assumed that agricultural production could skyrocket.[412] So the grain target for 1959 was raised, according to the recommendations made by Tan and Liao Luyan, from the Beidaihe estimate of 400–500m. tons

---

[406] *Mao Weikan*, xiii. 197, xiB. 138; *Mao Wengao*, vii. 575.   [407] *Mao Weikan*, xiii. 200, 209.

[408] Ibid. 211; Bo Yibo, *Huigu*, ii. 815.

[409] *Mao Weikan*, xiB. 135; Bo Yibo, *Huigu*, ii. 816. At the Second Zhengzhou Conference in March 1959, Mao continued in the same vein when he said, 'I'll ... firmly engage in rightist opportunism, and will persist to the end.' *Mao Weikan*, xiB. 174.   [410] Ibid. 203.

[411] *NJZWH*, ii. 206.   [412] For example, see *Mao Weikan*, xiii. 198, 215; xiB. 130.

to 525m. tons, and cotton from the Beidaihe estimate of 4.5m. tons to 5m. tons.[413] However, in the interests of restraint, it was decided that the new 40 Articles were too ambitious and should be shelved, although this was to remain secret.

The Sixth Plenum (28 November to 10 December)

Once Mao had made up his mind on the major issues, the Sixth Plenum met on the heels of the Wuchang meeting to flesh things out, to make a summation of the 1958 Leap, and to inform the Party of the policy changes. It considered the Resolution on the communes drafted under the charge of Mao, the 1959 economic plan, and the proposal that Mao would not seek further nomination as State President. Originally the Plenum was to be divided into seven groups to study the documents between 28 November and 1 December, but ultimately small group discussions between 29 November and 8 December took up the bulk of the time. On 30 November, Mao spoke to the Politburo Standing Committee, group leaders, and the directors of the Cooperative Regions to prepare them for the turnaround.[414]

In his major 9 December speech delivered to the Plenum, Mao urged the Party to tone down the rhetoric of transforming the country. Only a tiny percentage of the cadres who were guilty of the most tyrannical and abusive behaviour should be punished so that their enthusiasm would not be dampened. Here, Mao's concern was to protect those most amenable to his calls. The communes had to be overhauled and the cadres should pay attention to the well-being of the masses, not just production. The concept of level-by-level management should be introduced so that every level from the province to the production team should have some power, although no specifics were given. The timetable for achieving all-people ownership and communism should be slowed down, and all Party members should consult the Marxist classics. The high steel targets had been too exhausting, so the 1959 steel target should be set at 18–20m. tons.[415]

The three major documents of the Plenum were closely supervised and revised by Mao. The announcement of the resignation of Mao as the State Chairman was finalized by 9 December. The Resolution which was to be a definitive statement on the communes, was cobbled together by revising the Zhengzhou 'Resolution on Certain Problems Regarding the People's Communes'. It reflected a further development of the views articulated by Mao at Zhengzhou and the Wuchang Politburo meeting. After an explanation by Deng Xiaoping, the resolution was approved by the Plenum on 10 December, but was further considered and revised again *after* the Plenum (between 15 and 17 December) so that it was not published

---

[413] Cong Jin, *Quzhe Fazhan*, 168; Su Dong hai and Fang Kongmu, *Fengyun Shilu*, 579.

[414] *Mao Weikan*, xiii. 218–22; *Zhonggong Dangshi Jiliao*, 1997, lxi, 65 ff; also in Han Taihua (ed.), *Zhongguo Gongchandang Ruogan Wenti Xiezhen* (A true record of certain problems of the Chinese Communist Party) (Beijing: Zhongguo yanshi chubanshe, 1998), 592 ff.

[415] *Wansui* (1969), 259–69; an outline of talk is in *Mao Wengao*, vii. 636–42.

until 19 December.[416] It warned that the boundaries between collective ownership and all-people ownership, and between socialism and communism should not be blurred. The transition nationally from collective ownership to the all-people ownership would take a long time, fifteen, twenty or more years, it said. The attainment of the all-people ownership could not be equated with the realization of communism, which was contingent on the development of the productive forces and human consciousness. The most pressing task was to develop the productive forces, and in the lengthy transition to socialism, the principle of 'remuneration according to labour' was still applicable.

Therefore, those attempts to realize all-people ownership and communism had been rash steps and were to be avoided in future. Commodity production and exchange were reaffirmed, as commodity, value, currency, and price still served important functions. Commune members' personal possessions, such as housing, clothing, and bank deposits should forever belong to them. They could also keep isolated trees around the house, small farm tools, small livestock, and run small domestic sideline activities, if these did not hinder collective labour. The scope of the free supply system should not be too broad, as people's lives should not be uniform. A three-level management by communes, production brigades, and production teams should be introduced, although gains and losses should still be pooled in the communes.

Yet, the Resolution still insisted on radical policies such as the popularization of the mess halls, and the gradual implementation of the 'three-three' system as the super harvest of 1958 had been recognized as a fait accompli. The labour army was said to be indispensable for large-scale agricultural production, and the communes were required to imitate the organization and discipline of the military. A separate system of militia, therefore, was to be constructed. As to the cadres who were oppressive and who filed false reports, Mao wanted them to undergo self-criticism and education, not punishment, knowing that they were his staunchest supporters in the grass roots.[417]

The four months from December 1958 to April 1959 were to be used to rectify the communes along these lines. Finally, Mao ordered the distribution of the biography of Zhang Lu with his own commentary. Mao lauded Zhang's policy of free medicare, free rice supply, and mass campaigns, and said that these set a precedent for the communes.[418]

Mao also conceded that economic plans must be reliable and subject to the objective law of proportionate development, thereby abandoning his previous theory of disequilibrium, although he still had no regrets about the policy of 'steel as the key link', and the strategy of 'simultaneous development'. The steel target for 1959 was announced to be 18m. tons, not the 27–30m. tons projected at Beidaihe. Capital investment for 1959 was reduced to 36bn. *yuan* from 50bn. *yuan*. However, the 1959 targets for coal, grain, and cotton, as mentioned, were raised above the Beidaihe

---

[416] *Mao Weikan*, xiii. 224; *Mao Wengao*, vii. 643–4; *RMRB*, 19 December 1958.
[417] *Wansui* (1969), 259–60; outline in *Mao Wengao*, vii. 636.   [418] Ibid. 627–30.

estimates, showing that the euphoria had not subsided.[419] Peng Dehuai later recalled how the production figures for 1958 were decided at the North-West small group, one of the discussion groups at the Plenum:

Some comrades said that grain had reached more than 500m. tons. Others said that there were 450m. tons of grain and 3 to 3.5m. tons of cotton. Still others claimed that there was as much grain as they wished, and that industry had lagged behind agriculture. So when I said that there was not that much grain, a comrade gave me a friendly criticism, 'Old general! How can you suspect this and that?' To that I replied, 'If we publish lower figures, we will have more control if we have to revise them upwards, but if we publish figures that are too high, we'll have little room to manœuvre'. Later on when the Chairman said that the public figure should be 375m. tons, I acquiesced, although I still had doubts at heart.[420]

Li Fuchun shared Mao's illusion, and his zeal reinforced Mao's. The resolution for the 1959 plan submitted by him assumed that production of grain, cotton, coal, machinery, and other key products in 1958 had doubled or more than doubled that of 1957, so the new targets were set up on this basis in order to achieve another greater leap. More realistic estimates for grain, cotton, and coal production in 1957 were 185, 1.64, and 131m. tons respectively. In 1958, they were 200, 1.97, and 290m. tons respectively, even though the 1958 production figures for grain, cotton, and coal were assumed to be 375, 3.35, and 270m. tons. On this basis the 1959 targets for grain, cotton and coal were set at 525, 5, and 380m. tons, respectively, and steel at 18m. tons. The targets for cotton and coal even exceeded the estimates made at Beidaihe (coal 400–500m. tons; cotton 4.5–5m. tons). These targets were disclosed by the Plenum communique as the 'four big targets', and the ministries were instructed to work out the 1959 plan for other products accordingly.[421]

Among supporters Mao was more candid, although he ultimately reserved the right to decide what kind of opinion or feedback was appropriate. At the Politburo conference, Mao made only an implicit self-criticism, but this became explicit when he spoke to the Directors of the Cooperative Regions on 12 December:

I made a mistake at Beidaihe. My attention was focused on three things: the 10.7 million tons of steel, the people's communes, and the bombardment of Jinmen. I did not consider anything else. The resolution of Beidaihe should be changed. At that time (we were) enthusiastic, but did not combine revolutionary passion with the spirit of realism. We have combined the two at Wuchang.[422]

Now that Mao had turned around somewhat, Chen was emboldened to speak his mind a little more, albeit indirectly. Because he thought that the 'four big targets' were unrealizable, he advised Hu Qiaomu not to publish them in the Plenum communique, but Hu was too afraid to consult Mao, so the targets were made public.

[419] Bo Yibo, *Huigu*, ii. 817; Cong Jin, *Quzhe Fazhan*, 171; *Xinhua Banyuekan* (hereafter *XHBYK*), 1958, 24: 1–11. *Zhongguo Tongji Nianjian, 1983*, 162–3, 244.
[420] *Peng Dehuai Zishu* (The autobiography of Peng Dehuai) (Beijing: Renmin chubanshe, 1981), 265–6.
[421] Su Donghai and Fang Kongmu, *Fenyun Shilu*, 579; Cong Jin, *Quzhe Fazhan*, 171; *RMRB*, 18 December 1958.   [422] *Wansui* (1969), 258.

Hu's prudence was warranted, because when Chen told Mao (at a dinner party celebrating Mao's birthday on 26 December) that the 18m. tons of steel was probably not realizable, Mao shot back, 'These are the things I advocated; whether they are right or not will have to be verified by practice'. The Plenum announced that everyone would be given a coupon for 7m. of cloth, but this too was unrealizable.[423]

Only after Mao had changed his tone and offered self-criticism were officials more forthcoming with negative feedback, although they still had to be cautious not to make the chief commander appear with a chink in his armour and lose too much face. During the Plenum, the Ministry of Finance was emboldened to disclose the massive financial losses sustained as a result of the iron and steel campaign. Every ton of indigenous iron lost a minimum of 100 to 200 *yuan*, and the 1958 output of 10m. tons led to an estimated loss of 1.5bn. *yuan*.[424] Li Fuchun recommended that the losses should be borne by the state and regional governments, so that the collectives might be reimbursed. In December 1959, the Ministry of Finance reported that the losses were actually 4bn. *yuan*, more than one-tenth of the 1958 national budget of 38.76bn. *yuan*.[425] The transportation system was so clogged by coal, pig iron, and machinery for steel smelting that at the end of 1958, there were 30 to 40m. tons of resources awaiting shipment in the railway system alone. By the first half of 1959, light industrial production had plummeted.[426]

On 7 December, the Party Committee of the Ministry of Grain reported on the tense situation in grain supply. Between July and October, grain procurement was down 4.4m. tons, although sale and exports were raised to 2.6m. tons. At the end of October, the national grain reserve was reduced by about 5m. tons. Many localities, where grain reserves had gone down dramatically, swamped the centre with requests for grain transfer.[427] On the other hand, ministries that were seriously affected were still unwilling to deviate from the Leap priorities. For instance, on 7 December, the Politburo circulated an approved report by the party committee of the Ministry of Light Industry that revealed that because of the diversion of resources and labour to the iron and steel campaign since August, light industrial production had virtually ceased, leading to widespread shortages. Yet the ministry also maintained its full support for the running of industries in the communes, and even advocated that 80 to 90 per cent of the industrial products required by communes should be manufactured by themselves. Similarly, a directive by the Ministry of Transport issued on 17 December urged the emergency rush transport of daily necessities, provided that shipping for iron and steel production was guaranteed.[428]

---

[423] Bo Yibo, *Huigu*, ii. 715; Ye Yonglie, *Hu Qiaomu* (Beijing: Zhonggong zhongyang dangxiao chubanshe, 1994*a*), 129–30. For a more detailed discussion of the exchange between Mao and Chen, see Chapter 4.

[424] *Jingji he Shehui Fazhan Jihua Dashi*, 127. Su Donghai and Fang Kongmu, *Fengyun Shilu*, 580.

[425] Bo Yibo, *Huigu*, ii. 712.   [426] Ibid. 715.

[427] Ma Qibin *et al.*, *Zizheng Sishinian*, 156. By April 1959, Mao was informed that fifteen provinces had encountered spring drought, and 25 million people in five provinces were in urgent need of relief grain. *Mao Wengao*, viii. 209.   [428] Su Donghai and Fang Kongmu, *Fengyun Shilu*, 580.

In December, faced with chronic shortages of electricity in China's industrial areas, the SEC and the Ministry of Electricity and Water Conservancy convened a national conference to promote an 'all people run hydroelectric power' campaign in order to encourage the use of indigenous methods to produce electricity. The Ministry of Transport attempted to mobilize the peasants to ship up to 20 per cent of its freight volume, but without success.[429] Because of the premium put on speed, shoddy work, the dismantling of rules and regulations, and the use of substitutes, there were many serious accidents involving collapsed projects and loss of lives. In 1959, Bo reported to the Secretariat that more than 30,000 accidental deaths occurred in industry and transportation departments alone.[430] Hence, among the first tasks for Chen Yun as Director of the State Capital Construction Commission created in October 1958, was to convene a conference in December to address the matter. Now that Mao had changed his tone, Chen was emboldened to criticize the *duohao kuaisheng* formula in construction projects.[431]

Finally, the Plenum formally announced that Mao would not seek the nomination for the position of State Chairman. Although already proposed by Mao at the beginning of 1958, this still could only be seen as a partial admission of responsibility, especially in the context of his self-criticisms. In actuality, the shedding of this formal post was mostly symbolic; until his death in 1976 Mao maintained his dominance, as he was never contented to remain in the 'second line' of leadership.

At the Sixth Plenum, Mao had clarified some of the issues for himself. He was relieved by the Resolution from this conference, which was seen by him as a bit of closure, because he thought that the communes could be put back on the right track. Grain procurement and distribution might be a problem, but because of the supposed super harvest, grain was ultimately in the hands of the peasants. True, there was dislocation, confusion, and suffering on both industrial and rural fronts, and he felt a little apologetic about them, but ultimately he thought they could still be viewed in the context of one finger out of ten, and that there was nothing that could not be fixed.[432] He was satisfied that the 'four big targets' set were realistic. After the Sixth Plenum, Mao inspected Hubei and Hunan to talk to local officials, finally returning to Beijing on 30 December.[433]

In 1958, Mao had repudiated the planners, and dragged, goaded, and badgered them and the nation into the GLF that was designed to rush industrialization and changes in social organization and relations. He pulled out all the stops to get his way, but the sunk cost he had invested, in terms of his personal credibility and prestige and the well-being of the country was so enormous that a complete turnaround was out of the question, despite the severe problems. So the retreat at the end of 1958 was extremely limited, and Mao had not given up his utopian aspirations.

---

[429] Bo Yibo, *Huigu*, ii. 715; Su Donghai and Fang Kongmu, *Fengyun Shilu*, 583.
[430] Bo Yibo, *Huigu*, ii. 711.
[431] Chen Yun, *Chen Yun Wenxuan*, iii. 109 ff. Su Donghai and Fang Kongmu, *Fengyun Shilu*, 570.
[432] *Wansui* (1969), 272, 278.   [433] Bo Yibo, *Huigu*, ii. 819.

Criticisms by Peng Dehuai in July 1959 derailed the effort at moderation, and Mao plunged the entire country into the Leap again in mid-1959, though with less ferocity than he did in 1958. It would take the ensuing calamities to convince him of a temporary abandonment of the Leap. Yet, his insistence on reviving and defending the failed crusade would dominate his political agenda until his death a decade and half later.

3

The Ministry of Agriculture and Rural and Agricultural Policies in 1958

For all Chinese officials, the Great Leap Forward emerged with the force of a hurricane that could not be resisted. While many top leaders were repeatedly badgered and humiliated, still others who were untainted were under tremendous pressure to prove themselves, or better still, jump on the Maoist bandwagon. This was the strategy followed by Tan Zhenlin, General Secretary of the Secretariat who was also in charge of agriculture. As to the more junior officials such as Wang Heshou, the Minister of Agriculture, there was little choice but to go with the flow. The GLF began in the agricultural sector, and the obsession during the Leap with maximizing agricultural production and rural institutional changes thrust agricultural officials and the Ministry of Agriculture (MA) into the limelight. The MA owed its enhanced power and responsibilities entirely to Mao and his special attention to rural and agricultural affairs, but the trade-off was that it had to perform and constantly improvise according to the numerous conflicting policy initiatives and multiple goals continuously being mooted by Mao throughout 1958. As in most of the ministries, the leaders of the MA were veteran revolutionaries, and the ethos of the MA was rooted in the traditional values of peasant mobilization and revolutionary changes. This continuity with the past at least made the dogged pursuit of Mao's initiatives come more naturally to the MA than others. Unlike ministries such as the Ministry of Metallurgy, it did not have to subdue a partially modern constituency, as we shall see in Chapter 4. How did the MA propel the GLF? What role did it play? How did it implement Leap policies, especially under pressure? What policy instruments did it use? What kind of bureaucratic actor was it? Did it have any significant bureaucratic and institutional interests to defend?

The Institutional Setting

In the 1950s, Chinese agricultural policies were formulated and influenced by a number of sources at the centre. Mao was indeed the paramount decision-maker, but most other top Chinese leaders, especially those in the Politburo, also took an interest in agricultural development—a reflection of their rural roots and experiences—and intervened in agricultural and rural affairs from time to time. The MA was several layers removed from the nerve centre of central power, the Politburo, occupying junior status in the hierarchy of the centre. Organizationally, in the Central Committee, agriculture came under the jurisdiction of the Party Secretariat and the Rural Work Department (RWD), and in the government, under the State Council and its Number Seven Staff Office for Agriculture and Forestry, although the latter was really located within the RWD.[1] The latter in turn directed the MA and the Ministries of Forestry, State Farms and Land Reclamation, and Aquatic Products. At this time, Tan Zhenlin also had the responsibility of overseeing rural and agricultural affairs. In 1958 he was a fanatic of the Leap known for ramming crackpot ideas onto his subordinates. So at the Lushan Conference in 1959 when Mao accepted the main responsibility for the Leap, he also attributed many of the its misadventures to Tan's 'cannons'.

Before 1962, vice-premier Deng Zihui, a member of the Central Committee, headed both the RWD and the Staff Office for Agriculture and Forestry. The deputy directorships of these two central organs were held concurrently by Liao Luyan, the Minister of Agriculture, and Chen Zhengren.[2] This reflects not only the close supervision of the Party over agriculture, but also the direct relationship between the central organs and the ministry. Liao and Chen were only alternate members of the CC.

The MA was in charge of rural economic development, the drafting and implementation of annual and long-term plans, resource allocation, agricultural production and investment. More specifically, it supervised such matters as economic crops, land improvement, promotion of better agricultural varieties, agricultural mechanization, and the state farms between 1949 and 1956.[3] It also controlled the Chinese Academy of Agricultural Sciences and its branches in the provinces, the higher and middle agricultural colleges. The MA's bureaus were responsible for scientific research, agricultural machinery, grain production, and seed management. Before the decentralization of 1958, it directly supervised the departments and bureaus of agriculture at provincial, district, and county levels, and had the power to

---

[1] Su Shangyao and Han Wenwei, *Zhongyang Zhengfu Jigou*, 341–3; *Dangdai Zhongguo Zhengfu*, 177; Guojia Jigou Bianzhi Weiyuanhui Bangongshi, *Zhonghua Renmin Gongheguo Guowuyuan Zuzhi Jigou Gaiyao* (Outline of the organizational structure of the State Council of the PRC) (Shenyang: Dongbei gongxueyuan chubanshe, 1989), 115–18. See also, He Husheng, Li Yaodong, Xiang Changfu, and Jiang Jianhua (eds.), *Zhonghua Renmin Gongheguo Zhiguan Zhi* (A record of governmental officials of the PRC), expanded edn. (Beijing: Zhongguo shehui chubanshe, 1996), 214–15; Huang Daqiang and Wang Mingguang (eds.), *Zhongguo Xinzheng Guanli Dacidian* (A dictionary of Chinese public administration) (Beijing: Zhongguo wuzi chubanshe, 1993), 101–2; Ye Wensong (ed.), *Zhonghua Renmin Gongheguo Zhengfu Jiguan Zonglan* (A comprehensive survey of the governmental structure of the PRC) (Chongqing: Zhongguo wuzi chubanshe, 1993), 291–9.

[2] Despite recently available information about the Chinese governmental structure in the 1950s, Donnithorne's *China's Economic System* remains one of the best, see pp. 41–2; Kao, *Changes of Personnel*, 84–5, 155; *Chung Kung Jen Ming Lu* (Communist China's Who's Who) (Taipei: Institute of International Relations, 1978), 863–4. The latter, despite its anti-communist rhetoric, is clearly superior in terms of insights and details to the myriad of biographical dictionaries published in China today.

[3] Liu Lie, Zhang Shangping, and Zhu Bing (eds.), *Zhonghua Renmin Gongheguo Guojia Jigou* (Harbin: Harbin chubanshe, 1988), 122–3; Donnithorne, *China's Economic System*, 41–2, 93–4, 103, 112, 127, 129, 408, 423.

regulate production targets set by provincial agricultural departments. In March 1958, when the Ministries of Water Conservancy and Electricity were merged, responsibility for agricultural water conservancy was reassigned to the MA, to make it serve agriculture more closely.[4] In addition, the forty-five instructions, circulars, and regulations, issued by the MA from 1949 to 1963, either on its own or jointly with other ministries, included in the official collection of statutes are a good general indication of the nature and scope of the jurisdiction and activities of the ministry.[5]

Moreover, Liao and Chen, by virtue of their positions in the RWD, were in charge of promoting rural institutional changes prior to 1958.[6] Having worked with Mao closely on agricultural collectivization, Liao was highly attuned to Mao's changing moods and attitudes towards major policy decisions. In addition, Mao had prevailed over the moderate Deng Zihui in their quarrel regarding the tempo of collectivization (the changing of lower to advanced APCs) in 1955. Consequently, he was shut out of the inner sanctum of decision-making, although he kept his official positions. He was not involved in the drafting of the NPAD in 1956 and its revision in 1957, and illness prevented him from being particularly active in either 1956 or 1958.[7] In 1958, when Mao bulldozed his way into the GLF, leaving many of the regime's top leaders by the wayside, Deng, the eternal pragmatist, faced a difficult predicament. Ultimately, as we shall see later, he threw in his lot with the GLF, irrespective of his private view.[8] Only in 1959, when Mao began to turn around did Deng follow his instinct to retreat. Liao, on the other hand, appeared to be a staunch supporter of rural mobilization and transformation. He was chosen over other senior agricultural officials to deliver the authoritative explanatory speech on the Twelve Year National Programme on Agricultural Development (NPAD) at the Supreme State Conference two days after it was passed by the Politburo on 23 January 1956. Subsequently, the programme became the catalyst for the acceleration of collectivization and the 'leap forward' of 1956.[9]

The Beginning

As discussed previously, agricultural stagnation and shortages in grain, cotton, and other things near the end of 1957 led Mao to feel vindicated about pushing the 1956

---

[4] Su Shangyao and Han Wenwei, *Zhongyang Zhengfu Jigou*, 342.

[5] *Zhongyang Renmin Zhengfu Faling Huibian* (A compendium of the laws and regulations of the Central Peoples' Government) (Beijing: Falu chubanshe, 1982); *FGHB*, i–xiii.

[6] Liao's speech, in which he argued for a more radical approach to rural development, is in *FGHB*, iii. 12–23.

[7] Deng Zihui Zhuan Bianji Weiyuanhui, *Deng Zihui Zhuan* (Biography of Deng Zihui) (Beijing: Renmin chubanshe, 1996), 465–515.

[8] Current accounts tend to gloss over Deng's role in 1958 by stressing his reservations regarding Leap policies and practices (see *Deng Zihui Zhuan*, 525–7), although his public pronouncements in 1958 were all supportive of Mao's initiatives. Even Bo Yibo, who attempts to write party history as accurately as possible, portrays Deng as an inspiration and a paragon of integrity with 'unshakable resolve', completely overlooking Deng's responsibility in 1958 and the Leap. See his *Huigu*, ii. 1083. For Deng's conflicts with Mao, see Teiwes and Sun (eds.), *Agricultural Cooperativization*, 'Introduction'.

[9] The text of the programme is in *FGHB*, iii. 1–12. See also, Parris Chang, *Power and Policy*, 19–26.

Leap, and strengthened his case in favour of the NPAD as an outline for rural mobilization and development.[10] In August, a revised draft of the NPAD was introduced by the Party Centre, and at the Third Plenum (20 September–9 October), Mao turned the table on those who opposed *maojin* in 1957 and effectively stifled any dissenting opinion. He resurrected the NPAD and the slogan of *duohao kuaisheng*, both of which were partly responsible for the abortive 'leap forward' in agriculture in 1956. Although the issue of introducing the lower and advanced APCs had already been settled, Mao's diatribe against *fanmaojin* also silenced the planners and Deng Zihui, who had charged that in 1953 and 1955 that the hasty introduction of these collectives was a manifestation of *maojin*. As Deng was sidelined, other agricultural officials had no choice but to toe the line. Zealots and others who were at least more willing to pander to Mao, came to the fore.

The NPAD, a general and long-term agenda for rural development, was essentially a checklist of things to be done in the next twelve years. It was the catalyst that touched off the 1956 Leap, leading to economic dislocation and the overspending of 3bn. *yuan*. In the end, Mao had been persuaded by the planners (who criticized the whole affair as *maojin*) and had forced the temporary shelving of the programme, bringing an end to this short-lived 'leap forward'. Yet, at the end of 1957 Liu Shaoqi concurred with Mao about the need to revive the programme as an inducement to economic development, and Deng Xiaoping formally reintroduced it at the Plenum. Mao promised flexibility—the NPAD would be revised from time to time if the situation warranted,[11] and equally important, the revised draft of the NPAD was no longer the lightning rod as it had been in 1956 (see Chapter 2). The only exception was the output per unit projected for 1967, or the '4, 5, and 8' targets,[12] which specified that China would achieve the grossly unrealistic goals of 532m. tons of grain and 6m. tons of cotton. Yet, as an agenda for the next decade or so, the NPAD was not entirely farfetched, which explains in part the relative ease with which it was resurrected.[13]

However, as had been the case in 1956, Maoist initiatives and other events acted together to set the stage for the GLF. For instance, during the Third Plenum, a Party Centre and SC directive (24 September) launched a large-scale water conservancy and fertilizer accumulation campaign in the winter and spring of 1957 and 1958. On 26 October, Mao, in the name of the Party Centre, issued a directive calling on the entire population (including all rural units, factories, schools, arms units, etc.) to discuss the NPAD article by article for seven to ten nights in order to foment a production high-tide. From November to December, various party congresses

---

[10] Mao, *Xuanji*, v. 468–75; *Wansui* (1969), 141–3.

[11] MacFarquhar, *Origins*, i. 314–15. Mao, *Xuanji*, v. 474–5, 469. *Wansui* (1969), 142.

[12] Bo Yibo, *Huigu*, i. 523–4.

[13] It has often been alleged that the Third Plenum brought the eclipse of 'planners' like Chen Yun because his report, together with Zhou Enlai's, were not published. Roderick MacFarquhar, *Origins*, i. 315. However, new materials suggest that Chen not only addressed the problem of decentralization at this conference, he in fact masterminded the decentralization policies introduced a month later (Chen, *Wenxuan*, 58–69). See also Roderick MacFarquhar, *Origins*, ii. 60.

convened by the provinces took up the cause by criticizing 'rightist conservatism' by using the 'four bigs'.[14] Consequently, millions were mobilized to build water conservancy and irrigation projects, to raise pigs (for animal manure), and to improve the land to usher in the Leap. The number of mobilized peasants for this purpose climbed quickly as follows:[15]

October 1957	20–30 million
November 1957	60–70 million
December 1957	80 million
January 1958	100 million

The Ministry of Agriculture Mobilizes for the National Programme for Agricultural Development

Once Mao's strong position was revealed, more junior officials in the MA had no choice but to toe the line. For their part, Liao and Chen did their best to campaign for support for the NPAD within their circles, just beneath the apex of power. When the NPAD was shelved, Liao complied, but in 1957/8 Mao's displeasure with his alleged indifference was reflected in Mao's later criticism of him at the Nanning Conference in January (see below). This and Mao's complaints at the Third Plenum were sufficient to convince Liao of the need to be even more sensitive to Mao's wishes. In an article published on 1 December, Liao praised the NPAD as 'a great guiding principle for socialist construction', and called on the localities and the APCs to overcome 'rightist conservative' thinking and to deepen the high tide of agricultural production. He was perfectly confident that the NPAD could be realized because of what he claimed were the superiority of collectivization, favourable natural environment, and the abundant supply of labour.

Moreover, Liao claimed that grain production in 58 counties (or municipalities) had already attained the '4, 5, and 8' level, and one-third of all cotton fields had reached the production level specified in the NPAD, a full decade ahead of schedule. Yet, he also added a caveat—the APCs should not expect a massive infusion of investment. Although the state would raise its investment in agriculture, forestry, and water conservation, the APCs were expected to finance most rural development mainly on their own. Since the regulations of the APCs required 5 to 8 per cent of the total net agricultural value (assumed to be 40bn. *yuan* in 1957) be set aside for investment, the 2 to 3.2bn. *yuan* available was more than the annual state investment in agriculture, forestry, and water conservancy.[16]

---

[14] The 'four bigs' referred to the 'big blooming, big contending, big discussion, and big character' posters.

[15] Bo Yibo, *Huigu*, ii. 680–1; *Mao Wengao*, vi. 610–11; Cong Jin, *Quzhe Fazhan*, 109; Li Rui, *Dayuejin*, 119–28.

[16] *Zhongguo Qingnian* (Chinese Youth), 23, 1957, 8–11. The total state investment in agriculture, forestry, and water conservancy was just over 10bn. *yuan* during the FYP.

Chen echoed Liao in calling the NPAD the great guiding principle but noted that the huge construction and technical innovations required for the '4, 5, 8', targets were 'extremely strenuous', though perfectly realizable. Sixty-four counties had already reached the targets of the NPAD, Chen went further. He exuded confidence in the realization of the NPAD for the same reasons as Liao, but added two more: the industrial sector's support for agriculture (in supplying chemical fertilizer and agricultural machinery for irrigation and transport) and the Party and State's emphasis on agriculture and correct leadership. The chief obstacles, which would require uncompromising struggle, were said to be natural calamities, conservatism, subjectivism (including impetuosity), and capitalist thinking.[17]

So in contrast to the planners, the MA acted quickly at the end of 1957 to mobilize support for the Leap by convening a National Agricultural Conference (Beijing, 9–24 December 1957), to draw up plans both for the 2FYP and for the year 1958. Leading cadres of provincial agricultural departments and bureaus, as well as representatives from the central ministries and from agricultural science and education organizations gathered to hear Liao's argument that since the development of agriculture had lagged behind industry, agricultural departments had to catch up by rapidly raising production. The losses of 1957 were attributed to the dumping of the *duohao kuaisheng* principle, and the '4, 5, 8'; therefore it was necessary to wage 'unceasing struggle' against 'rightist conservatism.'

Liao's efforts received a boost when on 23 December, Zhu De, who was not normally involved in agricultural affairs, threw his weight behind the NPAD by giving an 'important instruction' at the Conference. He proposed a goal of transforming China into a rich and powerful socialist country with modernized industry, agriculture, and science and culture in ten to fifteen years. There were sufficient preconditions, Zhu asserted, to strive for a 'giant leap forward' in agriculture, and he ordered all ministries to redouble their support for agriculture. Deng Zihui also gave instructions but there is no record on what he said; his impact would be felt later.

Meanwhile, on the last day of the Conference, Liao called upon everyone to struggle hard for ten years to fulfil the NPAD, and all administrative levels from the province to the APCs were urged to work out measures to carry this out in order to promote the Leap in agriculture in 1958. He coined the following, 'the next ten years depend on the first three, and the first three years on the very first'[18] which indicated that 1958 was a very crucial year that required extraordinary and timely exertions. Slogans like this are notable in the Chinese context because the stress on hard work and the significance of 1958 influenced not only Mao, but inspired numerous variations on the same theme in that year. They contributed significantly to the spiralling expectations embodied in the slogans, such as 'hard struggle for three years, transform the face of the rural areas' drawn up later in the year. At the Conference, some representatives, such as those from Shanxi and Shunchang

---

[17] *Nongcun Gongzuo Tongxun* (Rural Work Bulletin), 1, 1958, 1–2.
[18] *RMRB*, 10 and 28 December 1957; *RMSC*, 1958, 514–16; Xie Chuntao, *Dayuejin*, 28–9. Mao said later that this slogan by Liao had inspired him, *Wansui* (1969), 153.

County, Fujian, were moved to raise their targets. Other pledged to overcome 'rightist conservatism' and learn from the advanced in order to strive for a 'great leap forward'.

One day after the conclusion of the Conference, Liao brought his campaign for the NPAD to the club[19] of the Departments Directly Under the Central Committee of the CCP.[20] To allay fears that the NPAD would mean further institutional change and disruption, he referred to its first article which stipulated that the entire 2FYP period or a little more time than that should be used to consolidate the APCs.[21] Anticipating queries about how all the rural programmes were to be financed, he argued that savings in the APCs could be raised in order to carry out capital construction, noting that about 20 per cent of total labour days in the APCs had already been used in such capital investment activities as sinking wells, digging ditches and ponds, soil improvement, planting trees, and so on.[22]

Liao then criticized the 'lopsided', 'unbalanced', and 'slow' development of agriculture during the 1FYP period. Many planned targets for economic crops, he said, had not been fulfilled because of the failure of the agricultural departments to fix the sown acreage of the crops in the APCs. In addition, one quarter of all China's twenty-four provinces and one out of three municipalities had not fulfilled the agricultural targets of the 1FYP, and the output of some counties and provinces in 1957 was lower than that of 1952. Echoing Mao, he attributed this to the retreat from the 'leap forward' strategy of 1956—the high tide of 1956, he maintained, was followed by the 'slump' of 1957. Total irrigated area, quantity of accumulated manure, and total sown areas as well as the multiple cropping index were all down in 1957. Specifically, the cultivated area in 1957 was 55m. *mu* less than 1956, and, assuming the 1957 average grain output/*mu* to be 202 *jin* (a realistic estimate), the net loss was 120bn. *jin*.

Hence he concluded that the Leap of 1956 was far better than the 'relaxation' of 1957, leaving no doubt that he favoured a mass mobilizational approach for promoting agriculture. Abandoning his superiors the planners, Liao threw his lot in with Mao and became a staunch promoter of Mao's policies, and some of his ideas articulated at this time might even have influenced Mao. For instance, Liao argued that, in agricultural development, it was normal for balance and imbalance to be temporary, and development meant the continuous struggle to overcome imbalance. This idea was later incorporated by Mao as Article 22 of the Sixty Articles, and the notion was expanded to encompass economic development as a whole. Similarly, the spirit of Liao's slogans 'the next ten years depend on the first three, and the first three on the very first', 'fulfil the NPAD ahead of time', were incorporated

---

[19] The club (*julebu*) was probably a recreational hall reserved for high party and state officials.

[20] *Nongcun Gongzuo Tongxun* 2, 1958, 1–7. A slightly different version is in *Xuexi* (Study), 3, 1958, 2–8.   [21] The full text of the revised draft of the NPAD is in *RMSC*, 1958, 502–7.

[22] Article 43 of the Model Regulations of the APCs (June 1956) stipulated that the accumulation fund (or savings) should be small in order to increase the income of their members. In lean years, no savings were allowed but in more prosperous years, the amount could be increased, but again subject to the principle that the income of the cooperative be guaranteed, *FGHB*, iii. 308.

into articles 12 and 13.[23] To gain Mao's trust, his subordinates often had to demonstrate their radicalism in order to eliminate any hint of 'conservatism'.

According to Zhou Enlai's not too congruous logic, Liao's 'the next ten years . . . ' slogan was what inspired Mao to think in terms of teleological planning. When Mao appended another phase, 'the first year depends on the first winter', the three phrases became his formula for economic planning. Since to overtake Britain in fifteen years required 45m. tons of steel, then the planners worked backwards to decide on the targets for the following ten, five years and the first year. As the success or failure of the entire GLF hinged on the crucial *first* year, timely exertion in 1958 was mandatory.[24]

Entering 1958, Liao continued to lobby for the NPAD and the mobilizational approach to agricultural development at various important central forums. For instance, he repeated his 25 December report, with modifications, to another venue, the Cadre Conference of the Offices of the Party Centre, Central Government Organizations, Beijing Municipal Party Committee, and Beijing Armed Forces of the PLA. His fervent support of Mao's vision contrasted sharply with the inaction of the planners.

Mao's Intervention and the Radicalization of Rural Policies

The Nanning Conference and the Sixty Articles on Work Method

As mentioned, the brainstorming at Nanning led to the creation of the Leap manifesto, the Sixty Articles. In matters pertaining to agriculture, Article 12, calling for the fulfilment of the NPAD in the entire country in five, seven, or eight years, was a major milestone. Consequently, all provincial units were required to explore this possibility. This time frame was meant to accommodate regional diversity, although in the months to come, uniform timetables, targets, and policies were often imposed from above, irrespective of local conditions. Article 54 cited examples of agricultural yields of 1,000 to 2,000 *jin/mu* and urged localities to attempt to match them. Therefore, at the end of January, Mao told the Supreme State Conference simply that the NPAD could probably be achieved in eight years.[25]

Another article (Article 18) which merits mentioning is the one on building experimental plots, designed to be run by the cadres in order to familiarize them with the 'hands on' experience of agricultural production, and to turn them into red 'experts'. At Nanning, Mao was impressed by a report on the experimental plots in Hongan county, Hubei, so the notion was translated into a central Party directive (14 February) calling for the popularization of the experimental plots in all localities (its extension to industry will be discussed in Chapter 4).[26] In 1958, however, rural

---

[23] *Mao Wengao*, vii. 48–9; Cong Jin, *Quzhe Fazhan*, 119.   [24] Ibid.

[25] *Wansui* (1969), 155; *Mao Wengao*, vii. 48–9.

[26] See Mao, *Xuanji*, v. 471; *Mao Wengao*, vii. 50. The Hongan report is mentioned in *Wansui* (1969), 146, and the central directive is in *RMRB*, 15 February 1958. The text of the Hubei report is in *NJZWH*, ii. 7–14.

cadres tended to lavish resources on their best plots and many of the most fantastic claims for agricultural output emanated from them.

Article 53 called on all provinces to set up institutes to study the 'reform' of farm tools and small and medium-sized agricultural machinery.[27] On the 28 January, an *RMRB* photograph showed Mao at a demonstration of the double-wheeled and double-shared ploughs at the Zhejiang Agricultural Research Institute, and an editorial in the *Zhejiang Ribao* extolling the ploughs appeared three days later. As mentioned previously, these ploughs were first introduced in the early 1950s and production climbed rapidly during the Leap of 1956, as the NPAD called for the manufacture of 6 million of them in the following 3–5 years. It was hoped that such a massive injection of these ploughs would kick off agricultural mechanization. Yet, as it turned out, these ploughs were too heavy and cumbersome for the draught animals, and were unsuitable for terraced or paddy fields, especially in south China. Slow sale and massive returns created huge stockpiles, forcing Mao to admit (in October 1957) that the target of 6 million of these ploughs was 'subjectivism', and mention of the ploughs was deleted from the revised draft of the NPAD.[28] Yet, in attacking *maojin*, Mao now wanted to resurrect this white elephant, as it was a symbol of the 1956 Leap. In January, Mao decided to 'reverse the verdict' and 'restore the reputation' of the ploughs.[29] Moreover, practically, they simply could not be thrown away, so it was hoped that some remodelling could make them functional after all.

Zhou Enlai's trip to Zhejiang to examine the ploughs prompted Mao's visit.[30] Acting on these cues, Liao duly convened a conference in February to promote the ploughs. All arguments against the ploughs were refuted one by one, and the MA itself was ordered to engage in self-criticism for not standing firmly behind them. As to the nagging problems with the ploughs themselves, Liao could only offer such advice as training the oxen, widening the farmland, leaders taking the lead, promotion committees, etc. Subsequently, the provinces reported plans to manufacture them, although Liao expected that these plans would be exceeded.[31]

In any event, this initiative, like so many of the shifting goals of the GLF, was never implemented. Mao might have finally realized that these ploughs were useless and lost interest in them. Different farm tools were invented in the middle of 1958 accompanied by national campaigns to promote them, and after February 1958, the double-wheeled and double-shared ploughs were finally forgotten.

Finally, Mao's fury at Nanning was directed most strongly at those he said were responsible for *fanmaojin*, but, as mentioned before, even his loyal followers like Liao suffered Mao's 'named' criticism. Mao accused them, Liao included, of being indifferent when the NPAD was shelved as a result of *fanmaojin*. Unlike the communist 'promoters of progress', these people failed to draw the line. Negative

---

[27] *Mao Wengao*, vii. 63.   [28] *Wansui* (1969), 142.
[29] *Mao Weikan*, ix. 160. At Chengdu, Mao argued that it was people's thinking, not the objective facts of the ploughs, which made them unusable. *Mao Wenkan*, xiB. 45.
[30] Xiao Xinlui, *Xunshe Dajiang Nanbei*, 102 ff.   [31] *XHBYK*, 7, 1958, 126–7.

remarks of Mao's like these, even made in passing, could be construed as criticisms that could break a person's career, so in 1958, Liao became even more earnest in reading the Chairman's intentions.[32]

As described in Chapter 2, Mao's persistent assault on *fanmaojin* at Nanning and Chengdu raised the political temperature tremendously. His diatribe against *fanmaojin* and his advocacy of a 'leap forward' encouraged the zealots and the opportunists. For instance, Mao praised Henan, which claimed that it had created an all-round GLF situation, and that it would complete water-conservation before the summer. Henan planned to realize mechanization in water conservancy work in two years, and semi-mechanization in five years. It claimed to have mobilized the masses, and to be striving for self-sufficiency in cement and iron production. The Sixty Articles, it vowed, could be realized by popularizing education, wiping out illiteracy, and the elimination of the four pests by 'surprise attack' (*tuji*).[33] It also vowed to fulfill the '4, 5, 8' requirements by 1958 or 1959.

Mao liked these ideas, but warned that other provinces should not try the same. Should Henan achieve some of these results, Mao warned, it should not be made public for fear that everyone would jump on the bandwagon. To achieve all these goals in one year, he maintained, would mean that work would be done 'crudely', and that the masses would be overtly 'tense'. Hence, he advised that it was perfectly all right to take anywhere from two to six years to accomplish the Forty Articles.

This mild admonishment did little, especially in view of Mao's later comments that it would be also wrong to insist on four or five years to accomplish the above tasks, even though he urged restraint at times.[34] Mao was far from consistent, and the combined effect of his exhortations pointed unambiguously in the direction of a further acceleration in the speed of development. This was further reinforced by developments in the next few months.

The Chengdu Conference

The Chengdu Conference raised the temperature of the GLF a few degrees. Three policy decisions regarding agriculture were particularly significant. First, with Mao's prodding, the conference decided to amalgamate the smaller APCs into larger ones. The massive water conservancy and irrigation campaign had created the impression that smaller APCs were too small to facilitate projects that would straddle large areas. Furthermore, smaller APCs were deemed unsuitable for agricultural mechanization that was to be achieved in a few years. In any case, the central decision made at Chengdu was only a recommendation, and provinces were given full discretion on the scale of amalgamation, timetable, and even whether to amalgamate or not.

Second, the Party Centre decided to launch a movement to 'reform' farm tools used in irrigation, cultivation, transport, and food processing, so that in seven years'

---

[32] *Mao Weikan*, xiB. 9.

[33] *Tuji* means a sudden and surprise attack, or a concentrated effort to finish a job quickly.

[34] *Wansui* (1969), 166–7.

time (striving for five), mechanization or semi-mechanization could be achieved. The emphasis was to be on small machinery supplied by local industries and produced by the APCs themselves.

Third, to complement the above, the Party Centre urged mobilization for the development of local industry to serve agriculture by forming small and medium-sized industries such as plants to manufacture and service farm tools, small mines, ore pits, etc. The provinces were also urged to strive to raise their GVAO to exceed their GVIO in five to seven years.[35]

An interesting case was Deng Zihui, Liao's superior and one of the few independent-minded top leaders who is generally regarded by analysts to be inactive during the Leap. In 1955, Deng lost out during a quarrel with Mao regarding the tempo of switching lower APCs to advanced APCs. As late as August 1957, Deng still insisted that excessively large APCs (those with 50–60 production teams, which in turn had 70–100 households and 100 to 120 labourers) were undesirable.[36] However, in 1958, even he buckled under pressure and changed his tone entirely. At Chengdu, Mao rambled on about history and chastised Deng in his interjections made during a speech by Chen Boda on 18 March, accusing Deng of opposing him in the past, and of being someone who remained attached to the ways of the 'bourgeois democrats' who argued for more freedom (in hiring labour, trade, renting out land, and so on) for the peasants. The major rift that had divided the Party was about how fast to build socialism, and the split was signified by disagreement between Deng and himself.[37] Yet, Mao now declared that Deng had turned around and had been 'convinced' by the GLF. In May, Deng duly published an article praising the small industries and the central decision to amalgamate the cooperatives.[38]

Meanwhile, Chen Zhengren, Deng's deputy weighed in with a report on Xushui, which claimed that the county had been totally irrigated after three months' hard work. A feisty 130,000 strong 'army' had created hundreds of 'reservoirs' and ponds connecting all the province's rivers and canals into a giant irrigation network. One 'reservoir' had been constructed by 480 women in three days and nights, and another by 700 students in just one day. This experience, it was said, showed that the face of agriculture could be altered in just two winters. The goal was to achieve an average yield of 500 *jin* per *mu* by year's end, even though average yield in 1957 was 216 *jin/mu*.[39]

The various decisions at Chengdu accelerated the momentum of the Leap. Beginning in May, many provinces had claimed that amalgamation was completed, and the number of households in the average APC had swollen to 2,000 to 4,000 households.[40] This was to give a great push to communization later on. We now turn to the campaign for water conservancy.

[35] *Jiaoxue Cankao Ziliao*, xxvii. 423–4.   [36] *Zhongguo Qingnian*, 21, 1957, 21.

[37] Li Rui, *Dayuejin*, 204; *Dangshi Yanjiu*, 1988, v. 37. See also *Mao Wenkan*, xiB. 34. The XXX in the stenographic records of Mao's speech refers to Deng Zihui, see *Deng Zihui Zhuan*, 525.

[38] *Deng Zihui Wenji*, 518–23.   [39] Li Rui, *Dayuejin*, 237–40.   [40] Bo Yibo, *Huigu*, ii. 730.

The Irrigation and Water Conservancy Campaign

Another policy area which was further radicalized by the MA during this time was irrigation and water conservancy. Although a water-conservancy and fertilizer-accumulation campaign was a routine conducted at the end of the agricultural season, the scale of the campaign launched throughout China in the winter of 1957/8 was unprecedented.[41] Tan Zhenlin who was the staunchest supporter of the NPAD, thought that the key to realization of the NPAD was irrigation and water conservancy. As early as September/October 1957, he was so impressed with water conservancy at Mang He that he wanted to turn it into a national model. In December, he had already summed up the experience with Mang He under the 'three emphases' slogan of storage, small-scale construction, and mass participation.[42] His preferences may likely have been derived from his interests and expertise, but they may also have been political, because they coincided with Mao's preferences. At Chengdu, Tan briefed Mao on how the numerous water irrigation projects north of the River Huai had water-conservation(ized) the area. Mao in turn praised Tan and others, claiming that these achievements could not be accomplished by the 'experts in a hundred years'.[43]

Like the many campaigns during the GLF, the water conservancy campaign was mobilized under the political pressure created by *fanmaojin* and carried out on such a massive scale in order to vindicate Mao. Right at the beginning, the campaign was embarked upon by criticizing 'rightist conservatism' in water conservancy work, and by counterposing the 'leap forward' approach against the gradualist approach. Soon Henan's experience with the Mang He and the principles of 'storage, small-scale construction, and mass participation' were selected as a model. These principles were then contrasted with established practices of the water conservancy departments, which were said to be 'drainage, large-scale construction, and state involvement'.

Since Henan had run a similar campaign in 1955 and later was criticized as *maojin*, its resurrection was symbolic of the victory of the 'leap forward' approach, and the campaign sparked a process of one-upmanship. When one locality announced a goal of full irrigation in two years, others trumped it by claiming one year, or even a few months. Anyhow, most irrigation projects turned out to be hasty fabrications that were wasteful and counter-productive. One example, according to Li Yunzhong, was a canal over 160 km long, which straddled 10,000 *mu* of wheat built by Luan county without advanced planning or prospecting. During the rainy season it was simply washed away. He himself had participated in many other futile 'toil hard for ten days' campaigns to, for example, double the number of pigs, wipe out illiteracy, and eliminate the four pests, etc.

---

[41] Parris Chang, *Power and Policy*, 65.

[42] 'Tan Zhenlin Zhuan' Bianzuan Weiyuanhui, *Tan Zhenlin Zhuan* (A biography of Tan Zhenlin) (Hangzhou: Zhejiang renmin chubanshe, 1992), 308–17.

[43] Li Rui, *Dayuejin*, 119; *Mao Wenkan*, xiB. 42.

Yet, the Ministry of Water Conservancy claimed that, from October 1957 to April 1958, 353.34m. *mu* had been brought under irrigation, or more than 30 per cent of the total acreage irrigated during the preceding eight years. As targets kept climbing in accordance with the requirements of the Leap, exaggeration, formalism, coercion, and neglect of quality became the norm. Yet, this malaise only served to heighten the tone of the GLF.[44]

In March, Chen Zhengren bragged that newly irrigated areas had already reached 160m. *mu*, exceeding the 1958 target by 180 per cent. Some provinces were said to have fulfilled the afforestation targets for 1958, and were successful in fertilizer accumulation and the elimination of the 'four pests'. A daily total of more than 100 million people were reported working at the agricultural front.

According to Chen, many provinces had already sought approval for their plans to attain the NPAD targets. Hubei, for instance, had decided to fulfil the planned increase in grain for the entire 2FYP period in just *one* year. Chen had no qualms in approving them, and added that most parts of the country could basically achieve full irrigation in two or three years, as Henan, Hebei, and Beijing had already proposed to do so in 1958.[45] All this enabled Liu Shaoqi to claim at the Party Congress in May that from October 1957 to April 1958, irrigated areas had increased by 350m. *mu*, exceeding the total acreage irrigated from 1949–57 by 807m. *mu*, and that the peasants had accumulated 15,000 tons of fertilizer.[46]

This formed the background to a reorganization of the central ministries which enhanced the formal power and responsibilities of the MA. The State Council decreed on 27 March that after the merging of the Ministries of Water Conservancy and Electricity, their duties of agricultural irrigation and water conservancy would be transferred to the MA. At the end of June, another State Council regulation put the MA in charge of small rural hydroelectric projects, planning and management of machinery for irrigation, and arbitration of disputes in rural water usage among the provinces. Two bureaus, including the Irrigation Control Bureau belonging to the former Ministry of Water Conservancy, were also transferred to the MA. All agricultural departments at the provincial level were required to consult the MA regarding this new division of responsibilities in their respective localities.[47]

This left the Ministry of Water Conservancy and Electricity with only the responsibility of planning for large river basins, and the role of the MA expanded, decentralization notwithstanding. The performance of Liao and the MA in the previous months to promote the GLF had earned the ministry the trust of Mao, so

---

[44] Li Rui, *Dayuejin*, 119–28; Li Rui, *Lushan Huiyi*, 48.

[45] Chen's report is in *Zhongguo Qingnian*, 6, 1958, 2–4. In the atmosphere of competition, Henan even pledged to achieve the '4, 5, & 8', total irrigation, elimination of the four pests, and illiteracy within one year. Mao doubted that this was possible, and therefore asked Wang Renzhong to telephone the 'responsible comrade' of the Henan PPC, but the latter could not be persuaded. Mao then commented that if everyone was fighting to be the first, there would be chaos. If indeed Henan could do it, it would probably be achieved with many defects. At the least the work done would be crude, and the masses would be too tense. *Wansui* (1969), 166. See also *Mao Zedong Tongzhi Bashiwu Danchen Jinian Wenxuan* (Collection of articles to commemorate comrade Mao Zedong's eighty-fifth birthday) (Beijing: Renmin chubanshe, 1979), 32–3.   [46] *HHPYK*, 11, 1958, 4.   [47] *FGHB*, vii. 359–60, 388–9.

the MA was rewarded accordingly. Such acclaim only encouraged the MA to become more extreme in discharging its expanded responsibilities.

The Great Leap Forward Takes Shape: The Second Session of the Eighth Party Congress (5–23 May)

As mentioned above, the Second Session of the Eighth Party Congress formalized all Mao's initiatives, launched the Party into the total mobilization effort, and solidified Mao's predominance with the addition of loyal Maoists to the Politburo. Mao's triumph was complete, and the Congress was bubbling with enthusiasm. In matters pertaining to agriculture, the Congress approved the second revised draft of the NPAD and Tan Zhenlin gave the authoritative speech on the programme. Now that the planners had been sidelined, loyal Maoists like Tan took centre stage. After the censuring of *fanmaojin*, Tan said, those who were sceptical of the NPAD and *duohao kuaisheng* had learned their lessons, and the 'autumn-account settlers' would finally lose. He credited the NPAD with the high tide of agricultural production—expanded cultivated acreage, and irrigated land in the winter/spring of 1957/8—and claimed that many localities had already over-fulfilled the targets of '4, 5 and 8' in 1958. Only a few things were changed in the revised draft, namely, the two articles on irrigation and water conservancy were merged to make room for a new one on close planting.[48]

Tan had become, next to Mao, the chief decision-maker and pace-maker for a mobilizational approach to agricultural policy; subsequently, he was to act zealously in implementing his pet projects, and in fleshing out Mao's general ideas. In his speech explaining the new draft of the NPAD, Tan argued that between October 1957 and April 1958, the stage for a 'great leap forward' had been set. Because of the 'remarkable' work in water conservation, fertilizer accumulation, reforms of agricultural tools, land improvement and other measures, the expected increase in grain output would be in the range of 10–20 per cent, barring large-scale natural calamities. However, he warned that in some counties, the 'progressive' targets had not been matched by concrete measures; they had not been sent down to the production teams or cooperative members. In others, not even the targets were 'progressive' and this, he urged, must be overcome.

Tan also paid lip service against crudeness, false reporting, and exaggeration in agricultural work, but, in the same breath, he observed that even though some units had set targets improbably high, he would consider them reliable if there were 'concrete measures' to implement them.[49] Turning to the changes in the NPAD since its approval in October 1957, Tan explained that oil-bearing crops should now be regarded as important as grain and cotton, because yield/*mu* had doubled or tripled. He was absolutely confident that this could be achieved, even ahead of schedule. As to the suggestion for raising the yield per *mu* for grain and cotton to

---

[48] Li Rui, *Dayuejin*, 313 ff.   [49] *RMSC*, 1959, 29–31.

more than 800 *jin* and 1,000 *jin* respectively, Tan considered that this should be left to the provinces to decide and it should not be included in the programme.

Tan now latched on to the idea of close planting, which seemed to have originated in a proposal from Guangdong,[50] as vital for achieving higher yield/*mu*. Although he argued that close planting should be reasonable, he noted that, like other 'progressive' measures for raising production, it was always resisted by 'conservative backward thinking'. This effectively cancelled out his appeal for caution, especially after his call for tripling the yield per *mu* for oil-bearing crops. In any case, close planting now was accorded its own separate article to underline its importance. The two articles on water conservancy were now merged into one, incorporating Tan's ideas of 'small scale, water storage, and operation by the APCs' (the wordings were slightly changed from the original). Yet, most water conservancy projects constructed this way were hasty and primitive concoctions, like the 600 dams at Andong County which were built with a mixture of straw and sand that would simply be washed away with the flood. These were useless in alleviating the drought situation in the summer of 1958, but continued to compete with regular agricultural work for manpower and resources. In fact, heavy rain in July destroyed many of the new 'reservoirs' in Henan.[51]

Tan was not unaware of the drawbacks of the water conservancy campaign in the winter of 1957/8, but was determined to continue it. In the rest of 1958, he actively championed both the campaigns for close planting and for water conservancy, as we will see later on. The NPAD also kicked off other campaigns, such as the increase in the target for chemical fertilizer and the popularization of primary education,[52] but these were less important.

In all, the Congress formally approved of the decisions made in the previous few months and its high profile further bolstered the momentum of the existing campaigns. Throughout the country, numerous propaganda meetings were held to spread the spirit of the Congress, and the groundswell multiplied. Immediately after the Congress, Tan was rewarded with a Politburo membership.

The Campaign for Summer Harvest and Planting

An important agricultural event which coincided with the Congress was summer harvest and planting, which demonstrated the MA's attempt to take charge by applying a wartime mobilizational style to routine agricultural work. In the years just prior to 1958, the summer grain harvest of winter wheat was roughly equivalent to one-sixth of the year's total output.[53] Summer harvest was traditionally a hectic affair as it had to be rushed to completion in just a few days because the frequent summer rains could cause grain drop, germination, and rot.[54] In 1958, the rhetorical hyperbole of the Leap had raised expectations, as the provinces had estimated that

[50] Ibid. [51] *Mao Wengao*, vii. 311; Parris Chang, *Power and Policy*, 73.
[52] *RMSC*, 1959, 31. [53] *Nongcun Gongzuo Tongxun*, 9, 1958, 1. [54] *RMRB*, 13 May 1958.

production increases would range from 15 to 100 per cent. Many of them had also expanded the ratio of multiple-cropping, and many wheat fields had been converted into rice paddies, the rationale being that rice was a crop with a higher yield than wheat. Correspondingly, the labour power required for harvesting was expected to multiply.

The MA acted quickly by issuing an emergency circular spelling out the measures to be adopted to fight this 'tense battle',[55] therefore assuring its continuing role in the direction of routine agricultural work, and also its power to demand that the provinces implement its decisions. Since the summer harvest, the summer planting and field management for crops sown in the spring had to be carried out simultaneously, it urged that all available labour power be mobilized and that the APCs should coordinate their activities. City dwellers, government offices, schools, and the armed forces were to be organized to help the peasants.

The ideas of this circular were publicly endorsed by an *RMRB* editorial.[56] Summer harvest, it said, was the first major step toward a GLF in agricultural production. Allegedly, there were 1bn. *mu* of high-yield fields and a spectacularly high yield of 1,000 *jin/mu* had already been reported.[57] However, since the crops were still in the fields, many special measures were needed to collect the harvest. Then the editorial detailed the long list of things which ought to be 'done well', the foremost of which was to continue fully mobilizing the masses. In the Shangqiu Special District (Henan), for instance, there had been district-wide mass debates on the summer harvesting and planting on the following questions. What was the effect of a well-executed summer harvest and planting on the total bumper harvest of the year? Should preparations for summer farm work be done early or late? Should harvesting and planting be done early and quickly or slowly and at a later date? How could cutting and threshing be done meticulously to ensure that not a grain was lost? Indeed, answers to these questions were predetermined so these 'debates' were designed to push the peasants to get the job done early, well, and quickly, and to silence dissent. That was why the editorial hailed this method of 'arousing and depending' on the masses the best guarantee of good summer harvest and planting, and admonished cadres of all levels to strengthen their part. The Party centre, with the *RMRB* as its mouthpiece, was now increasingly engrossed in day-to-day work, and in fact duplicated much of the work of the ministry. For the sub-national units, this was to mean excessive interference into their areas of jurisdiction, leaving very little room for initiatives of their own.

The Irrigation and Water Conservancy Campaign, Round 2

The MA jumped eagerly into its new shoes. Even before the conclusion of the Second Session of the Eighth Party Congress, it took the initiative of planning for

---

[55] *RMRB*, 13 May 1958.　　[56] Ibid.

[57] The average yields of wheat and barley in 1957 was only about 100 *jin/mu*, and the total cultivated area for both crops in 1958 was 5bn. *mu*.

irrigation and water conservancy for 1959 by convening a conference with the provinces between May and June, followed by another in June and July.[58] Both conferences were convened much earlier than usual and consequently, the provinces were said to have sprung into action much sooner than in 1957.[59] Since these conferences were rather similar in nature, we shall consider them together here.

The clarion call in both conferences was to 'go all out' in the autumn of 1958 and by 1 May 1959 to bring all farmland under irrigation in both North and South China. The ultimate goal was to ensure good harvests even in conditions of drought and flood. In the former conference, attended by thirteen provinces and representatives of three special districts, the delegates spent most of their time touring the water conservancy projects in nearby Xiangyang Special District and 'exchanging important experiences'. The latter conference (with delegates from fourteen provinces) was actually conducted en route by visiting three provinces and nine counties, starting from Baoding and ending at Zhengzhou. For four weeks, the delegates travelled and exchanged experiences, and discovered many models worthy of emulation.

Overall, the delegates simply suspended their disbelief about the 'unusual achievements' that were shown to them. For instance, Hebei's claim of a 166 per cent increase in summer crops despite the lack of rain for 300 days was attributed to the success of water conservancy. Wild exaggerations of this sort were constantly touted as advanced experiences to be copied, and were treated as 'facts' to refute the 'rightists' and 'dogmatists'. On this basis, even more far-fetched 1959 plans and targets were devised, even though everyone involved knew that they were unrealizable.

Invariably, the conferences issued numerous instructions—they demanded that all localities make early preparations, mobilize the whole party and people, get organized, train cadres, prepare the necessary resources, let 'politics take command', assign party secretaries to take the lead, criticize the complacent thinking that 'water control had reached its limits', and so on, and so forth. Superficially, these blanket statements appear to show a good grasp of the problems at hand, but in fact they contained so many diverse and ambitious objectives with no ranking of priorities that they were almost impossible to implement.

These two conferences organized by the MA did set in motion large campaigns for water conservancy. Invariably, the provinces would set even higher targets than those originally planned at the conferences.[60] In Guangdong, the peasants sustained exhaustive work and physical injuries to move mountains of earth to build reservoirs, canals, levees, for drainage and irrigation. Even temples and ancestral halls were demolished for building materials.[61] However, whether the numerous 'advanced experiences' were genuine or whether the goals were realizable was

---

[58] The two conferences were the South China Irrigation and Water Conservancy Work Conference (21 May–5 June), Wuhan, and Northern Areas Irrigation and Water Conservancy Work Conference (20 June–16 July) which was convened en route between Baoding, Hebei, to Zhengzhou, Henan. *FGHB*, viii. 9; *RMRB*, 9 June and 1 August 1958.   [59] *FGHB*, viii. 9.   [60] Ibid.
[61] Sulamith Potter and Jack Potter, *China's Peasants*, 76–8.

probably not a concern of the ministry, at least at this juncture. As long as the ball was set rolling, and the ministry was seen to have done its best, everything was fine. This is a good illustration of what can be called 'pass-the-buck' implementation.[62] The ministry's subordinates were left with the burden to make the alleged 'success stories' work for them and to fulfil the high targets they were encouraged to set for themselves. For the MA, the means were what counted, not the ends. In any case, as mentioned before, when the summer rains came, many of the reservoirs, dams, and levees, were simply washed away.[63]

The Minister of Agriculture's Call for a Great Leap Forward

Shortly after the Party Congress, Liao Luyan, in the spirit of the Congress, vouched for the policies and approaches to agriculture in a major *RMRB* article.[64] Attacking those cadres who insisted on moderation and more realistic goals, he argued that to have a leap in production, there must first be a leap in people's thinking. According to him, many cadres had failed to appreciate the zest and creativity of the cooperativized peasants. Therefore, they stuck to convention and conservatism, refusing to try things out even though they could be achieved 'objectively'. These people, Liao alleged, were actually being unrealistic and impractical.

Liao also reproved those who questioned the swift and indiscriminate way of spreading new and untested methods. He stressed the continued importance of struggling against nature through bold experimentation and creation. The advanced experiences, he urged, must be popularized by taking local conditions into account before adoption. However, a degree of risk was always inherent in agricultural production; some losses were unavoidable.

So Liao had no qualms with reports that dozens of counties had already fulfilled the targets in the NPAD, and that several hundred more could do the same in 1958 alone. He endorsed them all, praising them to be solid and practical.[65] This stand against moderation and negative feedback was to profoundly affect later events.

Spurred on by these prompts, in June/July, when the summer harvest was being completed, counties competed with one another in 'launching satellites' (or making claims of fantastic records). Counties in Henan claimed a wheat production record of 2,000 to 7,000 *jin/mu*. Not to be left behind, rice-producing counties in Jiangxi, Fujian, Hubei, Hebei, and Anhui tried to outdo one another by claiming records of *jin/mu* that spiralled out of control until they reached 10,000 *jin/mu*. In time, record yields per *mu* of wheat of 36,956 *jin* set by Hubei, and rice of 130,000 *jin* set by Guangxi, were touted in the *RMRB*.[66] Indeed, these claims were all fabricated. As documents from 1959 show, the Guangxi record was achieved by concentrating

---

[62] Robert Nakamura and Frank Smallwood, *The Politics of Policy Implementation* (New York: St. Martin's Press, 1980), 130–3.

[63] For instance, see *Mao Wengao*, vii. 311–12; Parris Chang, *Power and Policy*, 73.

[64] *RMRB*, 10 June 1958.   [65] Ibid.   [66] *RMRB*, 13, 27 August, 18 September 1958.

plants from 19 *mu* onto 1.9 *mu* so close together that a pair of hands could not push in. Others would sow 1,000 *jin* of seeds or pile fertilizer for hundreds of *mu* onto just one.[67] Anhui, Jiangsu, Hubei, and Henan, declared that they were early rice '1,000 *jin* provinces' (that is, their average output had reached 1,000 *jin/mu*). Sichuan, Henan, Anhui, and Gansu, announced that per capita grain harvest had exceeded 1,000 *jin*.[68]

Tan further fanned the flames by telling Anhui cadres that it was possible for their wheat production to reach 5,000, and even 10,000 *jin/mu*.[69] Provinces which did not play the game willingly, like Hunan, were given 'white flag' designation and suffered criticism.[70] This was the background when the MA presented its 2FYP which pledged to raise grain and cotton output to 425m. and 4m. tons respectively by 1962, so that each Chinese could have 600 kg. Mao had no qualms with the report, and in endorsing it, he retitled it 'The Future of Agriculture is Extremely Bright'.[71]

At this point, even Deng Zihui registered another turnaround. He pleased Mao with his report on 24 June on increased summer harvests. Statistics from twenty provinces, he maintained, showed that summer harvest had reached 47.5m. tons, or 17.75m. tons more than the 29.8m. tons of grains harvested in 1957. Hence, Deng estimated total grain for 1958 could reach 260m. tons, so that in just one year, the 1962 target set by the Eighth Party Congress could be surpassed.[72] Deng toed the Party line further in an article published by the MA entitled 'Battle hard for three years, transform fundamentally the countryside' in which he enumerated and supported virtually all Leap initiatives. For instance, he argued that targets contained in the NPAD could be realized in only three to five years. He reiterated the support for such GLF policies as water conservancy, small fertilizer plants, deep ploughing, afforestation, close planting, tool reform, and so on. Indeed, he even joined the chorus in denouncing *fanmaojin*, which he said had killed off the 'leap forward' of 1956, causing unnecessary harm to the cause of the revolution. Finally, vowing that this would not be repeated, he joined everyone in denouncing the 'tide-watchers' and 'autumn account-settlers' whom he said would be destroyed by the facts.[73]

Tan Zhenlin's Vision of a Great Leap Forward and His Role as a Decision-maker

In May and June, Tan Zhenlin, representing Mao, inspected the northern part of Jiangsu and Anhui and more than twenty counties, making many off-the-cuff

---

[67] *NJZWH*, ii. 207.

[68] Li Rui, *Lushan Huiyi*, 4; Cong Jin, *Quzhe Fazhan*, 139–40; Xie Chuntao, *Dayuejin*, 59–65.

[69] Chen Liming, *Tan Zhenlin Zhuanqi* (The legend of Tan Zhenlin) (Beijing: Zhongguo wenshi chubanshe, 1994), 325.

[70] Li Rui, *Lushan Huiyi*, 38–9.   [71] *Shizheng Sishinian*, 146–7; *Mao Wengao*, vii. 280.

[72] *Mao Wengao*, vii. 289–90.   [73] *Nongcun Gongzuo Tongxun*, 9, 1958, 1–8.

remarks during the tour. Though crude, ambiguous, and often contradictory, these utterances were venerated in the Party press as 'important instructions', and the provinces and other administrative units often felt obliged to follow them. As improvization and spontaneity became the norm, this kind of decision-making by oral instruction had become particularly pronounced in 1958.

At Fuyang Prefecture, for instance, Tan ordered that the grain production for the whole country in 1958 should increase by more than 20 per cent, regardless of the circumstances. He was also becoming more receptive to the idea that wheat was not a low-yielding crop, as conventional belief would have it, because a large area of high-yield wheat had been reported. Hence, he urged that people's thinking about high-yield crops should not be 'fixed', even though that cast doubt on the current policy of transforming farmland into rice paddy in order to achieve higher yield. In fact, Tan condemned attempts in some localities of turning paddy fields back into dry farmland when drought persisted. It was necessary, he urged, to 'advance boldly' and not to retreat.[74]

In addition, Tan also gave his blessing to grandiose projects. According to him, the taming of the Huai He was soon to be completed. He praised the people of Huaibei (north of the Huai River) for their efforts in water conservancy and their plans to construct a colossal network of canals and rivers so that it could be converted into rice cultivation to replace wheat. Yet, as it turned out, this pet project of the then first secretary of Anhui province was an unmitigated disaster, as the construction of numerous uncoordinated canals actually resulted in widespread salinization and alkalization.[75]

Finally, Tan also issued orders, made projections, and redefined rural policies freely. Of the twelve measures which were directly related to agriculture in the NPAD, Tan now maintained that eight particular items were the most crucial—water conservancy, fertilizer, deep ploughing, seed improvement, close planting, pest control, field management, and tool reform—and soon these were collectively known as the 'Eight Point Charter'. All the localities were instructed to make plans with regard to these matters well ahead of time, and water conservancy was to be carried out as early as October. Eventually, Tan began to entertain the notion of amalgamating the APCs into even larger collectives so that labour organization could be run like those in a factory with workshops. A finer division of labour would enable cadres and cooperative members to specialize—there should be people to take charge of maize or rice, and specific duties of field management should be contracted to the brigades, teams, and the households. As long as everybody 'battled hard' for three years, he maintained, the problem of grain deficiency would be solved when the average grain per individual reached 1,000 *jin* per annum. In some places, this could be achieved in 1958, and an absolute majority of places could do this the year after. The most important current task was the need to raise the yield for grain by more than 20 per cent. This would not only eliminate

---

[74] *RMRB*, 19 June 1958.   [75] *Wansui* (1969), 427.

the 'low-yield' thinking, but also throw cold water on the 'tide-watchers' and the 'autumn harvest account-settlers'.

The Further Mobilization of the Regions

In June and July, after the formation of the Cooperative Regions, Tan Zhenlin, Liao Luyan, Chen Zhengren, and the MA immediately linked up with them by a series of regional agricultural conferences (see Table 3.1) to push the GLF. Four of these conferences dealt with agriculture in general and two others were more specifically devoted to discussions of wheat and rice production, respectively.

Table 3.1. *The Regional Agricultural Conferences*

1. The First East China Agricultural Coordination Conference Among Four Provinces and One Municipality (Anhui, Jiangsu, Zhejiang, Fujian, and Shanghai) Hefei, 20–5 June.[76]
2. South-West Three Province Agricultural Conference (Sichuan, Guizhou, and Yunnan) Chengdu, 26 June–1 July.[77]
3. North China Six-Province Agricultural Coordination Conference (Shanxi, Hebei, Shandong, Henan, Shaanxi, and Beijing) Zhengzhou, 7–14 July.[78]
4. South China Promotion Conference for the Increased Production of Rice, Chengdu, 8–16 July.[79]
5. Central and South China Agricultural Coordination Conference (Guangdong, Hebei, Hunan, Jiangxi, and Guangxi) Nanchang, 16–24 July.[80]
6. Ten-Province Conference for the Raising of the Production of Wheat, Zhengzhou, July (?).[81]

Several of these conferences were labelled 'coordinating conferences' but this was a misnomer, as little or no coordination took place among the provinces. In effect, they were more 'appraisal-through-comparison' conferences in which the provinces attempted to outdo one another with their hyperboles of the size of their summer harvests.[82] Ke of the East China region led the pack by boasting that 1958 grain production could reach 60m. tons, an increase of 70 per cent over that of 1957. Hence, the goal originally designed to be accomplished in four to five years was now accomplished in just one. This fed Tan's fancy, who concluded that this was a flying leap, as the share of grain per capita in East China would be 1,000 *jin*. In three to five years' time, per capita grain would double to 2,000 *jin*. Accordingly, he declared that the problem of grain was basically resolved, and this was an idea

---

[76] *RMRB*, 28 June 1958; Tan's speech at the conference is in *Hongqi*, 1958, 6, 7–12.
[77] *RMRB*, 7 July 1958.   [78] Ibid. and 20 July 1958.   [79] Ibid.   [80] Ibid.
[81] Ibid. and 19 July 1958.
[82] Article 7 of the Sixty Articles specified that 'appraisal-through-comparison' meetings be held among the provinces, municipalities, counties, and APCs, *Mao Wengao*, vii. 47.

that Mao and other leaders picked up later. Based on the East China record, Tan estimated that total grain could reach 250m. tons in 1958, so the future goal was to ensure material abundance (*fengyi zushi*, literally well-fed and well-clothed) in two to three years. In order to ensure an all-round bumper harvest, Tan now prescribed the strengthening of field management, and the 'reform' of farm tools. Tan's conclusive speech to the East China Conference set the tone for the other conferences to come, as it pleased Mao, who then ordered it to be published in *Hongqi*.[83] This prompted other Cooperative Regions to inflate their output estimates, and to make 'leap forward' agricultural targets. Even the traditionally low-yield North-West region vowed to achieve per capita grain of 1,100 *jin* in 1958, 2,000 *jin* in 1959, and over 3,000 *jin* in 1962.[84]

Not surprisingly, all the provinces present reported spectacular summer harvests, notwithstanding the serious droughts being reported in East China and South-West China, and the increases in summer crops were said to be anywhere from 24 per cent (South-West) to more than 100 per cent (Central-South). Fantastic yields of wheat of 1,000 to 2,000 *jin/mu* were reported for 740,000 *mu*, and a smaller area was said to have produced a record of 7,320 *jin/mu*. Henan alone claimed that the size of the summer harvest was almost equivalent to the total production of 1957!

These conferences do give a sense of regional variation in agriculture, but these differences were overwhelmed by the imposition of uniform policies by the central leaders. These were reflected in the general shared themes of the conferences. For instance, while the North China provinces had traditionally been those with the lowest yield/unit and some provinces suffered varying degrees of natural calamity while others were spared, all of them vowed to make all-out efforts to strive for a spectacular autumn harvest on the basis of the alleged summer gain. All of them planned to achieve this by making arrangements according to the 'Eight-Point Charter'. For instance, all the conferences agreed on the continuation of the massive irrigation and water conservancy programmes. The 'new experiences' and 'new theories' which were responsible for the bountiful summer harvest were to be popularized with 'revolutionary style and creativity'. Hence, Huangyan county, Zhejiang, decided to deep-plough the fields from 20 to 36 cm, although the normal depth of ploughing was 7.6 to 10 cm, in order to double the rate of close planting. The Central-South conference also agreed on denser close-planting and further decided to launch a 'socialist competition' for raising production and for 'launching high-yield satellites'.

All the conferences agreed on the reform of farm implements made at the North China conference called by Tan, who demanded that all provinces should use mainly 'reformed' farm implements in the autumn harvesting and planting. In the irrigation and water conservancy work in the winter, the manual practices of 'carrying things on the shoulder with a pole' (*jiantiao*) and 'hauling by hand'

---

[83] Bo Yibo, *Huigu*, ii. 688; *Mao Wengao*, vii. 307–8; *Hongqi*, 6, 7–12.

[84] Gongheguao, *Daidian*, 557.

(*rentai*) should be eliminated. Semi-mechanized water-drawing tools were to be introduced by the coming winter/spring, and all 'backward' farm tools were to be replaced by 'reformed' tools within the year in order to dramatically double labour productivity by 200 per cent or more.

Beyond this, two conferences (the South-West and the North China) resolved to introduce a socialist education campaign in the winter, which in turn was adopted as a national campaign by the Politburo conference in August. At the North China conference, discussions surrounded the inadequacy of existing management and distribution methods in the APCs and it noted that 'higher stage communes' had already emerged in some places. Hence the conference demanded more investigations and studies about them. This undoubtedly gave another push toward the formation of communes.

The regional conferences strikingly demonstrate the imposition of uniform policies on the provinces, despite constant injunctions to 'suit measures to local conditions'. These conferences also continued the trend toward overloading the provinces with policy goals. Moreover, all these conferences were convened and chaired by central leaders, who were there to ensure that regions would stick to the 'leap forward' approach in implementing their policies. Even Deng Zihui gave the obligatory 'instructions' at one of the conferences. The MA and its ministers continued to issue direct orders and demands to provincial agricultural departments in these conferences. It is clear that the key decisions were imposed from above, and the 'creativity and initiative' of the provinces was to be given free play only in the implementation of these policies, or when they coincided with central whims and requirements.

Eventually, on the basis of provincial reports collected at these conferences, the MA took an unusual step on 22 July of publishing a communiqué on the results of the summer harvests. Apparently eager to take this first opportunity to vindicate policies pursued in the previous months, it made the far-fetched claim that the summer grain harvest had reached 50.5m. tons, a 69 per cent increase over the *total* summer grain of 1957. Average yield per *mu* was said to be 70 per cent over the 1957 figure. Winter wheat was 34.5m. tons, and together with the estimated spring wheat production of 4.5m. tons, the total came to 39m. tons.[85]

It goes without saying that these figures were hopelessly exaggerated; in fact, they were more than double the real output. Yet, the hyperboles did not end here. In July, the MA added up the new estimates submitted by the provinces and claimed that grain production in 1958 would reach a whopping 500m. tons. Even Mao found this incredible, so the figures made public were 300–350m. tons.[86] Yet the media

[85] *RMRB*, 23 July 1958. For Mao's buoyant acceptance of this estimate, see *Wansui* (1969), 228, 240; according to the reminiscence of Lu Gengmo, who was deputy director of the State Planning Commission in 1958, many cadres worried about the lack of storage facilities to accommodate increases of such a large scale. One of the perceived solutions was large-scale export of grain, and the reduction of the cultivated acreage was also contemplated. Lu was one of those who thought in these terms. *Jingji Yanjiu*, 2, 1980, 42. The Ministry of Grain was also being taken in by the extravagant reports, and it called a conference to discuss the problem of dividing the surplus grain. *XHBYK*, 14, 1958, 66.

[86] Xie Chuntao, *Dayuejin*, 65; *Mao Weikan*, xiB. 130.

continued to laud the miracles. A *RMRB* editorial on 23 July proclaimed that China had surpassed the USA in wheat production, and could produce as much grain as it wished. In one case, an 'unprecedented world record' of 7,320 *jin* of wheat per *mu* was said to be achieved by a production team leader in his experimental plot of *two mu*. This example was later cited repeatedly as if it was the general rule and to show that the sky was the limit. In fact, it seems likely that even the Chinese leaders accepted them as genuine at least for a short period of time.[87] For example, as mentioned before, Mao's conviction was reinforced by a report by Qian Xuesen, China's father of rocket technology, that if only the plants could utilize 30 per cent of the solar energy, then wheat production per *mu* could theoretically soar to 40,000 *jin*.[88] For the MA, the alleged triumph was important to score propaganda points. On 27 July, the MA convened a conference at Changge, Henan, on deep ploughing, tool and soil improvement, and demanded that localities immediately begin a campaign of deep ploughing and soil improvement so that all 1,600m. *mu* there could be completed by 1959.[89]

'Tool Reform'

As the initiatives from the centre (large-scale deep ploughing, water conservancy, fertilizer accumulation, etc.) crescendoed to a feverish pitch, activities in rural areas grew exponentially. Numerous new projects were started, but labour shortages were felt everywhere. To a certain extent, the top leaders expected this to happen and their panacea, expressed habitually, was 'tool reform'. This apparent obsession could also be explained by its congruence with Mao's notion of a 'technical revolution'. At the Chengdu conference, Mao had called for a mass campaign in tool reform as part of the 'technical revolution', believing that it would reduce the amount of labour power to a fraction of what would normally be required in agricultural work.[90]

At the Party Congress in May, Liu Shaoqi elaborated on Mao's notion of technological revolution, declaring that all work that could use machinery should do so, and urged the launch of mass movements to 'reform' farm tools and to revolutionarize techniques. In July, Chen Zhengren bragged that peasants in many localities had overcome their 'inferiority complexes' and conservatism, and boldly retooled hundreds of thousands of general farm tools, and irrigation,

---

[87] See also *RMRB*, 23 July 1958.

[88] *Zhongguo Qingnian Bao*, 16 June 1958; *Dang de Wenxian*, 4, 1994, 78; Zhang Suhua, Bian Yanjun, Wu Xiao Mei, *Shuibujin de Mao Zedong* (The inexhaustible topic of Mao Zedong) (Shenyang: Liaoning renmin chubanshe, 1995), 445.

[89] Peng Gangzi and Wu Jinming, *Zhonghua Renmin Gongheguo Nongye Fazhan Shi* (A history of agricultural development in the PRC) (Changsha: Hunan renmin chubanshe, 1998), 736.

[90] *Wansui* (1969), 165. For a discussion of agricultural mechanization from the Maoist perspective, see Benedict Stavis, *The Politics of Agricultural Mechanization in China* (Ithaca, NY: Cornell University Press, 1978), 117–22, and Jack Gray in Stuart Schram (ed.), *Authority, Participation, and Cultural Change in China* (Cambridge: Cambridge University Press, 1973), 139–43.

transportation, and food processing tools, thereby raising productivity by five and six times to over ten times.[91]

However, until August, progress in this campaign was slow, and acute shortages of labour threatened the production quotas. The situation was sufficiently severe that the Central Committee of the CCP and the State Council issued a joint directive on 13 July, ordering the launching of a campaign for the reform of farm implements.[92] The stated goal of this campaign was to deal with the expected bountiful harvest, to ensure that everyone had some leisure time, and to boost morale. Accordingly, the directive ordered that the campaign would replace all old-style farm implements quickly with new and improved ones so that labour efficiency could be doubled and tripled.

This policy became so central in the eyes of the leadership that in just slightly over a month, the Secretariat held two telephone conferences with the secretaries of the provincial party committees in August chaired by Peng Zhen and Tan Zhenlin.[93] At the first conference, Tan invented another new idea by declaring that the 'key link' of the agricultural campaign was now the installation of ball-bearings in all 'revolving tools' like transportation vehicles, pressing machines, water wheels, and the like, so that efficiency could be raised. This, he said, was the hallmark of semi-mechanization. In implementing this initiative, the Party Centre urged that separate battles (seven to ten days each) be launched to concentrate all efforts to fit all transportation vehicles, tools for carrying water, and processing tools with ball-bearings. This kicked off another major national campaign.

Mao followed the campaign with interest. After the first telephone conference, he specifically queried Tan about its progress, and expressed satisfaction with what he heard. Then he contributed more 'important instructions' of his own. Party committees at all levels, he ordered, must have a good idea of the numbers of farm implements to be reformed or to be installed with ball-bearings. Plans should then be drawn up to decide which tools should be reformed first, and which last, and when this could all be accomplished. The leadership would be considered 'strengthened' once all this planning had been done, according to Mao. These were trivialities, but the fact that they were disseminated as 'important instructions' demonstrates the aura surrounding the Chairman, and his paternalistic over-dominance of the policy process.

Following these instructions, the Secretariat again convened another telephone conference with the provincial party committees during which every province reported on their enthusiastic plans for tool reform and the progress made thus far. Some provinces vowed that all 'revolving tools' would be installed with ball-bearings by August or before autumn harvest. By year-end, all the implements in all the provinces would be 'ball-bearingized', and all other tools for capital construction would be 'reformed'. As to the 'mistaken' thinking widespread among the base-level cadres such as 'waiting for mechanization', 'perfection' (the notion that

[91] *Nongcun Gongzuo Tongxun*, 7, 1958, 1–5.   [92] *FGHB*, viii. 236–7.
[93] *RMRB*, 21 August 1958.

the effectiveness of the new inventions should be proven before they were popularized), and 'mystery' (the argument that tool reform was not that simple), the provincial authorities decided to overcome them by strengthening political education.[94] It is clear that grass-roots cadres' apprehension about these simplistic views of tool reform were justified. Most newly invented tools simply did not work, and fitting ball-bearings on moving vehicles did not increase efficiency to the extent hoped for by the leadership. By 1959, Liao Luyan admitted, almost all of these inventions had to be abandoned, and because of the large-scale destruction of tools during communization, old style sickles and cutters remained in common use.[95] Meanwhile, another major central conference unleashed several more campaigns on the entire country.

The Plunge: The Beidaihe Conference (17–30 August 1958)

As mentioned, the Beidaihe Conference was a major turning point for rural and agricultural policies in the GLF. Mao was fully confident that a huge bumper harvest had rendered the grain production problem a thing of the past. In rural policies, the conference called for formation of the people's communes throughout the country, and set agricultural targets for 1959, 1960, and 1962. It also issued five important directives (all on 29 August) on the socialist education movement, water conservancy, deep ploughing and soil improvement, fertilizer, and the elimination of the four pests.[96] The central authorities said and did relatively little about communes openly at this early stage, as formation of communes was assumed to be a more or less spontaneous grass-roots affair supervised by provinces and counties. The problems surrounding communization have already been discussed in Chapter 2, so the following will focus on the other major decisions made at the conference and their impact on the policy process.

On 25 August, the MA reported to the Politburo that grain production for 1958 had exceeded 400m. tons, more than double the 1957 record. Yet even Mao had reservations about this, so to be on the safe side, the communiqué of the Conference trimmed the number to 300–350m. tons, or a 60–90 per cent increase over 1957. On the basis of this the Conference set the 1959 grain target at 400–500m. tons, at 650m. tons for 1960, and 750m. tons for 1962.[97]

For many months since the Third Plenum, the Twelve-Year NPAD had been the guiding document for agricultural development. However, its scope was so broad and comprehensive that it had become rather unwieldy, and it contained no ranking of priorities. Furthermore, fantastic claims about extraordinary harvests in the summer of 1958 had rendered the '4, 5, 8' targets meaningless. Consequently,

[94] *RMRB*, 21 August 1958; *Mao Wengao*, vii. 351.   [95] *Extracts From China Mainland Magazines*, 181: 2.
[96] All these directives are in *FGHB*, viii. 1–16.
[97] Bo Yibo, *Huigu*, ii. 688–9; Zhang Suhua *et al.*, *Shuibujin de Mao Zedong*, 444; *Zhonggong Dangshi Ziliao*, xlvii. 226–8.

as we have observed, the document was pared down to the so-called 'Eight-Point Charter'.

However, even this distillation of the NPAD into eight points was still too imprecise, covering as it did almost all aspects of agricultural work. The introduction of the five directives at Beidaihe appeared to make things more specific, but the one on the launching of a socialist education movement in the countryside was to open up another Pandora's box. All the administrative units were already too overloaded with directives, instructions, and 'overridding tasks' that there was no realistic way to implement even a fraction of them. Of the seventeen issues Mao included for discussion at the first day of the Beidaihe Conference, Mao particularly emphasized deep ploughing, which, he said, was the principal direction for agriculture, as without it large quantities of fertilizer could not be added. Deep ploughing was also the basis for close planting, so in the North the ploughed depth should be 30 cm, whereas in the South, it should be 20 to 23 cm. After three year's hard work, Mao maintained, two-thirds of all farmland could be sufficient to support the population, and one-third could be used for afforestation.[98] In acceding to Mao's wish, the relevant directive puts it this way,

Many large-scale high-yield satellites have sprung up continuously during the agricultural great leap forward this year. This fully proved that deep ploughing is the heart of the technical measure in the increase in agricultural production. The central point of water, fertilizer, soil, good seed variety, close planting is soil [improvement] and that means deep ploughing.[99]

The directive also ordered that deep ploughing be accelerated. Mao and the Politburo arrived at this decision by the following chain of reasoning. Deep ploughing which had been carried out during the spring and summer sowing period, it was claimed, had covered only one-tenth of all farmland. At that rate, it would take more than ten years to complete deep ploughing in the country, but this was incompatible with the demand to raise yield/*mu* by two- to tenfold. So Mao's idea was that *all* farmland should be deep ploughed once within two to three years, and then the cycle would be repeated again. The standard depth laid down was more than 30 cm, and 60 cm for high-yield fields![100] This directive, apart from the decision to double steel output in 1958 and to form communes, was perhaps the most influential, as it was to quickly set in motion a massive campaign involving hundreds of millions of people in the winter/spring of 1958/9.

Meanwhile, other priorities had to be attended to. By early September, the MA seemed relatively satisfied with the 'tool reform campaign' as it declared that 221.7 million pieces (sic) of redesigned farm tools for harvesting, threshing, transplanting, processing, and deep ploughing were in use. In addition, 70 per cent of China's counties (or 1,530) were said to have manufactured 41.5 million sets of ball-bearings and 300,000 workshops had been set up for this purpose. Assuming that the former campaigns had been largely completed, the MA again convened another

---

[98] *Mao Weikan*, ii. 298; *Dangshi Jiliao*, xlvii. 216. See also *Mao Weikan*, xiB. 88.
[99] *FGHB*, viii. 11. See also the editorial in *RMRB*, 2 September 1958.   [100] *FGHB*, viii. 12.

national conference (?–19 September) with delegates from twenty-seven provinces to launch a new mass campaign to popularize cable-drawn ploughs.

A prototype of these ploughs had been picked up by Tan Zhenlin during one of his tours. According to Tan's chain of reasoning, communism resupposed the maximum development of agricultural production, and in the future, yield/*mu* of 10,000 to 50,000 *jin* would be attained. When the yield/*mu* reached 10,000 *jin*, then it would take only 0.3 *mu* to support each individual, and surplus land could be devoted to afforestation and parks. However, a prerequisite was close planting, which in turn required deep ploughing to depths of 30–90 cm. But as the shortage of manpower was acute, he declared that cable-drawn ploughs were the most significant means not only for the acceleration of socialist construction, but also for the gradual transition to communism.

Hence he urged that these ploughs be popularized to all production brigades *within one month*. The manufacturing of them should be carried out immediately after the conference, and each province should allot one such prototype to each county. In turn, the counties should make one available to each APC which was then required to copy them by launching mass campaigns.[101]

It should be noted that this was the second time the Party attempted to impose a farming tool uniformly over the entire country in an attempt to fully mechanize agriculture. As we have observed, the first attempt to introduce the infamous double-wheeled and double-shared ploughs between 1956 and 1957 nationwide had to be aborted, wasting tremendous resources, and Liao's efforts to revive them in February were futile. The cable-drawn ploughs turned out to be a repetition of this fiasco, but the new twist this time was that the grass-roots units were required to manufacture their own, using their own resources. Eventually, many localities tried to comply by making large numbers of these ploughs, but in the face of widespread resistance and/or apathy, this national campaign never really got off the ground, despite a great deal of exhortation and pressure from the centre, and the idea was finally discarded by late 1958.

Meanwhile, after the various national and regional conferences were over, the MA found it fitting to conclude the experience of the Leap for 1958 in an *RMRB* article entitled 'On the Experience of Leading the GLF in Agriculture'.[102] The ministry was so complacent it congratulated itself in September as if the year's work had already been completed and that the GLF in agricultural production was a foregone conclusion.

This sententious article is short on specifics and long on theoretical justifications, but it does reflect the thinking of the leaders in the MA at that time, and how ideology was enlisted to legitimize current policies. For instance, it pointed out that continued launching of the 'two-line struggle' was a main guarantee for a GLF in agriculture. The primary reason why some places had not boosted production was that leaders there were either 'capitalist elements' or 'rightist conservatives'. Only when 'unrelentless struggles were carried out against these leaders resulting

[101] *RMRB*, 20 September 1958.   [102] *RMRB*, 13 October 1958.

in their resignation' [*sic*], had the high tide for production emerged. In addition, the spirit of permanent revolution required that in every week, every ten days, or every half month at the most, a new task must be put forward, a new 'shock attack' must be launched. In general, the ranks of activists who were both red and expert had swollen; in some places they comprised 20 to 30 per cent of the labour force. Experimental plots were said to be the best leadership method because the cadres there had learned to become experts, overcoming the evils of 'subjectivism', coercion, and 'commandism'. Finally, the article praised the five-level inspections involving the provinces, special districts, counties, *xiang*, and cooperatives for promoting work through 'appraisal-through-comparison', and for eliminating 'superficialities'.

The MA had confused ideals with reality. In fact, frequent inspections meant that the control mechanism had become tightened and cadres were under tremendous pressure to report spectacular results, since nay-sayers would be vulnerable to charges of rightism and conservatism. Consequently, many of the most absurd claims of spectacular yields in crops emanated from cadres' 'experimental plots', and this generally fuelled the trend of false reporting and fabrication of statistics.

On the other hand, many goals were never met; in fact, many of the provisions had exactly the opposite effect to that intended. 'Departmentalism' had become rampant, and the mass line of broad consultation in decision-making was a sham. In many instances, outright coercion and 'commandism' had become the norm.[103]

Yet, the MA never wavered from pushing Mao's every preference. Sometime in September, Mao said that it was fundamentally wrong to run agricultural and forestry academies in the cities, as the students should integrate themselves with the peasants in order to 'toil hard' for three years. The MA took this seriously, so between 20 and 30 September it convened a national conference on combining education with labour, and decided that all students and staff of all agricultural academies should be sent into the countryside for labour training. Immediately after the conferences, 47,000 teachers and students from 28 academies were sent to the villages, ranches, and factories as labour.[104]

The Ministry of Agriculture and
the Destruction of the Statistical System

A defining characteristic of the GLF was hyperbolic misinformation for which the politicized MA was largely responsible. In the autumn, it expanded its role

---

[103] As Mao said of the cadres, 'Some people in the rural areas beat up people by the hundreds, and it will not be good not to punish them, because it will affect the people. However, regarding over 95 per cent of cadres, they must be protected.' *Wansui* (1969), 275. On the subject of 'blind command' during the GLF, one economist writes, 'The "communist wind" was also very prevalent, and the democratic management of the collective economy had suffered serious devastation. In some localities, a minority of cadres beat up and abused the peasants and this had become a usual practice. The peasants' personal rights were threatened.' Wang Haibo, *Shehuizhuyi Jingji Wenti Chutan* (A preliminary investigation of the economic problems of socialism) (Changsha: Hunan renmin chubanshe, 1981), 146.

[104] *Nongye Fanzhan Shi*, 737.

further by seizing the function of compiling national agricultural statistics from the State Statistics Bureau. In October, it had already published, in book form, the finalized statistics for 1957 which in turn were not issued by the Statistics Bureau until April 1959.[105] This dealt another fatal blow to a relatively reliable statistical system on agricultural production in China. On 13 October, the MA again took the limelight and announced in three separate communiqués an unprecedented bountiful harvest in early rice, spring wheat, and rapeseed.[106]

These jubilant communiqués reported many spectacularly high yields. These achievements were attributed to the 'brilliance' of the general line of socialist construction, anti-conservatism, hard work, the undaunting spirit against nature, and the success of a variety of 'technical measures' such as early sowing, experimental plots, better deep ploughing, more fertilizer, close planting, field management, and so on. Furthermore, on the basis of these records high yields, the communiqués called for even higher yields per *mu* for 1959.

On the next day, the MA issued another communiqué on the accomplishments of irrigation and water conservation in 1958 which claimed to have created a 'miracle in the history of the world'. It repeated the call for the need to 'battle hard' for another two winters and two springs to bring all farmland under irrigation. Finally, it ordered party committees and governments at all levels to obey these central instructions.[107]

The Last Battle

The jubilation of the MA was premature. Despite estimates of dramatic production increases, the major crops had yet to be collected from the fields and this was what occupied the agricultural policy-makers in the next few months. Three inter-related problems will be considered.

Grain Procurement

The procurement of grain by the government in 1958 was seriously affected by two rather incongruent government policies. First, there was the general belief that the 'grain problem' had been solved once and for all, so peasants were allowed, indeed encouraged, to consume as much as they wished. Second, large quantities of grain were being requisitioned from relatively rich villages, thereby depressing their living standards. As procurement allotment had been calculated on the assumption of an extraordinarily bountiful harvest that did not exist, a violent struggle for grain between the government and the peasants erupted in the autumn.[108] From July to October, procurement of agricultural products was slow

---

[105] Li Choh-ming, *Statistical System*, 89.   [106] *RMRB*, 13 October 1958.
[107] Ibid. and 14 October 1958.
[108] Kenneth Walker, *Food Grain Procurement and Consumption in China* (Cambridge: Cambridge University Press, 1984), 129–46, esp. pp. 139 ff.

and behind schedule. Procured grain was 4.4m. tons less than during the same period in 1957, but sales and exports had gone up. So at the end of October, state grain storage was down by 70 per cent. On 22 October, the Party Centre and the SC issued an emergency instruction demanding the procurement and shipping of agricultural product by 'surprise attack'. In fact, 1958 grain (grain year 1 July 1957 to 30 June 1958) output was up 2.5 per cent to about 200m. tons, but procurement was based on the assumption that there were 300–350m. tons. Actual grain procurement rose 22 per cent, from 48 to 58.75m. tons, and this greatly weakened the fragile rural economy.[109] According to reports by certain central ministries, as early as April 1959, 25 million people in fifteen provinces did not have enough to eat. Vegetables, oil, pork, and other subsidiary foods were also in short supply.[110] Uncollected grain (estimated at 10 per cent of total harvest) and reckless consumption and waste in the communes aggravated the situation.

As late as 17 December, Li Xiannian called for another mobilization campaign for procurement by 'surprise attack'.[111] At the end of October, many localities were pleading with the Centre for grain. In Hubei, for instance, bids for grain came from all over, with the most 'advanced' units most desperate in their entreaties.[112]

Acute Labour Shortages

In addition, labour supply for harvesting was extremely short, as large numbers of peasants had been dragooned to other activities such as iron and steel smelting and water conservancy. Autumn is traditionally the busiest agricultural season since harvesting, autumn ploughing and planting (for winter wheat, for example) all has to be completed in a short period of time. It has been estimated that the volume of work in the autumn of 1958 had been about four times as much as in past years. In many wheat-producing provinces, deep ploughing alone was 60 per cent of all rural work tasks.[113] In October, signs of trouble had already begun to occur—grain-drop and germination were being reported since ripe crops were not always being gathered on time. Likewise, unpicked cotton was being left to the influence of the elements in the fields.[114] The situation had grown so serious that the CC and the State Council issued a joint emergency circular on 7 October demanding immediate action. All localities were ordered to get organized to rush in the harvest on time; labour power was to be reorganized and other non-essential activities were to be postponed. In addition, local leadership was required to conduct inspections to ensure all these measures were properly carried out.[115]

Meanwhile, less than a week after issuing the emergency circular, a 'mammoth' mass campaign for a 'concentrated attack' on the three autumn tasks (harvesting, ploughing, and sowing) involving several tens of millions of people was said to have been unleashed nationally. On 12 October, an *RMRB* editorial rushed to

[109] *Jingji Bianqian*, 321–2; *Dayuejin he Tiaozheng*, 39; *Gongheguo Dadian*, 549. See also *Wansui* (1969), 274, 278.   [110] Bo Yibo, *Huigu*, ii. 714.
[111] Su Donghai and Fang Kongmu, *Fengyun Shilu*, 580.   [112] *NJZWH*, ii. 208.
[113] *RMRB*, 2 September 1958.   [114] Ibid. and 7 October 1958.   [115] Ibid.

proclaim a 'big victory' and claim that most autumn crops, except cotton, potatoes, and rice, were 'basically' harvested.[116] Yet according to the MA's estimate, uncollected potatoes and rice totalled 165m. tons, almost equivalent to the total grain output in 1957.

In the northern provinces, the opening of cotton bolls was almost complete, but the majority of the localities had not yet begun picking. Rain and frost would bring tremendous damage to the cotton crop. Potato crops, on the other hand, would be spoiled if the temperature fell below 8°C. It was absolutely necessary, particularly in October, to collect all potatoes and cotton around Frost Descent (the 18th solar term, falling on 24 October in 1958).

Yet, the Party was ambivalent. On the one hand, it called for an urgent mobilization and an 'all-out concentrated attack' on the autumn tasks. On the other hand, it refused to acknowledge the acute labour shortage, even though it admitted that the iron and steel campaign had crippled agricultural production by siphoning off agricultural labour. The mobilization of the masses, it maintained, could solve all problems. In Henan, it was said that although 6 million people had joined the iron and steel campaign, the three autumn tasks were progressing quickly. As to the other provinces, it was claimed that only a minority of counties were engaged in the iron and steel campaign anyway because not all of them had iron ore. (This is a devious excuse, as the Party knew full well that even provinces and counties with virtually no iron reserves had been ordered to join the 'all people smelt iron and steel campaign'). Estimates from the provinces, it argued, indicated that only one-third of all rural labour power was engaging in the iron and steel campaign, the remaining two-thirds were still occupied in agricultural production. In any event, it maintained, urban residents, government employees, workers' families, and students should make up for any labour deficiency. Clearly, in the face of a crisis, the Party was unwilling to make the choice of cutting back the number of peasants taken away for iron and steel production. Instead, it decided to pin its hope (unrealistically) on the mobilization of urban residents to replace the rural work force. However, the many problems associated with this venture, such as the logistics of transporting large numbers of people to the remote villages, were never addressed. The next chapter on Guangdong will examine how this decision was implemented, though in vain.

Deterioration in the Situation in the Communes

At the initial stage of communization in early September, Tan Zhenlin reassured Mao with a rosy report that claimed that communes had been formed rapidly and smoothly, and that only in a minority of places had the peasants resorted to slaughtering and selling of livestock, felling trees, and grain concealment.[117] However, an anonymous letter dated 5 September reached Mao in early October informing him that food shortages at several *xiang* in Anhui had killed over 500 people, and that many had become ill. The food shortages were attributed

---

[116] *RMRB*, 2 September 1958, 7 October 1958, and 12 October 1958.   [117] *Mao Wengao*, vii. 402–3.

to natural calamities, false-reporting, and administrative commands which forced the conversion of dry land into rice paddies.[118] As discussed in Chapter 2, Mao had single-handedly imposed the communes by following his instincts. The communes radically transformed rural economic organization and ways of life but were introduced hastily and virtually without advanced testing and preparation. Consequently, the countryside was plunged into chaos, as organization and incentives problems plagued the campaign from the start. As previously mentioned, only by October/November did Mao begin to realize the full effects of the 'communist winds' and the universal concealment of grain and slaughter of livestock among the peasants.[119] Coercive grass-roots cadres who exaggerated reports of yields had led to high procurement, which in turn deprived the peasants of grain, leading to deaths. Mao's confidence began to be shaken, but he still cherished the utopian ideal.

By winter 1958, some mess halls in the communes had run out of food, leading to outward migration, oedema, and abnormal deaths. Peasants were fleeing, begging, and battling for food. By early 1959, spring famine had already occurred, and many provinces affected, especially Shandong, Anhui, Hubei, Gansu, and Yunnan, were short of grain. Peasants plundered for food and those running away increased. Yet, the 20 million peasants that had been recruited into the cities in 1958 (30 million during the entire Leap) had to be provided for.[120] But China had just begun to experience the incredible hardships of the 1958–60 calamity, and even in June 1959, Mao thought that the food shortage problem was restricted to only a few provinces, and transfers from the centre or from other provinces would take care of the problem.[121] Meanwhile, at the Zhengzhou and Wuchang Conferences in November/December, Mao initiated a tactical retreat from the communes, and the Chairman's contradictions between utopian ideals and practical concerns would determine the zig-zag path of the communes for the next two decades. Back in 1958, before Mao made the authoritative decision, there was nothing the other leaders could do.

The Decision to Reduce the Sown Acreage in the Autumn of 1958

Meanwhile, another disastrous decision—the 'three-three' system—illustrates the impulsive and haphazard manner by which a general idea and long-term aspiration of Mao's could be snowballed into a major national policy. Many zealots, in particular Mao's lieutenant, Tan, vied eagerly in giving it substance. There was little planning or consideration of alternatives, fervour and intuition alone guiding all the decisions. In October and early November, a series of regional conferences were convened to discuss the plans for 1959 agricultural production, leading to a

---

[118] Ibid. 436; *Dangde Wenxian*, 4, 1994, 80.   [119] See also, *Mao Weikan*, xiB. 163–5.
[120] *Dangde Wenxian*, 3, 1995, 25; 4, 41; Li Rui, *Lushan Huiyi*, 13, 22, 113; Zhang Suhua *et al.*, *Shuibujin de Mao*, 445.   [121] *Dangde Wenxian*, 4, 1995, 44.

far-reaching decision to reduce the cultivated acreage for 1959 summer crops, which contributed greatly to the serious food shortages and famine in 1959. The earliest articulation of what turned into the 'three-three' system can be found in Mao's speech made at the Third Plenum in October 1957. He said:

In my opinion, China must depend on intensive cultivation to feed itself. One day China will become the world's number one high-yield country. Some of our counties are already producing one thousand *jin* per *mu*. Will it be possible to reach two thousand *jin* per *mu* in half a century? . . . we depend on intensive cultivation to feed ourselves, and even with a fairly large population we still have enough food. I think an average of three *mu* of land per person is more than enough and in future less than one *mu* will yield enough grain to feed one individual'.[122]

Mao was toying with the idea that high yields per unit would make the shrinking of the cultivated acreage possible in the future. Yet this was a tentative idea, because the much-heralded NPAD (revised draft) was ambiguous on this point. Article 4 called for intensive cultivation (*jinggeng xizuo)*, literally intensive and meticulous farming, but in the same breath, urged not only the reclamation of waste land and the expansion of cultivated areas, but the full utilization of ridges dividing fields, pool sides, ditch sides, and so on. (Article 16)[123]

In the spring and summer of 1958, the issue of reducing the cultivated areas received little attention. Liu Shaoqi's keynote speech at the Party Congress did not mention it. Yet, in the summer, Mao was convinced that a huge bumper harvest had finally created the preconditions for the 'three-three' system.[124] In September, extra high-yield 'satellites' were reported to have been mushrooming all over the country.[125] During his inspection tour to Jiangsu between 19 and 28 September, Liu Shaoqi was briefed by county party secretaries at Hebei and Henan who maintained that 'to plant little and reap more' was more 'economical' than 'extensive cultivation and reap less'. They said, in a few years' time, one-third of all farmland could be devoted to grain production, another one-third for planting trees, and the last one-third for fallowing. Apparently, Liu took this all in, and concluded that this was a 'fundamental principle in agronomy', thus putting his stamp of approval on the practice.[126]

At about the same time (10–29 September), Deng Xiaoping, Li Fuchun, and other top leaders inspected the Northeastern provinces (Liaoning, Jilin, and Heilongjiang) which were said to be lagging behind other provinces in agricultural production as *only* a production increase of 20–40 per cent was achieved. According to Deng's diagnosis, these provinces had fallen behind because their leaders had

---

[122] Mao, *Xuanji*, v. 469.   [123] *RMSC*, 1958, 504–5.

[124] Zhang Suhua et al., *Shuibujin de Mao Zedong*, 444.

[125] For example, *RMRB*, 23 September 1958. In 1957, only a few *mu* of wheat and rice were reported to have achieved 1,000 *jin/mu*. But in the GLF of 1958, grossly exaggerated reports claimed that there were over a million *mu* of wheat which yielded 1,000 to more than 8,000 *jin* of wheat per *mu*. Many so-called 'satellites' of high-yield rice reached the fairy-tale proportions by bragging outputs per *mu* of 10,000 and several tens of thousand *jin*. Propaganda also claimed that there were four '1,000-*jin*' winter-wheat provinces (i.e. provinces with average yield/*mu* of 1,000 *jin*), and many 1,000-*jin* counties and special districts.   [126] *RMRB*, 30 September 1958; *BR*, 32, 1958, 5.

not implemented Mao's 'eight-point charter'; instead, they were said to have followed the 'same old stuff' of 'wide spacing and shallow ploughing' and 'extensive cultivation and reap less', a 'reformist' leadership method. Since 'reformism' was incompatible with the GLF, Deng urged that a 'revolutionary campaign' be launched in agriculture.

At the Happiness and Rising Sun communes, Deng went a step further and instructed that they should experiment with high yields, and reduce the present cultivated areas so that all efforts could be concentrated on close planting and raising the output/*mu*. This, he maintained, would increase grain production, allowing the remaining area of land for fallowing or afforestation.[127] All of these paved the way for a formal decision to reduce the cultivated farmland, as we shall see later on.

Meanwhile, problems arising from the formation of the communes were discussed formally for the first time at the Agricultural Coordination Conference For North and North-East China, Xian, 10–18 October, attended by Tan Zhenlin, Li Xiannian, Liao Luyan, An Ziwen, Liu Ruilong, Chen Zhengren, Li Xiebo, secretaries of the PPCs, and the provincial directors of all Rural Work Departments and agricultural bureaus. The Conference covered a wide range of subjects, including the principle of production, labour organization, distribution, the supply system, social welfare, and the decentralization of finance, grain, and commerce departments below the counties. The Conference also decided to launch a campaign to create 'satellites' of extensive areas of high-yield fields, occupying about 10 per cent of all cultivated areas in all the provinces concerned. The concrete ratio would be determined by the provinces themselves.[128] This was another spur toward the reduction of cultivated land.

Shortly after the Conference, many counties from Hebei, Shanxi, Shaanxi, and Shandong were said to have sprung into action. These localities, led by the county or special district party committees, had designated certain pieces of farmland as 'high-yield satellite fields' and lavished large quantities of manpower and resources on them. Changzhi Special District in Shanxi jumped quickly into action, and 1.6m. *mu* of infertile, hillside, and small-terraced land out of a total farmland of 8.6m. *mu* were either retired for afforestation or used for extensive cultivation of subsidiary crops. The remaining 7m. *mu* of 'basic farmlands' were divided as follows: 1m. *mu* economic crops and vegetables; 6m *mu* basic farmlands (3m. *mu* of 'totally intensive fields', expected to yield 5,000 *jin/mu*, and 3m. *mu* of 'generally intensive fields', expected to yield 2,000 *jin/mu*).

In this way, total grain produced for 1959 was expected to reach 10.5m. tons, more than six times the 1.65m. tons estimated for 1958, and exceeding the total grain production of Shanxi province in the same year. This was clearly wishful thinking. However, as soon as the decision was made at Changzhi, other copycats promptly arranged to reduce the cultivated area, having assumed that production

[127] *RMRB*, 1 October 1958; *BR*, 35, 1958, 4.   [128] *RMRB*, 20 October 1958; *BR*, 35, 1958, 4.

in the 'extra high-yield fields' alone was sufficient to support the local population. Extremely intensive work, combined with irrigation, huge amounts of fertilizer, deep ploughing (ranging from 33 cm to 300 cm [*sic*]), and extremely close planting was said to make an average projected yield of 3,000 to 5,000 *jin* of wheat per *mu* 'perfectly possible', and the highest goal was 20,000 *jin* per *mu*.[129] Again, as we have mentioned before, these fantastic figures cannot possibly be accepted at face value, but they do give a rough indication of the calculations of these people. What is more important, many people did accept these figures and much 'planning' was done on this basis.

Accordingly, the Party hailed this in an *RMRB* editorial as a 'revolutionary' measure and the 'route' which all localities must travel in developing agriculture. As to the sceptical view held by some people that 'extra high-yield on a small plot of land was conceivable, but impossible for a large tract of farmland', the Party replied with the simple argument that 'largeness was developed from smallness' and 'what was small today could develop into something large tomorrow', completely dodging the problem of transferability. The Party admitted some difficulties might arise at the beginning, but maintained that they could be solved by the ability of the communes to organize large-scale labour power and by the reform in farm implements. It fact, it was argued, the exercise itself in the long run was the solution to the problem of inadequate labour supply because with reliable 'extra high-yield' fields, the total farmland could be cut back, releasing agricultural labour into other pursuits. Hence, the major advantage of these 'extra high-yield' fields, in comparison with the ordinary pattern of farming, was said to be the net saving in labour power.[130] So far all this talk about 'extra high-yield' fields was preparation for the ultimate and *future* goal of fulfilling the 'three-three' system. But in a little less than a fortnight, a New China News Agency report claimed that in Shanxi province, the farmland had *already* been reduced by 45 per cent but per *mu* yield had quadrupled, creating a record yield of more than 130 per cent more than 1956. This province was also said to be the first in converting non-fertile land ('mostly slopes with serious soil erosion') into forests, orchards, or plots for growing fodder. In view of this, the province planned to cut back another third of its farmland in 1959 but to increase grain output by two and a half to threefold. Henceforth, concentrated effort could be lavished on only about 20 per cent of the total cultivated land, and if the said targets had been achieved, further reduction of farmland would be effected. In other words, Shanxi was said to have put the 'three-three' system in practice in 1958![131]

To prove the correctness of this policy, the Party published a report from Shouchang county (Shandong) to publicize its claim that per *mu* output of maize was raised seven to sixteen times by adding three times more labour. In other cases, the provinces of Neimenggu and Qinghai, in anticipation of dramatic increases in output, planned to reduce their farm acreage by 21 per cent as well.[132] In late

[129] *RMRB*, 24 October 1958.   [130] Ibid.
[131] *SCMP*, no. 1893, 22–3; no. 1903, 23–4.   [132] *SCMP*, no. 1893, 22–3.

October and November, national leaders Tan Zhenlin, Chen Zhengren, and Liao Luyan attended three more regional conferences to discuss rural and agricultural issues.[133] Egged on by recent developments, they decided to promulgate the new policy of 'plant less, high yield, and reap more' *nationally*, and all the participating provinces were urged to implement this as early as 1959. The 'unprecedented harvests' which had doubled grain output in 1958 were assumed, and after some obligatory accounting of achievements, the provinces were asked to map out plans for implementation. The six-province conference, attended by Liao, decided to divide farmland into three types, the satellite, the extra high-yield, and ordinary fields, and turn 10–30 per cent (in Fujian, 50 per cent) into the second category. In the five-province conference attended by Chen, it was decided to concentrate labour and resources in the extra high-yield satellites comprising only 10–15 per cent of all farmland. On the other hand, infertile, eroded and dry, low-yield land was to be abandoned.

At the South China conference, Tan asserted that only with the introduction of this high-yield 'basic farmland' could large quantities of labour be redirected to develop industry and diversified farming. It would also accelerate rural mechanization and electrification because the equipment would be more concentrated, making the systematic application of the 'eight-point charter' easier. More importantly, Tan asserted, the resultant increase in production would make the elimination of the three big differences (between the cities and the rural areas, the workers and peasants, and between mental and manual labor) and the transition to communism possible.[134]

The first retreat from the communes did not bring about a corresponding change in the policy of high yield farmland. In fact, the resolution on the communes decided in the Sixth Plenum (28 November–10 December) reaffirmed it.[135] Consequently, the total sown acreage for 1959 was reduced nationally by 7.26m. hectares (or 110m. *mu*) compared with 1958. Assuming that the average yield per *mu* was 250 *jin* (Liao's 'conservative' estimate), 13.75m. tons less grain were produced. This would have meant a reduction of 50 *jin* of grain for every peasant, man, woman, and child in China, assuming that the peasant population was 500 million. Since the actual total grain production for 1959 was only 170m. tons (a 15 per cent decline from the 1958 level), this man-made policy error was another major reason for the widespread food shortages and starvation in many areas that began in 1959. Indeed, there were other contributing factors, such as widespread natural calamities and mismanagement associated with the policies of deep ploughing, close planting, and water conservation, but some argue that the shrinkage of the cultivated acreage was the most decisive.[136]

---

[133] *RMRB*, 10, 12 November 1958. They were the South China Agricultural Coordination Conference, Guangzhou, 27 October–4 November; the Five Province Autumn Agricultural Coordination Conference, Hohhot Shi, 27 October–4 November; and the Six Provinces (municipality) Autumn Agricultural Coordination Conference, 27 October–5 November.   [134] Ibid.
[135] *RMRB*, 19 December 1958.   [136] Kenneth Walker, *Food Grain Procurement*, 146–9.

In the ebullient atmosphere in the autumn of 1958, few could foresee the serious implication of this policy. But by early 1959, even Mao smelled danger, and sought to reverse the policy in a secret Party directive issued on 29 April 1959:

The 'small acreage and higher yield' plan is a long-range plan and is realizable, but cannot be realized wholly or in greater part within the next ten years. It can only be realized step by step within the next ten years, depending on conditions. Within three years, we should strive to sow *more* [emphasis mine]. The guiding principle for several years at present is simultaneously to expand small-yield acreage and to tend high-yield plots marked by a smaller acreage and bigger yield.[137]

Undoubtedly, the timetable of ten years was one of those random numbers which Mao pulled out of thin air from time to time, but his decision to backtrack came too late. Liao, sensing the shift of the wind, was emboldened to discuss the problem in the open.[138] Yet, serious loss in the summer crops for 1959 was irreversible. Moreover, the sowing of early rice, maize, millet, gaoliang, cotton, peanuts, soybeans, and hemp was not satisfactory in some areas. To rectify this situation Liao prescribed in 1959 some rather drastic remedial measures. All localities were ordered to revise their cultivation plans, and all 'small plots on land borders, along the roads and dykes, and near villages' (*sic*) were ordered to be planted if possible. For plots not suitable for collective farming, Liao went as far as to urge that they be cultivated by commune members, who in turn would be allowed to own the crops thus produced.[139]

The Three Autumn Tasks in November and Goal Conflict

Returning to November 1958, the need to attend to the heavy agricultural work had already become urgent, but the Party was still unwilling to face reality. According to an *RMRB* editorial (6 November), large quantities of cotton and potato crops were still not collected. Those collected were being left piled up in the fields and were not being shipped back to the communes because of the shortage of transportation vehicles, most of which had been diverted to the iron and steel campaign. Harvesting at some places was done sloppily as crops were scattered in the fields.[140] However, in the opinion of the Party, this need not be the case, because it argued that in places where the masses were thoroughly mobilized, their enthusiasm was so high that both iron and steel and harvesting were being done well. At the Hongqi commune, for instance, 11,000 farmers (out of a total of 24,000) were recruited into the iron and steel and the water conservancy campaigns (9,000 and 2,000 people respectively). The party committee was said to have mobilized women, children, old people, and urban dwellers, and used the method of 'trading the weak for the strong' to draw labour from the mess halls after much

---

[137] Kenneth Walker, *Food Grain Procurement*, 3; *Wansui* (1969), 293.   [138] *SCMM*, no. 181, 2–3.
[139] Ibid.   [140] *RMRB*, 6 November 1958.

'blooming and contending'. A nearby iron and steel army also used its intervals to help out.

The *RMRB* claimed all this had not only reversed the 'passive thinking' that the situation was 'an awful mess' and that harvesting could never be completed, it had actually led to the victorious conclusion of harvesting amidst the 'tense' iron and steel campaign, making the commune number one, in terms of speed and quality, in the county. One must take the outcome of this model with a grain of salt, but the story is indicative of the proportion of labourers being transferred to iron and steel production, and the desperate need to mobilize even children and old people for harvesting. Yet, it was doubtful if these people would ever be able to replace the regular agricultural labourers.

In fact, despite stubborn references to models like the one above to defend the iron and steel campaign, the Party now realized that labour must be reorganized if the harvest was to be collected. Hence the same editorial endorsed, for the first time, the 'immediate' transfer of manpower from iron and steel production back to agricultural production. At Yulin Special District, Guangxi, it was said, the majority of peasants were transferred back to autumn harvest after a 'great victory' on the iron and steel front. For the provinces, this could be an unmistakable cue to abandon iron and steel production if a 'victory' could be claimed.

Beyond this, 'second harvests' were launched in localities where large portions of the harvest had been left in the fields or at the roadside. Therefore in Shanxi 'second harvest armies' or 'teams for picking grain' comprised of women, children, and old folks (1 million strong) were said to have picked up the crops ear by ear, grain by grain, and recovered 600,000 tons of grain. However, some cadres complained that the various work tasks were so overwhelming that crude collecting and threshing was inevitable; others were disgruntled about having to reap throughout the night. Predictably, the Party criticized this kind of utterance, and its solution was to order all Party and government leaders to tighten their inspection and supervision of the campaign.[141]

By 9 November, according to the MA, still only 70 per cent of all cotton had been harvested, and the rest was beginning to rot. This situation was sufficiently serious that the MA demanded all cotton producing-areas launch 'shock attacks' to rush in the cotton in the next ten days or so, branding this as a 'most urgent' task. Nevertheless, the leadership of the MA was still reluctant to return manpower from iron and steel production to agricultural pursuits, although this had been approved by the Party. Instead, a 'responsible person' of the MA urged the emulation of the experience of the Shulu county (Hebei). This county had allegedly organized *all* its young and strong labourers into iron and steel and deep ploughing armies, leaving only the old, the weak, and the semi-able ones in the autumn-harvest army. From among the latter group, a hundred thousand people were assigned the special task of picking cotton, and it was said that this had greatly accelerated the reaping of cotton. Apart from this recommendation, the ministry also urged the widespread

---

[141] Ibid.

mobilization of all available hands from grass-roots level commerce departments, schools, urban residents, and government employees into large 'armies' to engage in 'shock attacks' for a few days. To promote enthusiasm, competitions for 'picking satellites' were ordered to be carried out among communes and brigades.

These were hackneyed solutions, especially in view of the persistent labour shortage in the countryside and the sagging morale in the communes. On the other hand, the behaviour of the MA is puzzling. One plausible explanation is that since the iron and steel campaign was so central in the eyes of Mao, the MA did not want to appear too anxious to negate it without exhausting other options. In any case, the MA did not appear to have significant institutional interests to defend, and its loyalty to the national leadership and to the Maoist vision seemed to be the paramount concern.

By the second week of November, autumn harvest was still largely incomplete even though the 'last hectic stage' had approached.[142] Although some provinces claimed that the harvesting of certain crops was 'basically completed', only 20 per cent of the task had been completed in many others. But even in the former, second harvest and threshing campaigns had to be launched in order to recover uncollected crops. In reaction to this and perhaps taking their cue from the centre, many localities were said to have begun releasing part of the labour force in iron and steel production and other activities (such as deep ploughing) into autumn harvest.

Meanwhile, on 13 November, the MA issued more instructions in an *RMRB* article. It 'pointed out' that the harvesting and threshing work was still crude and second harvests were urgently needed. In some areas, 40–60 per cent of the crops had not yet been threshed. Large quantities of cotton with open bolls had not been picked. A portion of sweet potato had not been dug out and those harvested were rotting because they had not been processed. This problem, it urged, must be taken seriously, especially in the north where it was getting cold. The localities should, in its opinion, mobilize all possible energy to rush through the harvest, threshing, and storage work in order to avoid or minimize loss.

All of this was rather repetitious, except for the fact that the report also mentioned localities which, 'having taken as a premise the completion of the iron and steel production', had transferred labour power from the iron and steel front back to harvesting. Even manpower distribution for the three autumn tasks were reorganized; for instance, the MA claimed that in Guangdong, the 4 million people originally assigned to deep ploughing were cut by half so that the harvest could be rushed in by 'shock attacks'. This could be construed that the MA, after some initial hesitation, had finally acceded to the need to reduce the manpower assigned for iron and steel production and deep ploughing.

Very little was heard about the autumn harvest after November, although much evidence suggests that it was far from being a success. In fact, according to a

---

[142] *RMRB*, 6 November 1958, and 13 November 1958.

speech made by the Deputy Minister of Agriculture in January 1959: 'Last year, a rich harvest of wheat was in sight but incessant rainfall caused heavy losses due to germination and mildew. The loss of crops was also great on account of crude harvesting.'[143]

Overall, some sources estimated that uncollected crops were equivalent to about 10 per cent of the total production of 1958.[144] As Bo Yibo had observed, the ratios of those who engaged in agriculture and those in industry was 13.8 : 1 in 1957, but declined sharply to 3.5 : 1 in 1958.[145] In January 1959, a report in the *RMRB* appealed for another autumn harvest by lauding some communes which had allegedly engaged in 'second and even third autumn harvests'. A commune in Fujian was said to have collected 250 tons of sweet potatoes this way. Hebei province had only recently launched a campaign to collect cotton remaining on the plants. In this way, 15 tons of ginned cotton was recovered by two special districts alone.

The *RMRB* admitted that there was an acute shortage in labour, but maintained that the assigned production tasks could still be accomplished if manpower was reorganized by using the work method of 'walking on two legs', better planning, and the avoidance of 'attending to one thing and losing sight of another'.[146] This kind of cant dressed up as advice had by this time became so expendable that it was doubtful if it could ever motivate the peasants for another harvest again.

Another report also described the abandonment and rotting of grain, as well as confused accounting procedures and practices, but it still tried to dodge the real issues by blaming this on the cadres who were said to have held the attitude that since there was a bumper harvest, some waste was unimportant. Finally in May 1959, in its discussion of the nature of the communes, the Party attributed the fiasco to the erosion of incentives:

... in last year's 'battles with large armies,' there was the phenomenon of serious waste as a result of sloppy harvest ... the major reason was that many people's communes had not persisted in the principle of 'distribution according to labour'. Another reason was that a strict responsibility system had not been formed. Whether reaping was done carefully or sloppily was treated the same. This naturally dampened the enthusiasm and the sense of responsibility of some commune members.[147]

This evaluation contains a small grain of truth although it was hardly the full picture. Sloppy harvesting had been aggravated by other factors. For example, in some places cadres insisted on shooting 'autumn harvest satellites'—harvesting of ripe crops was intentionally delayed until other fields were ripe so that huge quantities could be reported together.[148] At this point, the Party was still refusing to acknowledge the misadventure of the iron and steel campaign and its responsibility for the debacle.

---

[143] *RMRB*, 17 May 1959.   [144] Chu Han, *Sannian Ziran Zaihai*, 115.
[145] Bo Yibo, *Huigu*, ii. 714.
[146] Ibid.; *RMRB*, 15 January and 13 May 1959. See also *NJZWH*, ii. 136.
[147] Ibid., and *RMRB*, 17 May 1959, in *XHBYK*, 11, 1959, 115.   [148] *NJZWH*, ii. 208.

The Aftermath: The First Zhengzhou Conference (2–10 November) and the Sixth Plenum (28 November–10 December)

In late 1958, the national leaders finally had to review the year's work. As discussed in Chapter 2, between November and early December, Mao convened three important meetings to deal with the problems of the GLF and the formation of the communes. Yet Mao was ambiguous and contradictory. Although he wanted to tone things down and try to rectify the communes, he was ready to forge ahead on other fronts. At the First Zhengzhou Conference,[149] Mao made several speeches redefining ideology and the 'current tasks', and emphasizing a 'go-slow' and cautious attitude in the structuring of the communes. Now he put forward a 'revolution by stage' theory (in contrast with the theory of 'permanent revolution') represented by the notion of the 'two transitions'. He then declared that the communes should practise collective ownership, not all-people ownership. Even if the latter had been introduced, it still did not mean that communism had arrived, as was made clear by the above demarcations. In this regard, the principle of 'to each according to his labour' still applied as a distribution principle, as well as the ideas of commodity production and exchange, and exchange at equal value.

In practical terms, Mao now tried to dispel the prevalent idea, somewhat encouraged by him previously, that communes meant the arrival of communism. More urgent concerns were to come first, to put a halt to the indiscriminate transfer of produce and property from the communes without compensation (Mao said this amounted to the 'exploitation' of the peasants). Another effort by Mao was to reverse the decisions practised in some communes to eliminate commodity exchange (the trading of economic crops) in the belief that such exchanges constituted capitalism and that the communes should be self-sufficient units (one major characteristic of the commune was said to be its combination of the functions of agriculture, industry, commerce, education, and the militia all in itself). Such decisions, according to Mao, had rendered many counties unable to issue wages (because of the lack of cash income) after the free food supply system was introduced.[150]

As Mao made clear his second thoughts on the communes at Zhengzhou, Tan and Liao began to shift gear accordingly. In their report to Mao (16 November) which was approved as new policy for provincial authorities, they stated that:

- The 'three-three' system should be affirmed, although it should be implemented step by step. It would be too risky to reduce winter planting in 1958 and spring planting in 1959. Only when wheat, early rice, and other subsidiary grain had been harvested, then acreages for summer planting and late rice could be considered.

---

[149] Mao's talks in these conferences are in *Wansui* (1969), 247–68; *Mao Weikan*, xiB. 110–27; xiii. 173–95.

[150] *Wansui* (1969), 249. For a detailed account, see *Mao Zedong de Zuji*, 482–90.

- The 'three-three' system should not be applied uniformly; for instance, in highly populated areas, the emphasis was to raise output first, then reduce the number of crops per year, but not to shrink the cultivated farmland.
- Grain and cotton production had doubled in 1958, but other subsidiary agricultural products had not increased and had even decreased.
- The smelting of iron and steel by communes was mainly a losing proposition incurring large expenditure, and used up too much unpaid labour. Cash had become so short, some were even unable to pay out any wages.
- The scale of water conservancy for the winter of 1958/9 was estimated at three times larger than that of the previous year, and must be reduced as it would require 120 million people to contribute 100 days of work. The scale of water conservancy should be trimmed back to the 1957/8 level.
- Large numbers of problems in the communes must be dealt with in the next few months.

On the other hand, Tan and Liao still insisted that, despite the many false reports, a realistic estimate of 1958 output was 475m. tons, or at least no less than 375m. tons (or double the 1957 output) and advised that the latter figure be made public. They recommended that the grain target for 1959 be set at 525m. tons. The more sensible Chen Yun disagreed with publishing the 375m. tons figure, and told Hu Qiaomu, but Hu dared not pass this on to Mao.[151]

The Wuchang Politburo Conference (21–7 November) transmitted the decisions made at Zhengzhou and prepared for the Sixth Plenum. As Mao now decided to rein in the bravado he encouraged previously he was ready to swallow some pride and make an implicit self-criticism. The 1959 plan, which was on the table, had to be revised because the projections at Beidaihe were too optimistic. The steel target was reduced, and consequently all the other industrial targets as well. On the other hand, Mao had not cooled down with the super harvest, and the 1959 targets was set at 525m. tons, higher than the 400–500m. tons mooted at Beidaihe. The Sixth Plenum, which met between 28 November and 10 December, took a first step toward overhauling the communes by deciding on a major policy document, the 'Resolution of Some Questions Concerning the People's Communes'. This repeated the theory of the 'two transitions' as the ideological basis for slowing down the changes in communization and reaffirmed all the other decisions made at Zhengzhou. It also specified that 'means of livelihood' like houses, clothes, furniture, and savings should forever belong to individual commune members. It also ruled that these members could retain the trees around the houses, small farm implements, and small domestic animals, and could engage in sideline occupations. The 'three-three' system was affirmed, although its implementation was to be extended to a number (unspecified) of years and according to local conditions.

---

[151] *NJZWH*, ii. 104–9; Zhonggong Zhongyang Wenxian Yanjiushi, *Jianguo Yilai Zhongyao Wenxian Xuanbian* (A selection of important documents since the founding of the state) (Beijing: Zhongyang wenxian chubanshe, 1995), ii. 585–93; *Mao Wengao*, vii. 539–45; Li Rui, *Lushan Huiyi*, 37; Ye Yonglie, *Hu Qiaomu* (Beijing: Zhonggong Zhongyang Dangxiao chubanshe, 1994), 130–1.

Finally, it ordered that a movement to rectify the communes be carried out during the winter and spring of 1958/9.[152]

This was a first major step toward a retreat from the communes, although a number of pertinent problems were not addressed. The first was 'egalitarianism' within the communes, as agricultural products and property within the original APCs (some of them were more well-to-do than others) were pooled together, regardless of relative prosperity before amalgamation. Predictably, better-off APCs resented this levelling and would hide grain and slaughter farm animals which they feared would be confiscated.

Second, the Conference simply accepted the inflated grain and cotton estimates for 1958 and procurement on this basis would create tremendous resistance in the countryside. A third problem was the unchecked consumption of grain under the approved policy of 'eating rice without pay' or the free food-supply system. Since the actual amount of grain produced in 1958 was only a few percentage points more than 1957, much of the grain consumed came from reserves built up over the previous few years. This was to be largely responsible for the inability to provide relief in the famines in 1959 and 1960.[153]

A Pyrrhic Victory

The proceedings of the Zhengzhou and Wuchang conferences, and the Sixth Plenum were kept secret at the time, so the propaganda for the GLF continued. Between 23 December 1958 and 1 January 1959, the National Conference of Representatives of the Advanced Units of Socialist Agricultural Construction was held to celebrate 'victory' and 'great achievements' in agriculture in the GLF of 1958. However, because no new policy initiatives emanated from it, it was largely ritualistic, merely a 'public relations' gathering to swear loyal implementation of central policies. Six thousand delegates attended, representing counties or municipalities which had either overtaken the production targets of the NPAD with one year, or had basically eliminated flood or droughts. It is clear now that these 'advanced units' were mostly zealots and braggarts, but they were at that time commended with certificates of merits and souvenirs.[154]

Deng Zihui gave the opening speech, followed by speeches by Liu Shaoqi, Zhou Enlai, and Li Xiannian, among others. Deng, the cautious pragmatist who dared to disagree with Mao on collectivization in the past, now rhapsodized about the various aspects of the GLF, touting the 1958 and 1959 grain targets, the communes,

---

[152] *RMRB*, 19 December 1958.

[153] Luo Gengmo, *Jingji Yanjiu* (Economic research), 2, 1981, 42.

[154] *Dangshi Tongxun*, 11, 1987, 18–19. On the prevalence of fake achievements, Zhou Enlai said in 1962, 'In the past few years, I have participated in many large conferences and handed out many certificates of merit. If the deeds being commended are phoney, you should throw your certificates away.' *Selected Works*, ii. 350

the 'eight-point' charter, the 'three-three' system, and so on.[155] Liao reported on agriculture and merely parroted the official line and statistics.[156]

The Conference declared unprecedented harvests and achievements in agriculture, forestry, non-staple foods, and fisheries in 1958. Since the statistical system was no longer functioning, the statistics were provided by Tan and Liao and the targets for grain and cotton contained in the NPAD were said to have been accomplished nine years ahead of time. Grain and cotton production were stated to be 375m. and 3.35m. tons respectively, more than double the 1957 output.[157]

The 1959 targets for grain and cotton were set at 525m. and 5m. tons respectively. The ratio of increase (40 per cent and 49.25 per cent respectively) was set *low* (*sic*), Liao said, so that manpower could also be channelled to the production of other subsidiary crops such as oil crops, hemp (flax), and other industrial raw materials. It would also enable the masses to have some leeway to over-fulfil the targets which, he hastened to add, were still 'leap forward' targets.

In the section on the people's communes, Liao elaborated upon the 'Resolutions on Certain Problems Regarding the People's Communes',[158] maintaining that the system of ownership in the communes was still collective, although there were certain elements of 'all-people ownership'. The communes were still socialist and the current task was to build socialism, not communism. Hence, the communes must continue to develop commodity production (for exchange) and maintain the distribution principle of 'to each according to his labour'.

Apart from production, Liao maintained, the communes must pay attention to the livelihood of their members—to ensure sufficient sleeping and resting time and good food supply, and to run the mess halls and nurseries well. In 1959, the campaign for extra high-yield fields would be launched; the 'eight-point charter' must be carried out, and the practice of shallow ploughing and extensive cultivation would be changed to deep ploughing and intensive farming. When the campaign for 'large areas of extra high-yield fields' became successful, it would have laid the foundation for reducing agricultural farmland to only about one-third its original area, so that Mao's ideal of 'turning the entire country into a garden' could be realized. Finally, Liao urged the leadership to strengthen itself and to employ realistic work methods. Liao's speech was merely a rehash of decisions made in the Resolution.[159] Presumably these representatives of 'advanced units'

---

[155] *RMRB*, 26 December 1958. Whether Deng was speaking his mind is of course, a moot point.

[156] *RMRB*, 27 December 1958. For a description of the Conference and a selection of some of the speeches delivered, see *RMSC*, 1959, 437–45. For Deng's encounters with Mao, see Teiwes and Sun (1993), 'Introduction' Some of the texts are in *RMSC*, 1959, 438–40.

[157] Tan and Liao's report to the Party Centre is in *NJZWH*, ii. 104–9. Their private estimates of grain and cotton produced in 1958 were much higher, at 475 and 4.25m. tons, respectively. In June 1959, internal knowledge was 225m. tons. *Dang de Wenxian*, 4, 1995, 37. A more sober estimate is 200m. tons of grain and 1.96m. tons of cotton. This means that the production increase over 1957 were only 2.53 per cent and 20 per cent, respectively. See *Zhongguo Tongji Nianjian, 1983*, 158–9. Not until 1984 did China produce 400m. tons of grain. *Dangshi Wenhui*, 1993, vi. 10.

[158] *XHBYK*, 24, 1958, 3–11.   [159] Ibid.

would have read this Resolution a few weeks ago, yet Liao still found it necessary to repeat it all over again.

On the last day of the Conference, the delegates unanimously passed the 'Ten Great Proposals' which pledged to fulfil the 1959 production plans. The term 'proposal' is a misnomer because the delegates merely repeated the policies which were spelled out in the Resolution and in the speeches made by the various leaders during the conference.[160]

Finally, Mao led the other top leaders in a stroll around the conference hall amid thunderous applause, cheers, and rousing music, bringing the Conference to a close.

Taking Stock of the Lessons

In contrast to the ritualistic National Conference for the Representatives of Advanced Units, the MA convened a far more important conference in its wake attended by provincial party and government officials responsible for agriculture. In twelve days (2–13 January), the delegates discussed preliminary plans to fulfil grain and cotton targets set by the Sixth Plenum as well as other subjects associated with agricultural production.

Taking into consideration the nature of farmland, cultivated acreage, yield per *mu* and labour power, the Conference agreed that the grain and cotton targets were 'positive and vigorous', even though they represented increases of 40 per cent and 49.25 per cent over the extremely inflated estimates for 1958. In turn, the provinces duly put forward preliminary plans of cultivated area and production quantity. Many predicted a doubling in total production and output/unit, especially rice and wheat, so that the average grain per person could reach 2,000 *jin*. In effect, the preoccupation with grain as the 'key link' remained unabated, and this neutralized the other decision to improve the production of oil crops and hemp (flax).[161] In sum, all these measures reflect the continuation of the GLF mentality and the provinces' conformity with misguided central policies.

On the other hand, the conference also made several other important decisions reversing the policies still official a few days earlier, reflecting some of the lessons learned during 1958. For instance, the Resolution on the communes called for the implementation of Mao's ideal of turning the entire country into a garden through crop rotation:

People in the past often worried about our 'overpopulation' and relatively small amount of available land. But this idea has been overturned by the facts of our 1958 bumper harvest. In so far as we succeed in seriously popularizing the rich experience gained in getting yields through deep ploughing, intensive cultivation, layer-by-layer fertilization and rational close planting, it will be found that the amount of arable land is not too small but very considerable, and that the question is not so much overpopulation as shortage of manpower. This will be a very big change. In a number of years to come, local conditions permitting, we should try to

---

[160] *RMSC*, 1959, 444–5   [161] Ibid. 436–7; *XHBYK*, 3, 1959, 49–50.

reduce the area sown to crops each year, say, to about one-third of what it is at present. Part of the land so saved can lie fallow by rotation or be used for pasturage and the growing of green manure; the rest can be used for afforestation, reservoirs, and the extensive cultivation of flowers, shrubs and trees to turn our whole land with its plains, hills and water into a garden... This is a great ideal that can be realized.[162]

But after some deliberations, the Conference agreed unanimously that the yield/ *mu* must be raised *before* the farmland could be reduced step by step, thus reversing the previous attempt to accomplish this in 1958. Non-staple foods such as vegetables, meat, fish, and so on, were to be 'produced' energetically to improve their supply. The principle of 'intensive cultivation, small acreage and high yield' and 'turning the entire country into a garden' was to be carried out actively, but in a 'steady and down-to-earth' manner. It further qualified the idea by saying that 'without yields of 2,500 kg per *mu*', it would be impossible to reduce the farmland to one-third of its original size. In 1959, the amount of farmland could not be cut back by much. Specifically, the report stated, cultivated areas and sown areas should not be less than 90m. and 126m. hectares respectively. It went on to caution that established cotton areas should not be tampered with and that the acreage for potatoes should not be trimmed by too much. In addition, the reduction of multiple cropping must be prudent—only when there was a bumper summer harvest and autumn crops were in good condition should a reduction in late sowing be considered. This caution qualified the previous policy pronouncements. It was all the more significant in view of the fact that many localities had allegedly implemented the 'three-three' system as early as 1958.

Another definite change of policy introduced at this Conference was the role of industry in the communes. As we will see later, the goal of rural industry had swerved from serving local communities to 'serving heavy industry', particularly iron and steel. In no uncertain terms, the Conference declared that commune industry should from then on be concerned first with the production of agricultural implements and fertilizer, the processing of non-staple products, then other heavy and light industries. This effectively spelled the end for the iron and steel campaign in the rural areas. The delegates must have come to realize that the iron and steel campaign was a burdensome white elephant.

Closely related to this was the labour problem. In principle the conference declared that about 50 per cent of total labour power should be employed in agricultural production, and more during the busy season. It demanded that localities pay attention to the rational utilization of labour, to raising labour efficiency, and to continuing reforms of agricultural implements and fulfilling semi-mechanization.

Again, Tan's closing speech contained the usual bragging about unprecedented victories and diatribes against the 'tide-watchers' and 'rightist conservatives', but he also announced some policy changes. Water conservancy, he said, must be continued, but the scale should be limited, lest it affect quality and squeeze out other work. It would be sufficient to deep-plough one-third of the cultivated area every

[162] *RMRB*, 19 December 1958.

year, he now declared, and the depth of around one foot would be sufficient so that it would not use up too much labour. In close planting, Tan now declared that it was subject to 'certain limits' but, on the other hand, he urged all localities to examine the experience of producing 1,000–3,000 *jin/mu* as a reference point to devise their own standards.

On tool reform, Tan was unrepentant, and he dwelt on the subject in his speech. Agricultural mechanization in 1959 was still dependent on tool reform, he said, and it must be pushed ahead, in a 'down-to-earth' fashion. The fitting of ball-bearings must be continued. Toward these goals more research on technology, raw materials supply, and machinery repair should be conducted. Hence, he demanded that all localities build factories—county factories would manufacture more sophisticated instruments and communes more general ones, while the production teams should carry out tool reform. All counties and communes with 'preconditions' should establish factories for making ball-bearings. Finally, he demanded rapid restoration of the system of responsibility in the communes and the attainment of 'garden-ize', although no elaborations on this were made.[163]

In all, these decisions reflected the changing ideas of the Chairman and lessons learned in 1958, and they represented a limited retreat from the numerous ambitious and ill-conceived goals set in that year. But, on the other hand, decision-makers were still bent on sticking to many unworkable policies, and the 'leap forward' mentality had not abated, and would lead to the recrudescence of the GLF in 1959.

Overall, beginning from late 1957 and in 1958, agricultural and rural policy formulation and implementation were progressively radicalized to the full flowering of the GLF according to the dictates of Mao. At the end, reality forced the retreat from some of the ill-conceived policies, although most other assumptions and policies remained intact. As dissenters were silenced, other top national leaders vied to lend substance to Mao's diffuse ideas, often pandering to his every whim and intuition. Many rushed to the scene to add their own goals in what can be called the 'piling on' process. Some advanced their careers by complying with the Maoist vision. Even more seasoned leaders, like Deng Zihui, effected a 180 degree change to lend support to the GLF. Their optimism tended to reinforce one another, resulting in an endless spiralling of high expectations, and it would go a long way toward disaster before any turnaround could occur.

In this ebullient atmosphere, decision-making became a slipshod and haphazard affair; hunches, improvisations, and 'oral' instructions replaced planning and calculation of cost and benefits. As Mao remarked when he assigned responsibility for the GLF at the Lushan Plenum of July 1959, when most Leap policies were under attack,

... the main responsibility is mine. There is also the General Line. Whether it has any substance or not, you can share some of the responsibility for this ... As for the other big guns, other people should also take some of the responsibility. Boss Tan, you have fired a lot of big

---

[163] *XHBYK*, 3, 1959, 50.

shots, but your shooting was inaccurate, you had a rush of blood to the head and did not take enough care. You tried to introduce communism too quickly.[164]

Apart from this, Mao also harboured a desire to subject agricultural activities to the discipline, uniformity, and regimentation more characteristic of industrial production so that they could be more easily controlled in order to serve industry. The communes and the notion of the 'three-ize' were aspirations toward this direction.

On the other hand, the leadership of the MA jumped eagerly onto the GLF bandwagon. Despite decentralization, it had expanded its roles and influence throughout 1958, although it was even less bureaucratized than the MM, which contained a large contingent of experts and professionals (as we shall see in Chapter 4). The MA's leadership was dominated by veteran revolutionaries, which might have been radicalized by the experience of collectivization between 1953 and 1957. At the beginning, Liao campaigned for the relatively moderate approach to agricultural development as embodied in the NPAD, but embraced the more radical GLF line as soon as it took shape, becoming a zealot who shared Mao's vision. Throughout 1958, he crusaded actively for the GLF programmes. Under him, the MA stole the limelight by taking on many extra duties and functions, and was rewarded accordingly. However, in its zeal in promoting all the multiple and shifting goals emanating from the centre, the MA seldom gave much consideration to their implementability. Hence, the more recent claim that Liao maintained his sobriety and did not 'parrot the views of others' (*ren yun yi yun*) simply cannot hold water.[165]

[164] *Wansui* (1969), 304.   [165] *XHYB*, 4, 1979, 65.

4

The Ministry of Metallurgy and the Policies of Industrial Development in 1958

Single-handedly Mao pushed through the GLF by subduing the planners, stifling all opposition, and turning his harangued colleagues into either willing or reluctant accomplices of his personal crusade. The Chairman's obsession with iron and steel also thrust the Ministry of Metallurgy (MM) onto the centre stage. Communists from Stalin to Mao had always shown an exaggerated sense about the importance of iron and steel and the heavy industry-driven economic growth. From the mid-1950s onward, Mao increasingly was fond of using the quantity of steel to compare the achievements and capabilities of nations.[1] Consequently, the 1FYP placed tremendous emphasis on heavy industry—42.5 per cent of all capital investment was allocated for industry, of which 85 per cent was for heavy industry. The share of the metallurgical industry alone was 7.9 per cent of the total capital investment during the first plan, or 21.9 per cent of the total invested in heavy industry.[2] This preferential treatment had led to a remarkable tripling of output in steel, from 1.35m. tons in 1952 to 5.35m. tons in 1957.[3] Yet, this was regarded as inadequate, and during the GLF, the drive for steel turned into an all-consuming obsession, and the entire country was mobilized for this goal, despite the rhetoric of 'simultaneous development of industry and agriculture'. The new Maoist developmental strategy also necessitated a sharp break from the Soviet modus operandi, and the incorporation of many radical but unworkable policies. Subsequently, the MM was transformed into an engine for mass mobilization in the pursuit of an essentially self-defeating fantasy. How did a fledgling, modern, and professional organization reinvent itself? How did the MM fare under a Mao-dominated system? What was the MM's role in pushing forward the GLF? How was it transformed by the tidal waves of the GLF? Why and how did the ministry betray its own organizational and bureaucratic interests (best served under the Soviet model) in pursuit of alien and obviously unworkable policies? How did it implement central policies under pressure? These will be the major concern of this chapter.

---

[1] See Mao, *Xuanji*, v. 292, 295–6, 401, 474, 494–5; Mao, *Weikan*, xiA. 126, 136, 138, 158, 198; Mao, *Wengao*, vi. 356, 631–2, 634–5.
[2] *Zhongguo Tongji Nianjian, 1983* (Beijing: Guojia Tongjiju, 1983), 324–6.   [3] Ibid. 245.

The Ministry of Metallurgy on the Eve of
the Great Leap Forward

During the 1FYP, the Soviets provided generous aid and technological transfers to build up the small iron and steel industry in China. Soviet assistance established a solid foundation for iron and steel production, enabling China to absorb Soviet steel technology, then the most advanced in the world. The Chinese benefited by loans and experts supplied by the Soviet Union, and inevitably, the design, organization, arrangement, and production methods were carbon copies of Soviet practice. The Soviets emphasized the reconstruction and expansion of the existing iron and steel combines such as Anshan and Panzhihua, and the building of brand-new combines at Wuhan and Baotou. Nevertheless, they deemed it risky to build new plants on localities with uncertain supplies of iron ore and coking coal, and that they could not train the required skilled labour en masse. By 1957, Anshan alone had an annual capacity of 3m. tons, producing 60–70 per cent of China's iron and steel. The goal of this gradual method foresaw that China could produce 17.2m. tons of steel in 1967, the last year of the Third FYP. The Soviet emphasized large plants, but a couple, such as Wuhan and Baotou, were medium-sized by international standards.[4]

In 1958, when the modus operandi of the Soviet model was under attack, the MM bore the brunt of the pressure to reinvent itself. As mentioned, in 1956, external and internal events prompted Mao to rethink the Soviet model. Externally, the succession struggles after Stalin's death, the Soviet debate about the developmental strategy centred on heavy industry, the upheavals in Hungary and Poland, and the development of Yugoslavia led Mao to cast doubts on the old formulas. Mao felt that the likelihood of a world war was greatly diminished, thereby affording China a decade of peace to focus on economic development. Internally, questions were raised about whether the Soviet developmental strategy was really suitable to the peculiarities of China. After listening to reports from the ministries and major enterprises, Mao summed up the experience of the adoption of the Soviet model in the Ten Great Relationships speech, which stressed better balances in the relationships between: heavy industry, light industry, and agriculture; coastal and inland industries; economic development and national defence; the centre and the localities; Han and the ethnic minorities, and so on. One major conclusion of the document was the lowering of military spending in favour of economic development.[5] In a subsequent Politburo meeting, Mao substantiated this idea by the 'strategic thought' of slowing the development of industries for national defence in favour of metallurgical, machinery, and chemical industries, and more advanced weapons such as atomic bombs, missiles, and long-range aeroplanes.[6] Following this spirit, the Ministry of Heavy Industry was abolished in May 1956, and the

---

[4] Gardner M. Clark, *Development of China's Steel Industry and Soviet Technical Aid* (Ithaca: Cornell University Press, 1973), 4, 9, 16, 25, 36, 66–7; Ching-wook Chung, *Maoism and Development: The Politics of Industrial Management* (Seoul: Seoul National University Press, 1980), 31–3.
[5] *Mao Wengao*, vi. 87; Bo Yibo, *Huigu*, i. 466 ff.   [6] Ibid. 485.

former metallurgy, chemical industry, and building materials bureaux under it were turned into fully fledged ministries.[7] In addition, Mao entrusted Zhou Enlai with the direct leadership of the MM and the metallurgy industry.[8]

Another 'Great Relationship' was the encouragement of both the enthusiasm of the centre and the localities. The implication for the iron and steel industry was that tight central control and preference for giant projects should be relaxed, so that the localities could be encouraged to run the iron and steel industry. It was argued that the investment of 1.2 to 1.5bn. *yuan* required for building a large iron and steel combine (with a capacity of 1.5m. tons of pig iron), that would take nine years to complete, could be used more effectively to fund the construction of dozens of small iron and steel combines (with a total capacity of 1.7 to 2m. tons of pig iron) which would take only four years to complete.[9] Moreover, while the Chinese were incapable of producing equipment for large-scale iron and steel combines, they could manufacture equipment for medium and small iron and steel production. This produced the notion of the unity of the large, medium, and small, so that the bias toward Soviet-style 'giantomania' during the 1FYP could be addressed. Following Mao's 'Ten Great Relationships' speech, the Eighth Party Congress of September 1956 duly proposed to build 'a good number' of small and medium industrial enterprises throughout the country. These, the Chinese argued, could use scattered local resources (such as iron ores and coking coal) to serve local needs better without burdening the limited railway transportation facilities.[10]

In the late 1950s, it was simply assumed that 1,500 out of China's 2,000+ counties had coal reserves, and that twenty-four out of twenty-seven provinces had rich iron ore deposits, although little was said about their actual industrial potential.[11] This assumption informed the SEC conference in February 1957, during which the MM and eighteen provinces expressed interest in building small and indigenous blast furnaces with a total pig iron capacity of 0.4m. tons.[12] In March, a MM conference formally embraced the principle of combining of the large, medium, and small as its new orientation.[13] This was publicly endorsed by an 4 April *RMRB* editorial, which also revealed that the MM had trimmed investment in the three largest Soviet-aided iron and steel enterprises to fund the medium and small plants. Even equipments earmarked for Anshan were diverted for this purpose, and special funds were allotted by the SEC for regional metallurgical and coal industries. In any case, the small and indigenous blast furnaces (about 20 to 100 cu. m in capacity) considered at this time had nothing in common with the hundreds of thousands of primitive plants that mushroomed in 1958. For instance, the four blast furnaces planned by Hunan required investment of 1.8m. *yuan*, although *RMRB* on the same day reported that indigenous blast furnaces in Shangcheng, Henan, each

---

[7] *Zhongyang Zhengfu Jigou*, 221; *FGHB*, iii. 80–1; *Zhou Enlai Nianpu*, i. 555–6.

[8] *Mianhuai*, i. 69; *Women de Zhou Zongli* (Our own Premier Zhou) (Beijing: Zhongyang wenxian chubanshe, 1990), 210.   [9] *RMRB*, 4 April 1957.   [10] *RMST*, 1957, 15–16, 42, 60.

[11] *RMRB*, 8 August 1958; *BR*, no. 33, 14 October 1958, 15.

[12] *Jihua Jingji* (Planned Economy), 6, 1957, 10–11.   [13] *Mianhua*, 70.

costing only 20 *yuan* to build, could produce 230 tons of pig iron a year.[14] These indigenous furnaces were originally designed to utilize local ores to manufacture small tools for local needs, but at the height of the iron and steel campaign, they were pressed into service for supplying pig iron for modern steel smelting. In August, the MM announced its own plan to spend 600 to 700m. *yuan* to construct iron and steel mills in eighteen provinces. Construction work, which was to begin in 1958, was expected to be completed by 1962, and a total annual capacity of 2.5m. tons of iron and 1.7m. tons of steel was anticipated.[15] These outputs represented a small fraction of the total production. Therefore, this new strategy, which featured '3 large, 5 medium, and 18 small' iron and steel combines, designed for the 2FYP, might have changed the orientation of metallurgy, but overall, it was a modest and gradual modification of the Soviet strategy, and won the approval of Mao and even Chen Yun.[16] Nevertheless, the new strategy would be altered beyond recognition in 1958 once Mao had changed his mind.

Although almost a creation of Mao's new economic strategy, the MM was relatively low on the totem pole of central power hierarchy, being several steps below the apex of power, and subjected to multiple Party and governmental controls to ensure compliance with central policies. Unlike ministers of liberal democracies who are also members of the cabinet (roughly equivalent to China's Politburo), the minister of the MM since its creation, Wang Heshou, a veteran of the Chinese communist movement, was merely an alternate member of the Central Committee. The MM itself was supervised by the State Council's Number Three Staff Office that assisted the Premier in supervising the ministries. In September 1959, the eight State Council Staff Offices were streamlined into six and their titles changed, so the MM was placed under the Industry and Transportation Staff Office. In addition, the MM was also supervised by supra-ministerial organizations like the State Planning Commission (SPC), through its Heavy Industry Bureau and the Iron and Steel Department, and the State Economic Commission (SEC), through its Metallurgy Industry Planning Bureau. The directors of these commissions, Li Fuchun (SPC) and Bo Yibo (SEC), as observed, were badgered by Mao into becoming staunch supporters of the policies of the GLF. Zhou Enlai, whom Mao entrusted informally to 'lead' the MM, met with a similar fate. Therefore, from the perspective of Wang and the MM, to oppose or sabotage GLF policies was clearly not an option; it was easier and more feasible to go along with the tide.

In the party hierarchy, the MM was subordinated to the Department of Industrial Work of the Central Committee headed by a Central Committee member. This department was more important than the State Council Number Three Staff Office in directing the ministries, as it was responsible, with the Party's Organization Department, for assigning personnel to all governmental positions at the bureau level and above. It was also active in the drafting of annual plans, and in the

---

[14] *RMRB*, 4 April 1957; *JHJJ*, 6, 1957, 10–11.   [15] *RMRB*, 19 August 1957.
[16] *Mianhui*, i. 70–1.

monitoring of plan implementation by the ministries.[17] Within the MM itself, of course, Party control was ensured by the Party Committee.

Subsequently, the MM, like all the central ministries, enjoyed very little independence; the ministries were more administrative agencies to carry out the assigned tasks of the Communist Party. Indeed, the formal arrangement of powers is not the whole picture. Because soaring iron and steel production was close to Mao's heart, Wang and the MM were coopted into the inner sanctum of decision-making, replacing the central planners. So, although not major actors in national politics by design, their prominence was ensured when iron and steel were declared the centrepiece of the GLF. Yet ironically, the unrivalled access to the apex of power did nothing to promote the bureaucratic interests of the ministry; it only obliged the MM to cater to the whims of the Chairman.

Ironies aside, in the 1950s the MM was a large and complex professional organization that served many decision-making and management functions. The minister was served by four deputy ministers, and three assistants to the minister. The MM had fifteen to twenty departments, nine metallurgical construction corporations, and maintained (in 1957) control over more than forty-four building construction enterprises, nine designing institutes, five prospecting companies, sixty-three geological exploration units, eight reconnaissance units, and one geophysical prospecting unit, employing a total of more than 200,000 people of whom about 30,000 were technicians—a remarkable organizational achievement.[18] In addition, it also supervised many iron and steel plants, mines, and enterprises directly. In the GLF these included the Shanghai, Chongqing, Taiyuan, Ma'anshan, Baotou, Wuhan Iron and Steel plants and bases, and the great Anshan Iron and Steel base—the country's largest—which alone contributed the lion's share of the annual steel production (see Table 4.1). The ministry generally kept a tight rein over these enterprises, controlling not only their output targets, capital investments, resource allocations, and manpower ceilings, it also required them to submit monthly and even daily reports of plan fulfilment. On the other hand, these enterprises had representatives stationed at Beijing almost permanently.[19]

The MM also controlled directly metallurgical departments of the provincial governments, branch offices of the ministry, and some enterprises located in the provinces. The decentralization decrees introduced in late 1957 formally put these units under the dual control of the MM *and* the provincial party committees. This fact has often been cited to show the weakening of the centre, and the central ministries in particular. However, such pro forma redistribution of power did not affect the MM's continued dominance over its subordinates, as will be seen in this chapter.

[17] A. Doak Barnett with a contribution by Ezra Vogel, *Cadres, Bureaucracy and Political Power in Communist China* (New York: Columbia University Press, 1967), 21–3. *Zhongyang Zhengfu Jigou*, 217; Kao Chung-yen, *Changes in Personnel*, 157, 164–6; *RMRB*, 3 March 1957.

[18] Ching-Wook Chung, *Maoism and Development*, 113; M. Gardner Clark, *Development of China's Steel Industry*, 35. See also Ye Wensong (ed.), *Zhengfu Jiguan Zonglan*, 233–8; He Husheng, Li Yaodong, Xiang Changfu, and Jiang Jianhua (eds.), *Zhonghua Renmin Gongheguo Zhiguan Zhi* (A record of governmental officials of the PRC), expanded edn. (Beijing: Zhongguo shehui chubanshe, 1996), 208–9.

[19] Ching-wook Chung, *Maoism and Development*, 113–14.

Table 4.1. *Estimated crude steel production at major iron and steel plants in 1957 and 1960 (million tons)*

Plant	1957	1960
Modern plants		
Anshan	2.9	5.4
Shanghai	0.5	2.6
Chongqing	0.4	1.1
Taiyuan	0.3	0.5
Beijing	0	1.1
Ma'anshan	–	0.3
Bautao	0	0.3
Wuhan	0	0.2
Others	1.3	1.7
Total	5.4	12.5
Small plants	–	6.2
Total production	5.4	18.7

Source: *China: A Reassessment of the Economy* (Washington: Joint Economic Committee, Congress of the United States, 1975), 285.

Overall, the MM served two major functions that constituted its organizational mission. The first was the smelting and processing of ores into iron, steel, copper and aluminium, etc., and the production and processing of non-ferrous metals and rolled-steel products. The second was the production of raw materials, that is, the mining of iron, copper, aluminium, and a host of other metallic and non-metallic ores (except coal, petroleum, and other minerals).[20] Such activities required sophisticated technology and division of labour, and as such, the MM was greatly influenced by the Soviet experience.

Since the MM was a large professional organization, it was natural that it had established its bureaucratic outlooks and values, and that it had significant institutional interests to defend. However, one should not exaggerate the role of the MM as an independent bureaucratic organization, as both party leadership and control over the bureaucracy and the campaign style employed by the regime had impeded its bureaucratic institutionalization. For instance, the rectification campaign in late 1957 alone had led to the transfer of 64 per cent of the ministry's and 10 per cent of the enterprises' administrative cadres to lower administrative levels.[21] From the perspective of bureaucratic politics, the MM's organizational mission and interests were well served by the Soviet model, with its emphasis on the gradual, tried, and trusted methods, not by the radical and ever-changing policies of the GLF. Yet, although it became the star player in 1958, its Soviet connections were also a stigma and liability. Perhaps because of this, it was more inclined to overcompensate and err in the direction of excessive zeal than inaction. Furthermore, as Premier Zhou,

[20] *Zhongyang Zhengfu Jigou*, 221–5.   [21] Chung, *Maoism and Development*, 116–17.

who was in charge of the MM and the metallurgy industry, was disgraced, the ministerial leadership had no choice but to hang on Mao's every word, and to realize his every whim and policy. In so doing, it had almost reinvented the MM and exerted tremendous pressure on its subordinates.

The Ministry of Metallurgical Industry and the Iron and Steel Campaign

New Orientations and the Politicization of the MM

When Liu Shaoqi made public the slogan 'catch up with Britain in fifteen years' at the Eighth National Congress of the Chinese Federation of Trade Unions in early December, 1957, Li Fuchun chimed in with his prediction that yearly production of steel would reach 40m. tons in 1972, or 6.6 times the amount achieved in 1957, thereby exceeding the projected British production for the same year. The production of coal, machinery, cement, and chemical fertilizer, he asserted, would also exceed that of Britain in 1972.[22] In January 1958, the SEC, which was responsible for annual and shorter plans, proposed to the State Council the following 1958 targets: iron, 7.32m. tons; steel, 6.24m. tons; and rolled steel products, 4.82m. tons. These represented 24 per cent, 19 per cent, and 13 per cent increases over production in 1957. Simultaneously, in acceding to the need of 'overtaking Britain', the MM duly added certain construction items to its 1958 plan, and increased the planned production capability of iron and steel for 1958 by 1.38 and 1.03m. tons respectively, approximately 44 per cent of the total increases during the 1FYP. It also decided to accelerate the construction of the two modern iron and steel plants at Wuhan and Baotou, which had begun during the 1FYP. At this stage, the MM relied on the larger projects for the production increase, as 90 per cent of its investment was allocated to the fifty-seven above-norm construction projects. To maximize production, investment for 'non-productive' construction projects (such as housing for staff and workers) was slashed to only 4 per cent of the total investment—the lowest in comparison with any year of the 1FYP.[23] However, the planned increases in production, while significant in relation to previous plans, were still modest when compared to the escalations later. In subsequent months, the logic of mobilization and the Politburo's interferences raised these targets to unprecedented heights.

The development of local metallurgical industries, which received so much attention in 1957 accounted for only 15 per cent of the planned total pig iron production in 1958, and no steel was planned. Likewise, the indigenous production method was put on the back burner since Bo Yibo, vice-premier and minister of the State Economic Commission, did not mention it in his draft economic report for 1958 submitted to the National People's Congress in February. Bo also revealed that seventy-one new construction projects related to the metallurgical industry were to

---

[22] *RMRB*, 8 December 1957.   [23] *RMRB*, 26 January 1958.

begin construction in 1958—fifty-seven under the auspices of the MM, whereas the local authorities were in charge of fourteen. Therefore, the emphasis of the MM at this stage was clearly still on the large modern enterprises.[24]

As Mao no longer trusted and dealt with the central planners, beginning in 1958, he turned directly to the ministries. In January he summoned Wang Heshou, Lu Dong, Gang Yangwen (MM deputy director) and Xu Chi (assistant to the minister) to brief him on iron and steel production, and pushed his reasoning for the accelerated development of the local iron and steel industry. Many of China's provinces were as big, if not bigger, than some European countries, he argued, why can't they have one, or two, iron and steel plants. Hence he instructed the MM to promote seriously the iron and steel industry in these provinces, and to spend as much as 60 per cent of its resources to assist in building the plants.

The leaders of the MM understood the significance of this audience with Mao, viewing the Chairman's instructions as a sacred trust. After the Nanning Conference, the MM proposed to accelerate the development of the metallurgy industry (and by implication, all industries) by overtaking Britain in ten years, and the US in twenty.[25] In an eight-day meeting, the MM party committee weighed Mao's instructions carefully by adopting the *wuxu* method. The result of the deliberations was two reports penned by Wang and presented to the Party Centre and Mao in March, as we will see later.[26]

The MM Cleans House: The 'Two-Anti' Campaign (February/March 1958)

Blessed with Mao's confidence the leaders of the MM were ready to throw its full weight behind the Maoist initiatives. The new tasks and demands on the MM necessitated a fundamental shift in the ministry's outlook and priorities, and the leadership was ready for some extraordinary measures. Overall, the communists used the campaigns as weapons to break down bureaucratic routinization and specialization, to restrain the growth of institutional interests and identity, and to bend organizations to the wishes of the central leaders. For instance, in 1957 alone, the MM was subjected to the constant pressure of the rectification campaign, the 'anti-rightist' campaign, the 'sent downward' (*xiafang*) movement and several 'increase production and economizing' campaigns. During the rectification campaign, the MM's measures to combat the problem of bureaucracy included the decentralization of some enterprises to the local authorities, the expansion of the power of the enterprises, the simplification of forms, the merging of government organs, and the *xiafang* of cadres.[27] Some of these measures were subsequently incorporated into the national decentralization regulations. The MM itself had also cut its personnel by

---

[24] Ibid. Bo's report is in *RMSC*, 1959, 234–44 and a list of these construction projects is on p. 237.
[25] *Unpublished Chinese Documents*, 274.
[26] *Mianhuai*, 71–2; Sun Yeli and Xiong Lianghua, *Jingji Fengyun zhong de Chen Yun*, 155–6.
[27] *RMRB*, 27 October 1957.

sending 20 per cent of all bureaus and division-level cadres as well as 500 cadres to the lower administrative units or enterprises.

In 1958, the rectification campaign was merged with a new 'two-anti' campaign (*shuangfan*). In his Sixty Articles on Work Method (draft) dated 31 January, Mao called on every unit, factory, cooperative, school, armed force unit, and so on, to 'struggle' against 'waste' once a year, using the method of 'airing of views, rectification and reform'.[28] The MM responded quickly and in early February launched an anti-waste campaign aimed at the elimination of waste, bureaucratism, and 'lethargy' within all the units of the ministry.[29] Soon this campaign attracted much attention and the party committee of the central government organizations (*zhongyang guojia dangwei*) called a promotion meeting on 16 February to 'inspect anti-waste *and* anti-conservatism' (emphasis mine). Both the MM and the Ministry of Foreign Trade were commended for being advanced units. In particular, the MM was singled out for praise by the secretary-general of the State Council, Xi Zhongxun.

Buoyed by the activism for the rectification in the enterprises, Mao penned an *RMRB* editorial (18 February) which claimed that the worst enemies of the GLF were 'waste' and 'conservatism', so the current task of the rectification campaign was to get rid of these two vices. As mentioned previously, in early 1958 Mao had already demolished the economic planning system. Now his attention had shifted to the enterprises and all government units, arguing that the breaking of outdated rules and regulations could cut labour and cost, streamline all organizations, and change the relationship between the cadres and the masses so that production could be promoted using the *duohao kuaisheng* principle. This prompted the Party Centre and the State Council to convene many conferences to discuss the reform of the economic management system, leading to the acceleration of decentralization.[30]

The MM campaign encouraged the Central Committee of the CCP, which in a directive dated 3 March, formally decided to launch a 'two-anti' campaign against waste and conservatism nationally for two or three months.[31] The directive described the two-anti campaign as a campaign for 'socialist production and a cultural great leap forward'. Second, it claimed that if this campaign could be 'firmly grasped', then the same amount of manpower, funds, and supplies could increase or even double the outputs. Third, the methods of 'big-blooming, big-contending, big-character posters [*dazibao*], and big debate' and competitions among units were prescribed to see which ones were the most successful in fulfilling the slogan of *duohao kuaisheng*. The claim that this directive marked the effective beginning of the GLF might have been overdrawn, but the above assumptions and work methods were what informed the GLF campaign.[32] For the

---

[28] *Mao Wengao*, vii. 49.   [29] *RMRB*, 16 and 18 February 1958.
[30] Bo Yibo, *Huigu*, ii. 796–8.   [31] *RMRB*, 4 March 1958.
[32] The discussion in the following pages, unless otherwise stated, is based on *RMRB*, 16 and 18 February 1958, and *Yejin Bao* (Metallurgy News) (hereafter *YJB*), 7, 7 March 1958, 6–15. The latter contains two editorials and one report entitled. 'Oppose Waste and Conservatism', 'How to Mobilize the Anti-Waste and Anti-Conservatism Campaign', and 'The 160,000 *dazibao* in the Ministry of Metallurgy had Instigated the New Situation of Construction Great Leap Forward and Thought Great Leap Forward'.

MM, the campaign was employed to whip the ministry into shape according to Mao's goals and methods specified in the Sixty Articles, and to switch the MM onto the GLF mode. More particularly, it was intended to reorient the ministry to the goal of accelerating production and to quash any opposition, especially by its technicians.

Right from the beginning, the Party Committee of the MM, pitting itself against the engineers and technicians, controlled the campaign. The ostensible purpose of the two-antis campaign was the writing of *dazibao* to expose cases of waste and bureaucratism within the ministry, and the convening of meetings for debate, criticism, and 'appraisal-through-comparison' (*pingbi*). At the mobilizational meeting (6 February), the report of the party committee delivered by Lu took the form of sixty-two 'oral' *dazibao* to reveal cases of waste and conservatism.[33] Initially, the party committee estimated that an allotment of six *dazibao* per person was sufficient to expose all problems. Yet later, it discovered that although in the department of capital construction, the average *dazibao* put out by each member was ten, the problems were still not 'aired' adequately. Henceforth, the party committee raised the assignment to ten. It was said that within nineteen days, the average *dazibao* written per person had risen to twenty-five.

Initial response to the campaign, however, was lukewarm, and many units resisted the *dazibao*, citing their busy schedules. The officials were hesitant in encouraging their subordinates to write *dazibao*, fearing that this would cost them trouble. The subordinates, on the other hand, were afraid of antagonizing their superiors, who might retaliate. This initial reluctance prompted the Party Committee to apply more pressure on the individuals to write *dazibao*. For instance, the design department proclaimed the number of *dazibao* contributed by each person on a blackboard and conducted 'appraisal-through-comparison' to judge their quantity and quality. When a zero appeared under the name of a certain section chief, he lost no time in churning out several *dazibao*. The party committee also stipulated that the MM should inspect its departments and bureaus once every three days, and in turn these departments and bureaus were to inspect their own subordinates every day. The Party Committee also cited the example of the Non-ferrous Metal Design Institute, said to have used Tuesday, Thursday, and Friday evenings besides the stipulated rectification time (Monday, Wednesday, and Saturday afternoons) to write *dazibao*. As pressure mounted, the Party Committee finally got what it wanted. Between 9 and 28 February, it was said that a total of 160,000 *dazibao* was produced.

Apart from writing *dazibao*, the delegates were urged to overcome the problem of waste by revealing the problems at the many mobilizational meetings.

---

[33] According to Lu, he was criticized by a worker during one of his inspection trips who questioned the wisdom of the industrial departments in using the average rather than the advanced figures in their calculations. Lu said that he was greatly inspired, and concluded that to be satisfied with the average figures was to be afraid to upset the balance, and this was a manifestation of rightist conservatism. *RMRB*, 18 February 1958. This brought him in line with Mao's thinking.

Allegations made included:

- Sixty million *yuan*'s worth of equipment was kept idle in storage.
- Requests were made to write off as lost four rock drills that had been in storage for four years.
- One enterprise was fined 18,000 *yuan* because its accountant had forgotten to pay tax to the government.
- Ten thousand *yuan* were wasted in transportation as a shipment of goods designated for Shaanxi was shipped to Shanxi instead.
- A primary school for cadre children attached to the ministry had spent 1,400 *yuan* for a merry-go-round.
- A Shanghai plant had dispensed 150 raincoats for 15 individuals within three years.
- An engineer had accepted more than 10,000 *yuan* as salary over a period of three years but so far had not written any reports.
- A park planned by the Taiyuan Steel Plant was said to be as big as 54 hectares.

These cases, even if all true, are not surprising for an organization as large as the MM. What was significant was the reaction of Lu Dong, deputy minister of the MM, who used this to conclude that the investment for plant construction could be slashed by 30–40 per cent with no impact on normal production, if the alleged wastage could be overcome. By extension, he added, the same investment for a steel mill producing 6–7m. tons annually would be adequate to build one that produced 10m. tons.

Another objective of the campaign was to criticize the 'dogmatism' in copying other 'fraternal countries' (read Soviet Union) regardless of Chinese conditions. The MM's close Soviet ties made it the obvious target. For instance, it was charged that although China could not produce many large trucks, electric locomotives and power shovels, the method of opencast mining requiring this equipment was indiscriminately popularized. It was said that this mining method was 3.4 times more costly than that of shaft mining, a more labour-intensive method. Some people, it was said, resisted the idea of building more medium and small plants. They were said to have craved mechanization and automation, and have cited foreign data to prove that to industrialize, only large plants should be built. These charges were so damaging that Wang Heshou found it expedient to write an article denouncing 'dogmatism' himself.[34]

Finally, a more fundamental objective of the campaign was to spur production. Toward this end, the party committee under Lu Dong drew up another 'leap forward' plan that slapped another 0.4m. tons of iron and 0.45m. tons of steel onto the 1958 targets, making the grand totals 6.7m. and 7.75m. tons respectively. This dismayed those who were already sceptical about fulfilling the original plan; they were also disturbed by the revival of the discredited practice of *cengceng jiama* (raising the targets as they are passed down the administrative ladder).

[34] *Wansui* (1969), 177, *Mao Weikan*, xiB. 35; Li Rui, *Dayuejin*, 234.

Yet, this was exactly what the MM leadership wanted. By early March, it put forward another 'increase production, practise thrift' plan that raised the 1958 targets for iron and steel by 0.45m. and 0.55m. tons respectively, and the new national target was rounded off to 8m. tons of pig iron and 7m. tons of steel. Near the end of March, the MM again advanced the timetable for the completion of five medium-size integrated iron and steel enterprises (equipped with facilities for pig iron, steel, and rolled steel production) from the end of the 2FYP (1962) to 1960.

As to the outcome, some units might have learned a lesson and tried to play the game by sticking to the new rules. For instance, the non-ferrous metal bureau of Jiangxi had initially grumbled about the assigned state plan for tungsten. Under duress, it changed its tone, vowing to exceed the state plan by 14 per cent and to strive for a 23 per cent increase. The Yunnan Tin company had argued forcefully that the assigned state target was impossible. The campaign changed this and now it pledged to exceed the target by 14 per cent. Other issues were simply swept under the carpet. For instance, it was said, the nagging problems of wages and welfare, which had haunted the enterprises for many years, were quickly resolved once the mass mobilization, the *dazibao*, and the debates had taken their course.[35]

In any event, 1,500 leadership cadres with the rank of engineers and section chiefs and above were hardest hit. They were accused of harbouring conservatism and dogmatism and their performance during the first few days of the campaign was deemed unsatisfactory. Consequently, some of these cadres were said to have held meetings every day and even three times a day to criticize their alleged 'rightist conservatism' in underestimating the enthusiasm of the masses. In any case, all these cadres, it was said, were 'burned.'

The two-anti campaign was a shrewd device employed by the MM leadership to shake up the bureaucracy. Few leadership cadres were left unscathed. Instances of waste, both real and imagined, were disclosed. It dealt a blow to those who resisted drastic changes. By a combination of manipulation and group pressure, all dissenters within the ministry were intimidated into silence. The MM was thoroughly politi-cized. However, it is doubtful if the campaign did anything to alleviate 'bureau-cratism', as the Party had controlled it tightly from start to finish, using ritualistic and high-handed methods. Some might find some satisfaction in airing their com-plaints and in witnessing the self-criticism of the cadres. Yet, in the end, the ultimate goal of output maximization utilizing as few resources as possible undoubtedly encouraged and fostered overzealousness. When the demands departed from reality, the likelihood of cheating also increased.

The Ministry of Metallurgy: Star of the Chengdu Conference (8–26 March)

The leaders of the MM, particularly its director Wang, were caught up with the frenzy. As mentioned, in early March, after being coopted by Mao, Wang submitted

[35] Ibid. 235.

two reports to the Chairman during the Chengdu Conference on 20 March, and advanced the timetable of production further. At the beginning of the second report, Wang argued that the progress in metallurgy and in industry as a whole could overtake Britain in ten years, and the USA in twenty or a little more time. Enumerating Mao's ideas and language, the report claimed that if 'redness' could be combined with smelting steel, and if it could be liberated from the constraints of dogmatism, steel targets set by the Eighth Party Congress for 1962 (at 10.5 and 12m. tons according to the two sets of plans) could be surpassed. By applying the General Line of *duohao kuaisheng*, Wang continued, it was possible to exceed 15m. and strive for 20m. tons in 1962. At Nanning the target for 1962 was set at only 15m. tons, because the potential was not realized. Since there would be dozens of iron and steel bases by 1962, it would be realistic to project that in 1967, steel production could reach 30–40m. tons. The Soviet Union was hamstrung by one-man management, the experts, the central ministries, large plants, tedious methods and procedures, and reliance on material incentives. In contrast, the Chinese had done the exact opposite, such as reliance on the mass line and decentralization. In particular, because the Chinese had implemented the principle of large, medium, and small, the speed of construction could be accelerated 100 per cent but investment could be cut in half. Citing the two-anti campaign within the MM, Wang bragged that hundred of thousands of *dazibao* had led directly to the numerous pledges for technical innovations and the commitment to raise iron and steel production by 0.45m. and 0.5m. tons.

This was exactly what Mao wanted to hear, so he praised the reports three times in his speeches made on 22 and 25 March. Mao instructed other ministries to learn from the MM, to 'resolutely overcome the dogmatism, empiricism, "departmentalism", rightist conservatism, and the "indifference" to politics, and expert and not red'. When Mao was chiding the planners, Wang became one of those most willing to cater to his illusions. Mao was buoyant and infectious, but reports like these fed and reinforced his illusions, and the Leap must be understood in terms of this mutual reinforcement between Mao and his followers.[36]

The Ministry of Metallurgical Industry Mobilizes Its Subordinates and the Provinces

Having put its house in order after the 'two-anti' campaign, the MM turned to its subordinates and, more significantly, began to extend its control directly over the provinces, decentralization notwithstanding. Indeed, in doing so the MM was merely following Mao's instruction for promoting the local metallurgical industries. At the Chengdu Conference in March, the new iron and steel targets for 1958 had already risen to 8 and 7m. tons, respectively, or one-third more than the 1957 output.[37] Joined by the All-China Committee of the Heavy Industry Trade Unions,

---

[36] Bo Yibo, *Huigu*, ii. 693–5; Li Rui, *Dayuejin*, 234–6.   [37] *Jiaoxue Cankao Ziliao*, xxii. 415, 420.

the MM convened a national conference at the Tayeh Iron and Steel Mill—the National Conference on the Great Leap Forward in Iron and Steel Production, 27 March–2 April—to discuss the new 1958 production plan. Besides exchanging experience, the participants, comprising representatives from twenty state-owned and many local state-owned enterprises, not only expressed the 'unanimous' determination to surpass the year's iron and steel targets, but also drew up their new 'great-leap-forward production plans' on the spot, apparently without consulting their own units.

The Conference also embraced the latest appeal by the Party that required the leadership cadres to adopt the method of 'experimental plots', to conduct office work on the shop floor, to spend some time in the workshop, and to follow the practice of 'three togethers'.[38] The industrial 'experimental plots', which entailed the setting aside of a section of the factory for the cadres to experiment with new techniques, was intended to make the cadres both 'red' and 'expert'. Finally, the Conference also handed out awards to several advanced production units, blast furnaces, and open-hearth furnaces.[39]

Clearly, the MM maintained a tight rein over its subordinate units. The face-to-face interaction at the Conference made it easier for the ministry to secure agreement to higher production quotas from the representatives of its subordinates, especially when they had little opportunity to consult their experts and technicians. The ministry's speedy adoption of the new initiatives, on the other hand, demonstrated its readiness to toe the line, although they were profoundly disruptive of its routines and procedures.

In April, the MM shifted its attention to the regional authorities by convening the first National Conference on Local Metallurgical Industry. During this, the provincial authorities set up targets for blast furnace production for themselves, and the combined pig iron production for 1958 exceeded 2m. tons.[40] This reflected the renewed attention of local metallurgical industry, but more important, the new MM role of controlling the provinces. Previously, the MM provided leadership only to the enterprises and units under its functional chain of command, but the iron and steel campaign gave it the opportunity to expand its power and responsibilities. In subsequent months, the MM continued to order the provinces about in the campaign.

In any case, the conference spurred on the development of iron and steel mills in the localities. Goaded by slogans such as 'overtake Britain in less than fifteen years', *duohao kuaisheng*, 'twice the speed, half the investment', twenty-four provinces declared that they had planned to build more than sixty small ironworks, steel mills, and iron and steel mills. For example, Hebei, which had virtually no iron and steel industry, had started the construction of seven iron and steel mills and twenty-five small blast furnaces. Henan was said to have drawn up plans for more than 100 small blast furnaces and 1,000 indigenous blast furnaces; in Guizhou, an iron and steel integrated plant which could produce 40,000 tons of rolled steel products annually

---

[38] 'Three togethers' meant working, eating, and sleeping together.
[39] The Party's appeal is in *RMRB*, 24 March 1958. The report on the Conference is in *Nanfang Ribao* (Southern Daily) (hereafter *NFRB*), 4 April 1958.   [40] *RMRB*, 7 June, 22 and 27 August 1958.

had begun construction. Neimenggu expected that the fourth small blast furnace could be operational by July.[41] The MM itself announced its new plans of constructing one large and ten small seamless steel rounds plants in various provinces, to be completed in six months. Overall, the agitation by the MM had borne fruits.

Meanwhile, to ensure that the Party Congress would follow his direction, Mao summoned the heads of the Central Ministries (Metallurgy, Chemical Industry, Railway, Hydroelectric Power, and Geology) to Guangzhou (between 26 and 29 April) to discuss the issue of catching up with Britain in fifteen years. Incited by the extravagant reports and projections, Mao now posed the task of whether the USA could be surpassed in fifteen years as well. The most extravagant report, submitted by the Ministry of Hydroelectric Power, pledged the combination of large, medium, and small projects, so that half the responsibility would be given to the local authorities, and that all people would run electricity. Impressed by this, Mao ordered other ministries to submit reports imitating this ministry.[42]

The Great Leap Forward is Officially Launched

As mentioned, Mao scored a personal triumph at the Second Session of the Eighth Party Congress (5–23 May), as his ideas and policies developed since the Third Plenum were categorically affirmed, praised, and enshrined. Perhaps intoxicated by the adulation, the Chairman kept on pushing for more ambitious targets, thereby progressively shortening the timetable of catching up with Britain. Mao's prodding, praise, and pressure could not be ignored. Those around Mao had to be even more extravagant just to catch up. It was a game of one-upmanship, and at the Congress, a process of competitive bidding set in. So when Li Fuchun boasted that China could overtake Britain (in the production of industrial products) in seven or eight years, and the USA in fifteen, Wang Heshou, convinced that he had read Mao's mind correctly, went one step further. In his report entitled 'Catch up with the US in Fifteen Years' he exuded confidence that steel production could reach 12m. tons in 1959, 30m. tons in 1962, 70m. in 1967, and 120m. in 1972, so that China could surpass Britain in *five* years, and the US in *fifteen*. He said such speed signified the accelerated demise of the capitalist camp. The 30m. tons for 1962 was not speculation but based on careful and realistic calculations of increasing capacity; it might even be somewhat conservative. If 'realism' were combined with 'romanticism', he gushed, then 35 to 40m. tons of steel for 1962 was possible. Thanks to Mao's writings, his critique of *fanmaojin*, the general line, he was inspired and reeducated, and he was confident that China could surpass the US in fifteen years.[43] Such irresponsible bluffing might have unsettled the delegates and the planners, but Mao had the highest praise for it, comparing Wang's report to 'lyric poetry'. Thus encouraged, other ministries, such as the Ministries of Petroleum, Railway,

    [41] *RMRB*, 1 May 1958.
    [42] Liu Rui, *Dayuejin*, 262 ff; *Mao Wengao*, vii. 183–8; Bo Yibo, *Huigu*, ii. 692–3; *Dang de Wenxian*, 4, 1994, 77.   [43] Li Rui, *Dayuejin*, 302–3.

Reclamation, Transport, Textile, Forestry, Light Industry, Chemical Industry, and Coal, followed suit with similarly extravagant pledges.[44] On 7 May Mao mused that steel production for 1962 could probably reach 30 to 40m. tons, and 51m. tons by 1966.[45]

Mao had called for a faster speed of development than the 1FYP period and for the Party to become a 'promoter of progress' (*cujin pai*). This was precisely the role played by the MM at the Congress. The Congress also enshrined the principle of 'simultaneous development of national and local industries, and of large, small and medium size enterprises' by arguing that the medium and small required less time to construct, and were adept in absorbing capital from scattered resources but were quick in producing results. As Liu stated, the simple equipment required could be manufactured locally, transportation costs could be reduced. The spillover effect of these industries, he claimed, could promote industrialization in the countryside, help train skilled workers, and narrow the gap between the cities and the country-side, and between the workers and the peasants (two of the 'three big differences').

In addition, the implementation of this policy would involve the direct partici-pation of 'all central and local authorities at every level down to the cooperatives' and 'the whole party and population'[46] so that industrial plants would 'dot every part of the country like stars in the sky'. The production of iron and steel by the local industries, in particular, was planned to reach 1.73 and 1.41m. tons in 1958, an increase of 19 per cent and 78 per cent more than 1957 production respectively (the local iron and steel production in 1957 was 0.593 and 0.79m. tons).[47] Naturally, these new initiatives and demands generated a great deal of pressure on the central ministries, with the MM bearing the brunt. The implication of this restated policy for the MM was to emphasize the medium and small scales of production, since the large enterprises had already been well established. Mao realized this, although he thought it highly desirable to screw up the pressure constantly,

Imbalance and headache are good things. The First Ministry of Machine Building, the Ministry of Metallurgy, and the Ministry of Geology, for example, are experiencing a hard time and receiving pressure from all sides. Therefore, they must develop extensively, which is a good thing.[48]

Let us now look at the response to these policy initiatives by the MM and the rest of the country. As the MM was fixated on quantity alone, limited variety and shoddy quality of steel brought it into conflict with the First Ministry of Machine Industry. Yet these bureaucratic differences were totally suppressed. No evidence existed that the First Ministry had complained to Mao about its predicament; in fact, like other ministries, it joined the fray by submitting reports in June that pleased the Chairman, who promptly distributed them to the MAC conference. Furthermore, at the Lushan Conference of July, 1959, minister Zhao Erlu shipped boxes of sub-standard pig iron

---

[44] Bo Yibo, *Huigu*, ii. 695–6; Cong Jin, *Quzhe Fazhan*, 131–2; Sun Yeli and Xiong Lianghua, *Jingji Fengyun zhong de Chen Yun*, 156.   [45] Bo Yibo, *Huigu*, ii. 695–6.   [46] *XHBYK*, 11, 1958, 8.
[47] Ibid. 4.   [48] *Wansui* (1969), 213; *Mao Weikan*, xiB. 68.

to the conference to show his grievances, but changed his mind when tipped off by Zhou Enlai regarding the political climate.[49]

The Ministry of Metallurgy's Reaction to the Party Congress: Ten Thousand Blast Furnaces and Two Hundred Bessemer Converters

'When everybody adds firewood, the flames rise high'—this adage used by Liu in his report to the Second Session of the Eighth Party Congress[50] soon became a popular slogan guiding the acceleration of the development of the iron and steel industry. As mentioned before, this was a call for every organization and individual to participate in industrialization. It also set off the process by which new production targets were piled on top of one another by the mutually reinforcing efforts between the centre, the MM, and the provinces.

Following the Party Congress, an 'unprecedented' mass movement for building blast furnaces unfolded. Behind this was the MM, which duly convened the second National Conference on Local Metallurgical Industry at Beijing in late May or early June, just over a month after the first conference, to implement the new policies. During this conference, the provincial representatives proposed new plans to build more than 10,000 blast furnaces with capacities ranging from only 3 cu. m to 250 cu. m in the following twelve months, giving a combined total pig iron production capacity of 20m. tons. This output was said to be equivalent to the output of 40 modern blast furnaces with capacities of 1,000 cu. m. Emboldened by these pledges, the MM estimated that, because of the new blast furnaces being put into operation gradually, the local industrial enterprises in 1958 could produce 4m. tons of pig iron, doubling the target made at the previous meeting in April (or ten times over the 1957 production).[51] Apart from the large number of blast furnaces planned by the provinces, the inclusion of furnaces as small as 3 cu. m meant the incorporation of the indigenous technology into the state plan.[52] Even smaller furnaces were cited approvingly by the MM—it affirmed that a blast furnace in Sichuan (with a capacity of 1.8 cu. m) capable of producing 400 tons of pig iron annually was built in seven days, costing only 700 *yuan*. In addition, the MM also predicted that an 'all-people build blast furnaces' movement would soon sweep through the country.

As the temperature continued to rise, at a later stage of the conference, the provinces crossed another threshold by vowing not just to smelt iron, but also produce

---

[49] *Mao Wengao*, vii. 291; Li Rui, *Lushan Huiyi*, 40, 82, 84, 107; *Women de Zhou Zongli*, 150.

[50] *HHPYK*, 11, 1958, 8.

[51] *RMRB*, 7 June 1958; *BR*, no. 16, 17 June 1958, 4. Discrepancies between the figures listed here and the ones contained in Liu's report can be explained by the existence of the so-called 'three sets of plans' which were used widely during the GLF. Consequently, different people referred to different figures although they meant the same plan. This practice had contributed greatly to the confusion in planning and statistics collection during the GLF.

[52] According to one commentator, the capacity of the first blast furnace invented in Belgium five hundred years ago was 10 cu. m. Many indigenous furnaces built during the GLF had a capacity of even less that 1 cu. m. Ma Hong and Sun Shangqing (eds.), *Zhongguo Jingji Jiegou Wenti Yanjiu* (Studies on the structural problems of the Chinese economy) (Beijing: Renmin chubanshe, 1981), i. 304.

steel. Collectively they pledged to build 2,000 new medium and small Bessemer converters that might boost steel production instantly by 1m. tons in 1958 and another incredible 10m. tons within the next year. Even while Shandong, Jiangsu, Hebei, Anhui, Henan, and Sichuan each vowed to build 10–15 of these convertors, Zhejiang, Shanxi, Shandong, and Beijing claimed that theirs had already gone into operation.[53]

The MM's performance bolstered Mao's cause and perhaps even his confidence. Therefore, a Politburo meeting (26–30 May) adjusted the steel targets for 1958 to 8 or 8.5m. tons and for 1962, 40m. tons. This became the third account of 1958.[54] After the Politburo decision, Wang sought out Lin Te, and convinced him that the North China region could achieve production capabilities of 8m. tons by 1959. From 9 June onwards, the Party Committee of the MM dispatched cadres to all other Cooperative Regions to canvass support.[55] On 5 June, in acceding to Mao's wishes, Wang worked out a plan to raise the steel production *capacity* to 36m. tons annually from June 1958 to June 1960, which was then submitted to Liu. The Politburo on 9 June discussed and approved this plan. On 7 June, a MM report to the Politburo predicted that steel production for 1958 could be 8.2m. tons, so it set the target for 1962 at 60m. tons, doubling the highest estimates at the Party Congress.[56]

Mao thought highly of these estimates, adding that with 60m. tons for 1962, then surpassing the USA would be easy. Nevertheless, the more immediate task was to achieve 25m. tons in 1959 so that Britain could be surpassed.[57] In fact, Mao did his part to keep the competitive bidding alive. After the Congress, he gave a pep talk to the seven directors of the Cooperative Regions and first secretaries of the provinces on accelerating industrial and agricultural production.[58] Ke Qingshi, the newly appointed Politburo member, responded with relish. At the end of May, an East China planning conference chaired by Ke in Shanghai, 'aided' by many planners and ministers, pledged that the East China region alone could produce 6 to 7m. tons of steel in 1958 and 8m. tons in 1959. When other directors got wind of this, they followed suit with their own extravagant estimates. Accepting this at face value, the MM added up the estimates of the Coordination Regions, and declared on 21 June that steel output could reach 30m. tons in 1959, and 80–90m. tons in 1962. This was exactly what Mao wanted, for two days prior (19 June), he had already suggested to Bo to double the 1957 production in 1958.[59]

This simple-minded preoccupation with the expansion of smelting capacity and targets was the result of idealistic fervour. The corresponding problems such as the availability of raw materials, transportation support, power and labour supplies, and facilities for rolled-steel production, and so on, which plagued the campaign from the beginning, were not even mentioned, let alone addressed at this time. Inevitably,

---

[53] *RMRB*, 19 June 1958; *BR*, no. 17, 24 June 1958, 4.
[54] Bo Yibo, *Huigu*, ii. 696; Xie Chuntao, *Dayuejin*, 56.   [55] *Mao Wengao*, vii. 267.
[56] Bo Yibo, *Huigu*, ii. 696; *Mao Wengao*, vii. 278–9; Cong Jin, *Quzhe Fazhan*, 134.
[57] *Mao Wengao*, vii. 279.   [58] Ibid. 255.
[59] Bo Yibo, *Huigu*, ii. 701; *Mao Wengao*, vii. 282; Cong Jin, *Quzhe Fazhan*, 138; Li Rui, *Lushan Huiyi*, 36, 81–2; Xie Chuntao, *Dayuejin*, 56; Liu Suinian and Wu Qungan, *Daiyuejin he Tiaozheng*, 23–4.

the MM had to confront these issues, and two conferences were convened in June to deal with them. These conferences showed the ways the MM handled its sub-ordinates, as we will see in the following.

The Ministry of Metallurgical Industry and the Bottleneck Problems

Before it could be used industrially, ordinary crude steel has to be rolled into a variety of finished products such as bars, tube rounds, seamless tubes, steel plates, and rails. This complicated process requires large and modern machinery and highly technical and sophisticated equipment simply unavailable in large quantities in China in the 1950s. In June, the MM claimed to have 'predicted' the problem of rolled-steel production and subsequently convened the National Conference to Promote Rolled Steel at Shanghai. During this, the MM complained that the pro-duction of rolled steel had not received widespread attention. It claimed that some places had planned to produce some ordinary rolled-steel products such as bars and tube rounds, but generally the local authorities were reluctant. This was under-standable since this was an entirely new venture, and without the supply of funds, machinery and technological assistance from the centre, few would make com-mitments. Moreover, before the national conference, the centre and the MM had not set policy regarding rolled-steel production. The MM's complaint that the provinces had failed to make initiatives was a transparent attempt to shift the blame onto its subordinate units. In any event, the MM criticized the provinces' alleged failure to live up to their responsibilities as a kind of 'superstition'—the 'smashing of super-stition' was a favourite slogan used by Mao in 1958. It argued vehemently that a variety of rolled-steel products could be manufactured by using small, simple machinery and with indigenous methods. Hence, it urged that rolled-steel produc-tion should develop at the 'highest' speed, so the goal that in three years time, the variety of rolled-steel products would reach 10,000, doubling the 1957 record. It then demanded all the local authorities to 'uncover potentials' and to plan to increase rolled-steel production to match the soaring iron and steel production.[60]

These initiatives from the MM were a non-starter. In the rest of the year a frenzied drive to achieve the high iron and steel targets gripped the country, and rolled steel had to be set aside, for the obsession had become the fulfilment of astronomical targets, not production for use. In the winter of 1958/9, hoards of low quality and unusable crude steel swamped the country, but the supply of rolled steel was acutely short. It was not until the last week of 1958 that the MM convened another national conference, calling for a national campaign to raise production of rolled steel in 1959.

On the other front, to deal with the pressing problem of shortage of raw materials, the MM convened the National Conference to Promote the Construction of Ferrous Metal Mines at Handan, Hebei between 20 and 27 June. The avowed goal was to

---

[60] *RMRB*, 24 June 1958, 7 January 1959.

produce 200m. tons of iron ore by 1960, or thirteen times the output of 1957. Ironically, after spending months concentrating on the expansion of smelting facilities, the MM now came to the insight that 'to have a great leap forward in iron and steel production, the construction of mines must come before anything else'. In fact, the emergence of thousands of furnaces had created a tremendous demand for raw materials that were non-existent; the previous assumption that the scattered reserves would somehow supply the iron and steel furnaces were unfounded.

After hearing reports submitted to the meeting, the MM again expressed dissatisfaction over the provinces' handling of the developing of ferrous metal mines. According to it, some provinces had ignored this task; they had made plans but they wanted large-scale mechanized operations and resisted the working of small mines using the indigenous method. After criticizing these deviations, the MM brought out the Kuangshan Cun model that, it claimed, had overthrown the old accepted procedure and practice of operating mines. This new method combined the three different steps—design, construction, and production simultaneously (*biansheji, bianjianshe, bianshengchan*), using the 'small and indigenous' way. In effect, this meant that production was to begin immediately at locations even remotely suspected of having iron ore reserves, irrespective of the size of the deposits, cost, and feasibility.[61] In particular, two models from counties in Henan and Guangxi were chosen to be popularized. It was said that working independently of geological experts, the party secretaries there had mobilized the masses to search for ores. Allegedly, the ore deposits in their areas were well prospected quickly and without using state investments.

Finally, the MM demanded that the provincial party committees instruct their metallurgical departments to draft plans for the opening of mines immediately, especially the small and medium ones, to ensure that an uninterrupted supply to the numerous local blast furnaces could be assured.[62] The MM was making a virtue out of necessity by emphasizing the small mines, the indigenous method, and the mass movement. Fortunately, these measures were consistent with Mao's own thinking. The 1957/8 decentralization had stripped the ministries of many of their powers and responsibilities. Yet in issuing orders and demands over the provinces, the MM (or more accurately, its leadership) had overstepped its role. In contrast to many other ministries, the MM had increased its profile, power, and responsibilities, although it had simultaneously metamorphosed gradually from a bureaucratic actor to an agitator, model, and mobilizer. Internally the zealots had gained ascendancy and, in pushing for radical and unrealistic policies, its organizational mission was blurred. It had also begun to live with the consequences of its demagoguery and zealotry. Its attempt to make the provinces accountable for not anticipating the problems that accompanied the expansion of smelting capabilities was a clear case of buck passing. It also applied a great deal of pressure on the

---

[61] According to a visitor to Sichuan, during the GLF, an expensive railway was built leading to a remote mountainous area thought to have huge iron ore deposits. Only when the railway was completed did the people find out that the quantity of the ore was small and insignificant.

[62] *RMRB*, 3 July 1958; *BR*, no. 19, 8 July 1958, 6.

provinces to become self-reliant in the supply of raw materials and processing (rolled-steel) capabilities.

Steel as the Key Link (*yigang weigan*) and 'All People Smelt Steel'

Meanwhile, as Mao and the Party Centre had decided internally to double the 1957 output of steel for 1958 in June, the provinces convened a series of meetings on local iron and steel production between June and July to discuss how to implement the two important targets—10,000 small and medium blast furnaces and 2,000 small and medium convertors—made at the Second National Conference on Local Metallurgy. Yet even this must have been insufficient for the new tasks. A new turning point arrived when tens of thousands of blast furnaces were reported to have been built.[63]

Already at the end of July, one open report claimed that the output of pig iron, steel, and rolled steel in the first half of 1958 had exceeded the original plan by 25–32 per cent, and that there were 30,000 small and indigenous blast furnaces, far exceeding the target set in April and June. It bragged that some varieties of much-needed rolled-steel products had increased from 26 per cent to 142 per cent, although later reports on the severe crisis inflicting rolled-steel production contradicted this claim.[64]

A July report by the Director of the Bureau of Metallurgical Industry of the SEC predicted openly that steel production could soar to more than 10m. tons in 1958. The 'balanced' strategy was based on: first, the huge modern iron and steel mills such as Anshan, Shanghai, and Chongqing; second, many medium and small iron and steel mills; third, a 'myriad of small blast furnaces and small Bessemer converters'. An example of these small blast furnaces built by a farm tools plant in Suzhou (8 cu. m in size) had an annual capacity of 40,000 tons, and cost 100,000 *yuan* and three months to build. Although realizing that the indigenous blast furnaces and converters, being built with sand, stone, and fire clay, would not last, the Director argued that since they required little time and funds to assemble, their construction was amply justified by 'urgent need'.[65] As was made increasingly clear, the simple home-made small furnaces were used almost entirely to substantiate the hike in the targets and to support the vainglory of the Chairman.

Yet the small furnaces were from the beginning plagued by problems of shoddy construction, shortages of raw materials, and the lack of know-how. Furnaces already in operation were unable to function normally and the pig iron produced was sub-standard. Some were far from any mines, making the supply of raw materials difficult and forcing many to sit idle. The way the indigenous furnaces were developed at Shaoyang Special District, Hunan province, was typical and revealing, and is therefore worth quoting at length:

The Communist Party's first step was to call the residents of each locality to meetings where they discussed the importance of steel production to the national economy, the relation of steel

---

[63] *RMRB*, 8 August 1958.   [64] *RMRB*, 27 August 1958.   [65] *BR*, no. 22, 29 July 1958, 11–13.

to raising farm output, and basic information on steel-making. Through discussions and debates the farmers came to see that it was only a myth that one needed expensive equipment and highly trained personnel for steel-making, and decided that they could do it themselves. Once this idea was firmly established, the enthusiasm was so great that in one week the District Party Committee received letters from 500,000 people expressing their desire to join the project. Many volunteers brought along their own tools, food and materials, while others donated funds for the initial investment. One county collected 1.6m. *yuan* in this way. A million people were finally mobilized for steel, and most of them were set to comb the mountains for iron and coal known to be there. They said: 'We'll find coal and ore even if we have to dig to the other side of the globe.' In one county 14 iron ore and 8 coal mines were discovered and set up in this way.

Meanwhile the furnace-builders were at work. Their slogan was 'where there is ore there will be a furnace'. They set up whole forests of small furnaces near the deposits or on fields where crops had just been harvested. They were given names like 'Teacher's Furnace' to indicate the people who built and operated them—farmers, housewives, students, soldiers, and government workers. Through a five-day course, farmers were trained to be furnace workers. Each person who had learned how taught another ten people.[66]

Overall, pig iron production was inadequate for steel smelting. Internally it was known that total production of steel to July was only 3.8m. tons. Nevertheless, as the target had already been revealed to the Soviets, and Mao had shown a tremendous stake in its fulfilment, there was no turning back. By August, as the maximum pressure exerted by Mao began to be felt, a two-pronged policy change was adopted. First, steel was now designated the 'key link' in industry, and in the economy as a whole absolute priority was given to high-speed steel making in which everyone should participate. Steel was designated the key link because its phenomenal growth would also spur on other industries, and all sectors of the economy.[67]

Second, as the production targets kept spiralling out of control, the large and modern plants (including the small and modern plants) were no solution for the short-term goal of output maximization, as they required time and large investments. Hence, the Party increasingly counted on the small indigenous blast furnaces, which it claimed could be run not just by the MM, but also by other industrial ministries, government organs, arms units, schools, urban neighbourhoods, handicraft collectives, and APCs, as the determinant in the fulfilment of the 1958 iron and steel targets.

So in August, the Party proposed that the development of the iron and steel industry should rely *mainly* on the small and the indigenous (ways of production). It argued that since the large and medium enterprises required more investment, technology, and time to complete, they could not be popularized quickly. The small and indigenous furnaces were simpler, requiring little investment, and the technology could easily be mastered by local metallurgical and industrial departments, even factories, government offices, armed force units, schools, neighbourhood

---

[66] *RMRB*, 27 August 1958. *China Reconstructs*, December 1958, 14.
[67] *RMRB*, 8 and 22 August 1958.

committees, and handicraft and agricultural cooperatives. With tens of thousands of these small furnaces, a 'mighty torrent' of iron and steel could be formed. In turn, as the Marxist principle indicated, quantitative change would lead to qualitative change. The problem of quality could solve itself when large quantities were available.[68]

Again, taking the cue from the centre in August, Henan was said to have planned 30,000 indigenous and small blast furnaces within the year with a total capacity of 4m. tons of pig iron, which was equivalent to the total pig iron output of the Anshan Iron and Steel Works! As an *RMRB* editorial argued, if only one-quarter of all China's provinces could do the same, wouldn't it be like having seven Anshans?[69] As the Chinese leaders were consumed by delusion, this kind of reasoning by analogy was employed repeatedly in making decisions.

Again the MM took the lead in promoting the indigenous furnace campaign and disarming the opposition to it. It selected Shaoyang, Hunan, to be the first national model and called an on-the-spot conference there in August (6–14) with 400 representatives from the central and provincial authorities. The conference first affirmed the experience of using the indigenous method in smelting pig iron and then selected several 'workable' furnace designs to be copied throughout the country.[70] The Party alleged that this should solve the problem of the furnaces once and for all, and urged the leadership cadres at all levels to run 'experimental' furnaces. It was said that one deputy governor at a Hubei county had successfully led technicians in the use of charcoal to smelt pig iron. The on-the-spot training had cultivated more than 200 more 'technicians', who were now running 24 indigenous furnaces that could function normally. However, the Party also admitted that some people still scorned the small and indigenous way as too primitive. They still insisted on the large and medium furnaces. Other local authorities wanted to build small furnaces, but shunned the indigenous method.[71]

It was natural that the planners and technicians were reluctant to divert resources and energy to the primitive methods. Nor is it surprising that local cadres, who hoped that machinery and equipment would be supplied by the state to start small-scale productions, saw little point in extracting funds from the local populace to engage in the useless pursuit of smelting indigenous iron. Nevertheless, their concerns were totally stifled.

Steel Mania

The Expanded Politburo Conference at Beidaihe (17–30 August)

As mentioned, at the Beidaihe Conference, the intensifying pressure exerted by Mao and the official publication of the 1958 steel target defined steel to be a 'the most

---

[68] *RMRB*, 8 August 1958.   [69] Ibid.
[70] *RMRB*, 22 August 1958.   [71] *RMRB*, 8 August 1958.

important *political* task' (emphasis mine). Mao the supreme commander of the Leap realized that the iron and steel campaign had stalled, but since he had placed his personal credibility on the line, all-out herculean efforts were ordered by him for a desperate gamble. No let-down was permitted. Previous exhortations for action were deemed insufficient, so the party centre seized the direct leadership of the iron and steel campaign, and decided to throw its total organizational might into the campaign. All the nation's main resources were to be channelled into the campaign. New production quotas for steel were also assigned to each province, county, and *xiang*. The operational details of these decisions were worked out at a concurrent meeting of provincial secretaries in charge of industry (20–31 August) called by Mao. It decided to tighten control, as the progress of steel production was to be inspected weekly.[72] Other incentives to encourage iron smelting in September included the doubling of the MM's acceptable standard of sulphur content from 1 to 2 per cent, and the boosting of the state's purchasing price from 150 to 200 *yuan* per ton, with all the losses absorbed by the state.[73]

This obsession with iron and steel, which was incongruent with the strategy of all-round and balanced development envisaged at the beginning of 1958, showed the shifting goals of the GLF. In any event, the absolute priority accorded iron and steel production had created conflict with other departments and ministries. Nevertheless, the Party Centre was determined to vouch for steel. Hence an *RMRB* editorial of 27 August demanded that all industrial ministries (such as the Ministries of Machinery, Non-ferrous Metal Industry, Coal Industry, Power Industry, and Communication and Transport) should subordinate their own interests consciously (*zijue di*) to that of the MM, and elevate the support of the iron and steel industry as their foremost 'political tasks'. The machine-making enterprises, it claimed, had already adopted the slogan of 'stop the car and yield, let the supreme commander of iron and steel take command', and turned the manufacturing of metallurgical equipment, which was in short supply, into its top priority. At this phase of the iron and steel campaign, it was none other than Premier Zhou who took charge to ensure that 'other activities would give way' (*biede ranglu*).[74]

The immense pressure for steel set many provinces going. In Henan, all members of the PPC had participated in running 'experimental plots'. Roving iron and steel teams were formed to fix problems. Even the District Party Committees had switched their focus to iron and steel production. Luoyang and Xinyang Special Districts had organized an 'iron and steel army' of 570,000 that was subdivided into specialized transport, smelting, and mining teams, to throw into the campaign. Xinyang was said to have organized 'motor vehicle' and 'horse cart' divisions to transport ore and coal. The Hubei PPC, meeting on 1 September, pledged the immediate mobilization of a one million 'iron and steel army', and ordered all party

---

[72] *RMRB*, 1 September 1958; *BR*, no. 2, 1958, 4; *China Reconstructs*, December 1958, p. 15.

[73] Bo Yibo, *Huigu*, ii. 710, 712.

[74] Zhou Enlai, *Zhou Enlai Xuanji* (Selected Works of Zhou Enlai) (Beijing: Renmin chubanshe, 1984), ii. 406.

first secretaries of all levels to assume personal charge to smelt iron and steel and to run 'experimental plots'. On 2 September, a Hunan joint broadcasting conference of the PPC and PPPC demanded that the iron and steel quota for the year be completed in October.[75]

On the other hand, eight days after the initial call for 'everything for steel', another RMRB editorial called for the waging of an 'uncompromising struggle' against 'departmentalism' and 'dispersionism'. It reminded all ministries and localities again to accord the highest priority to iron and steel production. When conflicts arose regarding equipment, raw materials, electric power and manpower, they were to abandon their own requirements in favour of the iron and steel industry—now called the 'key point among all key points' of all industries.[76] The slogan 'politics takes command' took on a very unusual meaning as steel was now equated with politics.[77] However, despite the charged atmosphere, some rumblings could still be detected—some people in the industrial departments had chastised the mass movement running the steel industry as, in Mao's words, 'guerrilla habits', and 'unorthodox and irregular'. They either disagreed with the iron and steel campaign or resented having to suppress their needs and normal functions, to the single goal of the iron and steel industry.[78]

In any event, with the Politburo decisions, the colossal mobilization campaign for iron and steel finally caught fire, and many high-yield 'satellites' were claimed. In early September, Henan claimed that its daily production had exceeded that of Liaoning, Jilin, and Heilonjiang combined. It had accomplished this feat by building more than 50,000 small blast furnaces and mobilizing 3.6 million people.[79] The Ministry of Transport launched an 'all-people run transport' campaign and ordered its subordinates to devote all available transport vehicles and manpower to the shipping of ore, coke, and equipment.[80] These open exaggerations were matched by the equally extravagant internal report submitted to Mao by the Henan PPC on 25 September. It claimed that in 1957 the provincial pig iron production was a trifle of 3,000 tons, but daily production had soared to 1,000 tons, and one-day output on 15 September was 18,944 tons. Between 15 and 22 September, the total production was said to be 67,217 tons. Its aim now was to achieve a 'satellite' record of daily production of 20,000 to 50,000 tons before national day. Mao approved the report, and ordered its turning into a news report for the RMRB on 3 October, hoping it would rally the ranks.[81]

Nevertheless, this colossal spontaneous activism was soon soured by bad news. It was freely admitted that, of the total 240,000 small blast furnaces constructed so far, only one-quarter were operational.[82] Those in use simply could

---

[75] RMRB, 5 September 1958.   [76] Ibid.   [77] China Reconstructs, 12, 1958, 14.
[78] RMRB, 24 September 1958.   [79] Dangshi Yanjiu, 2, 1996, 63.
[80] RMRB, 18 September 1958.   [81] Mao Wengao, vii. 434–5.
[82] RMRB, 13 September 1958. In Sichuan, most blast furnaces were located in remote mountains far away from raw materials and inaccessible by roads so that food and fuel could not be shipped. NBCK, 29 September 1958, 4–5.

not produce normally; others were idle because of acute shortages of raw materials such as coal or iron ore. In 1958, 30,000 indigenous furnaces in Hunan were not even lit, perhaps as a bid to control the damage.[83] To remedy this situation, an *RMRB* editorial of 14 September urged the provinces to try to have half the blast furnaces already built start production and the remaining half produce regularly by 20 September.[84] The blast furnaces were clearly a sham, and the expectation about these furnaces at the grass-roots level was even lower. According to *Shishi Shouce*, a publication for grass-roots level cadres, if 'only one among one hundred blast furnaces can produce iron, it is very good; it means that a red flag has been hoisted'.[85]

Apparently the party counted on a spectacular success in pig iron production in September as a prerequisite to doubling the 1957 steel production to 10.7m. tons in the four remaining months in the year. However, this expectation was dashed once the production figures for the first half of September showed that most of the provinces had failed to fulfil substantial parts of their targets. This alarmed the centre, which admitted that the general situation was 'not good'. Nevertheless, it insisted that the task could be and must be done, and issued a stern warning to the provinces.[86]

To lend full support to Mao's cause, between the months of August and October, China's top leaders toured the provinces to inspect and promote the iron and steel campaign. Their comments and even casual remarks made during the trips were turned into policies that profoundly affected the turn of events. Many of them were impressed by what they saw. For instance, Liu Shaoqi thought he had found the solution to the problems of the small blast furnaces at Shijiazhuang, Hebei. Here, the people used several blowers for one furnace to raise the temperature; the iron ore was crushed and selected by hand, and low grade ore was baked to remove the impurities before being fed into the blast furnaces. An impressed Liu instantly instructed that this experience be popularized nationally.[87]

Operations like this were extremely wasteful, as one factory alone required five hundred people to crush the ore by hand. A few days later Liu reversed himself by announcing that such a waste of manpower was not that desirable after all; some form of mechanization, according to him, was preferable.[88] In any case, oral directives of this kind played an especially important policy role during the last part of 1958, as they were hailed as authoritative pronouncements to be implemented by the local cadres.

At Zhengzhou, Henan, Liu was briefed by Wu Zhipu, First Secretary of the Provincial Party Committee, who was worried about the critical labour supply. Liu replied that this shortage was a 'tremendously good thing', for this meant that surplus labour had disappeared in a country with a huge population, and that

[83] Li Rui, *Lushan Huiyi*, 39.   [84] *RMRB*, 14 September 1958.
[85] *Shishi Shouce*, 18, 1958, 13.   [86] *RMRB*, 16 September 1958.
[87] *RMRB*, 17 September 1958; *Hebei Ribao* (Hebei Daily), 16 September 1958.
[88] *RMRB*, 24 September 1958.

everybody was engaged in doing something useful.[89] Even at this stage, Liu seemed oblivious of the gravity of the labour problem. Even if he was aware, he could only offer stock answers. Li Fuchun, on the other hand, urged the workers at Anshan to 'emancipate their minds from all blind faiths and introduce bold measures to boost production' during a tour there on 25 September. In response, the steel workers were said to have revised the steel target for October upward and made many suggestions toward the fulfilling of this goal.

After the Politburo meeting in August Mao also toured four provinces to inspect and promote the iron and steel industry there. Upon his return to Beijing in late September he reiterated that the highest priority was the fulfilment of iron and steel targets. Yet, he also complained that some localities and enterprises had failed to organize large-scale mass movements in industry, belittling it as 'unorthodox, a rural style of work, and a guerrilla habit'. Having criticized this kind of thinking as wrong, he again called for general mobilization in industry.[90] One prototype that received Mao's blessing was the iron and steel plant run by the Anhui Provincial Party Committee. Managed mostly by cadres from the provincial administration, this 'experimental plot' was clearly very primitive, as many were engaged in crushing the ore by hand, and there was only one crusher.[91] However, this nod by the Chairman, together with other exhortations by the party, soon brought about another high-tide in the campaign.

The 'Reckless' October High Tide

29 September was designated by the Party Centre to be the day for 'launching satellites' to greet National Day, and the local authorities responded with aplomb. The total figure of small blast furnaces was said to have tripled from 200,000 to 600,000, and one day production of iron and steel had reached 300,000 and 600,000 tons, respectively. This accomplishment was attributed to the effective promotion of the '*xiao* (small), *tu* (indigenous), *qun* (mass movement)', or '*xiaotuqun*' method by the various levels of the party committees. So, an *RMRB* editorial declared that the

---

[89] *BR*, no. 37, 1958, 15–16. Deng Xiaoping, on the other hand, was pushing for urban communes in his tour of the northwest provinces in September. According to him, 'Urban communes must be formed. The rural areas of the entire country are being communized gradually. The cities should not be left behind.' *RMRB*, 1 October 1958. In his confessions made at the Red Guard trials, Wu Lengxi, Director of the New China News Agency (1952–66) and editor-in-chief of the *RMRB* (1957–66) recalled, 'During the Lushan Conference in July 1959, Liu Shaoqi severely criticized the NCNA and the *RMRB* in the small group discussions for having greatly stirred up an atmosphere of exaggeration in 1958. In particular, he stressed that the NCNA and the *RMRB* had published some opinions expressed by responsible comrades of the Central Committee during their tours in the provinces, and that these opinions were premature and erroneous and resulted in harmful effects throughout the nation. He also said that the NCNA had reported some opinions he expressed during his tour of Henan without consulting him before hand, that it had reported them inaccurately, and that he could not be held responsible.' *Liu Shaoqi Wenti Ziliao Xuanji* (A collection of materials on Liu Shaoqi) (Taipei: The Institute for the Study of Chinese Communist Problems, 1970), 609 (trans. in *Chinese Law and Government*, 2/4, 1969–70, 76.)

[90] *RMRB*, 1 October 1958.   [91] Jia Zhengqiu, *Mao Zedong Weixun ji*, 314–16.

pig iron 'hurdle' had been cleared 'basically', so it was time to switch the attention to the production of steel. Right on cue, reports from Sichuan, Zibo, Yuci, Lanzhou, Guangzhou, Shanghai, and Tianjin claimed that they had produced good quality steel using the indigenous method. Henan, they said, had constructed more than 5,000 converter furnaces within a few days, and the plan there was to erect up to 50,000 of these converter furnaces by the end of October. In Shanxi, a mass movement was formed to popularize the *xiaotuqun* method to smelt steel.[92] Clearly, these regional units were ready to cater to the illusion of the centre.

The campaign reached a boiling point when it was reported that an incredible 50 million people were working in the iron and steel production campaign to dig for coal, search for iron ore, fell trees, build furnaces, smelt iron and steel. Another 50 million people were involved in support functions. Apparently impressed by these reports, Bo Yibo, the head of the State Planning Commission, called for the October plan for iron and steel to double the amount achieved in September. October, he said, was the 'leap forward' month and was the key to the achievement of the year's target of 10.7m. tons of steel.[93]

Meanwhile, many of the 700,000 indigenous blast furnaces had such faulty designs that they produced only very low grade iron or no iron at all. For instance, Chunhua County had tried dozens of times and used up tons of charcoal, but failed to produce any iron. Other blast furnaces sat idle because of the lack of raw materials. Increasingly, the authorities found it difficult to feed, clothe, and pay the peasants-*cum*-workers. Logistics for the campaign were chaotic, wasting large amounts of manpower.[94] Nevertheless, the CCP was determined to commit all the resources at its disposal to accomplish the severely inflated targets. On 4 October, it issued another order and plunged the country into a new mass campaign for *steel* using the *xiaotuqun* method. This set off another craze to construct numerous furnaces such as converters, and open-hearth furnaces. In time, even crucibles were used.[95]

Clearly this was another uphill battle. First, the steel-smelting process, far more complicated than iron-smelting, required sophisticated technology and equipment unavailable to the general population. Second, the raw material obtainable, if at all, was the low quality pig iron produced by the small furnaces scattered throughout the country.[96] Attempts to transport them clogged the transportation system. Third, as the autumn harvest and sowing had become urgent tasks, and the other campaigns

[92] *RMRB*, 4 October 1958.

[93] *RMRB*, 1 October 1958. This would require the *daily* production of iron and steel to rise to over 60,000 tons and 100,000 tons respectively. In addition, this would require the 'appearance' of more than ten 'ten-thousand-tons provinces' and more than fifty 'thousand-ton counties' (that is, provinces and counties which could produce more than 10,000 tons and 1,000 tons of pig iron daily). Compared with the total iron and steel production at 5.93 and 5.35 m. tons respectively in 1957, these were indeed fantastic figures.

[94] *RMRB*, 10 October 1958; *NBCK*, 20 October 1958, 3–14.   [95] *RMRB*, 4 October 1958.

[96] According to Clark, *Development*, 70, 'The maximum allowable sulphur content for any type of pig iron is five-hundredths of one percent, usually much less is allowed. Native iron was frequently reported [during the GLF, author] to average 1%, and in many cases it averaged between 3 and 5%. A few pounds of such native iron could make tons of modern iron unusable in the manufacture of modern steel, but the attempt to use it also contaminated the high-quality iron and steel produced by modern standards.'

for copper and aluminium also made a heavy demand on manpower, it was impossible to retain as much labour at the iron and steel front as before. Finally, in north China, cold winter was approaching and autumn rain was more frequent in the south. Without adequate shelter against the cold and rain, the furnaces were unable to function.[97] Until now, the goal was simply to produce pig iron by hook or by crook, but now the problem of quality and cost had to be reckoned with,[98] although nothing was actually done.

Meanwhile, the condition of the blast furnaces deteriorated to such an extent that the CCP had to admit openly:

We cannot deny that the labour paid out by many people has come to naught. They have dug out the ore, transported it to the furnaces and tried to smelt day and night. However, because of the defects of the blast furnaces, no iron was produced. Although sometimes iron was produced, the quantity, quality, and cost were far behind the others.[99]

Yet, huge quantities of indigenous iron were already produced, so the Party tried desperately to convert it into steel, and designated 15–21 October 'high yield week'. Furthermore, the indigenous iron had been shipped, at large expense, to the steel mills, but the technicians shunned it, knowing that its high sulphur content had rendered it useless for steel smelting. Others adopted a wait-and-see attitude and some refused to use it outright.[100] The Party's response was to charge them for blindly worshipping things 'foreign', unwilling to search for the Chinese method by repeated experiments. Again, the MM had the unenviable task of trying to suppress this kind of sentiment by convening a national conference at the Xinxing Steel Plant at Tianjin between 7 and 9 October. Allegedly this steel mill had overcome the problems of using indigenous iron to smelt steel. The meeting then introduced some very elaborate, expensive, and wasteful methods to correct the faults of indigenous iron.[101] Although these technical remedies might be workable in a few places, they were unlikely to be duplicated in the rest of the country. As to the other drawback—the wide divergence in the chemical composition of the indigenous iron owing to its scattered origin and the small output per heat by the small blast furnaces—the meeting could only prescribe more laboratory testing to match similarly composed indigenous iron, whereas the only solution was to smelt it again in the regular blast furnaces.[102]

These manœuvres could not mask entirely the credibility gap, so the Party centre maintained that the only way out was to let 'politics' take command and to 'liberate' one's thoughts from the 'superstitions' that 'indigenous iron cannot make steel'.[103] The slogan 'politics take command' had acquired another new meaning in this context—it simply meant the suspension of one's disbelief and keep on doing what one was told.

Another stumbling-block for the iron and steel campaign was the shortage of coal affecting all provinces. As the target of iron and steel almost doubled once every

---

[97] *RMRB*, 10 October 1958. It was estimated that to produce 10m. tons of steel, 250,000 or 300,000 tons of copper and aluminum were required. Hence, an 'All-People Smelt Copper and Aluminum' campaign was initiated by the CCP in late September. See *RMRB*, 25 September 1958.
[98] Ibid. 10 October 1958.   [99] Ibid.   [100] *RMRB*, 12 October 1958.   [101] Ibid.
[102] Ibid. See Clark, *Development*, 70.   [103] *RMRB*, 12 October 1958.

month, the demand for coal was tremendous. Furthermore, the small blast furnaces consumed anywhere from 60 per cent to 400 per cent more coal than the modern blast furnaces. Besides, the transportation system was chaotic, as the widely scattered small furnaces had to be supplied by the large coal mines. Moreover, most of the coal originated from the northern provinces, and the necessity of shipping a huge amount of coal to the southern provinces aggravated the situation, making it impossible for coal to be shipped on schedule even inside the coal-producing provinces. In response, the Ministry of Coal Industry ordered the opening of small local coal pits in places with indigenous blast furnaces. The Party quickly endorsed this and on 13 October, called for a mass movement to develop coal pits using the *xiaotuqun* method.[104]

The centre was now totally wrapped up in the iron and steel campaign, yielding more than a few bizarre incidents. Beginning on 10 October, even national government units plunged themselves into the steel-smelting movement. The SPC, the SEC, and the State Science and Technology Commission joined forces to smelt steel with the participation of the Ministry of Education. The Ministries of Civil Affairs, Public Security, Railways, Geology, and Chemical Industry all had constructed their own furnaces. The First Ministry of Machinery searched its warehouses for scrap iron and the MM contributed by sending many staff members to supervise the proceedings.[105]

The Central Committee of the CCP was not to be outdone. The Propaganda Department and the Finance and Trade Department, among others, all took up the task. Chen Boda was reported to have joined the masses in crushing coke and iron ore.[106] Even Song Qingling, the respected widow of Sun Yixian, proudly displayed her own backyard furnace for steel at this time.[107]

---

[104] *RMRB*, 13 October 1958.

[105] Ibid. This lends credence to the report in the magazine *Zheng Ming*. According to it, Xue Muqiao recalled that the people at the State Planning Commission simply broke down the railings surrounding the Commission building and melted it down into iron and steel ingots, 10, 1979, 14.

[106] *RMRB*, 16 October 1958. The general atmosphere at that time is described in *BR*. 'In Beijing these days when government workers meet they greet each other with the extraordinary phrase "Are you making steel? And how much?" This has almost replaced the customary "How d'you do?" . . . Call at the ministries or make a tour of Beijing, day or night, and you will see just how steel-conscious the city had become in the last few days. Every organization has a special squad of men and women on the job who will not return to their desks, they pledge, until they have produced steel to their specifications and amount expected of them. These are no experts . . . practically all of them knew next to nothing about steel. But reading up on it in the newspapers, which are full of news and information about steel-making these days, and in the scores of newly published pamphlets on the subject, they have taught themselves not only the job of building native-style furnaces and smelters but also the technique of making the stuff themselves.

Leading cadres of the government offices and Party organizations give personal direction to the campaign. Many take an active part with the rank and file in this battle for steel. Yang Xiufeng, the Minister of Education, Chen Boda, an alternate member of the Political Bureau of the Communist Party's Central Committee, and many other cadres in leading positions have been in the role of puddlers at the furnaces installed in their office compounds.

The job of making steel continues day and night in many parts of Beijing. At night jets of flames from the furnaces cast a red glow and delineate the contours of eager-looking men and women, with shovel or rabble in hand, working with the excitement of explorers and discoverers who have found their own way to make steel from scratch.' No. 34, 21 October 1958, 4. For another similar report, see *BR*, no. 37, 1958, 15.

[107] *RMRB*, 9 November 1958. Song was then a vice-chairperson of the Standing Committee of the First National People's Congress.

Amid all this, the MM desperately tried to keep the steel-smelting campaign alive by convening a national conference on the indigenous method at Shangcheng, Henan, between 11 and 16 October to popularize two furnace models. These were primitive 'furnaces' built with mud paste, sand, and almost no refractory bricks. The bellows were made with wood, and the fuel and raw materials were wood charcoal, scrap metal, indigenous iron and steel, and broken cooking utensils.[108] Putting on a brave face, the Deputy Minister of the MM, Xia Yun, called for steel smelting by the indigenous method to dot the country. That indigenous steel was really steel must be affirmed, he insisted. To do this, he maintained that the 'conservative theory' and the 'sceptical faction' must be 'smashed' by an inevitable debate, as the promotion of indigenous steel was less a technical question than a political one. Finally, he urged that all the localities should learn from Henan and apply the *xiaotuqun* principle, the spirit of permanent revolution, and the method of 'launching satellites' to promote mass movements to smelt steel.

At this conference, attended by provincial party committee secretaries, heads of the provincial industrial metallurgical departments and many technicians, various indigenous steel furnaces and 'technical inventions' were displayed. The iron and steel factory of the Overtake Britain commune demonstrated by firing up sixty-six indigenous steel furnaces that were built overnight. They sufficiently impressed some delegates from Jiangxi that they vowed to build 10,000 such converters upon their return.[109]

So much political pressure was exerted by the MM that the delegates dared not express doubts, which would make oneself liable to the charges of being a 'rightist conservative' and 'sceptic', although the 'miracles' performed at the conference were hardly credible. Others were either anxious, or at least willing, to conform to the expectations of their superiors. Yet, it was in October that there was a general realization among the party ranks that the steel target for the year could not be fulfilled. However, the party centre, still not wishing to lose face, insisted that it must be reached, and not a ton less was acceptable. Faced with this unresolvable conflict, many units were said to have 'practised fraud and resorted to deception' (*nongs zuojia*), or in other words, goal displacement.[110]

---

[108] *RMRB*, 13 and 17 October, 24 December 1958; *Henan Ribao* (Henan Daily), 12 October 1958. Many over-zealous cadres had confiscated cooking utensils, iron fences, window frames, etc., and broke them down for scrap metal, since there was no iron in the localities. As mess halls were beginning to form in the people's communes, the confiscation of the cooking utentials was perceived to be a way of preventing the peasants from cooking at home. To smash the utentils was described as the 'smashing of private ownership and the conservative tendency of individual producers'. See *The Case of Peng Te-huai* (Hong Kong: Union Research Institute, 1968), 2 and 394. The noted Chinese economist, Sun Yefang, also reported that in many places, the smelting of iron and steel was in reality the wrecking of kitchen pots to fulfil the assigned quota. Ping Xin, *Lun Shengchanli* (Beijing: Sanlian Shudian, 1980), 11. The novel, *Pobiji* by Chen Deng Ke and Xiao Ma (Beijing: Renmin wenxue chubanshe, 1980), which belongs to the genre of 'report literature' popular after the fall of the Gang of Four and which was the first to examine the GLF and the Cultural Revolution in a critical light, also describes this phenomenon in some detail. See pp. 198–204.   [109] *RMRB*, 13 October 1958.

[110] *Xuexi 'Guanyu Jianguo Yilai Dangde Ruogan Lishi Wenti de Jueyi'* (Study the Resolution on certain historical problems of the Party after the founding of the state) (Guangdong: Renmin chubanshe, 1981), 81; Xue Chuntao, *Dayuejin*, 88–95.

Amid all this, it appeared that Zhou Enlai had come to realize the seriousness of the situation and was willing to sanction an exception. On the night of 16 October, Zhou Enlai visited the Beijing Steel Mills which, he was told, used nothing but 'foreign' (and therefore good quality, as opposed to poor quality indigenous) pig iron as raw material. After questioning the people in charge, the Premier expressed satisfaction with the performance of this plant. This is significant since it could be construed that the Premier had endorsed the exclusive use of 'foreign' pig iron in disregard of the indigenous iron in the modern enterprises,[111] especially in view of the MM's condemnation of those who resisted using indigenous iron and its declaration that to use indigenous iron to smelt steel was a 'political mission' only a few days before.[112]

This little interlude, like Zhou's many minor attempts to mitigate the harshest aspects of the campaigns that made him a hero to many Chinese, did not affect the overall iron and steel campaign whatsoever. The situation had reached the stage where backing down was regarded as impossible. In another telephone conference during the autumn, the central authorities again pressured the provinces to fulfil the 10.7m. tons of steel planned for 1958. However, some provincial cadres maintained that the iron produced by the indigenous furnaces were useless. Accordingly they pleaded for the reduction of the production targets, otherwise, they could only resort to false reporting. All the same, the conference concluded that since they had already announced the steel target 'to the world', it must be reached. The problem of false reporting was brushed aside.[113]

In fact, at this time, the centre, and perhaps Mao, were well aware that the production figures were meaningless, but to save face was more important. The 'sunk costs'—concerning not only the huge investment of material and manpower resources, but also the credibility of the Party and even international prestige—were so large that they precluded the consideration of other alternatives. The stated goal must be pursued until the end, although it might never be achieved.[114] On the other hand, some leaders might still entertain the idea that the inflated targets would somehow be fulfilled if constant pressure over the subordinate units was kept up.

The Eighteen Key-Point Iron and Steel Enterprises and the *Xiaotuqun* Campaign

So far we have described mainly the *xiaotuqun* movement, but the iron and steel industry also relied on the eighteen key-point enterprises for producing more than

---

[111] *RMRB*, 19 October 1958. Chinese leaders frequently *biaotai* (i.e. make known one's stand on certain issues) by having their names linked to certain policies, models, ways of doing things, etc. This is especially significant when they are opposed to, or want to modify existing policies and trends. The Chinese who are concerned with the issues will pay close attention to these manifestations.

[112] *RMRB*, 12 October 1958.

[113] Xue Muqiao, *Dangqian Woguo Jingji Ruogan Wenti* (Certain current problems of our national economy) (Beijing: Renmin chubanshe, 1980), 14.

[114] Once heavy investment has been sunk into policies and programmes (the building of airports, dome-stadiums, iron and steel mills are good examples), it is difficult or impossible to back down or to consider other alternatives. Thomas Dye, *Understanding Public Policy*, 5th edn. (Englewood cliffs, NJ: Prentice-Hall, 1984), 34, 36.

40 per cent and 80 per cent of the year's output of iron and steel, respectively. As could be expected, the normal production of these enterprises was not exempted from the commotion of the GLF. Until September, the call for a mass movement to smelt iron and steel was confined to the local industries. Yet, on 29 September, after touring the areas around the Yangzi river basin, Mao complained publicly in the press about the lack of progress in the organization of mass movements in some localities and enterprises. In other words, all units, including the large enterprises, were urged to mobilize mass movements for production, as an *RMRB* editorial on 23 October called upon them to do just that.

In any event, as early as May, the reform in management practice called the 'two participations and one reform' (labour participates in management, and cadres participate in labour and the reform of rules and regulations) had already been adopted in the nation's enterprises.[115] The call for mass movements was meant to complement this reform. However, given the high targets and the obsessive emphasis on steel ('steel is politics'), this meant the hasty destruction of existing rules, regulations, and routines with little or no alternatives. Numerous 'blooming and contending' meetings were held whereby the workers were enjoined to air views and to submit innovative ideas for the 'technical revolution'. A corollary of this was the downgrading of the role of the technicians. Since the speedy production of steel was elevated to supreme political significance, these mass movements, with the agitation of some activists, inevitably led to even higher production targets and the invention of timesaving and nonsensical ways to achieve them.

Therefore, it is not surprising that some leading 'comrades' resented these mass movements. In places where mass action had already been mobilized, they were said to be obstructionist. Some of them demanded more equipment as a precondition for raising production; others were said to have stuck stubbornly to the established managerial routines. These manifestations were categorically criticized as 'superstition, dogmatism, and empiricism'. A proud *China Reconstructs* article speaks volumes:

During the 'big leap forward' it was the workers and not the managers who decided when targets should be raised. Typically, meetings of workers raised production goals not once but several times during the year. For example, in January the 1958 target of the Shenyang No. 1 Machine Tool Works was 20 per cent more than the 1957 output. In the next eight months the workers raised the target four times, until the increase over 1957 was 135 per cent. In this plant production more than doubled, while the work force decreased 10 per cent.[116]

Apart from this, the key enterprises were also seriously affected by the nationwide iron and steel campaign. First, pig iron had not been shipped from the numerous scattered smelters on time to supply the large enterprises, many of which were located far from sources of raw materials. This problem was so acute that the MM and the Ministry of Transport convened a joint telephone conference (on 25 October) with thirteen provinces and issued an emergency call for action. The MM

[115] *RMRB*, 7 May 1958.
[116] *RMRB*, 23 October 1958. *China Reconstructs*, January 1959, 12.

ordered the metallurgy departments of the provinces to mobilize immediately to gather and ship pig iron to the key enterprises.[117]

Similarly, Wang Shoudou, Minister of Transport, ordered his subordinates to mobilize for a transport network to ship iron and steel. The provinces duly promised to accelerate transportation, build roads, and mobilize all sorts of land, water, and non-governmental means of support for this purpose. The key reason for this shortage, however, lay in the fact that the local authorities had consumed a large amount of locally produced pig iron and become major competitors with the key enterprises for fuel and raw materials. Other localities claimed (most probably, tongue-in-cheek) that since the *xiaotuqun* had created such wonders and even out-produced some key enterprises, the latter had become unimportant.[118]

Second, the most formidable problem was the high sulphur content of the indigenous iron. Much of the iron produced was really 'sponge iron' that could neither be used for casting nor converted into steel directly.[119] Therefore, no matter how much the CCP lauded the *xiaotuqun* campaign, the modern enterprises remained the backbone of the normal iron and steel production for the country. However, Angang, for instance, failed to achieve its targets in October and November, including those set for the 'high-yield week' (15–21 October) and 'make-up week' (25–31 October). Morale was low among the exhausted workers, and industrial accidents were rampant.[120] Daye Iron and Steel Mill had accomplished less than half its yearly quota by 15 November.[121] There came a point at which the harmful effects of the mass campaign for iron and steel on these key enterprises could no longer be overlooked, and this undoubtedly contributed to the leadership's decision to make adjustments. However, before we proceed to examine the retreat from the *xiaotuqun* campaign, we will turn to the planning process for iron and steel production for 1959 that occurred at this time, especially as it reflected the role of the MM in the campaign.

The Great Leap Forward for 1959: The Drawing Up of the 1959 Iron and Steel Production Plan

During the autumn and winter months of 1958 the top Party leaders were wildly fantastical. At the watershed meeting of the Politburo held at Beidaihe in August, the steel target for 1958 was doubled to 10.7m. tons, and the undisclosed preliminary targets for the key industrial products for 1959 included 30m. tons of steel.[122]

---

[117] *RMRB*, 27 October 1958.

[118] *RMRB*, 1 November 1958. [119] *RMRB*, 3 November 1958.

[120] *NBCK*, 24 October 1958, 3–4; 13 November 1958, 3. [121] *NBCK*, 24 November 1958, 7.

[122] *RMRB*, 1 September 1958; *Wansui* (1969), 252, 264. Li Fuchun was probably a supporter of high targets although under his auspices, the steel target was reduced. However, he did not go as far as Xue Muqiao would have wanted. When Mao talked about the need to reduce the steel target for 1959, he said, 'Is cold water being thrown on Li Fuchun this time? Plans must be positive and reliable, on a stable foundation . . . The enthusiasm at the Beidaihe Conference was for 30 million tons, of which 10 million tons was subjectivism'. *Wansui* (1969), 252. In a commemorative article on Li, it was said that he had made self-criticism for the mistakes made in economic planning during the GLF. *RMRB*, 9 January 1980, in *Xinhua Yuebao*, 1, 1980, 87.

At this time, the MM was totally wrapped up in the iron and steel campaign. According to Deng Liqun, it maintained that the priority was quantity—only when quantity was achieved then the problems of quality, variety, and balance could be tackled. The principle of 'comprehensive balance' was judged to be unsuitable for the planning for the GLF.[123] Indeed, one of the most important development strategies of the GLF being put forward now, as opposed to the notion of 'simultaneous development' advanced earlier, was the belief that the advancement of one sector could spur on (*daidong*) the other sectors. In other words, the MM took seriously Mao's philosophical outlook that 'imbalance is a universal objective law'.[124] Throughout 1959, it maintained this position and continued to champion high targets.[125]

In October, the Seventh National Planning Conference upheld the steel target of 30m. tons for 1959.[126] In the winter, the provinces were still eager to cater to the illusions of the centre, so their plans submitted to the centre also reached 30m. tons. Yet when Mao signalled his reservations at the Zhengzhou Conference things began to change. On 22 November, the Wuchang Politburo Conference considered specifically the issue of reducing the 1959 steel target from 30 to 18m. tons, with Mao concluding that even 18m. tons was unreliable. At a talk with the directors of the Cooperative Regions, he even made a self-criticism for the 'subjectivism' of aspiring for the high iron and steel targets. So after several discussion sessions, the Sixth Plenum decided formerly to set the published 1959 steel target at 18m. tons, although the internal target was still 20m. tons. The latter figure was championed by the SPC.[127]

Chen, sensing Mao's wavering, argued at an SPC meeting that 16m. tons were more than sufficient, but to no avail. According to Deng Liqun, it was not easy to hold down targets then, 'because everybody was hot-headed'.[128] Why this was the case can be explained by the cultural norm and the imperative of saving the face of the Chairman. As Mao had made concessions on strongly held beliefs, even offering a self-criticism, his subordinates knew that they should not appear too eager to go along, and to rub salt in his wounds, lest it would be interpreted as a sign of disloyalty (see Chapter 2).

In early 1959, the planners, pressed by this huge target, asked Chen to do something about it. Chen finally managed to persuade the SPC to lower the internal target to 18m. tons. But when Mao invited Chen to dinner just after Spring Festival in January, Chen took the opportunity to express his reservations regarding the 'four big targets', Mao paused and replied, 'That means that we have to forget it! Whether this General Line is correct or not, I have to keep observing. I am ready to revise the General Line anytime'. Although Mao said that he was willing to revise the General Line, he was ambiguous; yet the fact that he linked target revision with the General

---

[123] Deng Liqun, *Xiang Chen Yun Tongxi Xuexi Zuo Jingji Gongzuo* (Zhonggong zhongyang dangxiao chubanshe, 1981), 87. In a speech delivered to the staff and workers at Angang, Li Fuchun made a very similar argument, see *RMRB*, 26 September 1958.

[124] *Mao Wengao*, vii. 54.   [125] Lardy and Lieberthal, *Chen Yun's Strategy*, pp. xxiii–xxiv.

[126] *Lishi Changpian*, ii. 215.

[127] Sun Yeli and Xiong Lianghua, *Jingji Fengyun zhong de Chen Yun*, 166–7; *Mao Weikan*, xiB. 135–6.

[128] *Wansui* (1969), 252, 258. *RMRB*, 18 December 1958; Deng Liqun, *Xiang Chen Yun*, 13.

Line in the same breath raised the stakes tremendously, and suggested that he was not ready to do much. His lieutenants, including Chen, understood that they should not press on, so nothing was changed.[129] Only at the Shanghai Politburo Conference (March 1959), when Mao finally made up his mind, was the internal 1959 steel target adjusted to 18m. tons (with 16.5m. tons of 'good steel') although other economic targets remained unchanged. Yet even the revised steel target was deemed difficult to accomplish. Chen and other planners canvassed to lower it to 13m. tons, and this was finally approved by the Politburo and the Secretariat in May, over the opposition of the MM. The MM's overt reason was the fear that this would dampen enthusiasm, but the more fundamental reason was probably the unwillingness to spoil Mao's pet projects. In any case, this adjustment of the steel target was Chen's last act during the Leap before he took an extended sick leave, not to re-emerge until 1961.[130] On the other hand, in defending extremely high targets, the policy goals of the MM reflected closely the expressed preferences of Mao. These goals not only presupposed a continuous commitment to the campaign style in iron and steel production, they also imposed a tremendous strain on the Ministry. Yet, no evidence exists that the Ministry—or more probably, its leadership—had engaged in 'pulling and hauling' to realize some narrow institutional interests or advantages. It was a faithful and unquestioning executor of central initiatives and policies.

The Retreat from Popularization to the Elevation of Standards

By the end of October, even the MM had to admit the obvious, albeit in private. Its report (29 October) submitted to Mao finally spilled the beans, although in the usual language of stressing the positive and determination. It said that although the year's steel target could still be reached, the proportion of indigenous steel was high. The key-point iron and steel mills were unable to fulfil their own plans, so rolled steel produced would be short. The quality of pig iron was poor, and the indigenous method yielded only small lumps of 'steel', not large ingots that could be rolled into steel products.[131]

Between 4 October and 14 November, the unusually long National Conference of Secretaries of the Provincial Party Committees in Charge of Industrial Work, chaired by Bo Yibo, and attended by leading cadres of the SEC, the SPC, the industrial and transportation ministries, directors of the cooperative regions, and the provincial party secretaries in charge of industrial work, was held in Beijing. The timing (during the height of the iron and steel campaign) and the length (forty days) of the conference suggests important issues were being considered. In fact, items such as the mass movement to smelt steel and the future of the small and indigenous style of industrial production were under review. On the problem of whether the

---

[129] Sun Yeli and Xiong Lianghua, *Fengyung zhong de Chen Yun*, 167.

[130] Ibid. 173–85; *Mao Wengao*, viii. 294–5.

[131] Ibid., vii. 474–6. For another report on the sorry state of affairs in iron and steel in various provinces, see *NBCK*, 20 October 1958, 3–16.

'mass movement that took steel as the key link' had spurred on everything or 'crushed' everything, the conference was said to be unanimous in favour of the former. However, by this time, Mao had made clear his reservation about the excessively high steel targets at the Zhengzhou Conference. So after some further justifications of previous policies and the accounting of achievements, the Conference then decided to modify the small and indigenous style of production and to readjust the allocation of manpower, especially between industry and agriculture. While noting that in the previous stage the goal was to popularize the small and indigenous method by employing tens of million of people to achieve the 'quantity' and to enable the masses to be acquainted with this 'technology', it said, it would be a 'mistake' now not to 'advance further'. Therefore, the new policy was one toward 'elevation' or the raising of standards by turning the indigenous furnaces into integrated iron and steel centres using both the indigenous and 'foreign' (read 'modern') production methods.[132] The selection of these centres was to be guided by their proximity to raw material resources, transportation, and pools of labour supply. In practice, however, this was just a euphemism for the elimination of thousands of the useless indigenous furnaces and the reduction of the number of people who participated in the campaign, although the Conference also adopted the face-saving but futile injunctions that in places that had not already popularized the small indigenous furnaces *to do so* before 'elevating' them.[133]

This change of policy was undoubtedly motivated in part by the realization of the folly of the entire undertaking and in part by the practical consequences of the severe drain of manpower from the other sectors (notably agriculture) to the smelting of useless iron and steel. On the other hand, there might be some credibility to the claims by Henan that it had begun the reorganization of the indigenous furnaces like this as early as September and October. However, among the various proposals, it was the central authorities (the SEC or the SPC) which had the final say about which course of action to take. In any event, despite the alleged unanimity on the issue, many questioned the wisdom of building so many of these small indigenous furnaces only to discard them in favour of more advanced ones. Other dissenters maintained that since the small indigenous furnaces had worked miracles, there was really no point in modifying them.[134] The sarcasm was particularly humiliating.

Reorganization, Consolidation, and the Raising of Standards

By mid-November, the conditions of the iron and steel campaign continued to deteriorate. Of the one to two million indigenous furnaces said to have existed, most

---

[132] *RMRB*, 20 November 1958; Su Donghai and Fang Kongmy, *Fengyun Shilu*, 569; Ma Qibin *et al.*, *Zhizheng Sishinian*, 153. These sources give the dates of the Conference to be 4 October to 14 November, making for an unusually long meeting. There might be a typographical error here, as *HNRB*, 20 November 1958 cites 4 November as the beginning of the Conference. The context of the reports makes 4 November the more likely date.   [133] *BR*, 6 January 1959, 5; *RMRB*, 26 October 1958.
[134] Ibid.

were inoperative and the rest continued to compete with the major enterprises for scarce resources, churning out useless products. The shortages and low quality of the raw materials were as formidable as ever, causing many key enterprises to produce below capacity.[135]

Production figures for October showed clearly that most of the key enterprises failed to fulfil their monthly targets. Simultaneously, the State Statistical Bureau proudly showed that the quantity of iron and steel produced by the *xiaotuqun* in October had reached 91 per cent and 49 per cent of the national total, although these figures actually demonstrated that low-grade products comprised the bulk of the ouput, and that the key enterprises had suffered as a result. However, the Party finally realized a choice had to be made. Therefore on 25 November, it put forward the policy of 'Reorganization, Consolidation, and the Raising of Standards' and hailed it as a 'new stage' in the development of the *xiaotuqun* movement. Consequently, a 'five-fixed' system was also introduced.[136]

Xiaotuqun was defended vehemently as a 'major content of the long-term industrial policy' although the new decision was clearly designed to wipe it out. Now the centre no longer required places that had not built *xiaotuqun* to do so anymore. As integrated iron and steel centres were to be formed from then on, the provinces were given full discretionary power to decide how many they wanted to build according to local conditions. In retreat, Mao and the centre were more willing to give the provinces free rein, to let them restore some semblance of order out of a chaotic situation.[137] In effect, this is a good illustration of what can be called 'passing-the-buck discretionary implementation'. The centre was spared the embarrassment of having to preside over the retreat, and the provinces were granted the discretion to pick up the pieces, all in the name of 'suiting the policy to local conditions'.[138]

The Outcome

After much 'strenuous and even reckless' efforts in iron and steel production, MM statistics claimed that by 19 December, China had produced 10.73m. tons of steel.[139] By April 1959, the State Statistical Bureau revised the figure upwards to

---

[135] Clark, *Development*, 69; *RMRB*, 15 November 1958.

[136] The 'five-fix' policy meant: the fixing of points, the types of furnaces, the groups of furnaces, the staff, and the leadership. The fixing of points meant the selection of areas for iron and steel with better potential and the elimination of areas which were far away from the sources of raw materials, fuel, and transportation. Fixing the types of furnaces involved the selection of furnace types which were able to produce normally and to eliminate those which broke down frequently. Similar furnaces were now classified into groups to make it easier to inspect and to conduct production. Fixing staff and leadership meant the setting up of permanent staff and management with more established routines and organization.

[137] *RMRB*, 25 November 1958.

[138] Robert Nakamura and Frank Smallwood, *The Politics of Policy Implementation* (New York: St. Martin's Press, 1980), 130.

[139] *RMRB*, 22 December 1958; *BR*, 44, 1958, 6. The adjectives 'strenuous and even reckless' are Xue Muqiao's. See his *China's Socialist Economy* (Beijing: Foreign Language Press, 1981), 179; Mao referred to the same phenomenon as 'exhausting to death', *Wansui* (1969), 264.

11.08m. tons.[140] However, in August 1959, further verifications lowered the output of steel by 'modern equipment' which 'met the requirements of industry' to 8m. tons, a 49.5 per cent increase over the 5.3m. tons produced in 1957. The production and usage of indigenous steel would henceforth be left entirely to the local authorities.[141] This was another instance by which the centre shifted the responsibility for making a difficult decision to the provinces. Conceivably, some provinces might persist in making indigenous steel whereas the others would be glad to terminate this unenviable task.

As to quality, 40–50 per cent of the 9m. tons of pig iron smelted by the small blast furnaces was said to contain sulphur exceeding the minimum standard prescribed by the MM, making it useless for casting or smelting into useful steel products. It was a waste of labour and materials—and that was putting it mildly—according to a letter Chen Yun sent to Mao.[142] On the other hand, much of the steel produced during 1958, 1959, and 1960, which came from the *xiaotuqun* and the small blast furnaces, could not be turned into rolled-steel products. Most of it had to be re-smelted by the modern furnaces at very high cost but the quality was still low.[143] The cost of the pig iron produced by the *xiaotuqun* was also exceedingly high—the small blast furnaces consumed up to three times the coke normally required by the modern furnaces. Often the cost of the raw material consumed was larger than the value of the finished products.[144] Other mass campaigns to support iron and steel (such as the ones for electricity and coal mines) were similarly wasteful. In 1958, the Ministry of Finance already estimated that cost for each ton of indigenous iron was at least 250 or 300 *yuan*, although the transfer price was 150 *yuan*. Total losses for 10m. tons of indigenous iron in 1958 would reach 1.5 bn. *yuan*. In 1959, the Ministry of Finance re-estimated the cost to be 4 bn. *yuan*, or a little more than 10 per cent of the government revenue in 1958. This did not include the damages incurred by the large-scale denudation of the forests for fuel, or the opportunity costs incurred when huge amounts of investment, materials, equipment, and labour, were tied up in semi-finished and useless projects.[145] In addition, the iron and steel campaign also adversely affected the other sectors of the economy. Since factories had switched to the production of smelting equipment and since most of the transport facilities were requisitioned for shipping the goods and materials for the iron and steel industry, the production and shipment of other daily necessities, including food and agricultural products, were pushed aside, causing widespread shortages, particularly in the urban areas. The Ministry of Transport and its subordinate units were discernibly bitter about this.[146] The 90 million people recruited into the iron and steel campaign deprived the 1958 bumper harvest of much-needed labour, and anticipated gains. From October, construction projects built hastily with simplified plans and

---

[140] *RMRB*, 15 April, 15 January 1959.   [141] *RMRB*, 27 August 1959.

[142] Chen Yun, iii. 139–40.   [143] *Jingji Yanjiu*, 2, 1981, 43.

[144] Xue Muqiao, *Zhongguo Shehuizhyyi Jingji Wenti Yanjiu* (Studies on the problems of the Chinese socialist economy) rev. edn. (Beijing: Renmin chubanshe, 1983), 187.

[145] Bo Yibo, *Huigu*, ii. 712, Xie Chuntao, *Dayuejin*, 94–5; *Gongheguo Dadian*, 549, 563.

[146] *RMRB*, 9 November 1958.

substitute materials collapsed, and work-place accidents increased dramatically. Accidental deaths in the Ministry of Construction system alone numbered 435, or 2.2 times over that of 1957.[147] The Chinese were not ignorant of the costs, but the prevalent attitude then was that settling the account using 'economic' criteria (*suan jingji zhang*) was irrelevant.[148] That explains in part why Mao pushed the GLF further in 1959–60, and a much greater calamity was required to change his mind.

In addition, many small and medium-sized iron and steel mills that were planned in 1957 and were to be built during the GLF years simply fell by the wayside. More than half of these had not yet been completed by 1981. Those built with tremendous effort had so many 'congenital' defects that they remained inefficient.[149] For instance, the Liuzhou Iron and Steel Mill of Guangzxi, built with an investment of 3.7m. *yuan* during the GLF, was one of the most notorious examples of poor planning since it continued to carry a loss after more than twenty years, forfeiting a total of 1.92bn. *yuan* by the late 1970s. It had come into being more as a product of the scramble for construction projects, investment funds and resources; there was no careful prospecting of iron ore reserves before the factory was planned, and no coal reserves were available nearby to produce coke for smelting.[150]

The iron and steel campaign between 1958 and 1960 must have a negative impact on the national economy. Yet, one Chinese source suggests that 1958 was but a little interlude in the perspective of the entire GLF period and the damage could have been limited, if 'readjustment' was carried out in time. This did not come until 1961, however, and in both 1959 and 1960, the GLF policies persisted and the price paid also multiplied.[151]

To recap, in 1958 the MM played a pre-eminent role in directing and controlling the iron and steel campaign, despite decentralization that formally robbed the central ministries of many of their powers. As Mao had prevailed upon the planners, the MM had little choice but to respond with fervour. Yet, as the Maoist strategy necessitated a sharp break from the Soviet model and practices embraced by the MM, it had to totally reinvent itself. Subsequently, the MM had transformed itself from a fledgling professional organization into an engine for mass mobilization to promote radical Leap policies, to the extent of undermining its own organizational mission. Under the fervent leadership of Wang Heshou, the MM demonstrated itself to be the most loyal supporter of the Maoist ideal. It fed Mao's vision of a GLF, often going further than Mao himself. When Mao retreated, the MM backed down only slowly, being careful not to make Mao lose too much face, or appear to be too eager in dismantling the Chairman's pet projects. All of the Ministry's energy was expanded in the pursuit of one of the most colossal make-believe campaigns of the GLF. To a large extent, for the MM to get along and to get ahead seemed to be more important than to get things right.

---

[147] Chen Yun, *Xuanji*, iii. 109; Bo Yibo, *Huigu*, ii. 711. [148] Li Rui, *Lushan Huiyi*, 50.
[149] *Dang Qian Caizheng Wenti* (Current Fiscal Problems) (Beijing: Zhongguo caizheng jingji chubanshe, 1981), 22. [150] *Dushu* (Reading), 12, 1982, 17. [151] *Dang Qian Caizheng*, 45.

5

Agricultural and Rural Policies in Guangdong, 1958

Guangdong was a vanguard of the Leap in 1957/8, as its leaders had always been radical followers of Mao. Yet, nothing in the past could have prepared the province for the draconian measures of the Leap and the urges to change everything over-night. The Leap required the leadership to plunge into a bold social experiment, and to centralize direct control over the lives and daily routines of millions. It was totally uncharted territory. Why did the Leap policies appeal to the Guangdong leadership? How did it deal with the radical orientation and incessant demands for change? How did Tao Zhu and other leaders twist and steer the province into following their wills? In what manner were GLF policies implemented?

Guangdong in the 1950s

Guangdong was the southernmost province of China and enjoyed a tropical and subtropical climate with abundant rainfall. Agriculture and light industry were the dominant economic activities, so Guangdong was not highly urbanized. In 1957, only 14.75 per cent of the population were urban dwellers, and 81.7 per cent of the population engaged in agriculture.[1] The growing season is all year-round and agriculture was well developed. Cultivated lands, comprising about 20 per cent of the total area, were concentrated in the fertile river valleys, the Pearl River Delta, and the lowland along the coast. There, double-cropping or triple-cropping of rice, the most important crop, had made Guangdong the second in rank in grain output/*mu* since the mid-1950s.[2] Rice paddies occupied two-thirds of all cultivated land, with the rest devoted to dry crops. The most important commercial crops were sugar cane, silkworm mulberry, tobacco, hemp, jute, flax, and cotton, which supported many light industries such as sugar-refining, textile, paper-making, and food-processing. Since 1954, Guangdong had already contributed 40 per cent of the nation's yearly sugar output.[3]

[1] *Guangdong Sheng Tongji Nianjian, 1984* (Hong Kong: Economic Information and Agency, 1984), 73   [2] *RMRB*, 21 November 1958.
[3] Chang Ch'i-yun, *Chung- Kuo Ta Lu Fen Sheng Ti Tu* (Atlas of the Chinese Mainland by Province) (n.p.: The National Security Institute, 1966); Ezra Vogel, *Canton Under Communism* (New York: Harper Torchbooks, 1976), 15–16.

Rice was the preferred staple of the population and required irrigation for most of the year. In 1957, some irrigation facilities were available to 85 per cent of the total 45m. *mu* of paddy fields, although the majority were drought-resistant for less than thirty days. Seven million *mu* (15 per cent of the total) were labelled 'depending-on-heaven fields' (*wangtiantian*) which lacked any irrigation, and 5m. *mu* were subjected to either flood or drought every year. The Pearl River Delta was particularly susceptible to summer flooding. Fertile and high-yield fields were less that 10m. *mu*, of which only 3 to 4m. *mu* were of the best quality.[4] Therefore, the urge to introduce more irrigation and water-conservancy measures was understandable. Yet, the GLF attempt at turning the seasonal and under-employed rural labour into capital made little sense in Guangdong, as the year-round growing season had already kept the agricultural calendar busy. Moreover, the land had already been meticulously and intensively cultivated, and without a massive injection of machinery and chemical fertilizer, the mass campaigns were unlikely instruments for surges in production.

Guangdong's rural economy was fairly commercialized. The peasants raised silkworms, poultry, and pigs and cultivated sugar cane, vegetables, and tropical fruits. The products were sold at the many rural markets, contributing to relatively higher incomes, especially for those residing at the river deltas.[5] The Party's obsession with grain production displaced much of these economic activities, and the emphasis on self-sufficiency and autarky led to the closing of rural markets, fairs, and private plots. This partly explained the peasants' hostility to the GLF and communization. Consequently, the production of commercial crops dropped, the peasants lost their incomes, and the cities suffered shortages of non-staple foods.

Although agriculture was still the lifeblood of the Guangdong economy, like the rest of the country, its development during the 1FYP was disappointing. Grain production during this period grew by about 5 per cent annually, but it started with a very low baseline of approximately 8.5m. tons. In 1957, the average available grain per capita was a mere 270 kg.[6] Moreover, agricultural production fluctuated greatly, as the province was highly susceptible to natural calamities, such as flooding and drought, which affected an average of 5 to 6 million people yearly during the 1FYP.[7] In the same period, urban migration to Guangzhou and other cities not only aggravated the unemployment problem, but also generated heavy demands for grain from the countryside.[8]

The shortages of agricultural products in turn inhibited the development of industry.[9] In addition, Guangdong faced a perpetual dilemma of how to balance the conflicting demands for more grain for the population, and more economic crops to satisfy industry.[10] All these were the familiar problems of underdevelopment, and the key to further economic growth and the alleviation of poverty, in the context of

[4] *RMRB*, 14 December 1957; Vogel, *Canton*, 15; *NFRB*, 12 December 1959.
[5] Vogel, *Canton*, 18 ff.   [6] *NFRB*, 16 December 1957.   [7] *NFRB*, 16 November 1957.
[8] Vogel, *Canton*, 220.   [9] *NFRB*, 26 July 1957.
[10] *RMRB*, 14 December 1957; *NFRB*, 18 August 1957.

the 1950s, was to raise farm output. However, when large-scale capital investment was impossible, provincial leadership was attracted by the GLF development strategy of 'simultaneous development', irrigation, and water conservancy, the application of fertilizer, the increase in the multiple-cropping index, and the utilization of the abundant supply of manpower. It was eager to implement it during the 2FYP.

Moreover, the Guangdong leadership under Tao Zhu, who became first secretary in 1955, had been loyal to Mao and the centre.[11] In 1957, the battle against the so-called 'localist' and 'anti-Party' clique that led to the dismissal of two provincial governors had more to do with personal animosities, intrigues, and minor policy differences between a radical Tao and a more moderate Gu Dacun and less about the administration of Hainan Island.[12] Mao took Tao's side in the struggle, ensuring Tao's triumph, so Tao was indebted to Mao. Moreover, as Mao had rejected and humiliated the planners one by one, it was clear to Tao where to place his bet. Loyalty to the Chairman meant to follow him closely (*jingen*).[13] Therefore, on the eve of the GLF, a confluence of interests and viewpoints existed between the Maoist and the Guangdong authorities, and the GLF mentality for agricultural development took hold early in the province. In 1958, Tao was Mao's trusted lieutenant and a star promoter of the GLF, and his preference was shared by the equally radical Zhao Ziyang and Wen Minsheng.[14]

The Beginning

Three weeks after the re-enactment of the NPAD, the Guangdong PPC had already responded by drafting a Ten-Year Plan aimed at raising the average yield/*mu* from the current average of 500 *jin/mu* to 850 *jin/mu*, and total production from 12.25m. to 20m. tons by 1967 (approximately an accumulated increase of 5 per cent per

[11] Vogel, *Canton*, 220, 300. In the summer of 1959 when Peng Dehuai was seriously reprimanded for criticizing the GLF, Tao rallied behind Mao to denounce maliciously Peng and the others implicated with him. See Li Rui, *Lushan Huiyi*, 242–44, 257, 271–83. Even in the 1960s, Tao Zhu and Ke Qingshi were Mao's most valued and trusted among the secretaries of the six Regional Bureaux. See Xiao Donglian *et al.*, *Qiusuo Zhongguo*, 1079.

[12] *Dangdai Guangdong*, 2, 1997, 21–42; no. 3, 48–61. According to Vogel, 'localism' in Guangdong was expressed in the opposition of some Hainan cadres to the perceived excessive interference by the PPC in their local affairs, and its assignment of outside cadres to important leadership positions there. The 'localist' sentiment peaked in 1956 and 1967 and ended up in the dismissal of two provincial leaders, Feng Baiju and Gu Dacun, in late 1957. Vogel, *Canton*, 211–16. However, post-Mao information suggests that both the charge of localism and the punishment of these two leaders were exaggerated and overdone. See *Zhonggong Dangshi Renwuchuan* (Biographies of figures from Chinese Communist Party history) (Shaanxi: Renmin chubanshe, 1982), v. 304, 357–60.

[13] In her lengthy memoir, Zeng Zhi, revolutionary veteran and wife of Tao Zhu who was also deputy industrial secretary of the South Central Bureau, Head of the Guangzhou Electricity Bureau, and Party Secretary of Guangzhou MPC, devotes a few pages to the GLF, but is tight-lipped about Tao's role at that time. See her *Yige Geming de Xingcunzhe: Zeng Zhi Huiyi Shilu* (A fortunate survivor of the Revolution: The memoir of Zeng Zhi) (Guangzhou: Guangdong renmin chubanshe, 1999), 421–31.

[14] Both were secretaries of the PPC: Zhao was in charge of agriculture, and Wen, industry.

annum).[15] These were ambitious targets, although not entirely unreasonable, as rice production in Shantou Special District, a high-yield area, had already achieved 812 *jin/ mu* in 1956.[16] The PPC further argued that several favourable measures had made the hike in production possible: collectivization had been consolidated, and the introduction of water conservancy had already stabilized production. During the 2FYP, the state had earmarked 300m. *yuan*, an amount almost three times the total invested during the 1FYP, to invest in agriculture. Finally, available fertilizer would increase because of the plan to multiply the number of hogs from 8 to 15 million by 1967. Assuming that each hog could provide sufficient manure for 2 *mu* of land, the fertilizer required for 30m. *mu*, the total cultivated area in Guangdong, would be accounted for.

The cadres greeted these goals contained in the 10-year plan with scepticism, however. They were generally unwilling to accept high quotas, fearing punishment for nonfulfilment, and high priority tasks such as water conservancy and the expansion of winter planting meant extra work. For the PPC, this reflected a kind of 'rightist conservatism' (which it called the biggest enemy to the production high tide) which could be eliminated by ordering the cadres to go to the masses and to lead them with 'determination and stamina'. The best way to overcome the rightist thinking among the cadres, the PPC claimed, was by running well the activist oath-taking conferences. The PPC relied heavily on the motivation of the cadres, particularly the 'activists', because it understood that its organizational resources were the best guarantee for the realization of its ambitious goals. Criticizing 'rightist conservatism' was the PPC's way of intimidating or galvanizing its subordinates into action.[17] In the coming months, this technique was applied repeatedly so that the PPC finally got what it wanted.

This was made clear at the Second Session of the First Provincial Party Congress (21 November–5 December 1957). Billed as a gathering for 'the promotion of revolutionary progress', it formally repudiated the deviations of 'localism' and 'rightist thinking' within the Party in 1956/7. Tao, presiding over the Congress, called upon the province to implement resolutely the decision of the Third Plenum by using the greatest drive and speed, and the *duohao kuaisheng* principle. All counties were ordered to mobilize as if 'going to war'. Consequently, many targets originally set by the PPC were revised upward again. For example, despite the PPC's own initial reservations about the projected 1m. ton increase in grain for 1958, the Congress affirmed that it could be achieved. Likewise, the PPC's original hope that 2 million labour days would support winter production was exceeded by 1 million through pledges by the People's Liberation Army. The Congress also resolved to increase the 'send down' cadres from 160,000 to 180,000, raise the original target of 850 *jin/mu* for 1967 to 900 *jin/mu*, and boost the yearly investment for water irrigation from 70m. *yuan* to 100m. *yuan*. Finally, the PPC launched the slogan of turning the province into a 'thousand *jin* grain province' by 1967.

---

[15] More recent figures show that the actual grain production in 1957 and 1983 was 10.89 and 19.5m. tons, respectively. See *Guangdong Tongji Nianjian*, 1984, 119.   [16] *RMRB* 27 October 1957.
[17] *NFRB*, 13 November 1957; *RMRB*, 1 and 16 November 1957.

The Congress hailed these 'advanced' targets and the revolutionary enthusiasm, attributing them to the influence of the 'new revolutionary high tide' in the rural areas and the 'thorough criticisms' of the rightist conservative thinking and regionalism in the leadership of the Party. It also resurrected its own draft provincial programme for agricultural development (1956–67) drawn up when the NPAD was first promulgated in January 1956.[18] Like the NPAD, it was a long document that covered two full pages of the *NFRB*. Its thirty-six articles were a catalogue for comprehensive rural development containing numerous and diffuse goals. There were articles on targets for the consolidation of the APCs, increase in grain production, economic crops, fertilizer, acreage for multiple-cropping, elimination of droughts and floods, improvement of soil, afforestation, elimination of the 'four pests' and illiteracy, improvement of living conditions, education of landlords, 'reactionaries', and other 'bad elements', development of a rural small broadcast network, small hydroelectric stations, aquatic products, encouragement of overseas Chinese to develop socialism, and so on. Other articles covered intensive farming and the reclamation of wasteland, two things that would be regarded as incompatible later.

On the other hand, the Congress did not envisage any further rural institutional change, as it followed the proviso in the NPAD that APCs with more than 100 households would not be enlarged in the next 10 years. This stipulation that existing policy would not change for a long time (whether it be 10, 30, or 50 years) was frequently used in Chinese policy documents to reassure the public, but the promise was soon broken as the people's communes were introduced only eight months later. In any case, as spring planting was only two months away, Tao Zhu now assumed personal command of agriculture by ordering a 'surprise attack' campaign for 'spring ploughing' involving a 'labour army' of 8 to 15 million.[19] The aim was to mobilize the manpower during the relatively slack and frost-free winter to engage in fertilizer accumulation, soil improvement, reclamation, irrigation and water conservancy, which were traditionally not carried out until around the lunar new year (18 February in 1958).[20] All first secretaries were ordered to take charge of the campaigns, especially the water conservancy campaign. Therefore, at the end of 1957, the province was already a beehive of activities, setting the stage for the GLF. In the twenty days between December 1957 and January 1958, more than 6 million had participated daily in the irrigation and water conservancy campaign, and most of the county and *xiang* party committees had moved their offices to the work sites to lead the campaign.[21]

The Unfolding of the Great Leap Forward

Meanwhile, the provincial authorities sought to implement the NPAD by calling on the prefectural and county party committees to convene 'oath-taking'

[18] *NFRB*, 7 and 16 December 1957; 3 January 1958; *RMRB*, 11 December 1957.
[19] *RMRB*, 14 December 1957, *NFRB*, 16, 29 December 1957.
[20] *NFRB*, 23 December 1957.   [21] *NFRB*, 15 January 1958.

conferences to mobilize several hundred thousands of activists to spearhead the GLF. They regarded this as an effective way of overcoming 'rightist conservatism' and promoting 'high tides' in production.[22] The proceedings of one of these meetings—the Fourth Conference of the Representatives of Labour Models and Advanced Workers of Zhanjiang Special District, 30 December 1957–7 January 1958—will shed light on how this worked.

The declared goal of the Conference was to scrutinize production during the 1FYP, to recognize advanced models, and to promote enthusiasm. Significantly, some delegates, according to the *NFRB*, displayed varying degrees of 'rightist conservative' thinking at the beginning. Some claimed that production had already reached its limit and further increases were difficult. A proud APC delegate who announced the record of producing 7,000 *jin* of sweet potatoes/*mu* was shocked to be told that it was not good enough. Some were said to have been disheartened when presented with the alleged high production records of other localities; some expressed scepticism (at claims of rice yields of 2,663 *jin/mu* and sweet potatoes of 10,000 *jin/mu*) and were lukewarm toward the Conference's call to surpass them.

Not surprisingly, the labour models and advanced workers found the new alleged records hard to swallow at the outset. However, the PPC had raised the stakes to the ideological level—not believing was to commit rightist conservative error—so that most finally gave in. The conference then refuted the 'rightist conservative thinking' by the demonstration of 'all kinds of facts', by hearing more reports, and by organizing visits to advanced units. For instance, a delegate from the Victory APC with the highest record in sweet potato production was 'ashamed' to discover that his record had already been surpassed by another advanced unit. Confronted by these 'living' facts, the delegates were 'greatly educated' and they criticized their own rightist thinking 'one after the other'. All swore to fulfil the targets set for the next 10 years; some even vowed to do this in just one.

At the close of the Conference, Tao urged everybody to toil really hard for a few years to benefit their descendants. The advanced labour models, Tao maintained, ought to lead the masses along, and to promote technical reforms. Therefore, it became clear that this Conference was convened less for honouring the labour models than for telling delegates that old standards of excellence were no longer sufficient. In the extravagant atmosphere fostered by the PPC, the more opportunistic of its subordinates boasted of extraordinary achievements that became the new norms for everyone to follow.[23] The PPC got what it wanted, and the delegates began to learn the new rules of the game.[24]

The PPC's 'anti-rightist' efforts led to the expected misrepresentations. On New Year's day, *NFRB* reported that in Shantou Special District, 2,000 *mu* had already

---

[22] *NFRB*, 10 January 1958.   [23] Ibid.

[24] A commemorative article on Tao claims that at one conference, Tao had criticized a county party secretary for 'serious rightist error'. However, later development had shown that the party secretary in question was actually being 'practical and realistic'. When Tao realized his mistake, he was said to have apologized openly to this cadre. *Hongqi*, 1, 1979, 53. It was unlikely that this apology was given in 1958, because throughout the year, any reference to realism would be equated to 'rightist conservatism'.

achieved yields of 3,000 *jin/mu* in three crops. In particular, Denghai and Chaoan counties, which in 1955 were national models of 1,000 *jin/mu* fame, were said to have county-wide averages of 1,200 *jin/mu*.[25]

In the second half of January, four separate provincial conferences were held in Guangdong when the Nanning Conference was in session.[26] As mentioned, at Nanning, Mao struck back harshly at the planners who had opposed the Leap in 1956 and banned further criticism or even references to the so-called *maojin*, thus imposing a closure to more debate of the GLF strategy. As the planners were pushed aside, Mao took personal command of the Leap and presided over the drafting of its new manifesto—the Sixty Articles. Article 12 of the Sixty Articles, currently being discussed at Nanning but not yet promulgated officially, contained the first decision to accelerate the timetable of the NPAD. In Guangdong, this inside lead became a rallying point for the PPC. In all four conferences, the PPC vowed to take additional steps to implement the decisions of the Third Plenum and the latest central directive to eradicate rightism thoroughly. No evidence exists that the later was a formal directive; it was the more informal clue dropped by Mao at Hangzhou when he said that he was happy criticizing 'rightist conservatism'.[27] At the conference on 19 January, the delegates were said to have agreed unanimously with the central instructions and decided to revise the various production targets *again*, using '120 per cent revolutionary enthusiasm'.

On 20 January, the PPC, with the Hainan District Party Committee, the various prefectural party committees and more than 80 county and municipal party committees decided to revise their plans again—the planned grain output for 1958 was raised from 10m. tons to 14m. tons, and the output targets set forth in the NPAD (i.e. 800 *jin/mu*) was advanced *5 years* ahead of schedule to 1962. The latter did not match Henan's pledge to accomplish the provisions of the NPAD in just one year, but at Chengdu, Mao commended both the Henan and Guangdong decisions, praising the latter to be 'leftist'.[28]

To achieve the provisions of the NPAD ahead of schedule, the PPC decided to eliminate drought within two years by building even more water conservancy projects, thereby advancing the original timetable by three years. Accordingly, the original plan for water conservancy projects in 1958 was doubled, from 400m. to 800m. cu.m of earth, 650m. cu.m of which was to be completed before the lunar New Year. A total of 8 million to 9 million labour units would be mobilized. A second measure of the PPC was the accumulation of manure by mass mobilization, and the target to be reached by New Year was raised from 175 to 285m. tons. Moreover, the PPC ordered the organization of all 'subsidiary' labour, including old people and children, for this purpose.

---

[25] *NFRB*, 1 January 1958. Chen Jiyuan *et al.*, *Nongcun Jiangji Bianqian*, 293.

[26] They were the Fourth Provincial Planning Conference, 15–25 January 1958; the PPC Meeting 19 January 1958; the PPC Telephone Conference with the Party Committees of Prefectures, Municipalities, and Counties, 20 January 1958; and the PPC Telephone Conference, 20 January 1958 (night). These conferences are reported in *NFRB*, 22 and 30 January 1958, and *RMRB*, 24 January 1958.

[27] *Mao Weikan*, xiB. 1; Su Donghai and Fang Kongmu, *Fengyun Shilu*, 518.

[28] *Mao Weikan*, xiB. 46; Sun Yeli and Xiong Lianghua, *Jiangji Fengyun zhong de Chen Yun*, 143.

Echoing Mao's critique of the 'rightist' tendency, the conference claimed that the drop in production in 1957 was proof of the 'serious harm' brought to the masses by 'rightist' mistakes. Therefore, the Conference urged the unyielding destruction of rightist conservatism allegedly prevalent among party committees, especially at the middle level. These units were accused of failing to devise 'revolutionary measures' to surpass the most advanced. Subsequently, the party committees of Gaoyao Special District were accused of conservatism because with a population of 3 million people, its water conservancy plan was 'only' 30m. cu.m. That compared unfavourably with a certain county in Qingyuan which, having only a population of 500,000, had devised a 'bold' plan for a project reaching 21m. cu.m. Eventually, the PPC found that even the advanced units in Guangdong were still 'rightist conservative' when compared with other provinces.

Finally, in acceding to Mao's wish regarding the 'experimental plots', the PPC urged the improvement in 'leadership method' by imitating the experience of Hongan County, Hubei. According to it, every county must set up a model farm near the county seat (town); every *xiang* and collective must have a model field; all responsible cadres of the district and county committees must go down to the work sites, *xiang*, and collectives to discover advanced units and to help them to sum up and popularize their experiences.

These measures demonstrated the resolve of the PPC to follow both the letter and spirit of Mao and the central initiatives. Anticipating that its grandiose plans might have been resisted by the cadres, it relied heavily on the critique of 'rightist conservatism' to elicit compliance. Nevertheless, it had few other alternatives; it was pressured by the centre, as the progress among the provinces was frequently being compared. Apart from this, its own vision drove it to take extraordinary measures to transform Guangdong into a prosperous province.

Finally, the PPC also applied Mao's directive to itself. On 14 February, it trumpeted the opening of the experimental farm at Baiyun Shan (near Guangzhou), after more than one month's preparation. The PPC claimed that the farm, consisting of 660 hectares of terraced fields and paddy fields, would become the 'red and expert' training ground for all cadres belonging to departments directly under itself. A plot (0.4 hectares) was set aside for the leaders of the PPC, and Tao Zhu and Chen Yu *et al.*, had drafted comprehensive plans to reform rice cultivation.

The secretary-general of the PPC was selected to be the director of the farm whereas '*xiafang*' cadres and incumbent cadres formed production teams and rotated their responsibilities. Although these cadres knew little about agricultural production and were unaccustomed to physical labour, they had set up a 5-year plan to develop forestry, animal husbandry, orchards, and rice paddies, and predicted these would enable them to turn over profits to the state in three years.[29]

The goals of this experimental farm were to turn the top provincial leaders into 'red experts' and to set up advanced examples for the entire province. However, the involvement of the PPC leaders was only symbolic and eventually few

[29] *NFRB*, 15 February 1958.

spent much time there. It was another example of the many half-baked ideas dropped before they were implemented. In 1958, the farm was essentially a refuge for the provincial-level cadres who had been sent downwards.

'Battle Hard for Three Years'

The promulgation of the Sixty Articles further radicalized decision-making in Guangdong. In response, the PPC convened a plenary meeting between 7 and 12 February attended by all the members of the PPC and the first secretaries of the district party committees. Tao Zhu formally transmitted the instructions from Mao and the Party Centre. The plenum approved the slogan-cum-policy of 'battle hard for three years' (Article 13) and discussed the principle of 'fully arousing the masses and testing everything'. It adopted the method of 'overall planning and making frequent checkups' (Article 4) and considered the notion of permanent revolution (Article 4). Since implementation of the Sixty Articles required draconian measures, the PPC then decided 'rightism' among the cadres could not be tolerated, as all those who could not provide 'socialist leadership' would be removed 'resolutely'. This was no empty threat as it was carried out subsequently.

The meeting then ordered all APCs and party committees of *xiang*, counties, and districts to make 5-year plans, and urged all first secretaries of party committees to visit the localities that boasted advanced experiences to duplicate them. Organizationally, the PPC decided to amalgamate the Water Conservancy Bureau and the Institute for the Planning of Water Conservancy. Except for one or two 'responsible cadres' and one design team, all the technicians in these two organs were sent downward to the counties, not to return to Guangzhou for three years.[30] This 'decentralization' of responsibilities spelled the end of any coordinated planning for water conservancy at the provincial level, at a time when numerous such projects were being constructed. The rationale was that the small projects were more cost-effective than the large ones, and that the grass-roots units should take charge of them. According to Chen Yu, the Water Conservancy Bureau's 1958 plan would benefit only 5m. plus *mu*, but once the masses were mobilized, more than four times as much farmland had been irrigated in two to three months.[31] Chen's reasoning aside, the dispersal of the technicians to the 90 odd counties, the emphasis on the masses for running this mammoth campaign, and the designation of the APCs as the units to organize water conservancy resulted in numerous makeshift and uncoordinated projects that could resist neither floods nor droughts. In fact, as mentioned before, they not only aggravated the effects of natural calamities, they also caused widespread salinization and alkalinization.

In any case, at the end of February, the PPC was relatively satisfied with its efforts to compel its subordinates to raise their targets. Therefore, Zhao Ziyang convened a

---

[30] *NFRB*, 16 February 1958.   [31] *NFRB*, 12 March 1958.

telephone conference with the party secretaries of the district and county party committees (26 February) to discuss the 'important' changeover from the 'raising' to the 'realization' of the targets.[32] According to the conference, most targets had become progressive after being repeatedly raised but the main question now was more to find ways to fulfil them. Detailed reports submitted by the special districts and counties showed that the progress in various agricultural work was slow and uneven. Furthermore, much of the work done was sub-standard—a reservoir built with an investment of 41,700 *yuan* collapsed during the first rain. False reporting was rampant. Now, the PPC turned around and called for the exposure and criticism of those units that engaged in such 'empty talks' and in false reporting.

Specifically, the PPC adopted several measures. First, it continued to attack 'serious rightist conservative thinking' among the cadres, but added the enemies of 'lethargy', 'evil influence' (*xieqi*), a recognition of the emerging 'two-anti' campaign ordered by Mao. Therefore, the conference called for the rectification of the cadres (*zhengdui*, or dressing the ranks) 'from the counties to the *xiang*, and from the members of the Party and the Communist Youth League to the cadres of the APCs' so that teams with outstanding revolutionary drive and morale could be created to lead the GLF. Apart from this, the outstanding problems in all county party committees were to be resolved in the 'rectification meetings', using the methods of 'big character posters, big blooming and contending, and big debate' to 'praise a big batch and to criticize a small batch (of cadres)'. A 'big fanfare' was to be employed to commend those whose 'standpoints were firm, work enthusiasm was big, and methods were good', and then on this basis, the members of the Party or League branches were to be 're-elected'. In other words, this was a personnel shake-up by which zealous cadres were promoted and 'rightist-conservative' cadres were either demoted, dismissed, or replaced.

Second, the meeting ordered a 'great check-up' on the work for water conservancy, the accumulation of manure, sowing and afforestation to commend the good examples and to criticize the bad ones, especially those that gave false reportings. Presumably, these inspections would weed out the 'rightist conservatives' on the one hand, and the fraudulent practices on the other.

Third, the PPC set several deadlines because some agricultural work had to be ready before others could be conducted (e.g. the accumulation of manure should be completed before spring ploughing). In this regard, the PPC's projections are instructive. It relied on simple arithmetic and reasoning by analogy, ignoring completely the lack of resources or local situations. For instance, since the target for manure accumulation was 12,000 million *tan* (the dubious assumption was that half this amount had already been accumulated), the PPC ordered that 5 million people be mobilized in the next 20 days up to 20 March. If each person could collect 60 *tan*, then the daily accumulation rate could be 300 million *tan*, and the grand total of 6,000 million *tan* could be achieved in 20 days.[33] Crude projections like these were used extensively to justify the 'planning' of ambitious targets. Yet, the high-handed

---

[32] *NFRB*, 28 February 1958.   [33] Ibid.

but clumsy attempts to control activities normally the prerogatives of the collectives uniformly and mechanically turned out to be counter-productive.

Finally, to realize the NPAD ahead of schedule, the PPC and the Provincial People's Committee (PPPC) issued a directive ordering the 'revolutionary measure' of expanding the areas for winter planting in 1958 from 20m. *mu* to 30m. *mu*. The emphasis was on potatoes, beans, and oil-bearing crops, presumably because they weighed more, so that high yields per unit could be claimed. All localities were ordered to make advanced preparations in seed selection and land improvement. The later was deemed important because more than 30m. *mu* of farmlands were either made up of heavy clay or unsuitable for winter farming. Finally, acreage quotas were assigned to all special districts.[34]

At the Chengdu Conference (8–26 March), as mentioned, Mao blasted *fanmaojin* and introduced more Leap initiatives. Tao Zhu, on the other hand, rapturously supported Mao's view on the cult of personality and a more extreme case of decentralization (see Chapter 2), maintaining his status as one of the Chairman's most loyal allies. Between 13 and 30 April, Mao blessed Guangzhou with an inspection, and chaired the secret Guangzhou Conference, where he was planning to enshrine Leap policies at the coming Second Session of the Eighth Party Congress. His sojourn at Guangzhou not only galvanized the Guangdong leadership, he was spurred on by what he saw and heard. When commenting on a report by the Yingju APC that said it had toiled hard to change its appearance, Mao concluded that to overtake the capitalist countries would not take as long as previously thought. In fact, he was then considering the possibility of overtaking not just Britain, but also the USA by shortening the timetable.[35]

The 'First Victory'

In early April, spring harvest had just begun. However, based on *visual* estimates, the *NFRB* rushed ahead to announce the 'first victory' of the GLF—winter crops harvested alone were estimated to be 12.5m. tons, a 150 per cent increase over production in 1957. Therefore, it expected that the province could exceed the planned total of 17m. tons of grain for 1958.[36] In the third week of April, however, the Provincial Statistical Bureau revealed that the bulk of the spring harvest consisted of sweet potatoes (10m. tons), generally regarded as an inferior food more suitable for animals. Wheat consisted of 1.7m. tons, and other grain (other than wheat and rice) was only 0.8m. tons.[37] The PPC was so busy in defining and redefining new work tasks and slogans that the above incongruity attracted little attention whatsoever. As long as a dramatic increase could be claimed for the early crops, this minor inconvenience could be and was ignored.

[34] *NFRB*, 24 March 1958.
[35] *Mao Wengao*, vii. 177–84; Zheng Xiaofeng and Shu Ning, *Tao Zhu Zhuan* (Biography of Tao Zhu) (Beijing: Zhongguo Qingnian chubanshe, 1992), 259; Xiao Xinli, *Xunshi Dajiang Nanbei*, 147–63.
[36] *NFRB*, 4 April 1958.   [37] *NFRB*, 22 April 1958.

Nevertheless, such a flight of fancy did encounter a credibility problem, but the PPC was determined to stifle the sceptics. At the end of April, another four-day PPC conference called for the thorough 'liberation' of the thinking of the leaders by eliminating dogmatism, empiricism, and 'rightist conservatism'. The cadres were ordered to stress the 'subjective initiative' and the spirit of creativity, and to 'dare to think, to speak, and to act'. As soon as the leadership has liberated its thinking, the PPC asserted, miracles would happen. The 'tremendous achievements' in water conservancy and fertilizer accumulation were touted as examples to buttress this claim. This led to another massive escalation of the 1958 plan. By the end of the month, the planned output of grain for 1958 was inflated to 27.5m. tons, an amount equivalent to the total produced during the previous five years! Undoubtedly, this figure was chosen because of its propaganda value in claiming that production during the first year of the GLF matched that of the previous five years. As hyperboles became a habit in 1958, the PPC had no qualms about doubling, tripling, and quadrupling the output figures. The new target was cited as another 'miracle' resulting from the 'liberation of thinking'.[38]

Apart from forcing the total suspension of disbelief, this conference is worth mentioning because the themes and the wording corresponded exactly to that of Mao's three speeches given at the Chengdu Conference (9–26 March), which called for the elimination of dogmatism and the promotion of creativity and critical thinking, among many other things.[39] This reflects the extent to which the PPC stuck to and parroted Mao's initiatives. On the other hand, since the centre called repeatedly for the 'liberation of thinking', provincial and local cadres were emboldened to throw all caution to the winds.

Once the PPC was irrevocably committed to the astronomical targets, there remained the question of how to achieve them. The key might be a good early crop and a bountiful autumn harvest. Toward this end, the PPC meeting on 12 May decided to fire off the 'second high tide' in the campaign for water conservancy and fertilizer accumulation, and to overhaul the APCs. Then, rice transplantation had already been completed, but the early crop was threatened by drought in some areas and the inadequate application of fertilizer in others. On the other hand, the irrigated acreage of the autumn crops (rice and sweet potatoes, the most important crops of the year and regarded as the key to the agricultural GLF) was still limited. Furthermore, to raise yields the PPC ordered even denser close planting, but this required more fertilizer than usual.

Therefore, the PPC demanded that all localities start the 'second battle' by rearranging the labour to ensure abundant water supply for rice and sweet potatoes, and fertilizer application of 400 *tan/mu*. The PPC suggested that 40–50 per cent of all labour should be assigned to the accumulation of manure (3 per cent for running water conservancy projects) in areas with better water resources; in areas threatened by drought, 40–50 per cent of all manpower should be devoted to water conservancy. All water works should follow the principle of emphasizing the

[38] *RMRB*, 26 April 1958.   [39] See *Mao Weikan*, xiB. 25–50.

small-scale ones, and the 60,000 fertilizer 'factories' already built were ordered to begin production.

On the other hand, the PPC sought to tighten the controls over the leaders of the APCs by broadening the rectification campaign and by employing the highly ritualistic methods such as the promotion of 'democracy', the mobilization of the masses, and the launching of a 'high tide' in 'blooming and contending'. In an open invitation to misrepresentation, the PPC stipulated that places with the most *dazibao* would be judged to be the best and the most enthusiastic. It further ordered that the province should have millions and hundreds of millions of *dazibao*.[40]

Again, the grass-roots cadres bore the burden of these PPC initiatives. On the one hand, they were ordered to lead two new campaigns to solve two major perceived problems (water and fertilizer). On the other hand, they were required to deepen the rectification campaign and to carry out self-criticisms, or 'to draw fire to burn themselves', and to reorganize the management of the APCs by using the methods of the 'four bigs'. These imposed impossible demands on the time, energies and stamina of the grass-roots cadres, but that was not the end of it. We will turn to this in the following.

The Policy Instrument of Inspection

The Provincial People's Committee (PPPC) was overshadowed by the PPC in the GLF and little was heard about its activities. However, no organization could exempt itself from the hullabaloo of the time. Although their membership overlapped, the activism of the PPC also spilled over to the PPPC. In May, the 40 odd organs of the PPPC were turned into 347 work teams comprising a total of 2,853 members to carry out rectification and reform at the grass roots (villages, factories, etc.). This took several forms: first, 'leap forward' targets and methods of implementation were 'brought down' to the grass-roots organs. Second, some teams visited the advanced localities or units to conduct on-the-spot 'rectify and reform' meetings there. Third, experimental plots were created and these model experiences were used to solve problems that allegedly could not be resolved in the office. Fourth, 'appraisal-through-comparisons' were carried out at advanced units to 'liberate' people's thinking. Finally, the PPPC work teams conducted an inspection tour around the province and helped the grass-roots units to solve their problems of thinking and practice.[41]

The PPPC claimed that all this had helped to reveal advanced experiences so that they could be popularized, resulting in 'remarkable successes'. In effect, however, these practices exerted tremendous pressure on the local units, and many local cadres labelled rightists were punished. On the other hand, however, some work

---

[40] *NFRB*, 14 May 1958. Mikhail Klochko, a Soviet scientist residing in Beijing at that time, gives a vivid account of the competition to put up big-character posters. See *Soviet Scientist in China* (Montreal: International Publishers' Representatives, 1964), 70–4.

[41] *NFRB*, 25 May 1958.

teams simply went through the motions. This is not surprising, considering the contradictory objectives of the provincial authorities. Their subordinates were required to raise their targets to absurd heights, but on the other hand, they were also indicted for making exaggerated claims.

Despite its superficiality, this kind of inspection remained a favourable control method in Guangdong, as it was a grand display of the zeal of the provincial authorities. As mentioned, Tao was a star champion of Mao and the Leap policies at the Second Session of the Eighth Party Congress. His encomium of the 1956 Leap was accompanied by the necessary carping at its detractors and *fanmaojin*. The lesson, he alleged, was that one should never swerve from the correct line of Mao and the Party. He urged learning from Mao, not just foreign classics, especially Mao's ideas of smashing 'superstitions' and the liberation of thought. Echoing Mao, he stressed the importance of 'subjective initiative' and the use of the indigenous method (as opposed to 'foreign' or modern methods). Agriculture in Guangdong, he pledged, would reach the target of 800 *jin/mu* specified in the NPAD in 1960, at unprecedented speed.[42]

One example of the application of the 'subjective initiative' cited by Tao was close planting, originally initiated by the PPC Congress in December 1957, as an 'advanced' method to raise yields. Although close planting had doubled the rural work load, Tao was adamant to push it to 'smash' the 'conservative' way practised for 'thousands of years'. This inspired Mao, who later in 1958 ordered the national adoption of this method.[43] Tao earned Mao's trust, as he was selected the director of the newly formed South China Cooperative Region (which encompassed Guangdong and Guangxi).[44] These Cooperative Regions, as observed, true to their designed roles, were the most zealous and unaccountable promoters of Leap policies. Their frequent meetings to engage in 'appraisal-through-comparisons' were greatly responsible for the spiralling of targets.

Therefore, after the Party Congress, the PPC decided to mimic the PPPC by organizing a mammoth '10,000 member' inspection contingent to transmit the 'spirit' of the Party Congress and to promote 'another' GLF in agricultural production,[45] despite the inspection that had just been concluded by the PPPC. According to the formal document issued on 28 May by the PPC,[46] it planned to use the 40 days in June and July to inspect every *xiang* and APC in Guangdong. The inspection contingent, consisting of more than 10,000 cadres drawn from the provincial, special district, county, and *xiang* party committees and including Tao, Zhao Ziyang, Ou Mengjue, Lin Liming, and other members of the PPC, directors and deputy directors of the various provincial departments, was divided into four large contingents (east, west, south, and north). En route, they would also absorb some labour models into their ranks. Numerous goals were set for the inspection—it was to be a 'big promoter of progress', a 'big propaganda for the General Line',

---

[42] Li Rui, *Dayuejin*, 319–22. See also *Unpublished Chinese Documents*, 79–81. Tao returned to these themes in his contribution to *Shangyu* (Upstream), 1, 1958, 3–7.

[43] Li Rui, *Dayuejin*, 321; *NFRB*, 7 December 1957; 1 January 1958; *Mao Weikan*, xiB. 61.

[44] *Dangshi Jiliao*, xlvii. 207.   [45] *RMRB*, 26 May 1958.

[46] *NFRB*, 29 May 1958.

a 'big-appraisal through-comparison' exercise, a 'link-up' between the cadres and the masses, and so on. In particular, it was meant to promote various rural work such as early harvest, autumn harvest, and manure accumulation.

The guideline for measuring performance was the 'General Line' of 'going all out, aiming high, and building socialism by achieving greater, faster, better, and more economical results'. The goals were to have the principle 'strike roots in the hearts of the people' and raise the 'high tide' of production in the province even more. Many techniques, such as the 'drizzle' method (i.e. mild and gentle ways, as opposed to a 'rainstorms'), the 'looking at flowers from horseback' (i.e. quick scanning), the 'dismounting to examine the flowers' (a closer examination), and the 'dissecting of a few sparrows' (analysing a few typical examples) were to be employed. Small on-the-spot meetings were also to be conducted right in the fields to carry out 'appraisal-through-comparisons'. Ironically, after egging everyone on, the PPC also cautioned against bragging and exaggerations.[47]

A remarkable point is the close affinity in ideas and wording between the PPC's directive and editorial (on the inspection) with Mao's speeches delivered during the CCP Congress. For instance, Mao's injunction against 'fancy words without substance ... generalizations without detail' was reflected in the warning against exaggeration mentioned above. The 'sparrow-dissecting' method was mentioned in one of Mao's speeches and the 'flower methods' were outlined in the Sixty Articles. Mao's admonition that the cadres should appear like a common labourer was echoed, word for word, in the editorial that also devoted a long paragraph on how to be humble and to treat the masses and subordinates as equals. A comparison of these documents shows that Mao's remarks were not only repeated by the PPC verbatim, they were also treated as policy directives.[48]

In any event, this direct inspection of the grass-roots by the provincial authorities bypassed the normal bureaucratic procedures to promote a multitude of goals. It immersed the provincial leaders among the masses, and this was consistent with what Mao had advocated throughout 1958. Furthermore, these inspections were dramatic and ostentatious displays of the efforts and determination of the PPC to implement central policies, which explained the predilection of the PPC for such a policy instrument, though it duplicated the inspection just been completed by the PPPC. However, these massive inspections were essentially futile exercises, as Tao himself admitted later. In July 1959, even Mao admitted their futility.[49] Nevertheless, in 1958 the hyperactive PPC was bent on throwing everything at the perceived problems, and this overloaded the grass-roots masses tremendously.

Zhao Ziyang, Tao Zhu, and Technical Change

Obsessed with a dramatic surge in farm production and shunning the technicians, the provincial leaders Tao Zhu and Zhao Ziyang turned to yet another

---

[47] *NFRB*, 29 May 1958.   [48] *Mao Weikan*, xiB. 61; *Mao Wengao*, vii. 56.
[49] Li Rui, *Lushan Huiyi*, 72.

adventure—technical change. This was consistent with Mao's call for a 'technical revolution' as contained in the Sixty Articles. Just when the Great Check-up was about to begin, Zhao published the article 'The Pace of Grain Production Can be Accelerated' in the *NFRB*,[50] arguing that it was perfectly conceivable to apply the formula of *duohao kuaisheng* to accelerate grain production. Accordingly, he unveiled yet another set of new targets—grain production in 1958 should reach 30m. tons, and Guangdong was to be turned into an '800 *jin* province' in 1959 or the year after. Exuding confidence, he spelled out the measures toward this end.

Water, good soil, and fertilizer were essential for agricultural production, according to him, but they must be complemented by 'farming technique and system', that is, multiple cropping, the rotation of crops, and close planting. Apparently, close planting had met with most resistance, as he dwelt on refuting the arguments against it. By Zhao's reckoning, the peasants were experienced in production, but they were too set in their old ways. Many were said to be uninterested in 'bold' experimentation, and were opposed to early sowing and close planting. All these obstacles in 'thinking', Zhao insisted, could be overcome and the peasants could be led to abandon the 'old rules inherited from their ancestors' by intensifying ideological work.

Specifically, Zhao argued that the 'technical reform movement' could be introduced by several ways. First, the examples of close planting leading to high yield must be singled out as models. They must then conduct debates between the cadres and the masses and concurrently newly revised plans incorporating close planting could be drawn up.

Second, cadres from the *xiang*, APCs, and production teams, technicians, and experienced and 'reform-minded' old peasants would form 'technical teams'. The cadres should take charge for they had 'politics' and 'power' (presumably, political consciousness); the technicians had the scientific expertise and the old peasants had production experience. In this way, the 'red and expert' teams could elude the dangers of rightist conservatism and the departure from reality.

Third, all cadres were asked to study intensively, to become both red and expert, and turn into 'professionals' as quickly as possible. Finally, since such large projects as water conservancy, fertilizer accumulation, and close planting had multiplied the total amount of rural work, the issues of mechanization and 'tool-reform', according to him, had to be put on the agenda.

On the surface, technical changes to raise production were plausible. However, the extremely high targets, the desire to achieve dramatic increases in production instantly, the attempt to change the peasants' modus operandi by administrative fiat, and the substitution of overzealous cadres for technicians turned most of these projects into irreversible blunders. In the following months, the PPC became even more wrapped up in the frenzy of the GLF and even more fanatical schemes were devised.

Meanwhile, an example of how these proposed technical changes were forced upon the grass-roots APCs by the touring PPC inspection teams is revealing. In June,

[50] *NFRB*, 1 June 1958.

the North-Central PPC's inspection team led by Zhao descended on Vanguard APC, whose members were said to be uninformed about the advantages of deep ploughing and close planting. According to the experienced collective members, the *yield/mu* should be around 350 *jin*, as close planting yielded merely more stalks, not more grain. However, the PPC insisted that this estimate was too low.

To prove the APC wrong, the members of the inspection team sprang into action and harvested one field. After sun-drying on the same day, the grain was weighed and an alleged 476 *jin* was obtained. Thus vindicated, the inspection team urged the introduction of more technical reforms and proposed to raise the grain ration to whet the enthusiasm of the APC members after the anticipated bumper harvest.[51]

The inspection team made its point, although its exploit was dubious at best. In another case, when the upper level cadres compelled the reluctant peasants at Zengbu villages in south Guangdong to plant twice as many rice seedlings in the fields, the output/*mu* dropped from 650 to 350 *jin/mu*.[52] At any rate, the inspection shows how the PPC interfered directly with the grass roots, and how the relentless pressure for higher estimates had fostered exaggerations. The fantastic 'statistics' published by the provincial authorities at the end of June must be viewed in this context.

However, Zhao's other exploits drew Mao's attention and praise. His letter to the PPC on his experience of investigation at Conghua County claimed that *yield/mu* for early rice there had reached 300 to 400 *jin/mu*, although the record for 1957 was only 200 *jin/mu*. Although they had not met the demand of the Special District Committee for 600 *jin/mu*, they strove to achieve 500 *jin/mu* for late crops, so that the target of 800 *jin/mu* could be reached. Zhao attributed such achievement to close planting—the plants were placed only 7 cm apart, not the usual norm of 13 or 15 cm—and concluded that this measure was bound to raise production, if sufficient fertilizer were applied.

After the usual carping at *fanmaojin* for making the masses lose their enthusiasm, Zhao urged the cadres to listen to the masses more. The practice of working late into the night, even to dawn in some places, a good method, should be limited. Finally, *dazibao*, a useful tool in promoting production, should be encouraged until its use had become a social custom. When Mao got hold of this letter, he lauded Zhao for tackling the common problems nationwide and for the lack of intellectual 'tone', and ordered it to be published in *Hongqi*.[53] In July, Zhao cooked up another new method—on-the-spot evaluation and comparison, to be carried out in association with the experimental plots and *dazibao*—to pressure the 'backward' to learn from the advanced in close planting.[54]

On the other hand, in June/July, the inspection tour took Tao Zhu to the Shantou and Huiyang special districts for twenty days. Speaking on 27 June, he praised the large number of advanced elements that dared to experiment and set up 'bold and

[51] *NFRB*, 5 July 1958.   [52] Sulamith Potter and Jack Potter, *China's Peasants*, 72.

[53] *Hongqi*, 6, 1958, 13–17; *Mao Wengao*, vii. 302–4.

[54] *Shangyu*, 1, 1958, 15–20. Party Secretary Wu Nansheng also weighed in by declaring that close planting was the heart of the current technical revolution, citing the 'miracle' in Henan where 7,320 *jin* of wheat was harvested on one *mu* of land. The plants were so packed together that 'rats could not penetrate'. Ibid. 21–8.

unheard-of targets' such as 5,500 *jin/mu* of rice, 130,000 *jin/mu* of sweet potatoes, 200,000 *jin/mu* of sugar cane, and hogs weighing 1,000 *jin* each. Tao had no qualms about such hyperboles. According to him, the point was not whether these targets could be realized immediately, what counted was the overcoming of the 'super-stition' that 'the increase in grain production is limited'. The mere putting forward of these targets was certain to bring about new production measures and methods.

In the same breath, Tao also insisted that these wildly exaggerated claims were not fabricated to shock; they were backed up by 'scientific research and prepar-ations'. The centrepiece of the 'technical revolution' was the 'highest degree' of close-planting, he maintained. For this purpose, all the time-worn rules and regu-lations must be 'smashed'. To illustrate, he delved into some detailed calculations: when spacing in the rows was reduced by 1.5 cm to 10 cm, 300,000 bundles could be planted in one *mu*. Each bundle consisted of 5 ears of grain, making for 1.5 million ears of grain. Since each ear of grain had 90 kernels, the total would reach 135 million kernels of grain, and given that 20,000 kernels of grain weighed one *jin*, the amount of 6,750 *jin/mu* could be obtained! Allowing a margin of error of 15 per cent, the actual yield could reach 5,500 *jin/mu*, Tao asserted.[55] Such was the nature of his 'scientific research', although his output estimate was 7 to 11 times higher than that made by Mao and Zhao.

In concluding, Tao argued that the conditions of a technical revolution were 'perfectly mature', despite widespread resistance. Since this revolution appeared like a 'hurricane'—a most appropriate metaphor, considering the suddenness and the forcefulness with which the campaign was fired off—it was unavoidable that the masses had difficulty in adjusting to it. Therefore, he maintained that this 'technical revolution' entailed a serious struggle in 'thought', and not simply a technical matter. It was necessary therefore for all party committees to grasp 'action and thought' simultaneously. Once the problem of thinking was tackled, all problems could then be resolved easily.[56]

Such was the nature of the work of the inspection groups. Both the groups led by Zhao and Tao professed to popularize technical reforms. Both championed close planting and the various wonders they could bring. Nevertheless, in effect, both were urging the grass-roots cadres and masses to suspend their disbelief, to forget their own common sense and experience, and to embrace the wildest claims. This imposition of 'blind orders from above' was one of the most resented features of the Leap. With alternating pressure and exhortation by the PPC, many responded and played the game by becoming 'advanced elements', and the PPC embraced them without question. Such was the background to the spiralling estimates of agricultural outputs in the summer of 1958, and the so-called 'statistics' were gathered from such projections.[57]

[55] At the Second Session of the Eighth Party Congress, Mao used similar methods supplied by Guangdong to figure out that close planting could yield 800 *jin/mu*. *Wansui* (1969), 202.

[56] *XHBYK*, 14, 1958, 63–4.

[57] The novel *Pobiji* was the first in the post-Mao literature to give a vivid account of how 'statistics' were concocted in 1958. Xiaolin, one of the characters, was in the commune office when the county officer

Further Acceleration

Against this background, the Guangdong Statistical Bureau published a communiqué on 30 June on the achievements of the economic GLF in the first part of 1958. It now loudly trumpeted as a fact that the spring and summer harvest crops *alone* had exceeded 10 and 15m. tons, or roughly equivalent to the total output increase of the entire 1FYP period (at 25m. tons).[58] This was a fantastic claim, considering the total output in 1957 was only 10m. tons, and the 1958 plan was set at 14m. tons in January, 17m. tons in April, and 30m. tons in June. Nevertheless, in July, the PPC put forward another extravagant claim for the spring and summer harvests. The 25m. tons of grain announced twenty days before was now revised to 32.5m. tons (19.5m. tons of which was said to be early rice), enabling it to claim that the harvest of 'one crop' had exceeded the total production increase in the previous seven years since 1949! This spectacular outcome was attributed to huge production surges in many areas with more than 1,000 *jin/mu*, especially in former low-yield areas. In some areas, the yield had gone up 100 per cent. The PPC urged everybody to eliminate their 'inferiority complexes' and 'superstitions' to take advantage of the new techniques and new forms, such as close planting, which was most controversial. Although rice experts had warned that if 500 *jin/mu* was desired, the crops would wilt, the PPC advocated $7 \times 7 \times 12$ cm to replace the old standard of 20×17 cm and claimed that it was possible, if sufficient amounts of fertilizer were applied. The PPC claimed that it was vindicated by the dramatically increased output, and that these outstanding achievements strengthened the people's desire to 'subdue' nature. Now it bragged that they could produce as much grain as they wanted to. Finally, the PPC credited the surges in production to the thoroughness in rectification, the opposition to rightist conservatism, and localism. Places with the most *dazibao* were also deemed the most politically active.[59]

---

telephoned for the figure of chickens in the commune. Xiaolin obliged by supplying the numbers of roosters, hens, and even the number of eggs collected in detail. Then he called the switchboard to ask it to inform all production brigades to submit reports on the number of chickens (broken down into roosters and hens), as well as the number of eggs they had. A young girl present was astonished that Xiaolin would submit the figures to the county *before* collecting them from the production brigades. Xiaolin explains, 'Day in and day out, they telephone for the figures of hogs, sheep, and chickens. Who bothers to find out? Anyway, who would really look at these figures? Who cares if they are true or false? Everyone is just going through the motions!—Sometimes, you need to add a zero, or a few decimal points; only then they would believe you! At times, the county asks strange questions. The piglets are still in the bellies of the sows, but they want to know how many are males and how many are females. At the beginning, I told them honestly, but who knows, I had to bear the criticism by director Wang. [He said] "Fool! Wouldn't these piglets be born sooner or later!"' (Beijing renmin chubanshe, 1980), 211. Sulamith Potter and Jack Potter, *China's Peasants*, 72.

[58] *NFRB*, 1 July 1958.

[59] *NFRB*, 20 July 1958; *RMRB* 23 July 1958. Often, even hagiographic accounts are unintentionally revealing. For instance, Zhou Enlai, acting on Mao's instructions, inspected Xinhui county between 1 and 7 July, touting many of the GLF slogans, such as the goal of 2,000 *jin/mu*. See the two articles in *Dangdai Guangdong*, 1, 1998, 18–19, 23–30.

As expectations and ambitions kept spiralling out of control, the PPC Conference on 19 July (the first PPC Conference since the inspection tours of June/July) set forth another new 'battle task' of turning the province into a 'twelve hundred *jin/mu* province'. (To achieve an overall average yield of 1,200 *jin/mu* for Guangdong in 1958, the output of late rice would have to reach 800 to 1,000 *jin/mu*, and 4,000 to 6,000 *jin/mu* for sweet potatoes.) This task had become so important for the PPC that it ordered an emergency mobilization of the 'whole party and the whole people'. In large measure, this new initiative was made urgent by the alleged 'giant strides' in grain production in the other provinces. The total production increase of the country in 1958, according to Tao, was not 5 or 10m. tons, but 50 to 100m. tons. Members of the PPC and the prefectural party committees had visited neighbouring provinces and found that output of 3,000–4,000 *jin/mu* of rice was common. Henan and Anhui anticipated spectacular yields of 10,000 *jin/mu*. This development had led not only many provinces south of the Yangzi to declare themselves 'thousand-*jin* provinces' in 1958, but even provinces in the northwest had put forward similar slogans. Faced with this 'serious challenge', Guangdong, which had outperformed other provinces in the past, had now been left behind. In reality, the miracles reported in these provinces were hardly credible, but the competition among them had created a spiralling effect. More important, the rules of the game had been changed, as the centre not only did not dispute these claims, it joined the chorus in applauding them. Hence, Tao felt obliged to measure up to these achievements, and predicted a 'flying leap' in late harvest.

Many delegates of the prefectural party committees were ready to pander to Tao's wishes. All expressed concern over the 'urgency' of the situation and maintained that Guangdong could rejoin the 'advanced' by 'biting the bullet' and summoning up all its drive. The delegates from Gaoyao Special District pledged to hold a broadcast mobilization conference involving all cadres at the *xiang* level and above the next day, and that half a month would be devoted to the 'hard struggle' to transplant all rice seedlings. Huiyang Special District decided to organize an 'army' of 150,000 to go to the villages to propagandize the new tasks and to support the transplantation of rice seedlings. Hepu Special District decided to convene a telephone conference with all the secretaries of the county party committees the same night and ordered all of them to move down to the fields to conduct their official business there *by the next day*. Most cadres in the 'leadership organs' were to be sent down to the APCs and the production teams to strengthen the leadership of the grassroots level.

Finally, in Zhanjiang Special District, entire *xiang* party committees had already moved to live beside the experimental plots to lead production. Tao had nothing but praise for the Hepu and Zhanjiang decisions and ordered the entire province to learn from them. Except a few cadres, he urged, the rest should move to the sides of the experimental plots, build sheds and live there.[60]

---

[60] *NFRB*, 20 July 1958.

Guangdong was clearly under tremendous pressure to excel further. Although it was extremely active, it had fallen behind when measured against the other more zealous provinces. Therefore, even more drastic measures had to be taken. However, many far-reaching decisions were made impromptu. The delegates had not discussed among themselves before they made their pledges, let alone consulted their constituencies. They had scored points with the PPC but it is doubtful if these decisions could ever be implemented.

In any case, huge surges in production were now regarded as the norm. As mentioned, even Chen Yi, vice-premier and Minister of Foreign Affairs, in inspecting Panyu, Guangdong, in September, claimed that he had witnessed *yield/mu* of 500,000 kg of yams, 300,000 kg of sugar cane, and 25,000 kg of rice.[61] On the other hand, Tao tried to maintain himself at the forefront of the race to expedite production. In an article dated 15 July published in *Hongqi*, Tao strove to refute those who questioned the current quest to accelerate production as a form of 'subjectivism'. Although these detractors claimed that increases in yield of 20 per cent were impossible, Tao bragged that early crops in Guangdong had soared to 32.5m. tons, or more than 60 per cent of the yield of the previous year, so it would be possible for Guangdong to achieve 1,000 *jin/mu* in 1958. Citing Qian Xuesen's article that claimed that if only 30 per cent of the sun's rays could be fully utilized, then wheat could reach 40,000 *jin/mu*, Tao tried to show that the growth potential was almost limitless. In this vein, he argued that if wheat, commonly regarded as a low-yield crop, could achieve 7,000 *jin/mu*, then it should be possible for high-yield crops such as rice, which could also be raised in three crops a year, to reach 10,000 *jin/mu*. Reading between the lines, one senses that Tao blamed the other braggarts for raising the ante to incredible heights, but signalled that he was ready to play the game to the full. So he added that in some places, early rice had already reached 2,000 *jin/mu*, so with close planting, irrigation, fertilizer application, deep ploughing, good seeds, vigorous field management, yearly yield should reach 10,000 *jin/mu* without problems! According to him, Guangdong had harvested 10.5m. tons of grain in 1956, but production increased by only 2.5m. tons in 1957, because 'localism' and *fanmaojin* had poured cold water on the masses. Those who complained about high targets or exaggerations were really rightist conservatives.[62] In an article written for *Shangyu*, he went one step further, pledging that the 800 *jin/mu* target contained in the NPAD should be exceeded in 1958 to reach 1,200 *jin/mu*. It was perfectly possible for Guangdong to achieve 3,000 *jin/mu* in 1962 and 10,000 *jin/mu* by 1972, he added.[63]

[61] *RMRB*, 26 September 1958.

[62] *Hongqi*, 5, 1958, 1–5; Chen Jiyuan *et al.*, *Nongcun Jingji Bianqian*, 294. A post-Mao account claim that Tao tried to resist high targets and the Leap right at the beginning is inaccurate. See Zheng Xiaofeng and Shu Ning, *Tao Zhu Zhuan*, 259. Tao did feel pressured by the high targets mooted by the other provincial leaders at the Central South Coordinating Conference (16–24 July), but it was he who was willing to play the game of one-upmanship at the Party Congress in May. He never wavered from the numbers game in the rest of 1958.   [63] *Shangyu* no. 1, 1958, 4.

The August Interlude and the Beidaihe Conference

In August, the PPC continued to direct the day-to-day agricultural activities and to cope with the incessant central initiatives until the bombshell to form people's communes was dropped at the Beidaihe Conference. In early August, the transplanting of rice seedlings was almost completed and the PPC felt it was time to inspect the transplant work and to promote field management, both were regarded as the keys to realizing high production targets. It decided that three massive 'appraisal-through-comparison' inspections were needed in the coming two to three months (after rice seedling transplantation; this is traditionally regarded as a slack season).[64] A directive for the first such inspection (issued on 6 August) provided some details of operations.[65] To begin with, the PPC itself formed three inspection contingents going in different directions. The East Route was led by the Secretary of the PPC Secretariat, Zhao Ziyang, deputy provincial governor An Pingsheng, and deputy secretary of the PPC Secretariat Yang Yingbin. The North and Central Route was led by Secretary of the PPC Secretary Ou Mengjue, the Secretary of the Provincial Control Commission Li Jianzhen, and the Secretary General of the PPC Zhang Gensheng. The West Route was led by alternate Secretary of the PPC, Yin Linping, and the Director of the Rural Work Department of the PPC.

Second, the party committees from the special districts down to the *xiang* were ordered to engage in inspections and appraisals-through-comparison themselves. Third, the teams were to inspect such things as the number of rice seedlings, the general growing situation, the amount of manure applied, and the possible problems that might arise. One goal was to check the compliance with the 'close planting' trumpeted by the provincial leaders. In this way, the provincial authorities again immersed themselves among the grass roots. Paradoxically, the desire to impose greater direct control yielded only diminishing returns, a fact not recognized until much later. Meanwhile, another initiative from the centre had to be implemented.

Although the issue of the reform of farm implements had been discussed by the provincial authorities, it was the centre that formalized it as a national policy. In August, the Central Party Secretariat convened two telephone conferences with the secretaries of the PPC on the campaign to remodel farm implements and fit them with ball-bearings. Subsequently, Tao duly convened a provincial telephone conference,[66] and declared that mechanization was the only solution to the problem of the acute labour shortage created by the numerous activities of the GLF. Yet, since mechanization could not be realized immediately, the installation of ball-bearings on farm tools could be called 'semi-mechanization'. After some discussion, the PPC made several decisions. First, a small leadership group for the reform of farm tools, representing the PPC, would be invested with the authority of commanding, inspecting, and promoting the campaign. Similar groups were to be formed at the special district, county, *xiang*, and APC levels. Second, the PPC demanded that the

---

[64] *NFRB*, 21 August 1958.   [65] *NFRB*, 8 August 1958.   [66] Ibid.

province produce 25 million sets of ball-bearings, and quotas were assigned to the various municipalities, counties, and *xiang*. Third, the delegates were urged to start the campaign immediately after the conference.

The delegates were said to have agreed with the PPC 'unanimously'. Some resolved to hold emergency meetings to implement the PPC's directive; many special districts and counties decided to convene on-the-spot conferences in two to three days to popularize the experience in manufacturing ball-bearings. Again, the PPC's subordinates seemed to be obliging, as the various methods such as the critique of 'rightist-conservatism' and inspection tours had reduced them to docile agents. However, further challenges lay ahead.

As mentioned, the Beidaihe Conference, assuming that a huge bumper harvest was on hand, announced the doubling of the steel target and new and higher targets for 1959 and the 2FYP, and resolved to form people's communes. In response to the new initiatives set by the central Beidaihe conference, an expanded PPC Conference (3–6 September) on the iron and steel industry was called to discuss the central directives on shifting the emphasis of work from agriculture to industry, and the fulfilling of the target in steel production.[67] The meaning of the second task is obvious, but the same cannot be said of the first.

In fact, both industrial and rural problems continued to be so complex and onerous that no setting of priorities was possible, especially with the introduction of the people's communes. As the PPC anticipated, the communes would 'revolutionize' the labour organization and livelihood of the peasants, opening another Pandora's box. It foresaw the unavoidable misgivings among the peasants that would complicate the massive task of field management in the autumn.

For these reasons, it ordered that all party committees, especially their propaganda organs and newspapers, should convene meetings using the 'big blooming, contending, debates, and big character posters' method to propagandize the policy and the advantages of the communes. To allay the fears of the masses, and to 'handle well' the four major tasks (field management, the 'spectacular' autumn harvests, the iron and steel campaign, and the installation of ball-bearings), the PPC ruled that the APCs should be the unit to join the communes. This meant that what was produced by the individual APCs would still be distributed within themselves and not be pooled together in the communes.

The Second Great Inspection

At the end of the Conference, the PPC decided to launch the Second Great Inspection of Industrial and Agricultural work on 9 September as its last weapon to force the completion of the impossible targets.[68] Since this was a unique GLF phenomenon and was colossal in scope, it deserves detailed description.

First, the goals of the inspection were diffuse and wide-ranging. The teams were to scrutinize and promote work as diverse as autumn harvest, post-harvest work such

[67] *NFRB*, 10 September 1958.   [68] Ibid.

as state procurement, processing and the storage of crops, tool reform, the formation of the people's communes, and iron and steel production.

Second, the provincial inspection contingent of 100,000 people, drawn from the provincial government units, was organized into five sub-regiments; each was to merge with the members of the district, county, and *xiang* party committees. Each sub-regiment was subdivided further into two—one agricultural (to take charge of finance and trade, culture and education, law and politics *sic*) and one industrial (to take charge of iron and steel production, the fitting of ball-bearings on moving machines, and tool reform). More than 10 million of the masses were to be involved in this inspection campaign.

Third, the inspection sub-regiments would organize 'appraisals-through-comparisons' in the counties, *xiang*, and communes.[69] They would arouse the masses to launch *dazibao* campaigns to sum up experience by conducting commune test points, to promote the work of the various units through inspection, and to exchange and popularize experience.

The Great Inspection would last 45 days between 15 September and the end of October. On 5 October all leaders of the sub-regiments were to return to Guangzhou to submit reports. Between 5 October and 31 October, the main task was to participate in commune building and to carry out further inspections and to grapple with problems in production.[70]

Therefore this Great Inspection was meant to be a multipurpose campaign to promote work that the PPC regarded as most urgent. Its enormous scope and organization far exceeded the first Great Inspection Campaign conducted in May. The dispatching of large numbers of cadres down to the base level to inspect and mobilize work bypassed the normal bureaucratic control and procedure. The ideal was to involve as many people as possible and to promote national policies and to bring the leadership cadres into closer contact with the masses. Nevertheless, it turned out that the various techniques such as 'appraisal-through-comparison' and the *dazibao* placed a tremendous amount of pressure on the various administrative units for outstanding performance. When one unit announced high production targets, no matter how inflated or unrealistic, others were obliged to follow suit. The emphasis on establishing test points before the general introduction of people's communes reflected a certain degree of caution,[71] but the general frenzy for rapid commune formation, especially in Henan province, soon rendered these experiments superfluous.

Furthermore, it is difficult to see how the focus of the work of the PPC had been shifted to industry, as three of the four tasks to be inspected were associated with

---

[69] In Article 25 of the *Sixty Articles on Work Method*, Mao wrote, 'Members of the Central Committee and the party committees of provinces, municipalities directly under the Central Committee and autonomous regions—except those who are sick or senile—must leave their offices by turns for the grass-roots level, and spend four months each year there to make investigation and study to hold meetings. They should adopt both the method of looking at the flowers from horseback and the method of dismounting to examine the flowers. It is good even though they spend no more than three or four hours in one place.' *Mao Wengao*, vii. 56.   [70] *NFRB*, 10 September 1958.   [71] Ibid.

either agriculture or rural development. The province was saturated by so many goals that another injunction from the centre must be fused into current work, as any action could be justified in terms of some goals, and everyone was too busy to notice the difference anyway. In any event, this new 'big check-up', scheduled to last 45 days from September 15 to the end of October, meant that most of the province's most important leaders would again lodge themselves among the grass-roots. Therefore, there is no ground for the speculation that both Tao and Zhao disappeared from public view in the fall of 1958 because they were opposed to the communes, or that they adopted a wait-and-see tactic before committing themselves.[72]

At any rate, from September to the end of the year, rural agricultural affairs were immensely complicated by the hyperboles, campaigns, and institutional changes. To make the narrative manageable, the following will be divided into two sections. The first section explores the problems surrounding the introduction of the people's communes. The second examines the campaigns for autumn harvest and for another GLF in agriculture for 1959.

The Movement to Form People's Communes

The decision to introduce people's communes wreaked havoc in the everyday lives of the people and generated a great deal of conflict. In March, when the Party Centre issued the directive on amalgamation of the APCs, Liaoning and Guangdong were the two fastest-moving provinces.[73] In Guangdong, the 46,000 APCs had already amalgamated into 23,000 larger cooperatives.[74] This, however, did not lighten the impact, as the natures of the APCs and the communes were radically different, and the PPC had virtually no time to prepare, or to run test points. Since the formal decision at Beidaihe, communization proceeded in lightning speed. In September, it was announced that 42,000 APCs (with 8.16 million households) in Guangdong were merged into approximately 800 communes, with an average of 10,000 households each. Some huge communes comprised an entire county. Predictably, various economic and organizational problems emerged, and widespread grumbling and resistance among the peasants challenged the ability of the provincial leadership to deal with them. Yet, the PPC's hands were tied. Apart from homilies, there was little it could offer. Not until a policy change sanctioned by Mao and the Party Centre did the PPC have some leeway.

Belatedly, the PPC convened a conference (5–9 October) to review the so-called test-point communes selected by the party committees to come to grips with the economic and organizational problems, particularly the issue of acute labour

---

[72] David Shambaugh, *The Making of a Premier, Zhao Ziyang's Provincial Career* (Boulder, Colo: Westview Press, 1984), 19–20.

[73] For the amalgamation of APCs in Liaoning, see Alfred L. Chan, 'The Campaign for Agricultural Development, 61–2; Bo Yibo, *Huigu*, ii. 730.

[74] *Dangdai Zhongguo de Guangdong* (Contemporary Guangdong) (Beijing: Dangdai Zhongguo chubanshe, 1991), 86.

shortage. Without realizing the impact, the PPC also decided to push forward the policy of 'three-ize'—that is, 'militarize organization, combatize action, and collectivize living'. To 'militarize and combatize', the communes had to form two different sets of labour and military organizations. The first was a general labour organization whose members were also the general militia. The latter, acting as a reserve production unit as well as the backbone militia, were to consist of 15–20 per cent of all labour reserves. It was to be commanded by the communes and subject to regular military training. Its members were supposed to be all-rounders in production and they would also protect the motherland in times of need.

To collectivize livelihood, the PPC urged that the mess halls and the nurseries be run well to ease the transition to the communes. Hence the best cooks were to be transferred to the mess halls and the workers there were urged to work whole-heartedly for the commune members. The nurseries would gradually provide full room and board service.[75]

In singling out the problems of merging and distribution, the PPC clearly anticipated some fundamental problems of the communes that would eventually force the retreat from its original ideal. Yet, from October to December, situations in the communes continued to deteriorate. The fundamental problems and the ineffectiveness of the PPC's policies to deal with them will be discussed in the following.

Levelling

Communization meant the absorption of the public properties and savings belonging originally to the APCs into the communes. All means of production and agricultural tools were confiscated as common property. The shares given to the peasants and the appraisal values of their properties when joining the advanced APCs were abolished outright. The merging of better-off APCs with poorer ones and the pooling of their resources was bound to create serious frictions. For instance, the members of the Shikeng APC in Huilai county not only refused to merge with other poorer APCs, they tried to break away from the county and petitioned the secretary of the prefectural party committee to join a neighbouring county.[76] Levelling was soon aggravated by the free and unrestricted manner by which the communes requisitioned and moved land, labour, and property around for the iron and steel campaign, deep ploughing, harvest, and building industries. Land, animals, and raw materials were requisitioned to run farms or factories. Forest and trees were denuded to engage in tool 'reform', and cook-wares, utensils, metal windows and doors were taken to run the mess halls or for the iron and steel campaign. Funds were diverted to the building of such non-essentials as 'culture roads' and ceremonial arches. In time, other units such as the production brigades and production teams jumped into the fray, and scrounged whatever belonged to the commune members in an essentially free-for-all, or what the Chinese called 'communist wind'. In addition, the labour

---

[75] *NFRB*, 14 October 1958.   [76] *NFRB*, 15 and 18 October 1958.

requisition for the various water conservancy and iron and steel projects, and the construction of pig farms, estimated at nearly 10 million strong, was unpaid, and this lasted anywhere from a few months to half a year. Often, peasants had to supply their own food. One rough estimate put the value (discounting the value of land, forests, granaries, etc.) of property confiscated in Guangdong at 984m. *yuan*, and when the Party finally decided to pay compensation in 1959, it was done only perfunctorily.[77]

The PPC admitted that it was true that collectives had different endowments and income levels, but argued that it was the support by the state and other neighbouring collectives that had enabled some to become more prosperous than the others. Therefore, their 'departmentalism' was 'despicable'. It completely dodged the issues by maintaining that amalgamation benefited all concerned by citing some idealized examples. The collectives in the grain-producing areas could match perfectly with APCs from areas that specialized in commercial crops because the farmers had grain and the latter had money. The collectives in the hilly regions had rich resources and their merger with collectives in the plains would make possible the ideal of developing agriculture, forestry, animal husbandry, subsidiary occupations, and fishery simultaneously in the communes. The prosperity of some individual cooperatives was nothing in comparison with what the large communes could produce in the future.

As these reasonings were hardly credible, the PPC threatened serious punishment for those who persisted in the dividing of public property and disrupted production. A proposed communist education campaign was also outlined to weed out the 'impure' base-level organizations. Finally, the PPC ordered each county and commune to hold expanded cadre meetings to 'arm' and rectify all commune members and cadres.

The New Remuneration and Distribution System

A unified distribution within the communes despite the variation in production conditions and the income levels of the different APCs was a contentious redistributive issue.[78] The new remuneration system, which featured a combination of free-supply and wages, replaced the one based on work points and number of days worked. The more prosperous APCs felt that the unified distribution in the communes was tantamount to having 'the rich collectives subsidizing the poor collectives from their own pockets'. Subsequently, the cadres felt it was a waste of effort to have worked hard in the past for they ended up 'getting the worst of it'. Consequently, they lost all incentive for their work; others divided the public property and spent the savings extravagantly.

The free-supply system treated everybody equally and later became the only form of distribution. Although the ideal was to have a combination of wages and

[77] *Dangdai Zhongguo de Guangdong*, 87; Feng Ping, *Guangdong Dangdai Nongye Shi* (Contemporary history of agriculture in Guangdong) (Shaoguan: Guangdong renmin chubanshe, 1995), 45.
[78] See *NFRB*, 2 March 1959, in *XHBYK*, 8, 1959, 28.

free-supply, free-supply soon exhausted the limited resources of the communes, leaving nothing to be distributed as wages, and there was no way to tell the difference in the amount of work contributed by individual members. In addition, the distribution system based on free-supply favoured households with weak labour power (e.g. households with many children, old people, and few able-bodied members) at the expense of households with many labourers, and that created a great deal of disincentive for households with strong hands. Hence, the latter were opposed to it, claiming that it 'rewards the lazy ones but punishes the hardworking ones' and that it harmed the work incentive of the people. Others baulked at such a sudden and drastic change.

The PPC's defence of the new remuneration and distributions system was hackneyed. It ordered that the selfish thinking of 'caring only for oneself' and 'paying attention only to the present and ignoring the future' be 'ruthlessly' (*henhen*) criticized. On the issue of the system of ownership, the prescription was to debate the question: was it better to rely on the collective or on private (ownership)? To resolve the problem of distribution, similar debates surrounding the following questions were ordered: would those households with strong labour power get the worst of it by the introduction of the free supply system? Would a semi-free supply system reward 'lazybones' and deal a blow to the production incentive of the masses?

Second, the PPC accused those cadres opposed to communization as 'rightist conservatives' lacking communist consciousness. They were to be either disciplined or re-educated by a forthcoming communist education campaign using the method of 'big blooming, contending, and debate, and big-character posters'.

The PPC argued that the free-supply system represented the beginning of the transcendence of the principle of 'to each according to his labour'. Although the wage portion still operated under this principle (calculated from work points or number of days worked or both), it was modified because from now on the criterion of 'political attitude' was introduced for determining wages. The free-supply portion represented the 'sprouts of communism' and its scope would gradually expand, reaching gradually the communist ideal of 'from each according to his ability, to each according to his needs'. Meanwhile, the minimum aim was a combination of free supply of grain and the dispensation of monthly wages.

The PPC argued that the combination of free-supply and wages was more reasonable since it would close the income gap among commune members. It would also be easier to arouse their enthusiasm for production when they were provided with food and clothing. In due course, many communes began to extend free services to food, medicare, education, fuel, childcare, old age, burials, housing, and haircuts. Expenditures were so great that very soon the treasuries of these communes were empty, leaving nothing to disburse as wages.[79]

[79] Feng Ping, *Guangdong Dangdai Nongye Shi*, 40, 45.

Ownership

Another contentious issue was the abolition of private plots, and the confiscation of livestock, fruit trees, etc. As commune members were forbidden to profit by working in private plots and sideline occupations, they lost an important source of income. The few remaining small traders and vendors were closed down so they ceased to produce daily consumer goods. Quantity and variety declined.

According to an *NFRB* editorial, the defiant 'rich' peasants were quoted as saying, 'The policy of the CCP is changing again, it doesn't keep its word ... the collectivization of the means of production does not tally with the principle of mutual benefit; the poor peasants take advantage of the middle peasant ... [collectivization in the communes] is like expropriation of the landlords.' Still, what was worst, for the PPC, the people agreed with this kind of opinion.

In defence, the PPC argued that the chief advantage of the commune was that it was both big and more socialist (*yida ergong*, big, and also a higher degree of collectivity). Communization would eliminate forever all the private ownership of the means of production, and expand the scope of all-people ownership through collective ownership. However, the PPC pledged that 'all means of livelihood[80] would not be collectivized, but all the means of production (including private plots, animals, large production tools, small woods and orchards run by collective members) must be owned by the communes.'

It argued that the trouble-makers were the 'rich' peasants, since they owned more means of production. Therefore, it was necessary to let the masses carry out 'big blooming, contending, and debate' on the topic of 'whether the remnants of the private ownership of the means of production should be eliminated.'

Overconsumption: 'Eat Rice without Paying, Three Meals of Rice Each Day'

Though battered by the effects of the communes, the PPC leadership was confident that the grain-supply problem was resolved once and for all by a super early harvest and a projected bumper harvest. Tao, in particular, was concerned that no storage space was available for the huge amount of grain. So at the end of October, the PPC made the unusual decision that all communes should serve three meals of rice a day, and let their members eat all they wanted without paying.[81] At a cadre conference held at the Zhongshan Memorial Hall in Guangzhou, Tao personally called upon the peasants to 'stretch their bellies' to eat three meals of rice free of charge. Tan Zhenlin was quoted to have said that it was nothing to enter communism—'it was nothing more than beans and roast beef. It was very easy to do; it was happening before our eyes.'[82] Not surprisingly, policies that deliver collective goods are readily

---

[80] These included personal belongings such as houses, clothing, household goods, and savings. However, despite the PPC's rulings, these were often confiscated by the zealous commune officials.
[81] *NFRB*, 9 November 1958.   [82] Zheng Xiaofeng and Shu Ning, *Tao Zhu Zhuan*, 260–1.

implementable. For the peasants, this was a welcome change, for in the past rice was rationed and the staple diet was a combination of rice and other less desirable coarse food such as sweet potatoes. Many worried about not having enough to eat. When the new decision was implemented, jubilant celebrations took place in many localities. Moreover, starting on 15 November, the PPC had abolished grain rationing in Guangzhou, so the people could purchase as much as they liked.[83] Even in late November, Zhao reaffirmed that the policy of three meals of rice a day was a long-term one, and urged the masses to 'boldly loosen up their bellies' to eat.[84] Undoubtedly, the PPC also counted on this enticement to bolster the sagging morale in the commune, to make the mess halls more attractive, and to reward the peasants for a year of gruelling work. Unfortunately, this spontaneous outburst of joy was short-lived. The over-consumption used up commercial and reserve grain that was not there, and eventually contributed to the inability to provide relief in the disaster-ridden years following 1958. At the Zengbu villages, the peasants had consumed the normal rice supply for 6 months in 20 days. When rice was exhausted, the villages had to fall back on thin rice gruel, sweet potatoes, and herbs.[85] As the urban population grew, demand for commercial grain also soared, leading to high procurement that could not be sustained.[86] When grain was exhausted, the PPC blamed the peasants for hiding it.

Problems with the Mess Halls

By November, 85 per cent of the rural population took their meals in more than 200,000 mess halls. Yet, because they were formed overnight, only a few were economical, hygienic, and had enough for their members to eat well. Many did not have enough grain or vegetables or were unable to supply three square meals a day. Many mess halls were in the open air. The problem became so acute that the PPC issued a directive urging improvement in the management of the mess halls on 24 November.[87] Therefore, the stock formula 'attention by the party committees, strengthen leadership, secretaries take command, and the entire party participate' was prescribed as a remedy. A more tangible solution included the enjoinment on all *xiang* and commune cadres to join the mess halls themselves. At a PPC telephone conference on November 22, Zhao ordered all party committees to pay more attention to the material well-being of the masses. The communes were asked to distribute wages of 3–6 *yuan* per labourer per month and to ensure that their members should have eight hours rest every day and two days off every month. In addition, the 'democratization' of the management of the communes was to accompany the 'three-ize'.[88]

---

[83] *NBCK*, 49, 17 November 1958, 16.

[84] *NFRB*, 24 November 1958. According to one commemorative article on Tao, he had conducted several open criticisms not only for the 'three meals of rice a day' policy, but also for the unrealistic estimates of grain production in 1958. See *Hongqi*, 1, 1979, 53.

[85] Sulamith Potter and Jack Potter, *China's Peasants*, 73.

[86] *Dangdai Zhongguo de Guangdong*, 88.

[87] *NFRB*, 25 November 1958.   [88] *NFRB*, 24 November 1958.

Second, the PPC was adamant in the policy of 'three meals of rice every day, loosen bellies to eat one's fill', considering it a powerful incentive to spur production. Yet, many communes could not implement it because of the low grain stocks. To correct this, the PPC made the fateful decision of telling these communes to dig into the emergency reserves, or even to adjust the state's quota of grain procurement. This attests to the PPC's confidence in the overall 'bumper harvest' in 1958.

Third, some flexibilities in the mess halls were introduced according to the principle of 'large collective, small freedom'. Henceforth, if the grain rations were managed and cooked by the mess halls, the commune members were allowed to cook some dishes themselves, to take food home to eat, and to take some grain home for snacks. Finally, the PPC urged the elimination of the large number of open-air 'mess halls', and the allotment of some manpower to build some proper ones, especially when winter was approaching.

The above reflected the PPC's attempt to cope with some of the most glaring inadequacies in the communes, but its efforts did not seem to have much effect. Soon another decision made by the centre would sanction the retreat from the original concept of the communes.

At a time when labour was stretched to the limits, great leaps in other areas, such as industry and communication, culture and education, public health, sports, the militia, etc., also made huge demands on rural labour. According to one estimate, 2 million had gone to industry, 2 million were allocated to 'rear support' for the communes, 1 million were assigned to other special tasks, 300,000 grass-roots cadres had left production, and 180,000 mature students had returned to primary schools. Together, these took away 40 per cent of available rural labour.[89] Yet, work incentive plummeted. For instance, in Xinhui County, work attendance was down 50–60 per cent, and labour efficiency and qualities were both low.[90]

Confronted by these, the PPC had few tangible solutions but it persisted in soldiering on; again, the hackneyed method of educating people's thinking and 'big blooming, contending, debate, and big-character posters' were prescribed. Since these methods were ideologically correct, they could be appropriate for any circumstances, although they did not address the issues at hand.

During the rest of October, the problems arising from the communes persisted but the PPC's efforts to grapple with them were ineffective. The persistent criticism of 'departmentalism' did little. Then the PPC brought out the heavy artillery—the re-education of people's thinking.

The Communist Educational Campaign

The PPC's efforts to refute the disgruntled cadres and masses culminated in the promulgation of the PPC directive on the launching of a Communist Education

---

[89] *Dangdai Zhongguo de Guangdong*, 89.　　　[90] *Nongcun Shehui Jingji Bianqian*, 321.

Campaign on 26 October that took a much harder line toward communization.[91] It made clear that all savings originally belonging to the APCs must be transferred to the communes unconditionally. Second, it adopted the uncompromising policy of unified distribution in the communes, thus ending the more cautious approach set out in September to let the APCs divide their autumn harvest individually. In addition, it also decided to crack down more seriously on grain concealment,[92] 'selfish departmentalism', and the division of assets in the collectives.

Third, the PPC reaffirmed the semi-free supply and semi-wage system. To counter fears that this system benefited only households with a weak labour force, the PPC urged that the issue should be seen 'dialectically'—households with strong labour power would eventually turn weak whereas households with children would grow strong. The new distribution system would not only guarantee income security that would transcend the changes in the labour power in the households, but would also realize the communist spirit of 'all for one and one for all'. Fourth, the three '-ize' were said to be able to strengthen national defence and raise productivity. It would overcome the 'peasants' habit of slackness and laxness in discipline' (*ziyou sanman*) and encourage their spirit of collectivism.

Fifth, the PPC explicitly ordered the protection of the activists. This was necessary, one can surmise, because the activists were the staunchest promoters of unpopular or even hated policies among the grass-roots. Other customary injunctions, such as the rectification of the Party and the Communist Youth League, the resolute reliance on the 'class line' of the poor peasants and lower middle peasants, and so on, were also thrown in for good measure.

Coercion

The PPC did not rule out, and at times, even encouraged, the use of coercion to deal with peasant resistance and to implement GLF policies, especially the unpopular ones, such as close planting, 10,000 pig farms, tool refitting, etc. Some Leap policies were inherently coercive, such as the confiscation of properties and the organization of work along military lines. Many cadres equated 'militarization' with the right to order people about. Moreover, commune authorities used telephone conferences to bark out orders, so cadres at the lower administrative levels were pressed to use coercion to implement policies. For instance, those who doubted Leap policies and promises were labelled 'rightist-conservatives', 'tide-watchers', and 'white-flags' (to be uprooted). Cadres and peasants alike were subjected to a range of punishments ranging from criticism, fines, deduction of work points and grain, dismissal, transfer, and demotion. Physical abuses such as beating, forced labour, unlawful custody, and

---

[91] *NFRB*, 27 October 1958.

[92] According to MacFarquhar, anti-concealment drives in Guangdong in early 1959 resulted in criticisms, dismissals, and imprisonment of many grass-roots cadres. Even Mao soon decided that this practice was objectionable. *Origins* 141–2; *Wansui* (1967c), 4, 11, 13, 21, 29, 38, 40, 45. See also, Shambaugh, *Making*, 21.

home searches were rampant.[93] One recent account estimates that during 1958 and 1960, 142,000 party members and non-Party cadres were disciplined. Many others suffered criticism.[94]

The Retreat from the People's Communes

In two to three months, the PPC strove to defend and to implement the letter and spirit of the communes policy, amidst strong opposition from the peasantry. So it was relieved when the Sixth Plenum of the CCP finally decided to modify the extreme features of the communes. When the Congress was in session (28 November–10 December), the PPC had already received leads about the centre's wishes regarding how the communes were to be reorganized by taking cues from the First Zhengzhou Conference (3 December) and the Wuchang Conference. Therefore Zhao and Wen Minsheng convened a PPC telephone conference with the first secretaries of the prefectural party committees to arrange for rectifying the communes.[95]

It decided that the five months between December and April of 1959 would be set aside for the rectification of the communes. Zhao now turned around and conceded that the situation in the communes was chaotic—the general organization in the communes was deficient, the accounts were unclear, the organization of labour was confused, and there was no production planning. The formation of the communes coincided with the large-scale transfer of labour power to the iron and steel campaign and autumn harvest, leaving no time to resolve these problems. Therefore, the PPC decided to dispatch another 10,000-member inspection group for a province-wide general investigation, using the method of 'appraisal-through-comparison' meetings.

Specifically, Zhao wanted the strengthening of the commune executive committees, the various departments below them, and the commune party committees to provide a leadership nucleus. Then he ordered the division of the communes into three levels, each sharing some administrative responsibilities. The first level, the commune executive committee, was responsible for overall management of the communes. Second, the communes were to be divided into administrative districts (*guanli qu*, or former APCs), production brigades, or battalions to take charge of the five functions of agriculture, industry, commerce, education, and the militia. They were to be designated units for economic accounting, but the communes would still be responsible for their gains and losses. At the bottom, the production teams (*shengchan dui*) were the basic units to organize labour. Both the administrative districts and the production teams were to be granted certain powers in organizing production, capital construction, fiscal management, and the management of livelihood and welfare. The practice of turning an entire county into one huge commune was rejected.

---

[93] *Shangyu*, 1, 1959, 10–12. *Guangdong Dangdai Nongye Shi*, 46; Mao was cognizant of this, see *Mao Wengao*, vii. 614–15.   [94] *Dangdai Guangdong*, 2, 1997, 60.
[95] *NFRB*, 5 December 1958.

Zhao also urged the immediate auditing of all financial accounts, the taking of inventories, and the setting up of a system of storage. In labour management, Zhao emphasized that only when the routine day-to-day production and the division of labour were established could the methods of large labour armies and shock attacks be employed. In any case, normal production should not be disrupted. This was a reversal of the previous emphasis on the large-scale and haphazard transfers of labour for the numerous projects (iron and steel, deep ploughing, fertilizer accumulation) usually far away from the homes of the commune members. In addition, the 'unrealistic formalism' of 'launching satellites' for its own sake, previously encouraged by the PPC, was to be halted, although 'satellite launching' could still be done occasionally.

The other means to overhaul the labour organization was the introduction of the production responsibility system, or the 'four fixes' (the fixing of time, personnel, work task, and the area to be cultivated). It was hoped that these could set some standard for assigning work tasks and for the evaluation of individual contributions. Another decision was to connect the decentralized units such as industrial and commercial enterprises and schools more closely to correct the confusing situation in which no one claimed responsibility or took charge.

On the question of remuneration, Zhao was perplexed by the fact that many communes were unable to pay out wages once free-supply was introduced. Some of these communes made a virtue out of necessity by claiming that the communist principle of 'to each according to his needs' had already been realized. Yet, the damage to work incentive was profound. Zhao took pains to point out that although the new remuneration system already contained 'sprouts of communism', its underlying principle was still the socialist 'from each according to his ability, to each according to his labour'. Hence the scope of free supply should be limited, and the wage portion should gradually increase according to the development of production. Generally, the wage scale could be differentiated into six to eight grades, with the highest receiving four times as much as the lowest. In principle, 90 per cent or more of the commune members should increase their income whereas the remaining 10 per cent should not suffer losses in their earnings. To solve the problem of cash shortages in some communes, Zhao recommended the vigorous resumption of subsidiary production.

The policy that all 'means of livelihood' should still belong to the individual commune members was reaffirmed. While the communes could borrow unoccupied houses, ownership should still belong to the original proprietors. The isolated trees, small farm implements, small livestock should also belong to the individuals. If collective labour were not hampered, commune members were allowed to run some sideline productions.

Zhao urged the cadres to be more concerned with the livelihood of the masses and criticized those who were 'totally indifferent' to the well-being of the people. Henceforth, the working hours were to be tightly regulated, making allowance for eight hours for sleeping and four hours for resting and having meals. Even this implied a twelve-hour working day, and the fact that such modest provision had to be promulgated by Zhao reflects the breakneck pace of work to which the peasants were subject.

Zhao also urged that the mess halls and the nurseries should be 'run well'. The policy of 'three meals of rice' was to be guaranteed, but the communes were ordered to figure out how much grain was required so that they could arrange for state procurement, reserve, and animal feed. This was meant to make grain consumption accountable to avoid waste.

Zhao also decided that some labour must be released to erect buildings such as mess halls, nurseries, and hostels for industries and mines, no matter how tight the labour supply. Finally, Zhao urged the adherence to the work style of the 'mass line' and 'being practical and realistic', so that the phenomena of 'commandism' and false-reporting could be stopped.

All this represented the PPC's conclusive statement on the communes for 1958 and they showed certain departures from the original concepts. Zhao continued to grapple with the problems, seemingly able to identify the key issues such as the management system, decentralization within the communes, the reorganization of labour, the introduction of the responsibility system, the restoration of some degree of incentive, the diversification of rural production activities (as opposed to having 'grain as the key link'), and so on. There might be some learning from the experience of collectivization of 1955-6. Unfortunately, because of the chaotic situation in 1958 and 1959, more sensible policies were not finalized by the centre until 1960/1.

The fantastic claims of harvest led to equally great procurement quantities and increased demand, but shortages of grain, oil, meal, and vegetables. Even most of the grass-roots cadres conspired with the peasants to conceal and hoard grain. Leinan County, for instance, claimed an average yield of more than 1,000 *jin/mu*, but when procurement quotas were issued, the people there complained, and deflated their claims to 289 *jin/mu*. A determined County Party Committee effort to force the peasants to surrender the concealed grain spread grumbling and fear, and work incentive plummeted.[96] Yet, Zhao was slow to grasp the significance of this, and concluded that grain shortages were an illusion, as the villages had a great deal of grain, and urged tough measures. In early 1959, Guangdong embarked on general anti-concealment campaigns to seize grain from the peasants. Cadres who had failed to procure the assigned quota were forbidden to return home to celebrate Spring Festival.[97] In the end, the PPC claimed to have uncovered 2.5m. tons of grain.[98]

Overall, wages for the peasants declined. In the few months following communization, some communes could dispense 2 to 3 *yuan* per person each month, but afterwards, their funds dried up.[99] In December/January, when the communes at Xinhui disbursed meagre wages for the first time, morale sank and attendance rates and labour efficiency declined by 50–60 per cent. Many complained about the wide

---

[96] Cong Jin, *Quzhe Fazhan*, 173; Bo Yibo, *Huigu*, ii. 819.
[97] *Mao Wengao*, viii. 52–4; Zheng Xiaofeng and Shu Ning, *Tao Zhu Zhuan*, 261–3.
[98] *NBCK*, 10 March 1959, 2.   [99] *Guangdong Nongye Shi*, 47.

scope of the free-supply system, the small wage portion, and that they could not receive just reward for their labour. Because of the social guarantees, many, especially those who had seen their income reduced, were not willing to work. Even the cadres were won over by these sentiments, and took a passive attitude. Others used coercive methods. Labour assignment was confused and responsibility was unclear, leading to enforced idleness and slowdowns.[100] Meanwhile, Zhao had also to deal with the other agricultural campaigns in the province, to which we will now turn below.

The Campaign for Autumn Harvest and the Preparation for another Great Leap Forward in 1959

The PPC, and especially Zhao, vigorously implemented the policies of the communes, but the violent reaction to communization put it on the defensive. By contrast, other rural policies were pushed through with more aplomb and conviction, although they were equally destructive. As mentioned, by mid-September, a bumper harvest was deemed a certainty. Anticipating that a huge increase in grain would create new problems—from procurement, supply, and transportation to storage and processing—Zhao ordered all the localities to get ready early although harvesting normally did not commence until October. At the Provincial Industrial and Agricultural Work Conference (15 September–8 October, at Panyu and Xinhui, held on the heels of the 'great checkup'), Zhao tried to assure his subordinates of a bumper harvest by citing the following figures: total grain harvested in 1958 would reach a spectacular 30–40m. tons, making it possible for every individual in the province to have 1,500 to 2,000 *jin*. Clearly, Zhao was a victim of his own delusion, and the information supplied by his subordinates was biased to conform to his expectation. Yet, even discounting a dramatic bumper harvest, normal harvesting was hectic. In 1958, this was aggravated by the myriad of rural activities such as the campaigns for iron and steel, deep ploughing, soil improvement, and so on.

The situation at the Chenghai commune (a large commune comprising an entire county) is indicative of the extent of the problem. The 300,000 *mu* of late rice showed promise of a very good harvest, which meant that the amount of work (cutting, transportation, and the like) also increased tremendously. Yet, the additional tasks of deep ploughing and soil improvement had to be carried out simultaneously. However, 15, 000 able-bodied labourers had already been transferred out of the commune to become an iron and steel army, and farm tools were scarce. Furthermore, the system of labour organization was in disarray.

This situation was common in the newly formed communes in Guangdong at this time. To the PPC, the only obvious solution was to mobilize all other available sources of manpower, including government officers, students and teachers, workers, urban inhabitants, and the armed forces to join in the harvesting campaign.

---

[100] *Mao Wengao*, viii. 19–20; *NJZWH*, ii. 127–9.

Vacant houses and mess halls were turned into granaries, and many small machines were manufactured for processing the sweet potatoes (into slices, shreds, powder, and so on), to save labour. Plans were also made to repair and tune up available farm tools. Many schools were closed down for lengthy periods so the students could engage in campaigns such as water conservancy, fertilizer accumulation, afforestation, and planting. As dramatic production was the main concern, virtually any administrative unit could order school closing. Cadres, who feared punishment for non-fulfilment of quotas, had little scruples in working the students, often with coercion.[101]

However, in early October, the PPC's attention was diverted by another GLF in agriculture for the coming year, with Zhao Ziyang taking the lead by contributing many decisions.[102] As the PPC regarded deep ploughing and soil improvement the keys for another Leap in agriculture in 1959, it decided that 4 million people should be recruited immediately to form a 'specialized army' devoted to these tasks, which continued to function independently even during the hectic autumn harvest. Once harvesting was over, it would expand to 6 million members.

This policy of the PPC rested on the faulty premises that the problem of grain for Guangdong had already been solved once and for all, although in fact several major tasks, such as harvesting and the iron and steel campaign, had not yet been accomplished. It also planned to reduce the acreage devoted to rice paddies in 1959 to make room for more commercial or economic crops. Deep ploughing (to a depth of 30 cm) and soil improvement were meant to compensate for the shrinkage in rice paddies by raising their yield/*mu*. To tighten control, the PPC ordered the party secretaries of all levels to take charge immediately. Their offices were to be divided into two groups, one in charge of industry and the other, agriculture.[103]

About eight days after the initial call, however, the progress with deep ploughing and soil improvement was slow, as only one-third of the planned labour force was recruited. Apparently, the localities did not share the PPC's vision: Some complained that labour was unavailable because of the iron and steel campaign. Others claimed that there was no land to be deep ploughed (presumably the fields had not yet been harvested), and others believed that deep ploughing was unnecessary or counter-productive. In some localities, everything else ground to a halt when the iron and steel campaign was unleashed.

In response, Zhao convened another telephone conference on 14 October and chastised the various special districts, demanding that a 'specialized army' be formed immediately within two to three days without exception. He brushed off the reasons given by the localities as 'rightist' excuses and disputed their claims that the iron and steel campaign had siphoned off all labour power. Citing the earlier decision made by the PPC that 50 per cent of all manpower was to work at the iron and steel key points, 20 per cent at other localities, and 30 per cent in localities that

[101] *NFRB*, 28 October 1958; *NBCK*, 9 May 1959, 16–18.
[102] *NFRB*, 22 October 1958. Zhao had articulated these ideas on several occasions.
[103] *RMRB*, 9 October 1958.

lent support to other areas, Zhao argued that the issue was not whether this labour power existed or not, it was more a matter of 'subjective initiative' and organization, and 'good' leaders should try everything to overcome difficulties.

Second, Zhao ordered that tool reform be pushed ahead, especially in places where the manufacturing and installation of ball-bearings had stopped once the iron and steel campaign was introduced. Third, Zhao also demanded quality (especially in the manure accumulated) and specification (all fields must be ploughed to a depth of 30 cm). Finally, he also urged the elimination of all thinking unfavourable to deep ploughing by debates and 'real action'.[104]

The beginning of November was the busiest stage of harvesting, but so far only about 10 per cent of the farmland (3m. plus *mu*) was harvested, and the problem could not be neglected any longer. The solution was, indeed, to return more labour power to harvesting, but the PPC was heavily committed to many other campaigns.

As will be seen in Chapter 6, the PPC ingeniously organized a massive 'battle' for iron and steel on 1 November that produced a 'satellite' of 877,612 tons of pig iron. This figure not only exceeded the total production in the previous *ten* months, but also completed the production quota for 1958 in *one* day.[105] Having scored such a 'victory', the PPC promptly issued a directive on the very next day to order all rural areas to take harvesting as the 'central task'.[106] All county and commune party committees were commanded to transfer cadres and manpower from the iron and steel front, although 20 to 25 per cent of the total manpower in key point counties and around 10 per cent in ordinary counties were to be retained for iron and steel production. More adjustments were to be made after the harvest.

These figures reflect how much labour was diverted to iron and steel production. Now, the directive ordered all first secretaries of the county and commune party committees to take charge of harvesting at the front line and to form specialized teams. To cope with the shortage of tools, the directive urged the manufacturing of efficient, low-cost, and easy-to-make harvesters, threshers, shelling tools, and transportation equipment immediately. It further urged the mobilization of government employees, school staff and students, urban dwellers, and so on, to join in harvesting. The aim was to 'do well' simultaneously in harvesting, deep ploughing, soil improvement, and winter planting.

In an attempt to boost morale, the material incentive of the free supply system ('eating rice without pay') was initiated in early November to ensure success in the above tasks. The commune members were said to be so motivated that they volunteered to harvest throughout the night (not an uncommon practice then, but usually not voluntary), and work efficiency was reputed to have increased remarkably.

By 9 November, a record 10 million labour army had been thrown into the battle for rushing in the harvest. The announcement at the Seven-Province Agricultural Coordination Conference (South) that Guangdong could almost triple its grain

---

[104] *NFRB*, 16 October 1958.   [105] *RMRB*, 4 November 1958; see also *SCMP*, 1980, 23–4.
[106] *NFRB*, 2 November 1958.

output underlined the magnitude of the task ahead. By 7 November, 7m. plus *mu* had been harvested (roughly 20 per cent of the total acreage—probably not a satisfactory progress), and it was anticipated that harvesting should be completed around 20 November. All first secretaries of the County Party Committees were said to have 'assumed command', and specialized teams for cutting, threshing, transportation, and sun-drying were formed according to the skills and the strength of individuals. A new tool for cutting standing grain, six to ten times more efficient than an ordinary sickle and costing only 2–3 *yuan* to manufacture, was said to have been invented and popularized in the province.[107]

In the next few days, harvesting was accelerated as half of all cultivated farmland was reported to have been reaped. On the one hand, fantastic claims of yield/*mu* of 6,000–7,000 *jin*, even more than 10,000 *jin*, continued to be reported by the PPC in the press as a source of pride. On the other hand, the PPC also began to take measures to contain false reporting. It urged the careful verification of output so that 'not one more *jin* of grain or a *jin* less' should be reported. To this end, a PPC circular issued on 13 November ordered an end to the common practice of 'estimates based on experience' and 'verification without weighing' in the counting of grain harvested.[108] The cadres were ordered to pay attention not only to cutting but also to the threshing of grain (presumably they had only time and energy to supervise the former). Furthermore, it ordered party secretaries and technicians of every administrative level to go down to the fields with the highest yield to carry out cutting, threshing, sun-drying, and weighing themselves.

The PPC had two major concerns. The first was to prevail upon the masses the 'great significance' of the 'General Line' and the 'might' of Mao's 'Eight-Point Charter'. Second, the high-yield 'satellites' were to be used to refute the 'tide-watchers', the 'doubters', and the 'account-settlers'.[109] In fact, both boiled down to only one thing—since so much high expectation had been built around the 'General Line', and the leadership had staked its prestige, its integrity, and almost everything else (the 'sunk cost') on a dramatic harvest, it must be demonstrated that they were the best means for a spectacular Leap. Therefore, no let-down was conceivable, at least for the moment. Giving this contradictory intention, the insistence on the strict verification of production quantity was a feeble effort doomed from the start.

The Report of Victory

On 20 November, with only 22m. plus *mu* out of a total 34m. *mu* harvested, the Party simply could not wait to declare a super bumper harvest in Guangdong. An *RMRB* article claimed that the average yield/*mu* in the province had reached 1,100 *jin*, thereby fulfilling the requirements in the NPAD nine years ahead of schedule. This brought the total grain produced in 1958 to the ludicrous figure of 35m. tons (see Table 5.1), a 180 per cent increase over the 1957 output.[110]

---

[107] *NFRB*, 12 November 1958; *RMRB*, 11 November 1958.
[108] *RMRB*, 17 November 1958.   [109] Ibid.   [110] *RMRB*, 21 November 1958.

Table 5.1. *Guangdong: Harvest claims, 1958*

	m. tons
Early rice	8.6
Sweet potatoes (autumn harvest in 9m. *mu*)	7.85
Rice (autumn harvest in 34m. *mu*)	18.70
Total	35.15

As the province with the largest cultivated acreage of late rice, Guangdong was eager to claim a dramatic production increase. Yet, research by K. Walker shows that the total 1958 grain output for Guangdong was only 12.813m. tons (or 256.26 bn. *jin*)—or about 36.5 per cent of what was claimed. The actual increase over 1957 was only about 4.46 per cent, and furthermore, the increase was largely accounted for by potatoes, and the absolute quantity of rice produced actually dropped.[111]

This exaggeration of grain output led to two contradictory trends—on the one hand, the peasants were permitted, indeed encouraged, to consume as much grain as they liked, but on the other hand, a large amount of grain was requisitioned from the better-off villages in the communes, depressing the standard of living in these villages. Consequently, there was a violent struggle between the government and some peasants for grain in the winter of 1958/9. According to Tao, some villages were 'unwilling' to surrender their harvest to the communes and concealed grain amounted to 2.75m. tons (or 8 per cent of the revised figure of total grain production for 1958, 31m. tons).[112] Indeed, whilst these figures cannot be accepted at face value, they do reflect the perception of the provincial authorities regarding peasant resistance.

On the other hand, wastage due to the sloppy harvest was enormous. In Guangdong, a small piece of information buried in the rhetoric may show the extent of this problem. A letter to the *NFRB* editor revealed that in their anxiety to be the first in completing the harvesting, the cadres at the East Wind People's commune ordered the commune members simply to cut down the standing grain. As soon as this was done, they reported their success to their superiors. Nevertheless, since threshing was not done, the overripe crops were left to rot or be trampled, and the peasants grumbled about the heavy losses.[113]

Meanwhile, the provincial authorities played down these problems. On 22 November, Zhao[114] announced that the autumn harvest had now been 'basically'

---

[111] Walker, *Food Grain Procurement*, 136. *Guangdong Sheng Tongji Nianjian, 1984*, 119 gave figures for 1952, 1957, 1962, etc., but not 1958. Mao also referred to the grain crisis in Guangdong, in *Dangde Wenxian*, 4, 1995, 44.   [112] *NFRB*, 2 March 1959, in *XHBYK*, 8, 1959, 28.
[113] *NFRB*, 25 November 1958.   [114] *NFRB*, 24 November 1958.

concluded and the focus of work should be shifted back to deep ploughing and soil improvement, his two pet projects. The standard for deep ploughing was set at 30–45 cm and fertilizer was to be spread between layers of soil. All localities were ordered to mobilize into a large army of 6 million strong for this endeavour. In addition, another labour army of 3 million was also to be formed to complete 650 water conservation projects. The goal was to double the capacity for water storage so that all droughts or floods could be eliminated once and for all in the province. Finally, it was decided that the movement for tool reform should be resumed, and concurrently, the manufacture of the cable-drawn ploughs and vehicles that ran on tracks (another new invention, presumably used for the transportation of earth in the water conservancy campaign). These decisions effectively terminated the harvesting campaign and kicked off more new ones in the winter of 1958/9.

The Final Account for 1958

In December, the final account for 1958 was taken at the conference of the advanced units in 'socialist construction' in Guangdong (8–15 December). Those who were most willing to brag about their outputs were commended and rewarded with such things as large and small motor vehicles, tractors, or entire fertilizer factories.[115] This merely encouraged exaggerations, with Zhao taking the lead. He bragged that the total grain production had reached 35.15m. tons. Given the cultivated area of 42.5m. *mu*, the average yield/*mu* was calculated to be 1,654 *jin*, enabling him to claim that not only was the NPAD fulfilled nine years ahead of time, but the standard was also doubled (800 *jin*/*mu* was the original NPAD target). Each of the 38m. residents in Guangdong would have 1,820 *jin* of grain and 1,270 *jin* of rice each, and this, Zhao asserted, maintained the province's 'honour' in high grain production.

The other major achievement of 1958, according to him, was the resolute implementation of the 'Eight-Point Charter'. Yet in effect, he added, only two out of the eight items, close planting and field management, had been implemented adequately. Water conservancy was not satisfactory, the area of land deep-ploughed was small, the improvement of seeds was inadequate, the reform of farm implements was 'very bad', and many localities still had many problems with pests and diseases. Yet Zhao remained optimistic—the yield/*mu* had reached a dramatic 1,100 *jin*, although this left much to be desired; so, it would be certain to reach 4,000 *jin* or even 10,000 *jin* in 1959 if all eight items were done well.

Looking ahead, Zhao was sanguine that the grain problem that the country had wrestled with for the past nine years had finally been resolved. No longer was it necessary for the more than 30m. peasants to devote all their time in the year to working. In 1957, the average yield/*mu* was only 510 *jin* and average grain per

---

[115] *Guangdong Dangdai Nongye Shi*, 41, 44; *Dangdai Guangdong*, 2, 1997, 62.

person was 645 *jin*. Since the Leap in 1958 had allegedly doubled these figures, the province could finally elevate the development of diversified production and commune industry on the agenda. In 1959, the province would continue to raise the yield/*mu*, and the grain target was raised to 60m. tons. This would 'thoroughly' solve the problem of food supply in the province because each person in Guangdong would have 3,000 *jin* (assuming the population was 40m.). Zhao's projection of how this grain would be utilized is set out in Table 5.2.

Table 5.2. *Guangdong: Projected food supplies for 1959*

	Per. cap. (*jin*)	Total (bn. *jin*)	Total (m. tons)
Grain rations	600	240	12
Reserve grain	1,000	400	20
Rice seeds		40	2
Animal fodder		320	16
Surplus		200	10
Total		1,200	60

According to this projection, there would be 10m. tons of surplus grain even if reserve grain of 20m. tons were set aside in 1959. Henceforth, beginning in 1960, a total yearly production of 40m. tons was said to be sufficient. On this basis, the diversification of agriculture and commune industry would be promoted 'in a big way', and the production of oil crops, domestic animals, and poultry, was 'planned' to increase several folds in 1959. The development of other economic crops, such as sugar cane, mulberry leaves, hemp, flax, fruits, and vegetables, was to be pushed ahead. Indigenous commune industries such as chemical fertilizers and pesticide, the small machinery industry, the processing of agricultural products, as well as the iron and steel industry, would be encouraged.

Emboldened by his illusions, Zhao made the momentous decision of implementing Mao's 'revolutionary' method of 'plant little, high yield, and reap more' in 1959 to maximize yield/*mu* and total production. This ultra-intensive farming method was regarded as more efficient than extensive farming, paving the way for the introduction of the 'three-three' system. The past methods of expanding the cultivated acreage and the multiple-cropping index were to be abandoned, in favour of developing the 'gigantic' potential of single cropping. Therefore, the PPC made the fateful blunder of cutting back the acreage for early rice almost by half, from 33m. to 18m. *mu*, to run campaigns for 10,000 *jin* high-yield fields in 15 to 20 per cent of all cultivated fields, and to create many 10,000 *jin* counties, communes, and plots. Accordingly, the planned cultivated area of 60m. *mu* for 1959 was divided as shown in Table 5.3.

Zhao hoped that the early and middle crops of rice would yield an incredible 40 to 45m. tons, enabling a 'decisive victory' in the first half of 1959. Implicit in these calculations was that the entire autumn grain crop for 1959 could be eliminated in

Table 5.3. *Guangdong: Planned cultivation for 1959*

Land use	Area (m. *mu*)
Rice	22*
Sweet potatoes	3
Economic or commercial crops	22
Green manure, fruit trees, afforestation in the plains, and fallowing	15
Total	62

*18m. early rice; 4m. middle rice.

favour of economic and commercial crops. With supreme confidence he insisted that these plans were reliable, and went through the detailed 1959 targets for many agricultural activities, outlining the precise acreage, yield/unit, and the methods to be employed. Naturally, all these agricultural activities were to be 'developed in a big way', showing no sense of priority or constraint.[116]

These aside, Zhao's grand scheme and far-fetched targets were fully endorsed by the centre. Deng Zihui, now representing the State Council, had nothing but praise for Guangdong's plans when speaking to the Conference on 9 December.[117] After extolling the GLF principles and policies such as 'politics takes command' and the 'Eight-Point Charter' one by one, he praised the 'perfect correctness' of the 'plant little, high yield, and reap more' policy and its contribution to the 'three-three' system. Finally, vice-premier Li Fuchun also harped on the many 'important instructions' already delivered by Zhao and Deng.[118]

Both Zhao and the central leaders were totally blinded by the illusion of the extraordinary increases in output and it was on this basis that the 'planning' for 1959 was carried out. The cutting back of the acreage for early rice was one of the most disastrous decisions made in 1958, as we have had the occasion to observe. Eventually, the plan to eliminate the entire autumn crop could not be implemented, but Zhao's assumption must have reinforced the central decision to reduce the acreage for grain throughout the country in 1959.

The Outcome

Despite the extraordinary efforts, grain production for 1958 did not multiply several fold, it was only 10.53m. tons, or 3.27 per cent *less* than the harvest of 1957. The policy of 'three meals a day' for two to three months had consumed anywhere from 1 to 2m. tons of grain. Soon, food shortages led to oedema.[119] In the winter, hundreds

---

[116] *NFRB*, 9 December 1958.   [117] *NFRB*, 10 December 1958.
[118] *NFRB*, 16 December 1958.   [119] *Guangdong Dangdai Nongye Shi*, 47; *Tao Zhu Zhuan*, 262.

of thousands of migrants from Shaoguan swarmed into Hunan begging for food. The Hunan leadership, allegedly more cautious in 1958 (that is, they did not encourage peasants to eat as much as they wanted and terminated the iron and steel campaign early) was said to have more grain, which it used to support neighbours such as Hubei and Henan.[120] However, even in January 1959, Zhao insisted that grain shortages in Leinan County were an illusion, as the rural areas had large amounts of grain. A combination of anti-concealment drives, 'anti-departmentalism' struggles, education, and punishment had recovered 350 tons of grain. Mao approved of this approach, and on 22 February, disseminated the report to the top leaders and provincial authorities.[121] Yet, barely a week later, Mao backtracked, and took the side of the peasants at the Second Zhengzhou Conference in February/March 1959; Mao compared the levelling in the communes to robbery, and criticized the 'communist wind'. Overall, the procurement plan was unfinished, and food shortages persisted. In an implicit criticism of Tao and Zhao, Mao said that he did not believe there was so much Marxism in the Yangzi and Pearl River basins (Hubei and Guangdong).[122] So in early 1959, Tao had to write self-criticisms to Mao and the Party Centre for 'overestimating agricultural output, overconsumption of grain, and for extending the line of construction'. Wang Renzhong of Hubei did the same.[123] The Chairman, indeed, was much more tolerant of mistakes made by his allies, so these self-criticisms did nothing to harm the careers of these two men.

The numerous decisions and policies introduced by the Guangdong provincial authorities profoundly affected the lives of the people in that province, doing more harm than good. Although Guangdong's mortality rates during the Leap were not among the highest in the country, they did escalate from 8.4 per 1,000 population in 1957 to 9.1 in 1958, 14.6 in 1959, 18.4 in 1960, and 13.4 in 1961.[124] Beginning in 1959, many ill-conceived policies and hasty innovations, including the communes, had to be abandoned, although the regime persisted in implementing many other unworkable schemes. Yet, the provincial leaders deluded themselves with a phenomenal harvest, and drew up the 1959 plan on this basis. The uncontrolled consumption of grain after communization, on the other hand, cut deep into the reserves built up in the previous few years. In just one example, one family was said to have consumed four months' ration in just one. By 1959, grain rations had to be cut back,[125] and no relief was possible when severe flooding led to famine conditions in 1959.

---

[120] According to one source, the new provincial leadership in Hunan pushed the iron and steel campaign once more in 1959, and 600,000 people perished in that year. Hunan thus joined the top eight provinces which suffered the worst mortality rate for the entire Leap. *Tiandao*, 128–9; Tan Zhenqiu, *Mao Waixunji*, 251; Dali Yang, *Calamity and Reform in China: State, Rural Society, and Institutional Change Since the Great Leap Famine* (Stanford: Stanford University Press, 1996), 38–9.

[121] *Mao Wengao*, viii. 52–4.   [122] *Maso Weikan*, xiB. 173.

[123] Zheng Xiaofeng and Shu Ning, *Tao Zhu Zhuan*, 262.

[124] Dali Yang, *Calamity and Reform*, 38–9; Guojia Tongjiji Conghesi (ed.), *Quanguo Gesheng Zizhiqu Zhixiashi Lishi Tongji Ziliao Huibian* (Compendium of historical statistical materials for the nation's provinces, autonomous regions, and centrally administered cities) (Beijing: Zhongguo tongji chubanshe, 1990), 617 gives slightly different figures.   [125] *NFRB*, 22 October 1959.

The policy of 'plant little, high yields, reap more' mandated the reduction of 15m. *mu* of early rice, and 'several million' more *mu* were not planted because labour power was diverted to the deep ploughing campaign.[126] Furthermore, the extensive introduction of the round-grain non-glutinous rice (*jingdao*) from the north (presumably for its high output/unit) without testing led to unspecified losses. The same fate befell the 'direct-seeding rice' (*zhibodao*) which did not require nurseries and transplantation.[127]

Commmunization and the subsequent slaughter of livestock by commune members also contributed directly to the serious shortages in non-staple foods. Many draught animals died of overwork and exertion during the campaigns for water conservancy and deep ploughing. To maintain free-supply and self-sufficiency, some communes severed their supplies to the urban areas. Furthermore, the abandonment of fodder and subsidiary food production was the direct result of the numerous rural activities and the tremendous emphasis on multiplying grain output.[128] The drastic shortages of grain became evident in the spring of 1959, causing malnutrition, oedema, and unnatural deaths. In places, the peasants were forced to steal food or to migrate, and some mess halls were disbanded because of the lack of grain. One conservative estimate puts the number suffering from oedema in the first five months of 1959 at several hundred thousands, and deaths 'related' to grain insufficiency at more than 500.[129] The matter became so urgent that the PPC issued an order in May/June urging that commune members who utilized fragmentary or odd pieces of land would be entitled to the crops.[130] Soon, the PPC adopted a volte-face by announcing the policy 'expand the cultivated acreage, plant more and reap more' in a *Shangyu* commentary to complement intensive farming, and this was said to be the realization of the 'walking on two legs' principle.[131]

Most of the technical reforms introduced in 1958 were abandoned in 1959, as Zhao admitted they had been popularized prematurely and haphazardly and despite the valid doubts expressed by the peasants. Second thoughts were also expressed about close planting.[132] In May, a more sober PPC internal review of 1958 admitted it had made mistakes concerning high targets, close planting, goading, inflated crops estimates, the shrinkage of sown areas, the 'three meal a day' policy, the anti-concealment campaign, and cadre 'commandism'.[133] In June 1959, Tao concluded the obvious—deep ploughing, close planting, and other agricultural matters must be applied 'according to local conditions', not to a single common standard.[134]

Finally, in 1959, the number of communes in Guangdong was increased from 771 to 1,104 to eliminate the largest and most unwieldy ones, and continuous modifications ensued. For instance, food rations were allowed to be distributed to the households, and the free-supply portion of remuneration was lowered. Peasants were

[126] *NFRB*, 29 May 1959.   [127] *NFRB*, 26 May, 27 May, 12 June, and 14 June 1959.
[128] *NFRB*, 2 May, 25 September, and 1 October 1959; *Dangdai Zhongguo de Guangdong*, 370.
[129] *NBCK*, 10 March 1959, 3; 6 June 1959, 11.
[130] *NFRB*, 27 May, 4 June, 12 June, and 14 June 1959; Feng Ping, *Dangdai Nongye Shi*, 47.
[131] *NFRB*, 26 June and 30 June 1959.   [132] *NFRB*, 26 May 1959.
[133] *NBCK*, 31 May 1959, 2–7.   [134] *NFRB*, 14 June 1959.

once again allowed to own the proceeds derived from private plots and sideline occupations, so rural free markets were reopened in late April. Production quotas and calculation of work points based on the work done in the APCs were resurrected. Three-level management and accounting was adopted so that some powers to manage production were given to the production brigades (*guanli qu*).[135] Overall, this retreat from the original concept of the communes, despite some ups and downs, continued into the early 1960s when the household again became the fundamental unit for production. Yet, the damage was done. Grain production for 1959 declined to only 8.88m. tons and to 8.75m. tons in 1960. The production of cash crops, animal husbandry, and water products all shrank. This was compounded by the extra-ordinary natural calamities experienced in 1959 and 1960.[136] In three years of the GLF, grain production had dropped 5m. tons, the number of cattle was down by 1.2 m., and hogs by 3m. More than 1 million had suffered from oedema, and the widespread malnutrition, starvation, and deaths Guangdong experienced between 1959 to 1961 were largely the result of compounding policy mistakes, and not entirely attributable to 'natural disasters'.[137]

In Guangdong, the development strategy of the GLF took hold rather early, as it was viewed as the realistic solution to the existing problems at that time. Hence, once the momentum for an all-out mass movement developed, it underwent a progressive radicalization throughout 1958 almost unabated. This in turn was pro-pelled by the rising expectations and mutual reinforcement created by even more central initiatives and requirements, and the pressure to compete with the other provinces. The dynamics of the GLF must be seen in the context of this complex interaction between the centre and the provinces.

In dealing with the numerous goals and requirements of the GLF, the hyperactive PPC under Tao Zhu left no stone unturned, resorting to a whole range of campaigns and policy instruments to galvanize the masses into action. It seems that by throwing everything at the target, the provincial leaders expected that all goals would be achieved.

Moreover, the PPC also dictated the strategy for agriculture development by controlling the agenda, defining current tasks, and setting up rigid timetables to apply uniformly to the entire province, oblivious of diversities in agricultural realities. It was apparently carried away by the euphoria at the time. As the planners and technicians were pushed aside, it assumed all economic planning itself. Yet, as we have observed, the 'planning' of the PPC was based on the most faulty assumptions, and it was conducted by the use of inappropriate analogies and simple arithmetic with no reference to the real world. The obsession with the 'farming revolution', on the other hand, led directly to several rather disastrous campaigns including those for water conservancy, tool reform, the cutting back of the area of

---

[135] *NFRB*, 17 June, 15 and 18 July, 1 and 28 October 1959; *NBCK*, 18 May 1959, 3–5, 10–13. For Mao's praise of Guangdong's policy after the Second Zhengzhou Conference, see *Mao Wengao*, viii. 108–9. For a clarification of the terminologies used to refer to the internal administrative divisions within the communes, see MacFarquhar, *Origins*, ii. 181–4.   [136] *Dangdai Zhongguo de Guangdong*, 94.
[137] Vogel, *Canton*, 254–5.

cultivation for 1959, and deep ploughing and soil improvement. Despite the tremendous amount of resources and energy lavished on them, the final outcome was either futile or harmful.

Furthermore, the PPC expanded its control over its subordinates tremendously, bringing many new concerns under its control for the first time. Consequently, it found itself immersed in the day-to-day administration and the implementation of policies, even to the extent of interfering directly with the grass-roots units themselves. Yet, paradoxically, the attempt to impose more control resulted in even less control. Faced with the tremendous pressure of fulfilling impossible tasks and targets, the subordinates had no alternative but to resort to deception, and fed only the kind of information that conformed to the expectations of the PPC. The latter had become a victim of its own delusions.

More particularly, Tao's role in the GLF is consistent with the view that he was a most loyal Maoist party bureaucrat because of his zeal in promoting Maoist ideas and policies.[138] Zhao Ziyang, on the other hand, displayed similar zealousness as the principal instigator of Guangdong's agricultural and rural policies in 1958. As there was a great deal of stress for the provincial authority to implement central policies, and as the decision-making time and lead time were short, decision-making became a very personalized and haphazard affair. Therefore, the secretary in charge of industry would make all decisions regarding industry, and the secretary in charge of agriculture decisions regarding agricultural and rural affairs. Zhao was particularly obsessed with the reforms of the farming system as a means to boost production dramatically. Another of his pet projects was to change the alleged 'conservative' attitude of the peasants, a perception widely shared by the Chinese leaders at this time.

However, when a crisis developed at the end of 1958 over the communes, Zhao seemed to have sensed the underlying problems and was ready to introduce some modifications. Nevertheless, these solutions were not officially adopted until 1960, and other unrealistic expectations were carried over to 1959.

<hr/>

[138] Vogel, *Canton*, 300, 325.

6

Policies of Industrial Development in Guangdong, 1958

Chapter 4 makes clear the dilemmas faced by the Ministry of Metallurgy in implementing overambitious and often unworkable central policies, and the difficulty in motivating and mobilizing the ministry's subordinates and the regional authorities to totally reorient themselves. Here, the spotlight is on Guangdong province and the way it responded to the various 'industrialization' policies imposed upon it by the centre. As such, this chapter will also be organized chronologically, to explore the decision-making forums and the implementation process. It will demonstrate how the barrage of imperious and capricious demands from the centre had forced industrialization and the iron and steel campaign on agricultural Guangdong, although it did not have the preconditions and resources to do so. The PPC strove to implement all the centre's initiatives, although they were absurd, unattainable, and often unmindful of the capabilities of the province. Confronted by the impossible goals, the PPC had no choice but to mobilize its only true asset, its organization capability, to the fullest. In time, however, the Leap policies could not be sustained, goal displacement occurred—the PPC turned to concentrate on appearance rather than the substance of plan fulfilment.

Guangdong's Industry in the 1950s

For the Chinese communists in the 1950s, industrialization was almost synonymous with socialism and progress. So the aspiration of Guangdong provincial leadership was reflected in the oft-quoted slogan of 'Turning Guangzhou [Canton], the provincial capital, into the industrial base of South China'. However, the province was largely overlooked in the allocation of resources for industrial development during the 1FYP, because the central priority was to develop the medium-size inland cities.[1] Moreover, the dominant economic activities of the province had always been agriculture and light industry. Guangdong had a variety of mineral deposits in iron, manganese, tungsten, bismuth, tin, oil shale, and guano, but they were small and not easily exploitable, and the mining facilities and transportation system were backward. There was no significant coal deposit. All these accounted for the

---

[1] *NFRB*, 27 November 1957.

view that Guangdong did not have a future in developing heavy industry or industrialization.

During the GLF, this view came under attack, and the PPC often cited the mere existence of mineral deposits to prove its point.[2] Yet, when the centre planned to industrialize the entire country during the Leap, Guangdong was presented with a dilemma. On the one hand, it welcomed the initiative, but, it had to do so by relying on its own means. Furthermore, iron and steel smelting was a totally foreign task for the cadres, and the benefits it might bring were uncertain, so at the beginning they were uninterested. Moreover, as time wore on, industrialization simply turned into infinite central demands for raising production according to centrally-dictated development strategy. These difficulties were compounded by the inconsistent and shifting goals the centre set for the country throughout 1958.

In Guangdong, the replacement of the initial campaign to develop industry to serve agriculture by the iron and steel campaign was the most dramatic goal shift in 1958, and therefore, our discussion can focus on two periods in turn. During the first period, roughly from January to July 1958, the PPC groped for ways to promote industrialization to serve agriculture. In the second period, from August to December, everything was abandoned in favour of iron and steel production, the new essence of the GLF industrializing effort. This change of priority was dictated by Mao and the centre; correspondingly, the province simply acquiesced, demonstrating little independence.

The following discussion will focus on how the Guangdong authorities coped with the pressure exerted from above, the kinds of decision made by the PPC, and the manner by which it implemented central policies and mobilized its subordinates for the numerous campaigns in 1958.

The Beginning: The Provincial Planning Conference, 15–25 January

At the Third Plenum, Mao broached the idea of continuing giving priority development to heavy industry, but also the simultaneous development of industry and agriculture, so that both could be modernized.[3] Mao's notion of 'simultaneous development' was designed to address the problem of the bias toward industry and the neglect of agriculture. However, in November, when the idea of 'overtaking Britain in fifteen years' was introduced, industry, not just agriculture, had to be developed 'in a big way' as well.

In any case, 'simultaneous development' posed a dilemma for primarily agricultural provinces such as Guangdong, because their development strategy and economy had to be totally reoriented virtually overnight to take industry into account, and the expected opposition was correspondingly high.

---

[2] *RMRB*, 21 December 1958; Vogel, *Canton*, 17.
[3] *Mao Weikan*, xiA. 198; *NFRB*, 26 November 1957; 28 January 1958.

So it is not surprising that near the end of 1957, the province was lukewarm to a 'leap forward' in industrial production, and the sub-provincial units were either ignoring or resisting it. After the slogans of *duohao kuaisheng* and 'overtake Britain in fifteen years' were introduced in late 1957, the provincial authorities focused their attention on an agricultural leap, but the envisaged province-wide high tide in industrial production failed to take shape. In the rest of 1957, as the provincial authorities had done nothing noticeable for this cause, the cadres adopted a wait-and-see attitude. Many regarded the leap to be a spontaneous affair for the masses that did not require leadership initiative. Other cadres were pessimistic about the further production increases and economizing. Consequently, many resisted the raising of production targets and some 1958 targets were set even below the 1957 level.[4]

Entering 1958, the provincial authorities had to interfere, as Mao had called for the critique of 'rightist conservatism' at Hangzhou (3–4 January). Therefore, at the Fourth Provincial Planning Conference (15–25 January), the PPC issued a directive to eradicate 'rightism', criticizing the planning departments for their alleged over-emphasis on the reliability of the plans. Subsequently, many units were compelled to raise their industrial targets. The reluctance to do so and the mounting pressure for conformity can be seen in Guangzhou. The delegates of this city were obliged to revise their targets upwards three times, from a more modest 5.7 per cent increase over the past year to 10 per cent, 14 per cent, and then to 15 per cent. Since Guangzhou's industrial production comprised about half the province's total, it was the prime target singled out for criticism.[5]

At any rate, the Conference finally resolved to boost the GVIO (including handicraft industries) from an originally set goal of 11 per cent to 15 per cent over that of 1957. Of the 2bn. *yuan* assigned for capital construction, 1.1bn *yuan* was earmarked for local industries, an amount almost equivalent to the total sum invested in the same during the entire 1FYP period.[6] This was the first major attempt at rural industrialization, and the declared goal was to have industry serve agriculture. This meant the manufacture of irrigation and drainage machinery to satisfy the urgent demands of the large-scale irrigation projects undertaken throughout the province at this time. Other industries included the building of more sugar refineries, and the development of agricultural machinery, fertilizer, and pesticide plants.

However, it should be noted that the projected production of iron and steel, which became an obsession later in the year, was modest. The target for pig iron (excluding indigenous iron) was a mere 22,000 tons, although three iron and steel plants with a combined annual production capacity of 160,000 tons were planned and expected to be completed within the year. At the closing session, Wen Minsheng, the party secretary in charge of industry, attacked the so-called 'rightist opportunists', and the 'lazy fellows' who were said to be lethargic, and indifferent toward the Leap. Those who had allegedly set targets low deliberately to gain bonuses were not spared.

[4] Ibid.   [5] *NFRB*, 30 January 1958.   [6] Ibid.

Finally, he enjoined the party committees at all levels to organize a comprehensive and sustained high tide for industrial production.[7]

The Provincial Party Committee Assumes Leadership

A turning point was reached when central intention was made clearer by the drafting of the 'Sixty Articles On Work Methods'. One article of this document under discussion urged all production units to expand the GVIO to exceed the GVAO within five years, and the completion of this was regarded during the GLF, simplistically, as the indicator of industrialization. Although Mao's redrafting of the 'Sixty Articles' was dated 31 January, and the Central Committee did not formally promulgate it until one month later, the provincial authorities had caught wind of some of its content. Tao Zhu was present at the Nanning Conference, and probably had participated in the brainstorming for the Sixty Articles. After the Provincial Planning Conference, the Guangdong PPC began to take the proposed industrial GLF more seriously, although Guangdong was primarily agricultural. On 27 January a directive that set out the general programme for an industrial leap in the province showed that the PPC had assumed the leadership to push the development of industry.

The directive argued that the ongoing agricultural GLF must be accompanied by an industrial leap as well, because the many agricultural activities required equipment for water conservancy, transportation, and farm tools. It demanded that all production units should strive to ensure that the GVIO exceeded the GVAO within five years, and all plans inconsistent with this goal were to be revised. For 1958, all units were urged to raise their GVIO not by the previously agreed on 15 per cent, but 22 per cent. As the assistance from the upper levels was strictly limited, the enterprises were urged to use the 'poor' method (that is, starting from scratch) to harness the revolutionary enthusiasm of the mobilized masses. The crucial problems of production, supply, and sales (marketing) were to be solved by the production units themselves. In this way the enterprises obtained a high degree of autonomy but they were also expected to fend for themselves.

Simultaneously, the PPC complained that the projected province-wide high-tide of industrial production had so far not taken shape, because it was obstructed by the 'rightist conservatism' of the leadership cadres at the various administrative levels (i.e. the special districts, municipalities, counties, enterprises, and handicraft cooperatives). It is noteworthy that since the PPC had done very little itself in the month or so after the slogan of 'Overtake Britain in fifteen years' was broached, the reproach of its subordinates was a blatant attempt to shift the blame for inaction to its subordinates.

The various departments (such as transport, commerce, and agriculture) responsible for allocating goods and materials were admonished to cooperate actively, but the unavoidable problems of 'departmentalism' and wrangling, according to

[7] *NFRB*, 30 January 1958.

the PPC, were to be resolved by the continued criticism of 'rightist' thinking and the employment of the magic formula of 'blooming and contending' by the masses. Overall, at this early stage, the PPC had very little idea of how to implement a 'leap forward' in industrial production, especially when no additional resources were promised; exhortation was the only means.

Positive and Negative Models

Responding to the provincial directive, the party committees of various levels held a series of meetings. Many implementation measures were adopted, but the Foshan example was touted as a model. The municipality of Foshan had pledged to raise the GVIO and the total profit to be remitted upwards by 50 per cent and to improve quality to match or exceed national and provincial standards. It also put forward the 'five advances' slogan, that is, to seek out, to compare with, to learn from, to catch up with, and to outdo the other advanced units. To underline these points, Foshan had also challenged other municipalities to a 'revolutionary competition'.[8] For the time being, the PPC was satisfied with these initiatives.

On the other hand, the alleged 'rightist opportunist' thinking of the Kepu Special District and the Hainan District was openly criticized because their planned production increase was around 15 per cent. This percentage was the provincially approved figure only a week or so before, but since some units had set up even higher targets, the expectation of the provincial authorities also escalated, and without warning, these units that stuck to the previous standards were caught off guard. In addition, serious reprimands were handed out to units who had turned a blind eye to the production high tide.[9]

At any rate, the PPC was convinced that Foshan and the other advanced units were the harbingers of an industrial leap throughout the province. Subsequently, its pronouncements became progressively more ambitious. As an *NFRB* editorial argued, in drawing up production targets, the element of 'subjective initiative' must also be taken into account along with the objective factors. As everything depended on the human effort (*shizai renwe*) and revolutionary enthusiasm, it maintained, what was regarded as impossible could often be achieved. The alleged leap in agriculture then was used to prove this point. Although admitting that the experience in industrial management was lacking, it felt that the potential to be tapped was unlimited.[10] Other nagging problems, such as the slow sale of products owing to their shoddy quality, the lack of demand, and the shortage of raw materials were downplayed, although they continued to haunt the industrial enterprises.

---

[8] *NFRB*, 5 February 1958.   [9] Ibid.

[10] Ibid.; *NFRB*, 18 February 1958. For instance, threshing machines were said to have been returned by disgruntled peasants because of faulty design, slipshod production, and maintenance practices. Consequently, the supply and cooperatives suffered a loss of several million *yuan*.

**The Sixty Articles and the Guangdong
Provincial Party Committee**

The Sixty Articles on Work Method was formally promulgated by the General Office of the CPC CC on 29 February but the final version of the document must have been available to the Guangdong PPC beforehand because it convened a plenary meeting (7–12 February) during which decisions closely linked to the Sixty Articles were made. The Sixty Articles, like the NPAD, were wide-ranging in scope. Both of them contained a grand transformative vision, and many ambiguous goals with no order or precedence. However, at the provincial level (as at other subordinate levels), a central document like this had to be interpreted and operationalized for implementation. Article eleven of the central document stated:

The value of industrial output at all places...and the output value of the original local industrial and handicraft undertakings owned by the state...should strive to surpass the value of agricultural product in these places in the next five years, seven years, or ten years. All provinces and municipalities should set out at once to draw up plans for this on or before 1 July this year.[11]

This formal statement of the Sixty Articles allowed a leeway of 5 to 10 years to accomplish industrialization, but as we have noted, the PPC had already opted for the 'advanced' finishing time of 5 years. In the general climate of the time, it was probably prudent to do so to avoid any hint of 'rightist conservatism'. The PPC aimed to triple the output value of industry to 12,000m. *yuan* so that it would comprise 60 per cent of the gross output value of industry and agriculture in five years (in 1957 the percentage was 47.5 per cent). To implement the second part of the instruction, the PPC decided to overturn all the targets set up at the Provincial Party Congress in the previous December and to draw up a new five-year production plan so that by 1962, Guangdong would develop from a province with mainly light industry into one with a 'foundation' in heavy industry as well, thus achieving 'industrialization'.[12] For the PPC, to industrialize simply meant a dramatic projected surge in production in several key items by 1962 that would swell the GVIO to more than 60 per cent of the total output value of industry and agriculture (Table 6.1).

The assumption was naive, not to mention whether these ambitious targets could ever be achieved in such a short time span. Moreover, the premium put on quantity, speed, and output value often sacrificed quality and cost, and encouraged bragging and false reporting. In other words, the seeds for goal displacement were already planted.

Article 13 of the Sixty Articles introduced the slogan of 'battle hard for three years' (*kuzhan sannian*). The method was to mobilize the masses fully and to subject everything to experimentation.[13] To make good the 'hard struggle' slogan, the provincial forum adopted five specific measures. First, all government organizations

---

[11] *Mao Wengao*, vii. 65 and 48; *NFRB*, 16 February 1958.   [12] Ibid.   [13] *Mao Wengao*, vii. 49.

Table 6.1. *Guangdong: The PPC production plan, February 1958*
(m. tons, unless otherwise stated)

	1957	1958 (planned)	1962 (planned)
Sugar	0.4	–	1.50
Paper	–	0.08	0.37
Salt	–	0.47	2.00
Cement	–	0.32	0.90
Hydroelectric power (thousand megawatts)	–	0.36	1.33
Steel	none	none	0.10
Pig iron	2,596 tons[a]	0.022[b]	0.47
Chemical fertilizer	–	–	0.77

[a]*NFRB*, 14 May 1958.
[b]*NFRB*, 30 January 1958.
Source: *NFRB*, 16 February 1958, except for pig iron.

were to cut 10 per cent off their operating budget so that the savings could be turned over to the state treasury. The profit to be remitted upward by the enterprises was raised by 10 per cent. All capital investment was slashed, especially in the 'non-productive' portion (of housing, schools, and hospitals). Second, the government organizations were to organize an anti-waste campaign to uncover any surplus raw materials and funds to be remitted upwards. Third, another 20,000 sent-down (*xiafang*) cadres were added to the original target of 180,000 by the further simplification of government organizations. Fourth, a campaign was initiated for the cadres (district, army platoon levels, and above) to contribute toward the building of thirteen fertilizer plants. Fifth, the APCs and the handicraft cooperatives would expand their investment in construction while cutting back on consumption.[14]

These were austere measures designed to save and limit provincial spending, but they soon turned out to be difficult to follow because of the requirements of the GLF. Meanwhile, the higher cadres had to shoulder the dual burden of *xiafang* and donations for industry. Besides, a new plan for cadre study threatened to impose a tighter ideological control over them. The APCs and the handicraft cooperatives, on the other hand, were under growing pressure to supply funds and resources for industrial development.

---

[14] *NFRB*, 16 February 1958. Article 16 of the Sixty Articles incorporated the suggestions by some Hubei cadres that the production and distribution figures of 1957 should be used as a base and all subsequent increases in production should be subjected to the distribution (to cooperative members) and accumulation ratios of 4 : 6, 5 : 5, or 6 : 4. In better-off cooperatives, the suggested ration was 3 : 7. *Mao Wengao*, vii. 49. In Guangdong, the accumulation seemed to be across the board and not limited to the portion of subsequent production increases.

The Direction and Role of Local Industries:
The Xinhui County Model[15]

Article 11 of the Sixty Articles mandated that industry must serve agriculture, without much elaboration. This is not surprising since a massive development of local industries was a new task. The slogan that launched the GLF, 'overtake Britain in fifteen years', simply meant that China would catch up or surpass Britain in the production of certain key industrial products. It did not define the role of local industries and the direction they should take.[16]

It was not until 18 February that the PPC defined its position in the *NFRB* by referring to the Xinhui model. The Xinhui County Party Committee (CPC) resolved that local industries must cater completely to the needs of agriculture. In addition, it approved the measure of 'three demands and three provisions', which meant that all requests for agricultural implements (no matter the time, the variety, and the quantity required) would be satisfied. Furthermore, the peasants were promised brick houses to replace their straw huts, the elimination of the five pests, the beautifying of the environment, and the electrification of the rural areas. In busy agricultural seasons, the urban residents would be organized for agricultural labour. They were also required to accumulate 10 tons of refuse per person each year and to collect sewage water (*sic*) for use as fertilizer in the APCs. In addition, the county also planned to build a fertilizer plant with funds raised by itself. Not surprisingly, the cadres of the agricultural machinery factories opposed these ambitious programmes, fearing that they would lose money if too many trial products were produced, and there was no market for them. They were also worried that their limited technological capacity could not accommodate such a large-scale expansion.[17] However, these objections were summarily dismissed by the CPC.

The Xinhui policies, though ambitious, were intended to tie industry more closely to the needs of agriculture and to improve the livelihood of the peasants overall. The PPC felt it was on track, although the huge demands created by the GLF in 1958 put pressure on the limited supply of industrial products and agricultural machinery. For instance, the large-scale water works carried out in the autumn and winter months of 1957 and 1958 required large quantities of materials such as pumps, cement, and bricks. To raise the yield per *mu* large quantities of fertilizer and improved farm implements were required. More means of transportation were also needed to move the labourers. The PPC anticipated that local industries would have to shoulder the responsibility, especially when supplies from the central ministries were unlikely to be increased. However, the cadres on the

---

[15] *NFRB*, 18 February 1958.   [16] See *RMRB*, 4 and 8 December 1957; 1 January 1958.

[17] *NFRB*, 28 February 1958. Similarly, the cadres from Rongfeng County, Yunnan, argued that local industries could not be run without the goods, funds, machinery, and technicians, supplied by the higher authorities. Local industries could divert attention and resources from agriculture, and industry should be run with proper standards, equipment, and guaranteed funds. Mines should be properly surveyed before production began. See *Zhengzhi Xuexi* (Political Study) 7, 1958 July 9–13.

industrial front were uncooperative. Allegedly, they neglected agriculture when planning production; others were said to have set up very advanced targets but they had neither concrete plans nor confidence in their fulfilment.

Despite these obstacles, the PPC predicted the arrival of industrialization in five years, when the province would have networks for agricultural machinery, power, fertilizer, and the processing of agricultural products. However, this proved to be an unrealizable dream.

The First Wave

Soon a high tide of industrial production was said to have been formed, as many units in the province had revised their targets of GVIO several times upward to 40–60 per cent over that of 1957. The experience at Jiangmen gives a glimpse of how this was accomplished. The masses were aroused into 'big blooming and contending' around the preselected questions: was it possible to have a GLF in industry? Did the factories have more untapped potential for production? Predictably the leadership obtained what they wanted to hear, as the general political climate precluded any dissent. Consequently, in about ten days the target for the GVIO in Jiangmen was revised upward six times, from an original increase of 18.19 per cent to 60.5 per cent. Therefore, the *NFRB* was proud to report, 'the better the "debate", the more progressive the target.'[18] In this atmosphere, Hainan District, which had been openly criticized by the PPC, felt compelled to revise its planned increase to 54 per cent (expecting to reach 64.22 per cent). Foshan Municipality, the unit that started the competitive drive, also re-revised its increase in the GVIO to 60.2 per cent (expecting to reach 80.9 per cent).[19] In such a way, once a unit or locality had complied with the PPC's wishes, it was almost impossible for the rest not to do the same.

County-level Implementation and the 'Two-anti' (*shuangfan*) Campaign

By the end of February, the PPC was reasonably satisfied with the progress made at the prefectural and municipality levels; it was now prepared to mobilize the next administrative level, the county, where the progress in implementation was mixed. Some counties had 'conservative' (i.e. unacceptably low) targets, and other units complied with the high targets but had no concrete measures to implement them. Still, many other places emphasized quantity, but ignored quality, supply and sale.

To correct this state of affairs and to tighten control, the PPC convened a telephone conference on the 28 February. It ordered the counties to set up advanced

---

[18] *NFRB*, 23 February 1958. The revision of targets several times upwards was not unusual in other places. For instance, Nanjing Municipality was forced to do the same. *NBCK*, 10 January 1958, 3.
[19] Ibid., and *NFRB*, 26 February 1958.

industrial targets within seven days and report them to the district party committees (DPC) which in turn were to report to the PPC directly. The counties were also required to specify the time they would need for the GVIO to exceed the GVAO (i.e. the current Chinese definition of industrialization). All the first secretaries of the district and county party committees were required to devote some time to industry, and to nominate one party secretary exclusively to handle industry. A new system of evaluation (*pingbi*, i.e. appraisal through comparison) was set up—the districts and the municipalities were to assess the performance of the counties and the factories once a month. All the units below the province would be appraised in comparison with the advanced units, thus creating additional pressure for outstanding performance.

In addition, the meeting, taking its cue directly from Mao also launched a 'two-anti' campaign against waste and conservatism in the province's enterprises, handicrafts and transport cooperatives. In doing so, the PPC was a step ahead of the other provinces as the central directive on the two-anti campaign was not promulgated until 3 March,[20] and like the MM, its zealotry was designed to curry favour with Mao.

In Guangdong, the propaganda themes for the two-anti campaign were the slogans 'overtake Britain in fifteen years' and the values of frugality and hard work. The cadres were urged to 'draw fire to burn themselves' (*yinhuo shaoshen*), that is, to make self-criticism to encourage criticism from others. This was thought to be useful for getting rid of 'lethargy' and 'bureaucratic airs'. The criticism method was also to be employed to expose incidences of waste, theft of state property, and the false reporting of achievement to defraud bonuses.

The two-anti campaign was meant to be a direct assault on alleged bureaucratic practices, and more importantly, a means to spur production. However, in January and February, the province as a whole had raised production by only 14.4 per cent, not the 40 per cent planned increase more than 1957. Although some units had boosted production, many had suffered a decline of 30 per cent or more. Two special districts, Zhanjiang and Huiyang, were singled out for open criticism by the PPC. Invariably, their failure was attributed to their leadership and rightist-conservative thinking, serious charges indeed.

Immediate response to the two-anti campaign itself was unenthusiastic; it was virtually unknown in many places. To correct this, Chen Yu (who was also the Provincial Governor) and Wen Minsheng convened another PPC telephone conference on the 12 March.[21] The conference now decided to expand the campaign into a 'vigorous mass movement' and extend it to the organs of the special districts and counties, not just the factories and enterprises. All cadres were obliged to 'draw fire to burn themselves' and reforms were to be introduced after much 'blooming and contending'.[22]

Two things became clear at this point. First, many units failed to achieve the ambitious 'leap forward' plans, although the PPC was successful in compelling them to raise their targets to unrealistic heights. Second, the two-anti campaign was

---

[20] *RMRB*, 4 March 1958.　　　[21] *NFRB*, 14 March 1958.　　　[22] Ibid.

unwelcome, as it imposed extremely heavy demands on the cadres, who were required to arouse the masses to shake up the bureaucracy of which they were a part. Nevertheless, the PPC was convinced that the two-anti campaign was the ultimate weapon to neutralize opposition and to promote the GLF. However, in the context of high targets, it is doubtful if any of the formal goals could be reached. Places that heeded the spirit of the two-anti campaign announced that they would shrink the projected time and advanced the completion date.[23] In fact, they skimmed and cut corners. For instance, the Guangzhou Paper Mill claimed to have been inspired by the two-anti campaign to replace the 'crawling' plan with a 'leap forward' one. Its fame stemmed from the claim that it had utilized its by-products to create *eight* new factories for iron and steel, papermaking machinery, hydrochloric acid, alcohol, grinding stones, and the like.[24] Meanwhile, it is instructive to observe how the response of one special district to the new provincial initiative shed light on the bureaucratic procedure.

The Response of One Special District

As mentioned, the Zhanjiang Special District (which had eleven counties and one municipality), was criticized publicly in the provincial press for declining production. In response, it shifted its blame onto three counties and the Zhanjiang Municipality. At a subsequent inspection tour, the district party secretary charged that the leadership at Lianjiang and Hua counties had abandoned industrial production altogether since the launching of the rectification campaign. The industrial and transport department of the Zhanjiang MPC admitted not only that the leadership had wasted most of its time convening meetings and making plans, thereby ignoring the mobilization of the masses, it had not even transmitted the year's plan downward to the lower levels. However, in Wuchuan county, the head of the industrial section was openly defiant. He was quoted as saying, 'if neither machines nor technical cadres are supplied, no factories can be set up'. He also refused the request made by a jute factory to build an extension unless funds were provided by the state.[25]

In any case, these counties were ordered to reverse the trend of falling production as soon as possible. The pressure for conformity was transmitted effectively layer by layer until it culminated at the grass roots. However, before all of this could be resolved, another central initiative had to be implemented.

Red and Expert: The Experimental Plots in Industry

A central directive issued on 14 February ordered leadership cadres of all levels to set up experimental plots in agriculture.[26] As mentioned in Chapter 2, these were plots directly run by the cadres so that they could learn the skills involved in agricultural

---

[23] *NFRB*, 22 April 1958.   [24] *Shangyu*, 1, 1958, 33–6.   [25] *NFRB*, 24 March 1958.
[26] *RMRB*, 15 February 1958. For more details, see Chapter 3.

production. The goal was to turn these 'red' professionals into 'experts' on the one hand, and to overcome bureaucratism and 'subjectivism' by uniting the leaders and the masses on the other hand.

Guangdong's implementation of this order in agriculture has already been discussed in Chapter 5. However, on 15 March, the fervent PPC took this a step further and issued a directive calling upon all cadres to adapt the experimental plots to *industry and transportation*. All leadership cadres in charge of industry at the provincial level and below, including party secretaries, governors, mayors, heads of the provincial departments and bureau chiefs, were required to participate. It was also specified that they should acquire the skills of enterprise management in one to two years; become professionals (*neihang*) in three to five years, and experts in five to ten years. Similar rules were prescribed for party secretaries in the enterprises, factory managers, and chairmen of trade unions. The cadres in charge of industry at the provincial, district (municipality) and county levels were to spend four months of the year in the factories and mines. Industrial department and bureau heads were to take turns in becoming factory managers. These transferred cadres were enjoined to learn from older workers and technicians in order to acquire the desired skills. The PPC would monitor the progress made quarterly, and the various lower levels were to devise their own measures for implementation.[27]

Not surprisingly, this new provincial policy was unpopular. Some cadres claimed that it was fine for agricultural work, but was impossible to be applied to the more complicated industrial process, which required a higher level of technology. Some leadership cadres thought that to work at the lower levels would weaken their understanding of the overall situation. Others were sceptical but they kept silent. The cadres were also doubtful that they could turn into experts themselves in such a short time.[28]

The experimental plot was based on the simplistic view that the party members could replace the technicians with only a short stint of regular training. Some cadres resented the idea of having to spend one-quarter of their time participating in labour and 'learning' from their subordinates. Many found that even before they had a chance to establish themselves in their respective 'plots', they were already obliged to turn them into advanced units. In any case, the PPC's commitment to this policy was less than steadfast, as it was soon overshadowed by other new policies and priorities.

Industry in Every County

In a report submitted to Mao on 6 March, the PPC praised fiscal decentralization by claiming that the investment in capital construction originally assigned by the centre (at 119m. *yuan*) had risen to 226m. *yuan* by provincial contributions, thanks to the

---

[27] *NFRB*, 25 March 1958.   [28] Ibid.

anti-waste and economizing efforts.[29] By the time of the First Provincial Capital Construction Conference (?–20 March), the *NFRB* announced that the total capital investment for 1958 had reached 267m. *yuan*, or 66 per cent more than the total invested during the 1FYP period. Such funds had enabled virtually the building of a new factory or the expansion of an existing one every day, so that electricity, coal, metallurgy, construction materials, and chemical industries all benefited.[30] As mentioned before, this report encouraged Mao to consider a more radical version of decentralization. Moreover, he was impressed by the mass activism, so at Chengdu he broached the idea of a mass campaign to 'reform' farm tools to raise labour efficiency and to further mechanization, urging the provinces to promote tool reform and mechanization.[31] This Maoist initiative turned quickly into a central directive (passed at Chengdu on 22 March) which urged the reform of farm tools for irrigation, cultivation, transport, food processing, with an eye on semi-mechanization. The directive also urged the realization of agricultural mechanization and semi-mechanization in seven or five years by relying on the local industries and funds raised by the APCs so that this could be done in the *duohao kuaisheng* fashion.[32]

Taking this cue from Mao, the PPC announced in March that in 1958, all counties would run some industries. Moreover, the APCs, donations from cadres, local financial revenues and investment by local 'overseas Chinese'[33] had already raised 100m. *yuan*. In Zhanjiang Special District, half the 13m. *yuan* raised consisted of the voluntary contributions from the savings of the APCs, a heavy financial burden on them indeed. The PPC planned to use these funds to build 400 various medium and small factories, mines, salt works, and hydroelectric stations. Overall, they were closely linked to the needs and the conditions of the regions, as can be seen in Table 6.2.[34]

Pleased with the seemingly enthusiastic fund-raising activities of the localities, the Provincial People's Council (PPPC) decided to 'send downwards' fifty-four plants originally administered by the province to the county authorities as a reward. Likewise, ten other newly built sugar refineries would also be decentralized.[35] In this way, the decentralization policies initiated in late 1957 continued, but instead of acquiring more independence, the counties simply shouldered more responsibilities in the industrial campaign.

In March, the central ministries also assumed one of their new roles after the decentralization decrees, that is to design small factories and mines for the local authorities. The MM, for example, had designed several small blast furnaces with capacities ranging from 0.084 cu. m to 2.83 cu. m. Other designs included chemical fertilizer factories, power factories, cement kilns, and sugar refineries. Most of

---

[29] *Mao Wengao*, vii. 128.   [30] *NFRB*, 27 March 1958.
[31] *Mao Weikan*, xiB. 29–30.   [32] *Jiaoxue Cankao Ziliao*, xxii. 422.
[33] In the early 1960s overseas Chinese numbered about 6 million, or about one-sixth of the Guangdong population. In 1969, they comprised about one-fifth. These were people who had lived overseas, or who had an overseas Chinese connection, or had decedents, or were dependants of those who went overseas. Chang Chi-yun, *Chung-kuo Ta Lu*, and Vogel, *Canton* 20.
[34] *NFRB*, 27 March 1958.   [35] Ibid.

Table 6.2. *Funds raised by the Special Districts and*
the types of plants planned

Special District	General characteristics	Amount of funds raised (*yuan*)	Types of plants to be built
Zhanjiang	Producing mainly agricultural products	13 million	Processing factories, HEP stations, fertilizer factories, agricultural machinery factories
Shaoguan	Relatively rich in mineral ores	–	Mainly small mines
Huiyang	Poor soil	5 million	Mainly fertilizer factories
Foshan	–	–	Agricultural machinery, pesticide and fertilizer factories
Shantou	–	8 million	–

these were said to be suitable for the provinces, special districts, counties, and even the APCs. The guiding principle was to have every county run some sort of industry so that factories, mines and enterprises would 'proliferate like stars in a star-studded sky'.[36] It did not take much for the ministries to fulfil their new function; the onuses were really on the local authorities to turn out the equipment and machinery according to the designs and to find their own raw materials. The emphasis on small-scale industrial production had made local self-reliance the principle of operation.

The Yangjiang and Lianping Models

With this promise of 'technical assistance' from the central ministries, the campaign to develop local industries gained further momentum, and the goal of the Guangdong PPC escalated. Its original slogan 'industry in every county' was now replaced by 'industry in every *xiang*'. Again, the PPC utilized a model, this time from Yangjiang county, to illustrate how the new policy was to be implemented.[37] This county planned to have industry in every *xiang* by building 1,659 small factories. It also planned to increase the GVIO to 60–70 per cent of the gross value of industrial and agricultural output in three years' time, thus 'basically' achieving 'industrialization'. The county also promised to find its own funds, technology, raw materials, and market. The 2.78m. *yuan* to be invested in industry was to be collected from the *xiang* and the APCs, with an average contribution of more

---

[36] *NFRB*, 20 March 1958.   [37] *NFRB*, 28 March 1958.

than 20 *yuan* per household. All county cadres were to donate for several large fertilizer plants.

Lianping county, on the other hand, aimed at the 'industrialization'[38] of water conservancy within the year. This involved the construction of 17,000 small water conservancy projects (an average of 110 projects for each APC!), four hydroelectric stations that could introduce electricity to 15–20 per cent of the county's rural households, and hundreds of water mills and water-powered trip-hammers (for husking rice). When completed, they were said to be able to save 7.6 million labour units (*laodongli*) for agricultural production. In addition, the CPC urged that all rural areas, if conditions permitted, link all kitchens and canals (or ditches, *shuqu*) with bamboo tubes for running-water supply. This was meant to reduce labour used for carrying water. Soon, it was reported that the APCs were running an enthusiastic mass campaign to carry out these goals.

Because of the generally sanguine mood then, the opposition to rural industrialization embodied in the slogan of 'industry in every county' (or, in some places, 'industry in every *xiang*') was easily stifled. Industrialization, whatever it meant to the Chinese at that time, financed by the localities and serving local needs must have appeared to many people to be a rational choice. The provincial authorities were willing to stimulate the interest of their subordinates and to get them moving to develop their potential. The sending down of some enterprises normally belonging to the province was designed to encourage the counties to run local industries and to relieve the province of some of its responsibilities. The counties probably welcomed these initiatives for similar reasons but decentralization of enterprise management in the context of the GLF did not give them more autonomy. Some cadres remained convinced, perhaps rightly, that with no help from the state, the problem of funds, technology, raw materials, and markets were insurmountable. The provincial authorities were aware of these problems; however, their simple solution was the mobilization of the masses. As the Party kept on maintaining, 'once you arouse the masses, nothing can be a problem'.

The APCs probably bore the brunt of supplying funds although they were also the potential beneficiaries from the building of many small food-processing and oil-pressing plants, paper mills, hydroelectric stations, and so on. The grass roots, the local treasuries, and the 'overseas Chinese' were also pressured to make contributions.

In all, the programmes outlined by the models seem extravagant and even fantastic. However, most units probably took a more moderate course, which might yield positive results. Nevertheless, developments in the second half of 1958 soon overshadowed these initial efforts and shifted them onto a totally different course.

---

[38] This simply meant the popularization of hydroelectric power. The words 'to industrialize' were so much in fashion at this time that they were employed regardless of whether they were appropriate or not.

Industrialization and Mechanization: The Provincial
Meeting on Industry[39]

When statistics from the first quarter were available, the PPC was disappointed, but was determined to push forward. Despite the rhetoric of a 'great leap' on all fronts of the provincial economy, including the state-owned industries, the actual increases in local industry and light industry compared with 1957 were only 20.5 per cent (the target was 43 per cent) and 5.89 per cent respectively. In fact, certain localities and trades had reduced production. At a provincial meeting on industry which met on 21 April to review work and to set up new tasks, Wen Minsheng issued a new bugle call for accelerated industrialization, so that the GVIO would overtake the GVAO *within* 1958, and that mechanization and semi-mechanization would be achieved in five or three years. The province would, it was said, 'basically' achieve industrialization in five years. This meant that machinery would replace human power

Table 6.3. *Wen Minsheng's plan for Guangdong's industrialization*

Types of vehicles or machinery	Present numbers	Numbers required by 1962
Tractors	709	40,000
Ploughing and weeding machines	(probably few)	90,000
Double-wheel, double-share ploughs	10,000	160,000
Water pumps	–	90,000 hp
Variety of processing machinery	(probably few)	700,000
Hand-carts	–	5 million
Automobiles	–	40,000
Steamboats	–	20,000
A standard APC with 370 households, 1,500 people, and 3,500 *mu* of arable land, mechanization or semi-mechanization would need:		
Diesel engines, gas engines, and tractors		150 hp
Tractors		2
Ploughing and weeding machines		4 to 5
Automobiles		2
40-kilowatt HEP stations		
Steamboats or motorized sailing boats (for some APCs only)		1

Source: *NFRB*, 22 April 1958.

[39] *NFRB*, 22 April 1958.

in up to 70 of all major agricultural activities. In particular, 70 per cent of the 70m. *mu* of arable land projected for 1962 would be cultivated by machines. Table 6.3 lists the machinery required for Guangdong to 'basically' achieve mechanization or semi-mechanization as calculated by Wen Minsheng.

This was an ambitious plan, so Wen said that the only way to achieve it was to crush the 'mysterious' standpoints regarding industrialization and mechanization. This meant the abandonment of all worries and take a 'just-do-it' attitude, and in this spirit, he called upon the entire Party and all administrative levels to run industry. Wen was careful to throw in other rhetoric such as comprehensive planning, strengthening of the leadership, following the mass line, the combination of the large, medium, and the small, all-round development and 'letting the flowers [industries: author] blossom everywhere'.[40]

Yet the fact remained that existing machinery was few, and that the localities had to finance the industrialization drive themselves. Moreover, Guangdong simply did not have the heavy industrial base to produce these machines. Wen could not have failed to realize this, although his list of machinery was published in the *NFRB*. Wen and the PPC seemed to have tried to press the lower levels to exert as much as possible although privately they knew that their goals might not be realized. One purpose of the plan, however, was to demonstrate the determination of the PPC in implementing the central policies of rural industrialization although the likelihood of achieving them was slim. In any event, like many grandiose plans of the GLF, the plan for mechanization was soon abandoned as the provincial attention shifted again.

The Great Inspection Campaign[41]

In May, the PPC adopted a dramatically different method, the Great Inspection Campaign in industrial production, to monitor and promote the implementation of its policies among *all* the industrial units in the province. Apparently the progress made in the industrial campaign so far was disappointing. In some localities and sectors, not only was there not a 'great leap', but drops in production were reported. According to the PPC's diagnosis, this was due to the cadres' 'three winds' and 'five airs',[42] and their failure to 'rely on the masses'. These failings, the PPC claimed, had been uncovered extensively during the rectification and the 'two-antis' campaign, although the remedies were unsatisfactory. Therefore, the Great Inspection campaign, to all intents and purposes, was designed to be a more potent means to replace these ineffective campaigns.

Several aspects of this campaign merit attention. First, 3,000 odd cadres and secretaries from the province, special district, and county levels were transferred to

---

[40] Ibid.   [41] *NFRB*, 16 May 1958.

[42] The 'three winds and five airs' are bureaucratic, subjective, and sectarian work styles and arrogant, bureaucractic, extravagant, lazy and apathetic airs. See, Warren Kuo, *Comprehensive Glossary of Chinese Communist Terminology* (Taipei: Institute of International Relations, National Chengchi University, 1978).

the shop floors of factories and mines to organize the staff and workers and members of the handicraft cooperatives. There they were to conduct meetings to discuss the production plans by using the method of 'big blooming and contending, big-character posters and big debate'. The party committees at various levels were called upon to identify advanced experiences to popularize them, and instruct members of the factories and mines to mobilize the population to engage in the inspection of themselves.[43]

In the localities the work of inspection was farmed out to individual groups. In some areas, more specialized teams on capital construction, mines inspection teams and *xiang* and APC industries were set up. The special districts coordinated the counties and municipalities and set up a report system. In some areas, bulletins charting the progress of the campaigns were also published.[44]

The PPC was obviously impatient with its subordinates, so the dispatching of a large number of cadres to the base level to inspect and mobilize work bypassed the normal bureaucratic procedure and set up new methods of evaluation. The unstated assumption was that intermediate cadres were half-hearted about the industrial campaign. Therefore, one purpose of the inspection was to involve as many people as possible by bringing them in direct contact with the leadership—the mass line method. Another aim was to drum up support among grass-roots activists. Above all, it was an ostentatious display of the provincial authorities' determination to implement important central and provincial policies, and this also explains the predilection for this policy instrument. As noted in Chapter 5, this method was later applied to other areas and campaigns (such as agriculture) and it grew to mammoth proportions involving more than 10,000 leadership cadres.

However, the effectiveness of these massive inspections was at best limited. According to official reports, occasionally this inspection campaign was not taken seriously—the organizational efforts were small, and many units dragged their feet. In some counties and municipalities, the leadership cadres refused to take charge and delegated the task to the departments of industry and communications instead. Some leading cadres were bent on a superficial inspection (*zouma guanhua*) and tried to limit the time spent on it. Still other places had tried to evade the campaign altogether by claiming heavy work loads, or that they did not have sufficient industry to merit such efforts.[45] This general indifference, and its faulty design, doomed this campaign from the start. Two years later, Tao Zhu had this to say about the inspections:

Back in 1958, we had organized large-scale inspection groups to check on production work throughout the province. Nearly all the leadership comrades in the PPC had gone down. Wherever we went, the masses were warm and were bustling with activity [*xixi rangrang*] and they put up posters that read, 'Welcome the presence of the PPC Inspection Teams to give instructions' We ourselves were swaggering through the streets as if blatantly seeking publicity (*zhaoyao guoshi*)...Actually [we had] not examined anything thoroughly, and

---

[43] *NFRB*, 13 and 14 May 1958.   [44] Ibid.   [45] Ibid.

this made it impossible for us to discover and to solve problems. This method has been abandoned for the last two years.[46]

This frank admission was probably an accurate appraisal; the inspections must have generated more light than heat, and they failed to achieve the goals they set out to accomplish.

Iron and Steel to the Fore: The Second Session of the Eighth Party Congress (5–23 May)

As mentioned, Tao Zhu the loyal Maoist had another field day by 'closely following' (*jingen*) Mao and Leap policies at the Party Congress. His extravagant speech was followed inevitably by an equally extravagant pledge that Guangdong's industrialization would no longer take eight or ten years, but just one or two. Agricultural mechanization and semi-mechanization could be achieved in three to five years.[47] Furthermore, spurred on by the Party Congress, the PPC quickly proposed to the Party Centre that during the 2FYP, it would vigorously develop the iron and steel industry to lay the foundation for agricultural mechanization. A more immediate concern was that the industrialization drive over the past few months required raw materials and infrastructure that did not exist. In a major watershed, Guangdong vowed to build from scratch four iron and steel mills during the 2FYP period. Within 1958, 131 small iron-smelting plants were to be built throughout the province. By 1962, production by these small and medium iron and steel plants would amount to 1m. tons of pig iron, 0.45m. tons of steel, and 0.36m. tons of rolled-steel products. These were grand pledges, as Guangdong had never produced any steel or steel products before, and pig iron produced in 1957 was a mere 2,600 tons. Yet, not even Tao foresaw that rising expectations would force Guangdong to produce iron and steel in *1958*, and that his enthusiasm did not measure up.

One important point to note is that most of the factories proposed were to be equipped with electric motors and air-blowers so that the use of manual air-blowers with the indigenous blast furnaces was declared abandoned.[48] This was in tune with one of the 'original' goals of the GLF, the technical revolution. However, very soon afterwards, this plan was discarded when the urgent need to produce huge quantities of iron and steel let the indigenous method reign supreme.

However, after the Congress Mao continued to goad the directors of the Cooperative Regions to accelerate production, so Ke Qingshi of the East China Coordinating Region bragged in late May that East China alone could produce 6–7m. tons of steel in 1959. As soon as this bombshell was dropped, the other directors of the Cooperative Regions (including Tao) felt obliged to follow suit. Moreover, the two national conferences on local metallurgy industry convened by the MM (first one in April, second one in May/June), goaded by slogans such as 'overtake

[46] *NFRB*, 25 November 1960.   [47] Li Rui, *Dayuejin*, 321.
[48] *NFRB*, 14 May 1958; *Dangdai Guangdong*, 2, 1997, 63.

Britain in fifteen years', '*duohao kuaisheng*', and 'twice the speed, half the investment', put pressure on Guangdong to excel.

In early June, the PPC conformed by bringing forward the 1962 targets for iron and steel production by *five years to 1958*. New iron and steel targets for 1962 were raised to 6 and 4m. tons, respectively. It announced that more than 1,600 small blast furnaces *and* 28 large and small converters were to be built within the year. To make good these pledges, the First Provincial Conference on the Iron and Steel Industry (8–12 June) was convened by Liu Tianfu, the secretary-general of the PPPC at Qingyuan to switch the industrialization effort to iron and steel.

To mark the new departure, the PPC now declared that iron and steel were above all the most important raw materials, months after the industrialization push had already begun. As an *NFRB* editorial now put it, 'If you want industrialization, the first thing to do is to smelt iron and steel; if you want to mechanize agriculture, [you] must also smelt iron and steel. Besides this, there is no other way.'[49]

So the PPC now decided that everyone, every administrative level from the province to the *xiang*, and every department must spring into action immediately to build the iron and steel industry. At this time, the provincial authorities were vague about how to achieve this feat. As no modern equipment was available in large quantities, the conference made a virtue out of necessity by falling back on the small-scale production and the indigenous method. The small blast furnaces touted by the PPC were said to have many virtues—little investment but quick results. They required only a few weeks and several hundred to two thousand *yuan* to build, thus reversing the decision to abandon the latter made only weeks before. Fortunately for the PPC, these were consistent with the formula of 'relying on the masses', which was touted increasingly as a panacea. Accordingly, the conference called on everybody and all administrative units from the province to the APCs to run the iron and steel industry. The procedure was now said to be from 'indigenous' to 'modern' (*yang*, or literally, foreign), and from manual operations to mechanization, from 'low to high'.[50] Relying on the masses became a way to pass the buck.

However, the more sober delegates maintained that the iron and steel industry required modern, automatic, and sophisticated technology. Naturally, they had no use for the indigenous method. Other delegates did not even show up at the meeting when they found out beforehand that no new equipment was to be handed out. The sceptics of the new policy must have been numerous, judging from the length of an editorial in the *NFRB* (about one-quarter of it) devoted to rebuking them. The PPC was apparently impatient with any dissenting opinions, so the differences between itself and the critics were now elevated to the status of a two-line struggle.[51]

---

[49] *NFRB*, 15 June 1958, in Zhongguo Kexueyuan Jingji Yanjiusuo Ziliao Shi (ed.), *Gangtie Shengchan Dayuejin Lunwen Xuanji* (Selected articles on the Great Leap Forward in iron and steel production) (Beijing: Kexue chubanshe, 1958), 251. [50] *NFRB*, 9 June 1958.
[51] *NFRB*, 15 June 1958, in *Gangtie Shengchan*, 252.

A Statistical Triumph: The Half-Year Balance Sheet

On 30 June, the provincial statistical bureau published a communiqué on the economic leap which claimed that the funds raised by the localities had already reached the 1bn. *yuan* mark. This would be earmarked for the construction of more than 400 factories, mines, salt works, and hydroelectric stations, expected to be completed by the end of the year. Statistics from 99 counties also showed that more than 800 new factories had already been built. In the *xiang* and the APCs, industries were said to have spread like 'stars' in the sky, resulting in 150,000 factories or mines. On average each *xiang* had 76.2 units and each APC had 3.19 units. These were said to have been built with the 'poor' and indigenous methods by relying on the masses and by using the least amount of investment. This meant that all the necessary materials and equipment were requisitioned.[52] By July, Tao bragged that industrialization could be achieved not in seven or ten years, but in 1958, when the GVIO could exceed that of the GVAO.[53]

However, given the haste and the limitation of local resources, these small plants and mines that mushroomed overnight were primitive creations. Many never served the purpose for which they were designed. When the political pressure was high, the cadres exhorted the masses to build these industries. But once these industries were set up, they were left to drift along because the cadres regarded them as backward, unmodern, and ineffectual. In some places, virtually no demand existed for their products.[54] Furthermore, persuasive coercion was employed to appropriate buildings, labourers, and funds. By early 1959, the PPC finally ordered a halt to the building of these county and *xiang* industries.[55] Other established ones would be dismantled or simply abandoned in the next few years, not entirely due to the economic difficulties of the post-Leap years, but also because of the various unsolved problems of waste, inefficiency, and the lack of raw materials and demand.

In any case, although the original goal for the rural industries was to serve the local APCs and agriculture, by June and July, pressure from Mao and the centre forced the new orientation to supply raw materials for the larger industries such as iron and steel, and oil-refining. As the provincial policy continued to shift, the *xiang* were soon exhorted to build their own iron and steel plants and oil-refineries.[56]

In July, as competitive bidding for high targets at a South China Coordinating Conference (probably chaired by Tao) raised the iron and steel targets again—in 1962, iron output should reach 7m. tons, and steel, 5m. tons.[57]

By August, a province-wide mass movement for iron and steel was said to have unfolded, but production was slow. Among the 1,934 small indigenous blast furnaces being constructed, only 642 of them were in production. In Foshan Special

---

[52] *NFRB*, 11 July 1958.   [53] *Shangyu*, 1, 1958, 4–5.   [54] *NFRB*, 11 July 1958.
[55] *NFRB*, 5 April 1959.   [56] Ibid.
[57] *Dangdai Guangdong*, 2, 1997, 63. The 1958 quotas of 0.25m. tons of steel and 0.6m. tons of pig iron for Guangdong given by this source, which were lower than those set out in June, must be a variation of the 'two sets of plans'.

District, only three out of the 222 indigenous furnaces could function normally and this was a common province-wide phenomenon. Since the iron and steel drive began in June, iron and steel produced was a mere 7,942 and 2,197 tons respectively.

The PPC blamed this on the general apathy among the party committees, especially the first secretaries who had not taken charge personally, although the real obstacle for the iron and steel campaign was the lack of resources, equipment, raw materials, and expertise. Therefore, the cadres often waited for the higher authorities to supply equipment and technical personnel. Other localities had other priorities and concerns.

The Termination of the Rural Industrialization Campaign to Serve Agriculture and the Plunge into the Iron and Steel Campaign

When the decision for the doubling of the steel target to 10.7m. tons was being discussed at the enlarged Politburo at Beidaihe (17–30 August), national steel production was slow, accounting for only 3.8m. tons by July, leaving the bulk of the year's target to be accomplished in the few remaining months of 1958. As Mao had staked his personal credibility and applied the maximum pressure, any backdown was ruled out. At a meeting with the directors of the Coordinating Region on 19 August, Mao decreed that all first secretaries should also run industry personally.[58]

In view of this, the PPC promptly issued an urgent directive on 19 August to strengthen leadership by ordering all party first secretaries to take charge and to assure 0.3m. tons of steel and 0.5m. tons of pig iron for the province. Echoing Mao's concern that the plan might be non-fulfilled, the PPC now called the production quotas an 'important political mission'. The immediate task was to ensure that 4,000 blast furnaces would commence normal production by early September. Experienced workers and blacksmiths were to be recruited and to solve problems. In places with no bituminous coal, the use of wood charcoal, a wasteful and inefficient fuel for smelting, was condoned if no alternatives were found.[59] Other problems were simply ignored, as the PPC's panacea was the mobilization of the masses and the reform of farm implements to release more labourers to iron and steel production.

To tighten control, the PPC designated 22 key-point counties that were required to fulfil and over-fulfil the quota of 30,000 tons of pig iron. Special teams were to be organized to promote work in the other localities. Furthermore, the PPC also made Guangzhou and other municipalities responsible for steel smelting, whereas the counties were entrusted with smelting pig iron. However, even this limited realism was soon swept aside.[60]

---

[58] *Mao Weikan*, xiB. 84.
[59] For a discussion of the resultant problem of deforestation in China, see Smil, *The Bad Earth*, ch. 2.
[60] *NFRB*, 20 August 1958.

Meanwhile, the Yangshan county model for 'fully arousing the masses and the strengthening of technical management' was touted in the provincial press. This county was said to have rich coal reserves and iron ore in every *xiang*. Allegedly by putting 'politics' in command, ten blast furnaces were constructed, six of which could work normally. A further 351 blast furnaces were planned before year's end, and a total pig iron production of 45,755 tons was projected.

The first secretary there was said to have taken charge personally. Consequently, 15 per cent of the total labour force was set for pig iron production, no matter how busy agricultural production was. The concerns over the practicality of the blast furnaces and the lack of raw materials were to be resolved by propaganda and 'blooming and contending' meetings. For instance, since no refractory bricks were available, white clay and millstones were used instead. Iron ore and bricks were made available by voluntary donations from the masses and even houses were demolished for this purpose. However, some of these indigenous blast furnaces were so crude that they could produce only white iron (akin to iron ore).[61]

The emphasis of the entire campaign was on indigenous and small-scale technology, and those who were labelled 'greedy for the large [scale] and the foreign [modern]' were chastised. In Guangzhou, the slow progress made in the previous two months was blamed on the indifferent leadership cadres. Hence, the MPC decided to mobilize the population further. All party committees were asked to 'battle hard' for a month to fulfil the task of building furnaces before national day.

To strengthen control, the MPC decided to go down to the subordinate administrative levels to supervise and inspect their plans, schedules, and steps taken to ensure plan fulfilment. Apart from the three planned 'experimented plots' at the Guangzhou Iron and Steel Mill, Guangzhou Shipyard, and the First Heavy Machinery Plant, three additional pig iron 'experimental plots' were to be installed in Jiangcun District, Shijing District, and at Guangzhou Paper Mill. The MPC would ensure compliance by periodic on-the-spot conferences and 'comparison-and-appraisal' meetings.[62] This new obsession with iron and steel in the province spelled the end to the rural industrialization campaign.

When political pressure mounted and when production figures for August were available at Beidaihe, the Guangdong PPC responded by convening a series of emergency meetings between 25 and 27 August.[63] These meetings concluded that the condition of iron and steel production in Guangdong was 'really not wonderful'. Iron production up to 23 August was a mere 14,159 tons and steel 2,497 tons. Only 864 of the 2,290 small blast furnaces constructed had begun production. The 'serious danger' of plan non-fulfilment could not be ignored, since only four months were left in the year.

The PPC realized that the unreliable small blast furnaces and the shortages of fuel, raw materials, and labour were reasons for this poor showing, but insisted that the key was apathetic leadership. In fact, it can be said that since there was

[61] Smil, *The Bad Earth*, ch. 2.   [62] *NFRB*, 26 August 1958.
[63] *NFRB*, 29 August 1958; *RMRB*, 5 September 1958.

really no solution to the problem at hand, the only alternative was to rely on exhortation and the appeal to the human factor. Herein lies the voluntarism of the GLF.

To turn things around, the PPC now pinned its hope on the production of 50,000 tons of steel by the end of September, and took a series of extraordinary steps. First, the first secretaries of the Guangzhou MPC, the various district party committees, and the party committees of the 22 key-point counties were ordered to assume command immediately in iron and steel production. Tao Zhu had assumed personal command as the group leader of the iron and steel team of the PPC. The provincial governor, the secretary of the PPC secretariat, and the first secretary of the Guangzhou MPC had all become deputy team leaders.

The PPC also decided that the 22 key-point counties should guarantee the procurement of the required labour, raw material, technology, and equipment, and warned against 'dispersionism' and 'departmentalism'. As the task of steel smelting was assigned to Guangzhou, the special districts and the counties were enjoined to guarantee an abundant supply of pig iron to it. Failure to do this, the PPC added, was punishable by 'party discipline' and the 'laws of the land'.

At a telephone conference on the evening of 27 August, the PPC farmed out pig iron quotas to the localities and imposed several extraordinary measures. First, *all* machine factories were ordered to shift to the manufacturing of equipment for iron and steel production. Second, more small blast furnaces were to be built. Third, 300 automobile motors, 40,000 hp of irrigation and drainage engines, and all other available mechanical powers were turned over to the iron and steel front. Fourth, the localities were admonished to embrace the spirit of self-reliance and to open coal mines.[64]

These prepared the ground for the enlarged meeting of the PPC (3–6 September) on iron and steel. Tao formally transmitted the Beidaihe Resolution and Mao's speeches delivered at the Politburo meeting. Afterwards, the conference discussed the production plans for 1959 and for the 2FYP, but the more pressing concern was how to switch the gravity of work quickly from agriculture to industry, as demanded by the central directive, and to comply with the ambitious new assignment of producing 0.25m. tons of steel and 0.69m. tons of pig iron in the remaining four months of the year.

One major first decision was to mobilize 'all party and all people' to realize the aim of producing 50,000 tons of steel by the end of September. The PPC would focus its main strength to run industry (particularly iron and steel), the district committees and the party committees of the 22 key-point counties were to pay equal attention to agricultural and industrial work, and the remaining counties were to *begin* to pay attention to industrial work. Tao and Chen Yu now ordered the leading cadres to move and live alongside the furnaces and the mines to ensure plan fulfilment. Finally, the PPC also decided to organize 100,000 cadres and 10 million of the masses into five inspection teams to check the four most important kinds of work—the formation of the People's communes, iron and steel

[64] *NFRB*, 29 August 1958; *RMRB*, 5 September 1958.

production, autumn harvest and field management, and the movement to fit all revolving tools with ball-bearings.

Specifically, the September target of steel relied almost entirely on Guangzhou for achievement despite the persistent problems such as the shortages of pig iron, coking coal, manganese, aluminum, and technology. For sure, the various first secretaries of the district party committees pledged to ship pig iron to Guangzhou punctually, but without success. The Guangzhou MPC then promised to collect 34,000 tons of scrap iron and steel to smelt steel so that more time could be spared for the development of the small blast furnaces in the localities.[65]

In the remaining months of 1958, the smelting of iron and steel became an obsession and an end in itself as thousands of indigenous blast furnaces and converters (often called backyard furnaces) began to spring up in the countryside. The original rural industrialization plan to facilitate agricultural development was aborted, and little was heard about it in the rest of 1958. In this way, this was one watershed of the GLF. Despite its excesses, the rural industries programme was to a certain extent a reasonable response to the problems of that time although the same cannot be said about the ensuing iron and steel campaign. Some Chinese economists hold similar views when evaluating the GLF.[66] Furthermore, critics in China then who charged that the smelting of iron and steel 'in a big way' had 'squeezed out' everything else were probably correct. In any event, after August, the industrialization programme was to follow an entirely different course, as we will see in the following.

The Iron and Steel Campaign in Guangdong

A week into September, things were clearly not going well at the iron and steel front. Up to 8 September, 4,813 small blast furnaces were said to have been built and another 7,075 were in construction. A manpower of 550,000 had already been recruited for mining, coking, transportation, furnace building and other related activities. However, the amount of pig iron produced was pitifully small—3,000 tons in the previous days. Two-thirds of the completed furnaces had not yet started production, and those in production only did so erratically, as the scarcity of raw materials and machinery continued to plague the campaign. At a PPC telephone conference on the evening of 8 September, Tao argued that if only the completed furnaces could be put into production immediately, even at half their capacity, the daily production of pig iron could reach 6,000 tons. Since there were about 100 days left in 1958, the province could produce 600,000 tons of pig iron, bringing it closer to the quota of 690,000 tons.[67] Therefore, wishful thinking was passed off as rational calculation, for Tao ignored the objective constraints that had hampered

---

[65] *NFRB*, 10 September 1958.
[66] See *Jingji Yanjiu*, 5, 1980, 6. Xue Muqiao, *China's Socialist Economy* (Beijing: Foreign Languages Press, 1981), 206. [67] *NFRB*, 10 September 1958.

the campaign from the very start. Perhaps he really had no choice. Without resources, he could only emphasize the human factor; the 'mass movement' approach might be the only way out of the impasse.

The Second Great Inspection

As mentioned in Chapter 5, the PPC in September launched a mammoth Second Great Inspection involving 100,000 officials and 10 million of the masses as a desperate attempt to force plan fulfilment In any event, despite the scale of the operation, the sheer number of work units (factories, communes, etc.), and the multiplicity of goals, meant that the inspection could be carried out only super- ficially. As Tao Zhu admitted later, the entire undertaking was an extravaganza with more form than content. In fact, this is a good example of what is known as 'placebo policies'—policies designed to create the impression of action when action is being demanded, but they really do not address the problem.[68]

In fact, the PPC was disheartened when production figures were available to it on 21 September. Total iron and steel production to this date was a tiny fraction of the September target, not to mention the yearly target, although dozens of iron and steel divisions with a combined total of 6 to 7 million people were mobilized.[69] To head off a total collapse, Tao tried again to rally the troops at the First Session of the Second Provincial People's Congress (23 September). Tao and the PPC blamed the various party committees for not having paid sufficient attention to this 'solemn' task. Up to then they had come up with only a few dozen tons of iron and steel just to go through the motions. So, a great mass movement had not been unleashed. The PPC finally admitted the obvious—there was no basis for an iron and steel campaign in Guangdong. The equipment was too inferior and time too limited. However, it refused to budge. According to its own calculations—which it called the 'objective basis'—the province now had 10,500 furnaces and another 10,000 more were under construction. Suppose by the end of September all these could be put into producion and suppose only 30 per cent of these could produce normally, and each could produce one ton of pig iron per day, then about 180,000 tons of pig iron could be had in October. If in October, 2,000 more blast furnaces could be built and if the percentage of furnaces that could produce normally could rise to 40 per cent, then by the beginning of November, 240,000 tons of pig iron could be produced. If in November, the total number of furnaces could increase by another 2,000, then by December, the amount of pig iron should reach 400,000 tons. With regards to steel, the planned smelting capacity in Guangzhou alone was 700,000 tons annually, and existing equipment could handle 500,000 tons. There- fore, in the remaining three months of 1958, 140,000 tons of steel could still be produced.

[68] Hogwood and Peters, *The Pathology of Public Policy*, 172–4.
[69] *NFRB*, 29 December 1958.

Armed with these calculations, the PPC again called for the immediate mobilization of the masses, and the strengthening of the Party's leadership over the iron and steel campaign. According to Tao, this campaign must be run with the same scale and 'boldness of vision' as land-reform and collectivization. The first secretaries were urged to shoulder the responsibility '100 per cent'. The key-point counties were ordered to mobilize and to organize 'shock troops' into iron and steel divisions of 20 to 30 thousand people and to send them where the need arose. Only success was allowed, he added. Taking note that the grain problem had been 'basically' resolved, the PPC decided that iron and steel were more important than grain at this stage. Should conflicts occur, the PPC ordered that iron and steel be accorded the highest priority. Other kinds of work would have to yield. Therefore it called on *everybody in the province* to join in the campaign for iron and steel, if not to work directly at the furnaces, to participate in the various support activities.[70]

Late September and October coincided with the busiest period for autumn harvest and winter planting, but according to the instructions of the PPC, millions were drafted to smelt iron and steel. At its height, 7 million, or half the labour force, were engaged in the campaign. As the equipment and raw materials were lacking, brick and limekilns, and blockhouses were pressed into service. The masses were mobilized to search for metals by breaking up window frames and cooking utensils, and to denude forests for wood. Quality was not of concern, as long as the quantitative aspects were satisfied. This folly was conducted in the name of 'liberation of thought', and 'dare to think, say, and act'.

The Intensification of the Iron and Steel Campaign in October

In October, several developments led directly to the further intensification of the iron and steel campaign in Guangdong. First, on the eve of national day, the various provincial authorities competed with one another in 'launching satellites' (*fang weixing*), that is, to publish grossly exaggerated claims for iron and steel production. The alleged spectacular yields of Henan, Shandong, Hebei (the three front-runners), Shanghai, Beijing, Guangxi, Anhui, Guangdong, Jiangxi, and Zhejiang were lauded in the *RMRB*.[71] The 'demonstration effect' and the atmosphere of competition combined to make for more pressure to excel. Second, as mentioned, Mao's speech of 29 September criticized the cadres for being unwilling to launch a large-scale mass movement in industry. Third, Bo Yibo, the head of the SPC, had issued a call for the October plan for iron and steel to double that achieved in September. Fourth, on 4 October, the CCP issued the order for a new mass campaign to smelt steel using the *xiaotuqun* method. Fifth, the MM had convened a national conference at the Xinxing Steel Plant at Tianjin between 7 and 9 October and claimed to have overcome the problem of using indigenous iron to smelt steel.

[70] *NFRB*, 24 and 26 September 1958.   [71] *RMRB*, 1 and 2 October 1958.

This foreclosed any further complaints that the indigenous iron was useless for anything.

Smaller! More Indigenous!

These developments could not be ignored, so the PPC convened a telephone conference on 6 October to promote the *xiaotuqun*. It admitted that iron and steel production in Guangdong was slow and 'not very wonderful'. Although by that time 1.8 million people had already participated in the campaign, a 'real all-people smelt iron and steel' mass movement had not yet materialized. The real reasons, indeed, were the lack of raw materials, equipment, skills, and transportation facilities.[72] Yet, at this time, the PPC blamed the lacklustre performance on the fact that the *xiaotuqun* principle had not been implemented thoroughly. Up to that time the capacity of most of the small blast furnaces was about 0.03 cu. m, large enough to require air-blowers (which the machinery industry failed to provide in quantities) and large amounts of fuel to operate. Therefore, they were too difficult to be managed by the masses (*sic*). That Henan was able to launch so many high-yield 'satellites', the PPC claimed, was because it had popularized the smaller, and more indigenous method—they used crucibles and a kind of furnace that did not need blowers. Since this method could be mastered by everybody, the PPC maintained, it was also the best means to mobilize millions of people to participate instantly in the iron and steel campaign. It claimed, 'the indigenous method is the method of relying on the masses. The wisdom of the masses is boundless. Only if [we] rely on the masses, mobilize them, will unexpected miracles happen'.[73]

So, the PPC had found a magic formula—to produce iron and steel at high speed, the smallest and more indigenous furnaces were the best. The immediate goal was to clinch the '10,000-ton province' status by 10 October. In response to criticisms that these methods were too backward, the PPC argued that they were really well-tested treasures handed down by the ancestors for thousands of years.

According to the PPC, in Lian county, a dozen or so tons of pig iron were produced by simply placing 'grains' of ore in crucibles and heating them in a limekiln. Slaked lime was produced simultaneously, without any need for blast furnaces or air-blowers. If this method could be popularized throughout the province, the PPC speculated, the effect would be tremendous!

As to steel, the PPC admitted that since the pig iron 'hurdle' had not been cleared, Guangzhou still shouldered the responsibility for smelting steel. In a rare moment of realism, the PPC admitted that steel could be smelted only with pig iron and not just scrap iron alone. Therefore, it demanded that the localities fulfil the September transfer quota of pig iron in two or three days. In addition, it also handed out the quota for October and demanded that the localities produce 150,000 tons of pig iron and transfer 80,000 to 100,000 tons of pig iron to Guangzhou. In the end, the PPC

---

[72] *Shangyu*, 1, 1959, 13–14.   [73] *NFRB*, 7 October 1958.

also urged that another mass campaign using the indigenous method to smelt steel be launched alongside the drive for pig iron.[74]

It was clear that the iron and steel campaign in Guangdong had hit many snags. One account states that Tao Zhu had suggested to a central telephone conference that the indigenous blast furnaces were a hoax, and that the steel target should be lowered to stop the fabrications, but was ignored.[75] The PPC had no choice but to fall back on the 'the smaller, more indigenous, and even more primitive method'. In this regard, Henan province[76] had pointed the way, and although the miracles it had created were clearly a ploy, they were accepted by the centre, so the PPC had to play the game by forging ahead. Since the accepted premiss was that the indigenous method was the method of the masses, it was deemed the most effective way to launch a mass movement, which in the frantic atmosphere in the GLF, became a goal in itself. The distinction between means and ends was blurred. From the perspective of the PPC, to get the mass movement going was perhaps the only way to give the appearance of doing something.

Goal Conflict and the Redefinition of Priorities

In any event, despite the absolute priority attached to the iron and steel campaign, the resources and labour power were limited. Other obsessions of the GLF, such as the preparation for another agricultural leap, also demanded attention. Therefore, on the evening of the 6 October, another PPC telephone conference issued a 'battle call' for deep ploughing and soil improvement, which was now said to be the 'most important measure' toward another leap forward in agricultural production in 1959.

Henceforth, the PPC decided on 6 October to transfer 4 million people from various activities to form a 'professional army' for deep ploughing and soil improvement. It was envisaged that this army would work non-stop even after autumn harvest, when it would swell to about 6 million people.[77] An *RMRB* editorial (9 October) accompanying the report on Guangdong called for the immediate reallocation of labour, although it also downplayed the seriousness of the situation. It maintained that the labour sources had not yet been fully tapped. For instance, in Shanxi, labour was recruited among government offices, shops, and urban residents. All schools were either turned into half-work, half-study schools or closed to allow students to participate in labour. There was really no need to make choices, and the principle of 'simultaneous development' could still be maintained.[78]

---

[74] Ibid.

[75] Xue Muqiao, *Xue Muqiao Huiyilu* (Memoirs of Xue Muqiao) (Tianjin: Tianjin renmin chubanshe, 1996), 255.

[76] Henan was a constant pace-setter in the iron and steel campaign. On 15 September, it became the first province to produce more than 10,000 tons of pig iron in one day, thus acquiring the status of the 'ten-thousand tons' province. By the end of September, the estimated daily pig iron production was inflated further to over 90,000 tons. *RMRB*, 22 September, 1 October 1958.

[77] *RMRB*, 9 October 1958.   [78] Ibid.

The implementation of the 6 October decision turned out to be slow. By 14 October, it was clear that only one-third of the 4 million people planned for were mobilized. Therefore, another 'battle call' was issued ordering the localities to organize the required number of labour in two or three days. Now the PPC admitted that labour management was chaotic, and efficiency was low. In some localities, it complained, everything else stopped when the iron and steel campaign was set in motion.

The paramount importance attached to the iron and steel campaign made the turnaround difficult to achieve at short notice. In addition, local cadres doubted that deep ploughing and soil improvement would bring about dramatic increases in yield. The PPC refused to believe that in some localities, 70–80 per cent of the total labour force was committed to iron and steel production, and insisted that rearrangement must be possible. Subsequently, it specified that in the key-point iron and steel areas, it would be sufficient to devote 50 per cent of all manpower to iron and steel production. In other areas, 20 per cent would suffice.[79] This was the first attempt to put a ceiling on manpower that could be channelled into iron and steel production.[80]

As time wore on, even deep ploughing and soil improvement gave way to the imperatives of autumn harvest, a more direct concern as it affected the immediate well-being of the population. By the first part of November, the proposed 4 million 'professional armies' for deep ploughing and soil improvement were slashed to 2 million. Even workers in the iron and steel front were beginning to be transferred to autumn harvest.[81]

The 1 November 'Breakthrough'

Up to the end of October, iron and steel production was progressing extremely slowly, despite the continuous efforts of the PPC to exhort, cajole, and pressure. Only 21,100 tons of pig iron were produced by the end of September and during October, 59,865 more tons.[82] However, the PPC claimed that in the twenty-four hours of 1 November, a record-breaking 870,000 tons of pig iron was produced, greatly exceeding the entire 1958 target of 500,000 to 600,000 tons. In one day, more than 7 million people, including peasants, workers, cadres, officers and men of the People's Liberation Army, and students, and nearly all the secretaries and members of the local communist party committees participated, using more than 100,000 blast furnaces, adobe furnaces, brick kilns, cement kilns, and the like. Tao Zhu and Chen Yu personally directed this colossal undertaking. So, the PPC claimed that the success of 1 November was a breakthrough because it demonstrated that the 'laws' of iron production had been mastered by the broad masses. It was the victory of the indigenous and 'poor' method.[83]

---

[79] *NFRB*, 16 October 1958.   [80] *NFRB*, 22 October 1958.   [81] *RMRB*, 13 November 1958.
[82] For the precarious situation in iron and steel production in September and October in Guangdong, see *NBCK*, 18 October 1958, 30–5. For the situation in other provinces, see ibid. 3–30.
[83] *RMRB*, 4 November 1958; *SCMP*, no. 1890, 23–4.

In one day, an all-out effort had allegedly brought about a production bonanza that exceeded the entire year's target for pig iron. This contrasted sharply with the slow and tortuous development in the previous months, despite repeated prodding by the PPC. Apparently, the reported achievement was a hoax. There was no attempt at verification, but this was besides the point. When other more urgent tasks now required attention, it was simply absurd to tie up too much manpower and resources in the iron and steel campaign. A final big push could dispose of the year's pig iron quota, giving the appearance that the assigned task had been fulfilled, and completed with the fanfare of the indispensable 'mass' line. Other provinces had done the same—Shanxi was said to have over-fulfilled its yearly pig iron target by producing 690,000 tons on 31 October; allegedly, Henan had maintained its national champion's status by producing more than 3m. tons of pig iron between 29–31 October[84]—and the centre had embraced these figures without questioning. Guangdong was merely following the new rules of the game. In fact, a provincial directive issued on 2 November finally redefined autumn harvest as the central task for all rural areas.[85] The province quickly trimmed and removed the iron and steel contingent, and in early November, 10 millions of manpower were said to have been transferred back to autumn harvest.[86]

The Battle for Steel

On the other hand, steel production, which was the task of Guangzhou and some municipalities, had yet to be tackled, but they did not experiment with smelting steel by the indigenous method and did not mobilize a mass movement until October. Many special districts and counties had adopted the two primitive furnace models introduced by the MM at Shangcheng, Henan in October. The Huiyang Prefectoral Party Committee sent an observation team to the Shangcheng national conference and upon its return, had published pamphlets on the method of smelting steel using the indigenous method. A three-day course was held to train ninety technicians in the application of this 'advanced experience'.

The women of Tongping district were said to have perfected the technique of smelting steel with their cooking stoves, producing several ounces of steel per heat. Dismantled bicycles and waste wood were turned into manual and pedal-powered bellows.[87] Not surprisingly, the PPC endorsed and encouraged these practices, but this was less a matter of conviction than a conscious attempt to play the game, once the tacit rules were made known. In any event, the PPC claimed that a new production record had been reached in steel production on 20 November.[88] This one-day wonder was so dramatic that it almost fulfilled the year's target for steel, in the same way the 1 November record had done for pig iron production. It satisfied the

---

[84] *RMRB*, 2 November 1958; *SCMP*, no. 1890, 24. [85] *NFRB*, 2 November 1958.
[86] Ibid.; *RMRB*, 11 November 1958. [87] *NFRB*, 6 and 9 December 1958.
[88] *NFRB*, 6 December 1958.

PPC's claim that the 1958 iron and steel targets, which had given it so much trouble for months, were simply resolved in two record-breaking days.

Reorganization, Consolidation, and the Raising of Standards

As mentioned, on 25 November the CC introduced the new policy of 'Reorganization, Consolidation, and the Raising of Standards' and a 'five-fix' system to implement it. In Guangdong, these measures were dutifully enforced, as some 'better' furnaces were grouped together to form base areas, and furnaces that were far away from sources of raw materials, fuels, or transportation facilities were simply abandoned. This reversed the former policy of 'the more indigenous, the better'.

However, this 'reorganization' process was carried out very slowly. As there was general demoralization after the retreat policies were announced, some argued that the '*xiaotuqun*' were only a temporary expedient and nothing could be done to improve them. Some wanted to wait until the next year and then mobilize a 'sudden assault' lasting for two to three months, just like what was done in 1958. Others contended that since all the targets were fulfilled, there was no need to carry on any further. Subsequently, the iron and steel 'armies' were disbanded. Many were only too glad to use the reorganization policy to abandon the indigenous furnaces altogether.

On the other hand, the PPC criticized some localities for 'fixing' too many points, showing that some cadres were still wary about the policy change. Therefore, the PPC was forced to specify that points should only be 'fixed' at places with ores, fuel, and transportation facilities. In rural areas with neither iron nor coal, the policy was 'resolute contraction and elevation'. An explicit order was issued for cadres not to force things.[89]

Preparations for 1959

Meanwhile, however, another central demand had to be dealt with. The centre called for consolidation and the raising of standards, but the 1959 target for iron and steel handed down was another 100 per cent hike over the alleged output in 1958. So far, the centre seemed to have turned a blind eye to the quality of iron and steel products as long as the targets were claimed to have been over-fulfilled; however, from now on, the new quality standard was set higher. Given the meagre resources and its limited technological capabilities to build new modern furnaces, the PPC had no choice but to fall back on the past practice by concluding (at a meeting on 4 December) that the bulk of the iron and steel production ultimately had to be dependent on the *xiaotuqun*. Therefore, it called for the tightening of the reorganization procedure to reduce the work force and to raise efficiency and quality. It was unthinkable, it maintained, to simply repeat what was done in 1958.

---

[89] *NFRB*, 6 December 1958.

So the PPC ordered the counties to convene industrial meetings and to plan for work in 1959. The prefectural and the county party secretaries were ordered to divide their attention equally between industry and agriculture whereas the first secretaries were to be in charge of both. Industrial departments or bureaux containing metallurgy, fuel, machinery, general industrial communication and political sections were to be established by the county party committees and the county people's council.

In the communes, one party secretary and one deputy commune director were to be assigned to industrial work. In addition, rearrangement of the rural work force would ensure that 25 per cent of it was to be devoted to industrial work permanently, so that the extensive waste of labour resulting from the frequent reorganization of labour in 1958 could be avoided.[90]

This was the final attempt at dealing with the iron and steel campaign in 1958. The emphasis was on the raising of efficiency and by reducing manpower directly involved in production. A second way was to strengthen the organizational resources by putting more functionaries directly in charge of production. Without the necessary resources, these things were what the PPC could resort to.

The Final Outcome

On 19 December the MM claimed that national steel output was 10.73m. tons, a 100 per cent increase over the 1957 production. At the end of the year, steel production was expected to soar to 11m. tons, and it was anticipated that all provinces and key enterprises would fulfil or over-fulfil the state target across the board, scoring 'an all-round victory'.[91] In Guangdong, the steel target was not completed until 25 December. According to reports, 204,022 tons of steel were produced (78 times more than the 1957 production), exceeding the 0.2m. ton target assigned by the state by 0.2 per cent. Of this, 'foreign' (i.e. good quality) steel was 40,069 tons (14 times more than the 1957 production). Good quality pig iron reached 419,929 tons, 0.5 per cent over the state target of 400,000 tons. In addition, there were 631,667 tons of low-quality pig iron. According to one account, in 1958, 43 iron and steel factories, 630 modern blast furnaces, 293 steel converters, more than 70,000 small indigenous blast furnaces, and more than 120,000 small steel furnaces were built.[92] However, there was virtually no rolled-steel produced, and a widespread shortage of metals began to appear in the winter of 1958/9 to the extent that even small items of houseware, nails, and iron wire were in short supply. The 150,000 tons of indigenous steel were probably unusable, because by early 1959, the PPC still could not decide what to do with it.[93] Most likely, it was closer to iron ore than refined metal. Further verifications showed that good-quality pig iron and indigenous iron were only half and a third, respectively, of the amount previously

[90] Ibid.   [91] *RMRB*, 22 December 1958.
[92] *Dangdai Guangdong*, 2, 1997, 63.   [93] *NFRB*, 4 February 1959.

reported—a tacit admission that plans were unfulfilled. Moreover, the product was of extremely low quality and this was reflected by a new order to raise the quality standard of 1959 more than a dozen times more than 1958.[94]

After much self-congratulatory comparisons with the past, the PPC revealed that 1.1m. people, or approximately 6.9 per cent of the total labour force of 16m. were now employed permanently for iron and steel production alone.[95] Regarding iron and steel bases, it was reported that 430 odd had now been fixed. Except a few large ones that were now administered by the province and the special districts, nearly 100 of these bases were put under the jurisdiction of the counties, and more than 300 were under the communes. It was said that the consolidation and construction work of these bases were now being carried out in earnest. Except for the existing small blast furnaces that were under 'elevation', a group of new blast furnaces—more than 90 with a capacity of 0.8 cu. m, and 100 with a capacity of 0.23 cu. m—was now being built. This belies the fact that thousands upon thousands of indigenous (or 'backyard') furnaces had been wiped out, a far cry from the policy of 'the more indigenous, the better' pushed through by the PPC only two months before. It was also doubtful if the new blast furnaces could ever be constructed. In February 1959, a further reduction of the number of these bases (to 300) was ordered. According to the PPC, the bases that were far away from raw materials, fuel and, communication facilities were to be 'resolutely eliminated'.[96] In fact, most of the furnaces would have been eliminated if this criterion were observed. In any case, this brought the *xiaotuqun* movement of 1958 to an end.

Overall, Guangdong simply did not have the preconditions and the wherewithal to implement the ambitious and contradictory industrialization policies prescribed by Mao and the centre. It welcomed the prospect of industrialization but, without the massive support from the centre, it showed little interest at the beginning, especially when the Leap in industry merely meant the raising of production and further economizing. Nevertheless, as political pressure mounted, the PPC, under the fervent leadership of Tao Zhu, strove to implement the numerous central initiatives one by one, even though they were absurd, unattainable, and often took no account of the capabilities of the province. The situation was aggravated when central policy shifted from the ambitious initial plans to develop rural small industrialization to the total obsession with iron and steel production. Although Guangdong was not endowed with natural resources for developing heavy industry, it threw itself into the campaigns with abandon.

In addition, in the absence of resources commensurate with the tasks at hand, the PPC had little alternative but to mobilize its organizational capability to the fullest. Inevitably, this led to goal displacement—the PPC turned to concentrate on appearance rather than on the content of goal fulfilment. Mass movements were unleashed for their own sake, as they were a pompous display that satisfied Mao and the centre's penchant for the loud, large, and the showy. The means seem to have overshadowed the ends.

[94] *NFRB*, 4 February 1959.   [95] *NFRB*, 22 October 1958.   [96] *NFRB*, 4 February 1959.

Even policy instruments which were originally designed to ensure the PPC's direct control over the grass roots by bypassing the bureaucracy, such as the Great Inspection Campaigns, were reduced to mere 'formalism'. Yet, in the end, choices had to be made, and the agricultural labour which had been siphoned off to the smelting of useless iron and steel had to be returned to the agricultural front. The PPC attempted to change its course, but its efforts were hampered by its previous commitment to the iron and steel campaign.

On the other hand, the behaviour of the provincial leadership created tremendous pressure on its subordinates. Although there was no lack of zealots who responded earnestly to the provincial decisions and policies, many critics and dissenters were not won over by the development strategy of the GLF. When pressed, all these cadres played the game by devising elaborate efforts and procedures. Yet, ultimately, no amount of exhortation and mobilization could have prevented the total collapse of the industrial development policies in 1958. The tremendous energies and resources expended on these efforts were largely wasted.

7

Conclusion: Policy-making in a Mao-dominated System

The most striking feature of the policy process in 1958 was a dominant Mao bent on exerting his power and consummating his personal vision. With supreme confidence, he took personal charge of running the economy by bullying all his detractors into submission. Mao was firmly committed to the Leap strategy of an all-out effort requiring the mobilization and participation of virtually every Chinese citizen. Since he had invested tremendously of his personal political capital in the Leap campaign, he was anxious to achieve results. Timetables for production increases were constantly advanced, and production tasks multiplied. Numerous policy instruments ranging from exhortation to coercion were approved by Mao and hurled at the general population. All these are classic examples of hyperactivity, over-instrumenting and over-targeting.[1]

The implementers, such as the MA, the MM, and Guangdong were under tremendous pressure to achieve spectacular results in a short period of time. They too may have been caught up in the euphoria but at any rate all had no choice but to be compliant with Mao's vision. Yet, without physical resources commensurate with the tasks at hand, mass mobilization and exhortation were the only option, and increasingly, mass mobilization became the only means toward the goal of output maximization, and then ultimately became an end in itself. As the prospect of achieving the unattainable goals became more remote, the implementers became more obsessed with following rules and procedures that would enable them to ward off pressure and to evade responsibility and possible punishment. This explains the very elaborate and grandiose mass mobilization campaigns and techniques that were used by the ministries and Guangdong, even though they must have been aware of their futility. Because of such strong advocacy by the central leaders, critical information and criticisms were unwelcome, or viewed as signs of weakness or opposition to innovation, particularly at a time when the bureaucracy was suspected of undue caution and conservatism. Subordinates were obliged to supply information that would reinforce or conform to Leap policies, and suppress information that challenged the centre's expectations. For these reasons, the implementers stuck knowingly to unworkable policies. In this regard, even though some GLF policies were not implausible on the surface, the way they were implemented and piled onto one another made successful outcomes impossible. The distance between ideals and

[1] For detailed discussion of these concepts, see Hogwood and Peters, *Pathology*, 44, 149, 167–8.

reality has been observed clearly in our discussion of the policy implementation process. We will summarize these themes further in the following.

The Central Decision Process

The Dominant Mao

While this book focuses primarily on 1958, the consideration of central decision-making also covers the period of *fanmaojin* up to the Third Plenum of September/October 1957 during which Mao still sought to consult and cooperate with his colleagues. At that time he did not seek to prevail upon his subordinates on *every* issue. From the end of the Third Plenum onward, however, his supreme confidence over the GLF led to a sharp break in the policy process. Impatient with slow economic progress and even more so with the alleged conservatism of planners, he pushed his personal views relentlessly, to the extent that he thought he could dispense with the planners altogether and run the economy himself. His grand millennial vision of a dramatic economic breakthrough shaped most GLF policies, and his interventions were decisive. An extremely activist Mao got every policy he wanted, and his dominance reached a zenith in 1958. Like other charismatic leaders, Mao also showed a preference for flair, élan, improvization, 'showcasing', and direct appeals to the enthusiasm and ideological commitment of the masses.[2] As Mao improvised, his every hunch, intuition, and whim was adopted and accepted as central policy. All of the most egregious policy blunders of the GLF were masterminded by Mao: the destruction of the planning system, the extreme decentralization measures, the communes, the 'three-three' system, and the iron and steel campaign. Yet, even the most far-fetched policy, such as the campaign to double steel production in the last third of 1958, were given the full mobilization treatment.

Mao's ability to dominate the decision-making process was phenomenal, and we have explored in detail how he did it. As we have argued, his charisma, unshakeable confidence, and forceful personality were crucial. Yet, like all politicians who try to keep on top, he also employed a range of strategic and tactical manœuvres to maintain his supremacy, particularly in 1958. His foremost asset was his position as the regime's chief ideological authority who could define the class configuration and fundamental contradictions, and set the current task and goal for the nation. He used this skilfully in 1958, although his many definitions and redefinitions of 'the principal contradiction', designed to bolster his current obsession, was inconsistent—at times it was equated to the struggle between the bourgeoisie and the proletariat, at times to high-speed development, and at times to 'steel as the key link'. He branded *fanmaojin* as a kind of anti-Marxist 'rightist conservatism' and an error in principle, and put forward the theory of permanent revolution to justify radical changes. A no-less potent weapon was his revival of the

---

[2] In this respect Mao is typical of charismatic leaders, see Caiden and Wildavsky, *Planning and Budgeting in Poor Countries*, 196.

cult of personality so that his pronouncements must always be obeyed.[3] Another important source of Mao's power was his direct control of the media starting in 1957, achieved by the insertion of loyal Maoists into key positions and his own contribution of articles to promote Leap policies in such publications as the *RMRB* and *Hongqi*.

Mao utilized his position as Party Chairman to control such things as the timing and agenda of meetings, the drafting of policy documents, the handing out of rewards and punishments, etc., in order to assert himself. He also vetted speeches and policy documents of such meetings. He often handpicked participants at meetings, and often sprung surprises that caught his colleagues off-guard, or left them with little room to manœuvre. He would also invoke the Leninist principle of democratic centralism, of 'unifying thinking and action', and raise the spectre of a split in the Party to force a consensus behind him. Since as Chairman he always had the final say in policy matters, he could and did use as leverage ambiguity (often deliberate) and refusal to cooperate. His deliberate absence from central meetings meant that his lieutenants had to report to him the proceedings which he could then either approve or reject. When he declared a meeting to be a rectification meeting, it meant that all must engage in criticism and self-criticism to 'unify thinking' under his Thought. In time, Mao himself became the Party Centre, as he often issued personal directives in the name of the Centre without consulting the Politburo. In 1958, when he decided to take matters into his own hands by rejecting the planners, he cultivated his own 'inner court' of advisers and supporters among the central and regional leaders, among them the directors of the Cooperative Regions. Around his person, he gathered a coterie of aides, secretaries, and followers to act as his eyes and ears, and to flesh out his ideas on the Leap. Even his personality traits, such as anger and temper tantrums, were deliberately used for maximum effect to intimidate and to disarm. In these many ways, Mao towered above his colleagues, turning himself into their overlord and chief commander.

Any of the above tactics alone would not have ensured Mao's predominance, but a combination of them made Mao almost invincible. Planners who were opposed to *maojin* were totally humiliated, and forced to make an extraordinary turnaround and to rally around the Leap policies. The supra-ministerial agencies such as the SPC, the SEC, and the State Capital Construction Commission under the planners were all immobilized. Most central leaders, including alleged moderates and pragmatics, such as Liu Shaoqi, Zhou Enlai, and more independent minds who had disagreed with Mao openly in the past, such as Chen Yun and Deng Zihui, showed strong support for Leap policies in 1958. Mao's ability to prevail upon his colleagues and turn them against their own wills and better judgement to follow him was impressive. Other more opportunistic lieutenants, such as Tan Zhenlin, Ke Qingshe, Liao Luyan, Wang Heshou, and Tao

---

[3] Mao clearly viewed the cult of personality as an instrument of power. Edgar Snow, *The Long Revolution* (New York: Vintage Books, 1971), 70, 169–70, 205; *Mao Wengao*, xiii. 164, 174, 176.

Zhu added fuel to the fire of Mao's imagination. Over-optimism and collective wishful thinking overcame rational deliberations. By 1958, decision-making at the centre had become a ritualized group approval of Mao's ideas, predilections, and policies.

The Improvisational Mao

Mao might have dominated his colleagues, but consistent with his approach of improvization and spontaneity, he had no blueprint for the Leap, just general ideas about how to run the economy. Hence, decision-making became a slipshod and haphazard affair where hunches, impulses, improvisations, and even whims became policy decisions. Everything was touch-and-go, and there was little or no consideration of alternatives. When the planners and their carefully and laboriously drawn-up plans were jettisoned, Mao fell back on past methods and experiences deemed successful in the 'revolutionary wars', such as mass mobilization campaigns, organization of labour along military lines, shock attacks, etc., and applied them indiscriminately to the most disparate situations, in both industry and agricultural production.

Mao was so over-confident about Leap policies that decisions were made as if all values could be maximized at once, and doubts regarding these policies were branded ideological errors or 'rightist conservatism'. Mao's opinions expressed during interviews with reporters could, and were intended to, unleash mass movements.[4] His injunctions at the end of September 1958, for industrial enterprises to run mass movements is a good example. Similarly, his seemingly off-hand remark 'People's communes are good!' was designed to launch the commune movement throughout the country even before the Politburo had a chance to discuss the issue, let alone make official decisions.

Mao's over-confidence also encouraged braggadocio. Like the sorcerer's apprentice, Mao's colleagues rushed in to heap on the pile their own personal goals and objectives.[5] Decision-making had become more personal and informal so that individual Politburo leaders were more and more turning their personal views into policies. This was done by giving instructions during the numerous inspection tours they took throughout the country. These were the 'big shots' Mao referred to when he tried to assign responsibility for the GLF at the Lushan Plenum of July 1959 (see pp. 156–7).

Consequently, one of the most striking features of Chinese policy-making in 1958 was the numerous, diffuse, inconsistent and contradictory goals Mao and the

---

[4] In 1959, Mao tried to absolve himself from the responsibility for initiating the commune movement throughout the country by blaming the reporters. In a rather contradictory section of his Lushan speech he said, 'I do not claim to have invented the people's communes, only to have proposed them. The Beidaihe Resolution was drafted according to my suggestions. At that time, it was as though I had found a treasure in the regulations of the Cha-ya-shan [commune]. When I was in Shangdong a reporter asked me: "Are the people's communes good?" I said: "They are good", and he published it in a newspaper. There was a spot of petty-bourgeois fanaticism there, too. In future reporters should be kept away.' Schram (ed.), *Mao Tse-tung Unrehearsed*, 145; *Mao Weikan*, xiB. 197.   [5] Bardach, *Implementation Game*, 85–90.

leadership had set for themselves, and the extremely short time limit allowed for their attainment. Countless new objectives were heaped upon old ones as new goals were continually defined throughout 1958. The profusion of extreme goals was epitomized by the slogans of 'simultaneous development' and *duohao kuaisheng*. Mao was bent on pushing development in all sectors and on all fronts, be it in agriculture, industry, commerce, finance, education, social welfare, or the military and militia. He was also determined to maximize all values at once by striving concurrently for speed, quantity, quality, and economy. Consequently, he avoided completely the setting of priorities. In this situation, intervention by other Politburo leaders was legitimate, even in areas in which they had had no previous involvement. So Zhu De discoursed on both agricultural and industrial policies, and argued for the acceleration of the NPAD. Deng Xiaoping spoke freely on the necessity for a 'revolution' in farming methods, the communes, the future of communist society, and for his pet project of establishing urban communes. Liu Shaoqi toured the country praising and promoting indigenous methods in smelting iron and steel. The important fact is that no matter how casually these remarks or instructions were made, they were then transmitted as authoritative and binding decisions to be implemented.

This behaviour by the Chinese leaders gave rise to severe goal conflict.[6] Implementers were overloaded with a multiple of conflicting goals that could not be attained with available resources, or attainable only at excessive cost. Consequently, these profuse goals were seldom pursued to their logical conclusion. Since they were conflicting and contradictory, they shifted continuously, depending on how the 'current task' was defined. Some goals were pursued vigorously only to be aborted halfway in favour of others. For instance, the much-heralded rural industrialization campaign to serve agriculture in Guangdong gave way to the iron and steel campaign even before getting off the ground. Similarly, the ambitious rural mechanization campaign soon succumbed to the campaign to reform existing farm tools by the uniform introduction of ball-bearings and cable-drawn ploughs, and then to the all-important iron and steel campaign. Sympathizers with the GLF who argue that its principles are 'not irrational' overlook this and assume a consistency of goals. In fact, the only consistent goal of the leadership was output maximization, although the leadership insisted until the end that equal attention be paid to quality, efficiency, and economy.

Despite the waste of resources, most of the goals set by the leadership went unfulfilled. For instance, despite the manifest goal of giving more attention to agriculture (the 'walking on two legs' strategy), the Stalinist preoccupation with heavy industrial production was undiminished, and normal agricultural activities were seriously hampered by the diversion of manpower and resources to the iron and steel campaign.

In this regard, the attempt to explain the origins of the GLF by bureaucratic politics is wide of the mark. To make such a case, one must demonstrate that *policy formulation at the centre* was an outcome of competition, bargaining, conflict, and

---

[6] For the notion of goal conflict, see Hogwood and Peters, *Pathology*, 22–8.

'pulling and hauling' among competing bureaucratic actors driven by their concerns with the bureaucratic interests of the institutions they represented, not simply the existence of bureaucratic perspectives and rivalry.[7] In fact, in 1958, institutional and organizational interests were all subordinated to Mao's single-minded drive for production maximization. There were no interest groups or factions that could have an impact on policy-making. The bureaucracy might be tempted by the promise of larger budgets at the beginning of the Leap, but soon had to succumb to the irrational policies of the centre, and its ever-increasing demands for output maximization and economizing. Furthermore, the entire Leap enterprise, with its emphasis on mass mobilization, spontaneity, improvisation, destruction of routine, rules and regulations, was profoundly antithetical to bureaucratic preferences for routinization and stabilization. Granted that ultimately Mao and his lieutenants fell back on the bureaucracy to implement Leap policies, the resultant administrative process was radically different from previously more 'bureaucratic' periods. Moreover, scholars in bureaucratic politics had pointed out that bureau heads are not always champions of the bureaucracies they represent, and our studies of the MA and the MM are consistent with this view. One may object that our consideration of the Leap from 1955 to 1958 is limited, and that Mao's dominance was only ephemeral, but research by Teiwes and Sun has demonstrated convincingly the centrality of Mao's absolute power from the 1950s to 1976. During the catastrophic years of the early 1960s, Mao was willing to let his colleagues pick up the pieces. No longer upfront as he was during the Leap, he nevertheless reserved the right to have the final word, striking back if he wanted to, and occupying centre stage during the 'Cultural Revolution'.[8] Indeed, the use of 'bureaucratic politics' to explain policy formulation in other periods or other issues (such as foreign policy) in Mao's China cannot be precluded, but in view of our exploration of the origins and conduct of the GLF, it is at best secondary, or at worst, irrelevant.[9] Our discussion of the MA and the MM further illustrates this point.

Two Policy Areas

Notwithstanding decentralization, the centre's supervision and direction of industrial development actually tightened, and similarly, a firmer grip was extended to agricultural units, which traditionally had a great deal more discretion in how to go about production. One hallmark of policies in both sectors is uniformity, as some general notions were regarded as applicable to all. In 1958, the centre attempted to control and transform agricultural production directly, although it had explicitly

[7] For the classic statements on 'bureaucratic politics' see Graham Allison, *Essence of Decision: Explaining the Cuban Missile Crisis* (Boston: Little, Brown, 1971).

[8] As MacFarquhar has pointed out, even when Mao was not involved in the day-to-day business of governing during the early 1960s, he was always in overall charge. MacFarquhar, *Origins*, iii. 468.

[9] This view is fully collaborated by Teiwes and Sun, *China's Road to Disaster*. One can add that since the assumptions of the bureaucratic politics model are based on the working of semi-autonomous actors in federal systems of governments like the US, it has relatively less utility when applied to more unitary political systems.

avoided doing so in the past. The ever-increasing agricultural targets were imposed on agricultural cooperatives, along with numerous centrally directed campaigns, rural activities, and technological policies such as irrigation and water conservancy, deep ploughing and soil improvement, tool reform, the accumulation of manure, the elimination of the four pests, and above all, the iron and steel campaign that was meant to serve heavy industry. There was also the fatal decision to cut back total farmland by one-third to implement the 'three-three' system. Most of these schemes were ill-conceived, but what was worse, they were required to be implemented uniformly throughout the country, regardless of regional diversity.

The need to run these campaigns gave rise to the notion that agricultural units should and could be run with the same organization and discipline as the factories. Attempts to create a division of labour in the collectives (such as the creation of specialized labour armies) reflected this kind of thinking, which also explains the general enthusiasm of top leaders for the introduction of the communes. In all, the centre, more than ever, attempted to centralize the direction of agricultural production by imposing excessive control and interference, and by the setting of targets for all kinds of rural activities irrespective of their appropriateness.

The same pattern of policy-making was applied to industrial development which, to some extent, was more amenable to uniformity. In industry, a few Politburo leaders monopolized decision-making, and depended mostly on their intuition to churn out a series of decisions and policies, virtually at the snap of a finger. There were no formal groups which were able to influence industrial policies. In fact, over-dominance by the centre had nullified the previous intention of expanding the decision power of the enterprises.

In 1958, industrial enterprises were saddled with many unfulfillable targets. Rules and regulations were hastily obliterated in the belief that this would, first and foremost, spur production, and concern for workplace democracy was decidedly only derivative. Large enterprises were urged to become self-sufficient and to create new facilities to supply their own raw materials. Since the method of mass movement and mobilization was deemed mandatory, the most primitive methods and simplistic solutions were encouraged as something that accorded with the nature and aspirations of the masses, as was the denigration of technical expertise and specialization. This disrupted normal production, and magnified a preoccupation with quantity at the expense of quality and economy. It is not without reason that these practices were criticized as backward 'guerrilla habits' and 'rural work style'.

The Ministry of Agriculture and the Ministry of Metallurgy During the High Leap

A Mao-dominated central decision-making system, with an emphasis on improvisation and an anti-bureaucratic slant, constituted the policy environment and context in which the MA and the MM had to implement central policies. Both ministries were led by veteran revolutionaries, but the MA had been radicalized by the experience of collectivization between 1955 and 1957, and was less 'bureaucratized' than the MM, which was a fledgling professional organization containing a large contingent of experts, engineers, and professionals. The MM's Soviet ties and organization became a stigma. Therefore, to switch into the GLF mode, the MM re-invented itself by such means as the 'two-antis' campaign and the advocacy of indigenous methods. Eventually, it was transformed into an engine for mass mobilization in pursuit of radical and self-defeating policies. Both ministries, which had been relatively low on the totem pole of central power, were thrust into the limelight in 1958 less because of their own efforts and more because their spheres of responsibility coincided with Mao's priorities. As their superiors among the planners were repeatedly humiliated, and as Mao's intentions were clarified, ministers Liao Luyan and Wang Heshou had no choice but to jump onto the GLF bandwagon, and turned into staunch supporters of the Leap. As they escaped the wrath of Mao and were coopted by him, they pandered to the wishes of the Chairman even more. In late 1957 these ministers may have entertained the idea that the Leap might serve their bureaucratic interests, but as time wore on, it had turned instead into an infinite central demand for both raising production and economizing which quickly reached irrational proportions.

Despite decentralization, both of these ministries expanded their role, influence, and responsibility throughout 1958 according to the inflated demands of the Leap. Under Liao, the MA stole the limelight by taking on many extra duties and functions, and was rewarded accordingly. For instance, the MA took over most of the responsibilities of the defunct Ministry of Water Conservancy, and played a major role in directing the irrigation and water conservancy campaign. It also overshadowed the State Statistics Bureau and began to collect agricultural statistics on its own. On this basis it published several communiqués on agricultural production, closely identified itself with the most exaggerated reports of achievements in 1958, and summed up the year by claiming to speak for the development of agriculture. The MM, despite the decentralization measures of 1957–8, continued to play a pre-eminent role in directing the iron and steel campaign, convening decision-making conferences, initiating campaigns, making policies, issuing orders, and making demands over its subordinate units, including the provincial authorities.

Another new function of these ministries was to coordinate central policies. One common way to do this was the convening of national conferences with representatives from the provinces, but most of these conferences were merely used to announce new central initiatives, policies, directives, and demands, and little coordination actually took place. It was as if, in the zeal to promote the multiple and shifting goals emanating from the centre, the MA seldom considered their implementability in any way.

Policy Instruments

Yet, despite their differences, the ultimate choice of policy instruments by the two ministries was similar—mass mobilization with a heavy dose of exhortation, combined with such means as 'blooming and contending', the 'four bigs', 'appraisal-through-comparison', the 'two-anti' campaigns, the 'changing of people's thinking', and so on. What is remarkable about this is that principles and methods deemed suitable for industrial production were regarded as appropriate for agricultural pursuits, and vice versa, as if they were infinitely transferable. For instance, agricultural experimental plots, small-scale production, and indigenous methods were applied to the iron and steel campaign, and strict planning and control were applied over agricultural activities including the setting of compulsory targets, the acreage sown of various crops, tool reform, technical reform and technology transfer. In addition, there was a desire to subject agricultural activities to the discipline, uniformity, and regimentation more characteristic of industrial production. The communes and the notion of the 'three -ize' were aspirations toward this direction. Hence, instead of fostering spontaneity, the GLF campaigns imposed even more centralization and uniformity.

Bureaucratic Politics?

More importantly, neither the MM nor the MA were able, or even attempted, to articulate and defend their institutional interests. Decision-making became a relatively simple process during the GLF in the sense that it did not involve significant, complex, and protracted bargaining by bureaucratic actors. It was not the outcome of 'log-rolling', competition, or bargaining, and factional struggle was not involved. The hyperactivity of the ministries was motivated more by a high-pressure political climate involving ideology, optimism, and anti-conservatism, and less by any perceived bureaucratic interests. In 1958, it was more important for the MA and the MM to pander to the preferences of Mao, than to protect the interests of their constituencies. In fact, both of these ministries espoused and implemented many policies that were either detrimental to the institutional interests of their own organizations or simply unworkable.[10] For instance, the MA was reluctant to divert manpower away from the iron and steel campaign back to agricultural production even when a crisis was imminent. The MM had reinvented itself in order to promote mass mobilization and 'indigenous' methods relentlessly in its enterprises and in the entire country without questioning their efficacy. Despite its continuing prominence, the MM did not articulate or defend any institutional or narrow interests or advantages. Its policy goals were always in accord with the stated intentions and preferences of the top leadership. Most of the ministry's effort was expended to ensure the implementation of central desires and policies. In many ways, these ministries were mainly docile tools of the centre, with orientation and loyalty squarely directed toward the centre. Furthermore, there was no perceptible

---

[10] This is consistent with Lucian Pye's insight about the weak articulation of institutional interests, and why such organizations as the Chinese Air Force and the municipality of Shanghai vouched for radical, anti-bureaucratic, anti-industrial positions. See his *The Dynamics of Chinese Politics* (Cambridge: Oelgeschlager, Gunn Hain, 1981), 15, 86, 119–20.

competition between these bureaucratic actors, let alone any bargaining, and 'pulling and hauling'. As a result, the 'bureaucratic politics' model is irrelevant for our analysis. To a large extent, 'getting along' seemed to be more important in that period than getting anything right.

Guangdong and the High Leap

In 1958, Guangdong province and its leadership played complex roles in the policy process, but ultimately became the willing pawn of Mao's crusade. When the top national leaders were enfeebled, the provincial leaders knew that they too had little choice but to toe the line. A 'higher' loyalty to the ultra-dominant Mao became paramount compared to their loyalty to the interests of their constituencies. As pressure mounted, the haughty and arbitrary style of decision-making at the centre came to be repeated at the provincial level, and much energy was expended in maintaining a make-believe world of leaping production.

During 1958, Tao Zhu and some provincial authorities participated in most of the important central decision-making forums, but given tremendous pressure for unanimity and conformity, they were very wary of overstepping their limits and falling into the abyss of 'rightist conservatism'. Members of the PPC, such as Chen Yu and Wen Minsheng, became staunch supporters of the Leap, and Tao Zhu and Zhao Ziyang distinguished themselves as the most zealous in substantiating and promoting Mao's ideas.[11]

In implementing central policies, Tao and the PPC churned out decisions and policies of their own according to central requirements as if by reflex action, paying little or no attention to objective constraints. In 1958, Guangdong followed obsequiously every initiative and directive from the centre, including every hunch and utterance made by Mao and other central decision-makers. This was reflected in the close affinity between the remarks made by Mao and the wording of the provincial directives and decisions. Numerous conferences were held to synchronize with central decision-making forums to operationalize and implement central decisions. Although many central directives were extremely demanding and disruptive, and although the provincial authorities were already reeling from the numerous demands already made, no stone was left unturned in Guangdong to promote the Leap.

The agricultural leap took hold early, and it underwent a progressive radicalization throughout 1958. This in turn was propelled by rising expectations and mutual reinforcement created by even more central initiatives and requirements, and the pressure to compete with the other provinces. The dynamics of the GLF must be understood in the context of this complex interaction between the centre and the provinces. The industrialization and iron and steel campaigns are good examples of Guangdong's steadfastness in sticking to central policies.

---

[11] This is consistent with Ezra Vogel's view that he was 'the more Maoist party bureaucrat'. See his *Canton Under Communism*, 300, 325.

Guangdong was under a great deal of pressure to excel in all agricultural fronts, and to implement many impossible tasks. The political survival of the leaders was at stake. Frequently, the performances of the provinces were compared with each other, leaving very little room for them to manœuvre. As political pressures mounted, the PPC strove to implement the numerous central initiatives to promote industrial development, although they were absurd, unattainable, and often unconcerned with the capabilities of the province. Guangdong simply did not have the infrastructure and resources to develop these industries, let alone on the scale and in the time limits prescribed by the centre. Yet it threw itself into these campaigns with total abandon, and was kept constantly on the run by the multiple and shifting goals emanating from the centre. As the decision-making time and lead time became shorter, decision-making turned into a very personalized and haphazard affair. Central policies, like the formation of the communes, were pushed down the throats of resisting peasants. Zhao Ziyang whipped up numerous policies for agriculture according to his pet ideas of reforming the farming system to boost production, and altering the alleged 'conservative' attitude of the peasants.

In dealing with the numerous and diffuse goals of the GLF, the hyperactive PPC set in motion many campaigns and utilized a whole range of policy instruments to galvanize the masses into action. Such techniques as the encouragement of competition, ideological education, the 'four bigs', the critique of 'rightist conservatism,' large-scale inspection tours, material rewards, the threat of discipline and dismissal, and so on, were employed repeatedly to elicit compliance, although their efficacy was questionable. More specifically, the gathering of 'activists' was seen to be an effective way to implement ambitious central targets, although it encouraged mendacity and opportunists. The critique of 'rightist conservatism' was probably the quickest and most effective means of stifling overt opposition to GLF programmes and policies, but its effect was transient. The free grain-supply system was a means to raise the incentive of the commune members, although the communes could not afford it.

The massive and highly publicized PPC inspection tours among the grass roots were ostentatious displays of the province's determination to enforce central policies, although they were largely ineffective. It seems that by throwing everything at the target, the provincial leaders expected that all goals would be achieved. The discussion of policy issues was often raised to the ideological level, so that many cadres were labelled 'rightist conservatives', and others were under the constant threat of replacement or dismissal. In addition, lacking resources commensurate with the tasks at hand, the PPC had little alternative but to mobilize its organizational capability to the fullest. In time, this led to goal displacement, and the PPC turned to concentrating on the form rather than the content of goal fulfilment. Mass movements were unleashed for their own sake, as pompous displays that satisfied the centre's penchant for the loud, the large, and the showy. The means seem to have completely overshadowed the ends. Witness, for example, the two separate days in November during which the mass mobilization of iron and steel production was said to have produced sufficiently huge quantities to fulfil the year's target at one stroke.

The provincial authorities blatantly invited misrepresentations, and in turn, these inflated and untrustworthy claims were accepted by the centre. This contravened other efforts by the centre to introduce a certain reliability in the reporting of achievements by their subordinates. However, at this point, as long as it could be demonstrated that mass movements had been unleashed, the centre was satisfied. Provincial authorities were not averse to playing the game, once the new rules were tacitly formed and understood.

Hence, a great deal of goal shift occurred, the initial goal of rural industrialization gave way midstream to the iron and steel campaign, and the PPC had the unenviable task of having to justify every about-face to their subordinates. There is no evidence that they attempted to use the discretionary powers inherent in any large organization to slow or stall the implementation of central programmes and policies. Yet, in the end, practical concerns such as agricultural production and harvesting could not be entirely ignored, and choices had to be made. The agricultural labour siphoned off to the smelting of useless iron and steel had to be returned to the agricultural front. The PPC attempted to change course, but its efforts were hampered by its prior commitment to the iron and steel campaign.

Moreover, the PPC also dictated the strategy for agriculture development by controlling the agenda, defining current tasks, and setting up rigid timetables to apply uniformly to the entire province, regardless of the diversities in agricultural production. Carried away by the euphoria, what occurred at the centre was being repeated at the provincial level. As the planners and technicians were pushed aside, provincial leadership assumed all economic planning itself. Yet, the 'planning' of the PPC was conducted by faulty analogies and simple arithmetic with no reference to the real world. Obsession with the 'farming revolution' led directly to several disastrous campaigns including ones for water conservancy, tool reform, cutting back of farmland for 1959, and deep ploughing and soil improvement. The tremendous amount of resources and energy lavished on them were wasted.

Furthermore, the PPC tightened its grip over its subordinates tremendously, bringing many new concerns under its control for the first time. Consequently, it found itself immersed in the day-to-day administration and implementation of policies, even to interfering directly with grass-roots units itself. Yet, paradoxically, the attempt to impose more control resulted in even less control. Although there was no lack of zealots who responded earnestly to the provincial policies, many critics and dissenters were not won over by the development strategy of the GLF. Between these two extremes was a range of behaviour that encompassed evasion, stalling, muddling along, 'buck passing', false reporting, and 'tokenism'. Moreover, there were probably attempts to wreck or discredit the GLF by taking it to ridiculous extremes. Many subordinates fed only the kind of information that conformed to the expectations of the PPC. The PPC had become a victim of its own delusions. Cadres in the industrial systems who were under the most intense pressure demonstrated clear resistance to unworkable policies. The rural cadres, on the other hand, lacked experience in running industrial campaigns. Agricultural and food production were their main concerns, and they were reluctant to divert their energies and resources to what appeared to be totally alien tasks. They also had to contend with peasant resistance to unpopular policies, especially the communes. When pressed, all these cadres either played the game by devising elaborate procedures or simply went through the motions. So, essentially, the dilemma faced by the sub-provincial units was the same as that of the provincial authorities.

Despite tremendous pressure from above, the fact remained that conflicting and unrealistic goals could not be implemented, leading to goal displacement. In turn this was aggravated by the PPC's own inclination toward ritualistic behaviour. Yet, ultimately, the total collapse of the industrial development policies in 1958 can be attributed to the overambitious goals and the objective constraints that no amount of exhortation and mobilization could overcome.

When it encountered problems, Guangdong was unwilling to address them or to decide, especially when central intentions on those issues were vague, or when the demands of centrally designated priority tasks clashed. At this juncture, Guangdong's hands were tied; either no decisions were made, or hackneyed solutions like the persistence in educating people's thinking and the application of the 'four bigs' were put forward. In effect, these solutions were non-decisions, as they did not require making hard choices or the finding of resolutions. However, by the end of 1958 when Mao appeared to have turned around, the provincial leaders did make some important adjustments (those that dealt with the communes were good examples), although they had to be consistent with the Chairman's wishes. In the end, despite the tremendous efforts expended on the various mobilization campaigns, the objective constraints reasserted themselves, and nullified most, if not all, the goals of the GLF in 1958.

Bibliography

Publications in Chinese

Chinese Journals and Newspapers
Bainianchao (The Hundred Years' Tide). Beijing.
Caizheng (Finance). Beijing.
Dangdai Guangdong (Contemporary Guangdong). Guangzhou.
Dangdai Zhongguoshi Yanjiu (Research on Contemporary Chinese History). Beijing.
Dang de Wenxian (Selected Documents of the Party). Beijing.
Dangshi Ziliao Zongkan (Collected Party History Materials). Beijing.
Dangshi Yanjiu Ziliao (Materials on Party History Research). Beijing.
Dangshi Tongxun (Party History Bulletins). Beijing.
Hebei Ribao (Hebei Daily). Shijiazhuang.
Hongqi (Red Flag). Beijing.
Jiaoxue yu Yanjiu (Teaching and Research). Beijing.
Jihua Jingji (Planned Economy). Beijing.
Jihua Yu Tongji (Planning and Statistics). Beijing.
Jingji Yanjiu (Economic Research). Beijing.
Mao Zedong Sixiang Yanjiu (Research on Mao Zedong Thought). Beijing.
Nanfang Ribao (The Southern Daily). Guangzhou.
Neibu Cankao (Internal Reference). Beijing.
Nongcun Gongzuo Tongxun (Rural Work Bulletin). Beijing.
Renmin Ribao (Peoples' Daily). Beijing.
Renmin Shouce (Peoples' Handbook). Beijing.
Shangyu (Upstream). Guangzhou.
Shishi Shouce (Handbook of Current Events). Beijing.
Xinhua Banyuekan (New China Semi-monthly). Beijing.
Xinhua Yuebao (New China Monthly). Beijing.
Yejin Bao (Metallurgical News). Beijing.
Zheng Ming (Contend). Hong Kong.
Zhengzhi Xuexi (Political Study). Beijing.
Zhonggong Dangshi Wenzhai Niankan (Annual Digest of CCP Party History). Beijing.
Zhonggong Dangshi Yanjiu (Research on the History of the Chinese Communist Party). Beijing.
Zhonggong Dangshi Ziliao (CCP History Materials). Beijing.
Zhongguo Nongbao (Chinese Agricultural Bulletin). Beijing.
Zhongguo Qingnian (Chinese Youth). Beijing.
Zhongguo Qingnian Bao (China Youth Daily). Beijing.

Translation Series
Current Background. American Consulate General, Hong Kong.
Chinese Law and Government. White Plains, New York.
Extracts from China Mainland Magazines. American Consulate General, Hong Kong.

Joint Publications Research Service. National Technical Information Service, Arlington, Virginia.

Survey of China Mainland Press. American Consulate General, Hong Kong.

Union Research Institute. Hong Kong.

Books, Monographs, and Documents in Chinese

Bai Fulin, Chen Shaochou, and Wang Zuokun. *Yidai Gongpu Liu Shaoqi* (A public servant of his generation, Liu Shaoqi). 2 vols. Changchun: Jilin renmin chubanshe, 1998.

Bin Zi. *Mao Zedong de Ganqing Shijie* (The emotional world of Mao Zedong). n.p.: Jilin renmin chubanshe, 1990.

Bo Yibo. *Bo Yibo Wenxuan, 1937–1992* (Selected works of Bo Yibo, 1937–1992). Beijing: Renmin chubanshe, 1992.

Bo Yibo. *Ruogan Zhongda Juece Yu Shijian de Huigu* (A review of certain major policies and events), i. Beijing: Zhonggong zhongyang dangxiao chubanshe, 1991, repr. 1997.

Bo Yibo. *Ruogan Zhongda Juece Yu Shijian de Huigu* (A review of certain major policies and events), ii. Beijing: Zhonggong zhongyang dangxiao chubanshe, 1993.

Cao Junjie. *Zhongguo Erqiao* (China's two Qiaos). Nanjing: Jiangsu renmin chubanshe, 1996.

Ceng Yingwang. *Zhongguo de Zong Guanjia Zhou Enlai* (China's chief steward Zhou Enlai). Beijing: Zhonggong dangshi chubanshe, 1996.

Chang Ch'i-yun. (Kung Fei Chieh Chu Hsi Ti) *Chung-kuo Ta Lu Fen Sheng Ti Tu*. (Provincial Atlas of the Chinese Mainland). n.p.: The National Security Institute, 1966.

Chen Boda. *Chen Boda Yigao: Yuzhong Zizhu ji Gita* (The posthumous manuscripts of Chen Boda: His account written in prison). Hong Kong: Cosmos Books, 1998.

Chen Dengke and Xiao Ma. *Pobiji* (The smashing of the wall). Beijing: Renmin wenxue chubanshe, 1980.

Chen Jiyuan, Chen Jiaji, and Yang Xun. *Zhongguo Nongcun Jingji Bianqian, 1949–1989* (The economic changes in China's countryside). Taiyuan: Shanxi jingji chubanshe, 1993.

Chen Liming. *Tan Zhenlin Zhuanqi* (The legend of Tan Zhenlin). Beijing: Zhongguo wenshi chubanshe, 1994.

Chen Mingxian. *Wannian Mao Zedong, 1953–1976* (Mao Zedong's twilight years, 1953–1976). Nanchang: Jiangxi renmin chubanshe, 1998.

Chen Shaochou, Lu Xiaojia, and Zhang Feihong (eds.). *Liu Shaoqi Yanjiu Shuping* (Commentary on the research on Liu Shaoqi). Beijing: Zhongyang wenxian chubanshe, 1997.

Chen Yun. *Chen Yun Tongzhi Wengao Xuanbian, 1956–1962* (Selected manuscripts of comrade Chen Yun, 1956–1962). Beijing: Renmin chubanshe, 1980.

— *Chen Yun Wenxian* (Selected works of Chen Yun), 3 vols. ii (1949–56); iii (1956–85). Beijing: Renmin chubanshe, 1995.

Cheng Bo. *Zhonggong 'Bada' Juece Neimu* (The inside story of the CCP's Eighth Party Congress). Beijing: Zhongguo dangan chubanshe, 1999.

Cheng Ping (ed.). *Zhongguo Gongchandang Lishi Dacidian* (A dictionary of the major events of the CCP). Beijing: Zhongguo guoji guangbo chubanshe, 1991.

Chu Han. *Zhongguo 1959–1961: Sannian Ziran Zaihai Changpian Jishi* (China 1959–1961: A detailed record of the three years of natural calamities). Chengdu: Sichuan renmin chubanshe, 1996.

Chung Kung Jen Ming Lu (Communist China's who's who). Taipei: Institute of International Relations, 1978.

Cong Jin. *1949–1989 Nian de Zhongguo, ii. Quzhe Fazhan de Suiyue* (China 1949–1989, ii. The years of tortuous development). n.p.: Henan renmin chubanshe, 1989.

Dangdai Zhongguo de Guangdong (Contemporary Guangdong) Beijing: Dangdai zhongguo chubanshe, 1991.

Dang Qian Caizheng Wenti (Current fiscal problems). Beijing: Zhongguo caizheng jingji chubanshe, 1981.

Deng Liqun. *Xiang Chen Yun Tongzhi Xuexi Zuo Jingji Gongzuo* (Learn how to do economic work from comrade Chen Yun). Zhonggong zhongyang dangxiao chubanshe, repr. by Guangdong renmin chubanshe, 1981.

Deng Zihui Zhuan Bianji Weiyuanhui. *Deng Zihui Zhuan* (Biography of Deng Zihui). Beijing: Renmin chubanshe, 1996.

Deng Zihui Wenji Bianji Weiyuanhui. *Deng Zihui Wenji* (Collected works of Deng Zihui). Beijing: Renmin chubanshe, 1996.

Ding Shu. *Ren Kou: Dayuejin yu Dajihuang* (Man-made calamities: The Great Leap Forward and the great famine). Hong Kong: Jiushinaindai zazhi she, 1991.

Dong Baocun. *Tan Zhenlin Wai Zhuan* (An unofficial biography of Tan Zhenlin). Beijing: Zuojia chubanshe, 1992.

Dong Bian, Zeng Zi (eds.). *Mao Zedong he Tade Mishu Tian Jiaying* (Mao Zedong and his secretary Tian Jiaying). Beijing: Zhongyang wenxian chubanshe, 1989; expanded ed., 1996.

Fan Xianchao, Li Youxin, Li Hui, Cheng Xiaojun, and Tan Zhenmang. *Mao Zedong Sixiang Fazhan de Lishi Quiji* (The historical tracks of the development of Mao Zedong's thought). Changsha: Hunan renmin chubanshe, 1993.

Fang Weizhong (ed.). *Zhonghua Renmin Gongheguo Jingji Dashiji, 1949–1980* (A record of the major economic events of the PRC, 1949–1980). Beijing: Zhongguo shehui kexue chubanshe, 1984.

Feng Ping, *Guangdong Dangdai Nongye Shi* (Contemporary history of agriculture in Guangdong). Shaoguan: Guangdong renmin chubanshe, 1995.

Gao Zhi and Zhang Nieer (eds.). *Jiyao Mishu de Sinian* (The remembrances of the confidential secretaries). Beijing: Zhonggong zhongyang dangxiao chubanshe, 1993.

Gong Guzhong, Tang Zhennan, and Xia Yuansheng. *Mao Zedong Hui Hunan Jishi, 1953–1975* (A record of Mao Zedong's revisits to Hunan, 1953–1975). Changsha: Hunan renmin chubanshe, 1993.

Gong Li, Zhu De, and Chen Shu. *Mao Zedong Zai Zhongda Lishi Guantou* (Mao Zedong and critical historical junctures). Beijing: Zhonggong zhongyang dangxiao chubanshe, 1993.

— Zhou Jingqing, and Zhang Shu, *Deng Xiaoping zai Zhongdai Lishi Guantou* (Deng Xiaoping at critical historical junctures). Beijing: Zhonggong zhongyang dangxiao chubanshe, 2000.

Gong Yuzhi, Pan Xinzhi, and Shi Zhongxuan (eds.). *Mao Zedong de Dushu Shenghuo* (Mao Zedong's life of reading). Beijing: Sanlian shudian, 1986.

Gu Longsheng (ed.). *Mao Zedong Jingji Nianpu* (Chronicles of Mao Zedong and the economy). Beijing: Zhonggong zhongyang dangxiao chubanshe, 1993.

Gu Shiming, Li Guangui, and Sun Jianping. *Li Fuchun Jingji Sixiang Yanjiu* (Research on Li Fuchun's economic thought). Xining: Qinghai renmin chubanshe, 1992.

Guangdong Sheng Tongji Nianjian 1984 (Statistical yearbook of Guangdong, 1984). Hong Kong: Economic Information and Agency, 1984.

Guojia Jigou Bianzhi Weiyuanhui Bangongshi. *Zhonghua Renmin Gongheguo Guowuyuan Zuzhi Jigou Gaiyao* (Outline of the organizational structure of the State Council of the PRC). Shenyang: Dongbei gongxueyuan chubanshe, 1989.

Guojia Tongjiju Conghesi (ed.). *Quanguo Gesheng Zizhiqu Zhixiashi Lishi Tongji Ziliao Huibian* (A compendium of historical statistical materials for the nation's provinces, autonomous regions, and centrally administered cities). Beijing: Zhongguo tongji chubanshe, 1990.

Guo Simin (ed.). *Wo Yanzhong de Mao Zedong* (Mao Zedong in my eyes). Shijiazhuang: Hebei renmin chubanshe, 1992.

—(ed.). *Wo Yanzhong de Chen Yun* (Chen Yun in my eyes). Beijing: Zhonggong dangshi chubanshe, 1995.

Han Taihua (ed.). *Zhongguo Gongchandang Ruogan Wenti Xiezhen* (A true discussion of certain historical problems of the CCP). Beijing: Zhongguo yanshi chubanshe, 1998.

He Husheng, Li Yaodong, Xiang Changfu, and Jiang Jianhua (eds.). *Zhonghua Renmin Gongheguo Zhiguan Zhi* (A record of governmental officials of the PRC), expanded edn. Beijing: Zhongguo shehui chubanshe, 1996.

He Li (ed.). *Zhonghua Renmin Gongheguo Shi* (A history of the PRC), expanded edn. Beijing: Dangan chubanshe, 1995.

Ho Ping (ed.). *Mao Zedong Dacidian* (A dictionary of Mao Zedong). Beijing: Zhongguo guoji guangbo chubanshe, 1992.

Hu Qiaomu. *Hu Qiaomu Huiyi Mao Zedong* (Hu Qiaomu's reminiscences of Mao Zedong). Beijing: Renmin chubanshe, 1994.

Hu Qiaomu Wenji (Collected writings of Hu Qiaomu). Beijing: Renmin chubanshe, i, 1992; ii, 1993; iii, 1994.

Hu Sheng (ed.). *Zhongguo Gongchandang Qishinian* (The CCP's seventy years). Beijing: Zhonggong dangshi chubanshe, 1991.

Huang Daqiang and Wang Mingguang (eds.). *Zhongguo Xinzheng Guanli Dacidian* (A dictionary of Chinese public administration). Beijing: Zhongguo wuzi chubanshe, 1993.

Huang Kecheng Zishu (The autobiography of Huang Kecheng). Beijing: Renmin chubanshe, 1994.

Huang Yunsheng. *Kaiguo Lingxiu Mao Zedong Yishi* (Anecdotes about Mao Zedong, founding leader of the country). Beijing: Zhongyang wenxian chubanshe, 1999.

Huang Zheng (ed.). *Gongheguo Zhuxi Li Shaoqi* (Liu Shaoqi, Chairman of the Republic). Beijing: Zhonggong dangshi chubanshe, 1998.

Jia Sinan (ed.). *1915–1976: Mao Zedong Renji Jiaowang Shilu* (1915–1976: Records of Mao Zedong's interpersonal contacts). Nanjing: Jiangsu wenyi chubanshe, 1989.

Jia Zhengqiu (ed.). *Mao Zedong Waixun Ji* (Mao Zedong's inspection tours). Changsha: Hunan wenyi chubanshe, 1993.

Jiang Mingwu *et al*. *Zhou Enlai de Licheng: Yige Weiren he Tade Yige Shiji* (Zhou Enlai and his journey: A great man and his century). Beijing: Jiefangjun wenyi chubanshe, 1996.

Jin Chongji (ed.). *Zhou Enlai Zhuan* (Biography of Zhou Enlai), iii. Beijing: Zhongyang wenxian chubanshe, 1998.

—and Huang Zheng (eds.). *Liu Shaoqi Zhuan* (Biography of Liu Shaoqi). Beijing: Zhongyang wenxian chubanshe, 1998.

Jin Fu. *'Wenge' Qianshinian de Zhongguo* (The ten years prior to the 'Cultural Revolution'). Beijing: Zhonggong dangshi chubanshe, 1998.

Jin Ye (ed.). *Huiyi Tan Zhenlin* (Remembering Tan Zhenlin). Hangzhou: Zhejiang renmin chubanshe, 1992.

Jin Zhao. *Lushan Michuan* (A secret history of Lushan). Beijing: Zhongguo dangan chubanshe, 1995.

Kao Chung-yen. *Changes of Personnel in Communist China*. Hong Kong: Union Research Institute, 1970.

Ke Yan. *Mao Zedong de Licheng: Yige Weiren he Tade Yige Shiji* (Mao Zedong and his journey: A great man and his century). Beijing: Jiefangjun wenyi chubanshe, 1996.

Li Fuchun. *Li Fuchun Xuanji* (Selected Works of Li Fuchun). Beijing: Zhongguo jihua chubanshe, 1992.

Li Haiwen (ed.). *Zhou Enlai Yanjiu Shuping* (Discourses on research on Zhou Enlai). Beijing: Zhongyang wenxian chubanshe, 1997.

Li Jiaji and Yang Qingwang (eds.). *Mao Zedong yu tadi Weishimen* (Mao Zedong and his bodyguards). 2 vols. Beijing: Zhongyang wenxian chubanshe, 1998.

Li Jian. *Zhonggong Lishizhuanzhe Guantou: Guanjian Huiyi Qinli Shilu* (The historical turning points of CCP history: A real record of personal experience of key meetings), i. Beijing: Zhonggong zhongyang dangxiao chubanshe, 1998.

Li Jie and Yu Jundao (eds.). *Dongfang Juren Mao Zedong, 1956–1976* (Mao Zedong, the great eminence of the East), iv. Beijing: Jiefangjun chubanshe, 1997.

Li Ping. *Kaiguo Zongli Zhou Enlai* (The PRC's first premier, Zhou Enlai). Beijing: Zhonggong zhongyang dangxiao chubanshe, 1994.

Li Qi (ed.). *Zai Zhou Enlai Shenbian de Rizi: Sihuating Gongzuo Renyuan di Huiyi* (The days working at Zhou Enlai's side: The memoirs of the staff of Sihuating). Beijing: Zhongyang wenxian chubanshe, 1998.

—*Huiyi yu Sikao* (Remembrances and contemplation). Beijing: Zhongyang wenxian chubanshe, 1999.

Li Rui. *Li Rui Wangshi Zayi* (A random recollection of past events by Li Rui). Nanjing: Jiangsu renmin chubanshe, 1995.

—*Dayuejin Qinliji* (A record of my personal experience of the GLF). Shanghai: Shanghai yuandong chubanshe, 1996.

—*Li Rui Wenji, ii. Mao Zedong de Wannian Beiju* (Selected works of Li Rui, ii. The tragedy of Mao Zedong's last years). Haikou: Nanfang chubanshe, 1999.

—*Lushan Huiyi Shilu* (A true record of the Lushan Conference). Beijing: Chunqiu chubanshe, and Changsha: Hunan jiaoyu chubanshe, 1989; New and expanded edn pub. as *Mao Zedong Mishu Shouji: Lushan Huiyi Shilu* (The personal record of Mao Zedong's secretary: A true record of the Lushan Conference). Zhengzhou: Henan renmin chubanshe, 1994; repr. as *Li Rui Wenji, i. Lushan Huiyi Zhenmianmu* (The real story of the Lushan Conference). Haikou: Nanfang chubanshe, 1999; 3rd expanded and rev. edn. retitled *Lushan Huiyi Shilu* (A true record of the Lushan Conference). Zhengzhou: Henan renmin chubanshe, 2000.

Li Shengxiao, Yi Feixian, and Wu Zhenhua. *Zhou Enlai Moulue* (Zhou Enlai's Strategy). Changsha: Hunan renmin chubanshe, 1998.

Li Xiannian. *Li Xiannian Wenxuan 1935–1988* (Selected works of Li Xiannian). Beijing: Renmin chubanshe, 1988.

Li Xiannian Wenxuan, 1935–1988 (Selected works of Li Xiannian, 1935–1988). Beijing: Renmin chubanshe, 1989.

Li Yinqiao. *Zai Mao Zedong Shenbian Shiwu Nian* (Fifteen years at Mao Zedong's side). Shijiazhuang: Hebei renmin chubanshe, 1991.

Li Yong and Xiao Wen. *Buhuide Hezuo: Mao Zedong yu Peng Dehuai* (Cooperation without regrets: Mao Zedong and Peng Dehuai). Huhhot: Yuanfang chubanshe, 1996.

Li Yuehan, Tan Deshan, Wang Chunming. *He Shengwei Shuji Men* (With the Provincial Party Secretaries). Beijing: Zhongyang wenxian chubanshe, 1994.

Li Zhuang. *Renmin Ribao Fengyun Sishinian* (The trials and tribulations of the People's Daily over four decades). Beijing: Renmin ribao chubanshe, 1993.

Liao Gailong, Zhao Baoxu, and Du Qinglin (eds.). *Dangdai Zhongguo Zhengzhi Dashidian, 1949–1990* (A dictionary of major events in contemporary Chinese politics, 1949–1990). Changchun: Jilin wenshi chubanshe, 1991.

Lin Yunhui, Fan Shouxin, and Zhang Gong. *1949–1989 Niande Zhongguo, i. Kaige Xingjin de Shiqi* (China 1949–1989, i. The period of triumphant advance). Henan: Henan renmin chubanshe, 1989.

Liu Guoguang (ed.). *Guomin Jingji Guanli Tizhi Gaige De Ruogan Lilun Wenti* (Certain theoretical problems regarding the reform of the system of economic management of the national economy). Beijing: Zhongguo shehui kexue chubanshe, 1980.

— and Wang Ruisun. *Zhongguo De Jingji Tizhi Gaige* (The reform of China's economic system). Beijing: Renmin chubanshe, 1982.

Liu Guoxin and Liu Xiao (eds.). *Zhonghua Renmin Gongheguo Lishi Changpian* (A detailed history of the PRC). 2 vols. Nanning: Guangxi renmin chubanshe, 1994.

Liu Jintian (ed.). *Deng Xiaoping de Licheng: Yige Weiren he Tade Yige Shiji* (Deng Xiaoping and his journey: A great man and his century). Beijing: Jiefangjun wenyi chubanshe, 1994.

Liu Lie, Zhang Shangping, and Zhu Bing (eds.). *Zhonghua Renmin Gongheguo Guojia Jigou* (The state organizations of the PRC). Harbin: Harbin chubanshe, 1988.

Liu Shaoqi. *Liu Shaoqi Xuanji* (Selected Works of Liu Shaoqi), ii. Beijing: Renmin chubanshe, 1985.

Liu Shaoqi Wenti Ziliao Xuanji (A collection of materials on Liu Shaoqi). Taipei: The Institute for the Study of Chinese Communist Problems, 1970.

Liu Shaoqi Yanjiu Lunwenji Bianjiju (ed.). *Liu Shaoqi Yanjiu Lunwenji* (Collected Research Essays on Liu Shaqi). Beijing: Zhongyang wenxian chubanshe, 1989.

Liu Suinian and Wu Qungan (eds.). *Dayuejin he Tiaozheng Shiqide Guomin Jingji, 1958–1965* (The national economy during the GLF and the adjustment period, 1958–1965). Harbin: Heilongjiang renmin chubanshe, 1984.

Liu Zhende. *Wo Wei Shaoqi Dang Mishu* (I was Shaoqi's secretary). Beijing: Zhongyang wenxian chubanshe, 1994.

Lu Haijiang and He Mingzhou (eds.). *Mao Zedong he ta Tongshidaide Ren* (Mao Zedong and his contemporaries). Zhengzhou: Henan renmin chubanshe, 1992.

Lu Ruilian, Zhang Yunying, and Liu Zhigao (eds.). *Gongheguo Lingxiu de Jueceyishu* (The republic's leaders' art of policy-making). Changsha: Hunan renmin chubanshe, 1997.

Lu Xingdou (ed.). *Zhou Enlai he Tade Shiye: Yanjiu Xuancui* (Zhou Enlai and his enterprises: A collection of research). Beijing: Zhonggong dangshi chubanshe, 1990.

Lu Yanyu. *Zhonghua Renmin Gongheguo Lishi Jishi: Quzhe Fazhan, 1958–1965* (A true historical record of the PRC: Tortuous development, 1958–1965). Beijing: Hongqi chubanshe, 1994.

— and Han Yinghong. *Zhonghua Renmin Gongheguo Lishi Jishi: Jiannan Tansuo, 1956–1958* (A true historical record of the PRC: The strenuous search, 1956–1958). Beijing: Hongqi chubanshe, 1994.

Ma Hong and Sun Shangqing (eds.). *Zhongguo Jingji Jiegou Wenti Yanjiu* (Studies on the structural problems of the Chinese economy), i. Beijing: Renmin chubanshe, 1981.

Ma Qibin, Chen Wenbin, Lin Yunhui, Cong Jin, Wang Nianyi, Zhang Tianrong, and Bu Weihua (eds.). *Zhongguo Gongchandang Zhizheng Sishinian, 1949–1989* (The CCP's 40 years' rule, 1949–1989). Beijing: Zhonggong dangshi ziliao chubanshe, 1989; Zhonggong dangshi chubanshe, rev., enlarged edn. 1991.

Ma Yongshun. *Zhou Enlai Zujian yu Guanli Zhengfu Shilu* (A true record of Zhou Enlai's organization and management of the government). Beijing: Zhongyang wenxian chubanshe, 1995.

Mao Zedong. *Mao Zedong Sixiang Wansui* (Long live Mao Zedong's Thought!). n.p. 1967*a*.

— *Mao Zedong Sixiang Wansui* (Long live Mao Zedong's Thought!). n.p. 1967*b*.

— *Mao Zedong Sixiang Wansui* (Long live Mao Zedong's Thought!). n.p. 1969.

— *Mao Zedong Xuanji* (Selected Works of Mao Zedong), v. Beijing: Renmin chubanshe, 1977.

Mao Zedong, *Maozhu Weikan Gao, 'Mao Zedong Sixiang Wansui' Beiji Ji Qita* (Unofficially published works of Mao Zedong, additional vols. of 'Long Live Mao Zedong's Thought' and other secret speeches of Mao). 15 vols. Oakton, Virginia: Center for Chinese Research Materials, 1990.

— *Jianguo Yilai Mao Zedong Wengao* (Manuscripts of Mao Zedong since the founding of the state). 13 vols. Beijing: Zhongyang wenxian chubanshe, i (1949–50), 1987; ii (1951), 1988; iii (1952), 1989; iv (1953–4), 1990; v (1955), 1991; vi (1956–7), vii (1958), 1992; viii (1959), 1993; ix (1960–1), x (1962–3), xi (1964–5), 1996; xii (1966–8), xiii (1969–76), 1998.

Mao Zedong, *Mao Zedong Wenji* (Collected Works of Mao Zedong). Beijing: Renmin chubanshe, vi (1949–55), 1999; vii (1956–58), 1999; viii (1959–75), 1999.

Mao Zedong Tongzhi Bashiwu Danchen Jinian Wenxuan (Collection of articles to commemorate comrade Mao Zedong's eighty-fifth birthday). Beijing: Renmin chubanshe, 1979.

Mao Zedong Tongzhi Jiushi Danchen Jinian Wenxuan (Collection of articles to commemorate comrade Mao Zedong's ninetieth birthday). Beijing: Renmin chubanshe, 1984.

Mao Zhuxi Zoubian Zuguo Dadi (Chairman Mao travels all over the country). Taiyuan: Shanxi renmin chubanshe, 1993.

Mianhuai Mao Zedong editorial group. *Mianhuai Mao Zedong* (Cherish the memory of Mao Zedong). 2 vols. Beijing: Zhongyang wenxian chubanshe, 1993.

Mu Xin. *Ban 'Guangming Ribao' Shinian Zishu, 1957–1967* (A personal account of running the Guangming Daily for ten years). Beijing: Zhonggong dangshi chubanshe, 1994.

Nan Guang (ed.). *Mao Zedong he Ta de Sida Mishu* (Mao Zedong and his four major secretaries). Guiyang: Guizhou minzu chubanshe, 1993.

Peng Dehuai Zishu (The autobiography of Peng Dehuai). Beijing: Renmin chubanshe, 1981.

Peng Gangzi and Wu Jinming. *Zhonghua Renmin Gongheguo Nongye Fazhan Shi* (A history of agricultural development in the PRC). Changsha: Hunan renmin chubanshe, 1998.

Qiu Shi (ed.). *Gongheguo Yishi, ii. Gongheguo Zhongda Shijian Juece Shilu* (A true record of the major events and policies of the PRC). Beijing: Jingji ribao chubanshe, 1998*a*.

— (ed.). *Gongheguo Yishi, iii. Gongheguo Zhongda Juece Chutai Qianhou* (Tales of the PRC, iii. The formulation and consequences of major policy decisions of the Republic). Beijing: Jingji ribao chubanshe, 1998*b*.

Quan Yanchi. *Hong Qiang Neiwai: Mao Zedong Shenghuoshilu* (Inside and outside of the Red Wall: A record of Mao's Life). Beijing: Kunlun chubanshe, 1989*a*.

— *Lingxiu Lei* (Tears of the leaders). Beijing: Qiushi chubanshe, 1989*b*.

— *Zouxia Shentan de Mao Zedong* (Mao Zedong when he descended from the altar). Hong Kong: Nanyue chubanshe, 1990.

— *Gongheguo Dizaozhe de Qinggan Shijie* (The emotional world of the founders of the Republic). Hohhot: Neimenggu remnin chubanshe, 1992.

— and Huang Lina. *Lushan Huiyi Xinlun* (A new interpretation of the Lushan conference). Beijing: Dashidai chubanshe, 1997.

— and Huang Linuo. *Tian Dao: Zhou Hui yu Lushan Huiyi* (Heaven's way: Zhou Hui and the Lushan Conference). Guangzhou: Guangdong luyou chubanshe, 1997.

Renmin Ribao Baoshi Bianjizu (ed.). *1948–1988 Renmin Ribao Huiyilu* (1948–1988 recollections about the People's Daily). Beijing: Renmin chubanshe, 1988.

Renmin Ribao She Guonei Ziliao Zu and Zhongguo Gongye Jingji Xiehui Tiaoyan Zu (eds.). *Zhonghua Renmin Gongheguo Gongye Dashiji, 1949–1990* (A chronology of major events in the industrial sector in the PRC, 1949–1990). Changsha: Hunan chubanshe, 1992.

Shao Kang (ed.). *Mao Zedong he Dangwai Pengyou Men* (Mao Zedong and his friends outside of the Party). Beijing: Tunjie chubanshe, 1993.

Shaoshan Mao Zedong Jinianguan (ed.). *Mao Zedong Shenghuo Danan* (Life file of Mao Zedong). 3 vols. Beijing: Zhonggong dangshi chubanshe, 1999.

Shi Jing. *Tebei de Jiaowang: Shengwei Diyi Shuji Furen de Huiyi* (Special relationships: The memoirs of the wife of a provincial first secretary). n.p.: Jiangsu wenyi chubanshe, 1992.

Shi Zhongquan. *Zhou Enlai de Zhuoyue Fengxian* (Zhou Enlai's outstanding contributions). Beijing: Zhonggong Zhongyang dangxiao chubanshe, 1993.

— Shen Zhengle, Yang Xiancai, and Hang Gang. *Zhonggong Badashi* (History of the CCP's Eighth Party Congress). Beijing: Renmin chubanshe, 1998.

Shou Kaohe, Li Weifan, and Sun Shuyu (eds.). *Zhongguo Shengshi Zizhiqu Ziliao Shouce* (Handbook of Chinese provinces, municipalities, and autonomous regions). Beijing: Shehui kexue wenxian chubanshe, 1990.

Song Yixiu and Yang Meiye (eds.). *Mao Zedong's Renji Shijie* (Mao Zedong's personal relations). Beijing: Hongqi chubanshe, 1992.

Su Donghai and Fang Kongmu (eds.). *Zhonghua Renmin Gongheguo Fengyun Shilu* (A real record of the major events of the PRC). 2 vols. Shijiazhuang: Hebei renmin chubanshe, 1994.

Su Shangyao and Han Wenwei. *Zhongguo Renmin Gongheguo Zhongyang Zhengfu Jigou* (The government structure of the PRC). Beijing: Jingji Kexue chubanshe, 1993.

Su Xiaokang, Luo Shixu, and Chen Zheng. *Wutuobang Ji: Yijiuwujiu Nian Lushan Zhixia* (An epitaph for utopia: Lushan in the summer of 1959). Beijing: Zhongguo xinwen chubanshe, 1988.

Sun Baoyi. *Mao Zedong de Dushu Shengya* (Mao Zedong's reading career). Beijing: Zhishi chubanshe, 1993.

Sun Yeli and Xiong Lianghua (eds.). *Gongheguo Jingji Fengyun zhong de Chen Yun* (Chen Yun in the midst of the economic upheavals of the republic). Beijing: Zhongyang wenxian chubanshe, 1996.

'Tan Zhenlin Zhuan' Bianzuan Weiyuanhui. *Tan Zhenlin Zhuan* (A biography of Tan Zhenlin). Hangzhou: Zhejiang renmin chubanshe, 1992.

Tan Zhenqiu. *Mao Zedong Wai Xun Ji* (The records of Mao Zedong's inspection tours) Changsha: Hunan wenyi chubanshe, 1993.

Tao Zhu. *Tao Zhu Wenji* (Collected works of Tao Zhu). Beijing: Renmin chubanshe, 1987.

Tao Zhu Zhuan (Biography of Tao Zhu). Beijing: Zhongguo qingnian chubanshe, 1992.

Tong Xiaopeng. *Fengyu Sishinian* (Trials and tribulations over forty years), ii. Beijing: Zhongyang wenxian chubanshe, 1996.

Unpublished Chinese Documents on Opposing Rash Advance and the Great Leap Forward, nos. 1–6. n.p.: *c.*1992. Deposited at the Fairbank Center Library.

Wang Dongxing, and Qiu Zhizhuo. *Wang Dongxing Gongkai Mao Zedong Sishenghuo* (Wang Dongxing reveals openly the private life of Mao Zedong). Hong Kong: Mingliu chubanshe, 1997.

Wang Gengjin, Yang Xun, Wang Ziping, Liang Xiaodong, and Yang Guansan (eds.). *Xiancun Sanshi Nian: Fengyang Nongcun Shehui Jingji Fanzhan Shilu, 1949–1983 Nian* (The countryside over three decades: A true record of rural socioeconomic development in Fengyang, 1949–1983). 2 vols. Beijing: Nongcun duwu chubanshe, 1989.

Wang Haibo. *Shehuizhuyi Jingji Wenti Chutan*. (A preliminary investigation into the economic problems of socialism). Changsha: Hunan renmin chubanshe, 1981.

Wang Junwei and Li Jianjun (eds.). *Zheng Feng: Cong Dayuejin, Yangyuejin dao Ruanzhelu* (Strife and confrontation: The Great Leap Forward, the foreign leap forward, and the soft landing). Beijing: Jincheng chubanshe, 1998.

Wang Yifu. *Xin Zhongguo Tongji Shigao* (Draft history of new China's Statistics). Beijing: Zhongguo tongji chubanshe, 1986.

Wei Gang (ed.). *Peng Dehuai*. Chengdu: Sichuan renmin chubanshe, 1993.

Wen Yu. *Zhongguo 'Zuo' Huo* (China's 'leftist' scourge). Beijing: Chaohua chubanshe, 1993.

Women de Zhou Zongli (Our own premier Zhou). Beijing: Zhongyang wenxian chubanshe, 1990.

Wu Lengxi. *Yi Mao Zhuxi: Wo Qinshen Jinglide Ruogan Zhongda Lishi Shijian Pianduan* (Remembering Chairman Mao: Fragments of certain historical events which I personally experienced). Beijing: Xinhua chubanshe, 1995.

Wu Shihong and Gao Yi (eds.). *Deng Xiaoping yu Gongheguo Zhongda Lishi Shijian* (Deng Xiaoping and the major events of the Republic). Beijing: Renmin chubanshe, 2000.

Wu Xiaomei and Li Peng. *Mao Zedong Zouchu Hongqiang* (Mao Zedong emerges from the Red Walls). Beijing: Zhonggong zhongyang dangxiao chubanshe, 1993.

Wugong Renmin de Zhandou Licheng. (The Wugong people's course of struggle). Beijing: Zhonghua Shuju, 1978.

Xiao Donglian, Xie Chuntao, Zhu Di, and Qiao Jining. *Qiusuo Zhongguo: 'Wenge' Qian Shinian Shi* (China's quest: A history of the decade before the 'Cultural Revolution'). 2 vols. Beijing: Hongqi chubanshe, 1999.

Xiao Ke, Li Rui, Gong Yuzhi *et al. Wo Qinilguo de Zhengzhi Yundong* (The political campaigns I have experienced personally). Beijing: Zhongyang bianyi chubanshe, 1998.

Xiao Shimei. *Mao Zedong Moulue* (Mao Zedong's strategy). Changsha: Hunan chubanshe, 1993).

Xiao Xinli (ed.). *Xunshe Dajiang Nanbei de Mao Zedong* (Mao Zedong's inspections tours north and south of the Yangzi). Beijing: Zhongguo shehui kexue chubanshe, 1993.

Xie Chen. *Zhonghua Renmin Gongheguo Wushinian Huigu yu Sikao* (Reminiscence and contemplation on the fifty years of the PRC). 2 vols. Beijing: Xinhua chubanshe, 1999.

Xie Chuntao. *Dayuejin Kuanglan* (The raging waves of the GLF). Zhengzhou: Henan renmin chubanshe, 1990.

Xing Chongzhi, Jiang Shunxue, Liao Gailong, and Zhao Xuemin (eds.). *Mao Zedong Yanjiu Shidian* (A dictionary of events for the research of Mao Zedong). Shijiazhuang: Hebei renmin chubanshe, 1992.

Xiong Huayuan and Liao Xinwen. *Zhou Enlai Zongli Shengya* (Zhou Enlai's career as premier). Beijing: Renmin chubanshe, 1997.

Xue Muqiao. *Shehuizhuyi Jingji Lilun Wenti* (Theoretical problems of socialist economics). Beijing: Renmin chubanshe, 1979*a*.

— *Zhongguo Shehuizhuyi Jingji Wenti Yanjiu* (Studies on the problems of the Chinese socialist economy). Beijing: Renmin chubanshe, 1979*b*.

— *Dangqian Woguo Jingji Ruogan Wenti* (Certain current problems of our national economy). Beijing: Renmin chubanshe, 1980.

— *Xue Muqiao Huiyilu* (Memoirs of Xue Muqiao). Tianjin: Tianjin renmin chubanshe, 1996.

Xuexi 'Guanyu Jianguo Yilai Dangde Ruogan Lishi Wenti de Jueyi' (Study the 'Resolution on certain historical problems of the Party after the founding of the state'). Guangdong: Renmin chubanshe, 1981.

Yan Chang and Yang Xuemei. *Liu Shaoqi Moule* (Liu Shaoqi's strategy). Beijing: Hongqi chubanshe, 1996.

Yan Changlin. *Jingwei Mao Zedong Jishi* (The notes of Mao Zedong's bodyguard). Changchun: Jilin renmin chubanshe, 1992.

Yang Mingwei, *Zouchu Kunjing: Zhou Enlai zai 1960–1965* (Escape from dire straits: Zhou Enlai in 1960–1965). Beijing: Zhongyang wenxian chubanshe, 2000.

Yang Qingwang (ed.). *Mao Zedong Zhidian Jianshan* (Mao Zedong commands and appreciates the country). 3 vols. Beijing: Zhongyang wenxian chubanshe, 2000.

Yang Shengqun and Tian Songnian (eds.). *Gongheguo Zhongda Juece de Lailong Qumai* (The origins and developments of the PRC's major policies). Nanjing: Jiangsu renmin chubanshe, 1995.

Ye Wensong (ed.). *Zhonghua Renmin Gongheguo Zhengfu Jiguan Zonglan* (A comprehensive survey of the governmental structure of the PRC). Chongqing: Zhongguo wuzi chubanshe, 1993.

Ye Yonglie. *Zhang Chunqiao Zhuan* (Biography of Zhang Chunqiao). Beijing: Zuojia chubanshe, 1993.

— *Hu Qiaomu*. Beijing: Zhonggong zhongyang dangxiao chubanshe, 1994*a*.

— *Mao Zedong de Mishu Men* (Mao Zedong's secretaries). Shanghai: Shanghai renmin chubanshe, 1994*b*.

— *Fan Youpai Shimo* (The history of the Anti-Rightist campaign). Xining: Qinghai renmin chubanshe, 1995*a*.

— *Mao Zedong de Wenmi* (Mao Zedong's secretaries). Xining: Qinghai renmin chubanshe, 1995*b*.

— *Wuqi Nian de Xuelei* (The tears and blood in 1957). Xining: Qinghai renmin chubanshe, 1995*c*.

— *Chen Boda Zhuan* (Biography of Chen Boda). New edn. Beijing: Renmin ribao chubanshe, 1999).

— *Mao Zedong yu Liu Shaoqi* (Mao Zedong and Liu Shaoqi). n.p.: Yuanfang chubanshe, 2000).

Yin Jiamin, *Gongheguo Fengyun zhong de Mao Zedong yu Zhou Enlai* (Mao Zedong and Zhou Enlai in the stormy years of the Republic). Beijing: Zhonggong zhongyang dangxiao chubanshe, 1999.

Yu Jundao and Li Jie (eds.). *Mao Zedong Jiaowang Lu* (Records of Mao Zedong's social contacts). Beijing: Renmin chubanshe, 1991.

Yu Shicheng. *Deng Xiaoping yu Mao Zedong* (Deng Xiaoping and Mao Zedong). Beijing: Zhonggong Zhongyang Dangxiao chubanshe, 1995.

Zeng Zhi. *Yige Geming de Xingcunzhe: Zeng Zhi Huiyi Shilu* (A fortunate survivor of the Revolution: The memoirs of Zeng Zhi). 2 vols. Guangzhou: Guangdong renmin chubanshe, 1999.

Zhang Sai (ed.). *Zhonghua Renmin Gongheguo Tongji Dashiji* (A chronicle of statistics in the PRC). Beijing: Zhongguo tongji chubanshe, 1992.

Zhang Suhua, Bian Yanjun, and Wu XiaoMei. *Shuibujin de Mao Zedong* (The inexhaustible subject of Mao Zedong). Shenyang: Liaoning renmin chubanshe, 1995.

Zhang Suizhi, *Hongqiang Neide Jingwei Shengya* (The career of a security guard within the Red Walls). Beijing: Zhongyang wenxian chubanshe, 1998.

Zhang Taozhi. *Zhonghua Renmin Gongheguo Yanyi* (A historical novel of the PRC). Beijing: Zuojia chubanshe, 1996.

Zhang Wenhe and Li Yan. *Kouhao yu Zhongguo* (Slogans and China). Beijing: Zhongyang dangshi chubanshe, 1998.

— and Li Yifan, *Zoujin Liu Shaoqi* (Getting close to Liu Shaoqi). Beijing: Zhongyang wenxian chubanshe, 1998.

Zhang Yeci. *Zhang Yaoci Huiyi Mao Zedong* (Zhang Yaoci remembers Mao Zedong). Beijing: Zhonggong zhongyang dangxiao chubanshe, 1996.

Zhang Wuxuan, Liu Wuyi, and Xiao Xing (eds.). *Gongheguo Fenyun Sishinian, 1949–1989* (The Republic's forty stormy years, 1949–1989). 2 vols. Beijing: Zhongguo zhengfa chubanshe, 1989.

Zhao Qihua, Tian Jujian, and Cheng Zhongyuan (eds.). *Huihuang de Sishiwunian* (The glorious forty-five years). Beijing: Dangdai zhongguo chubanshe, 1995.

Zhao Wei. *Zhao Ziyang Zhuan* (A biography of Zhao Ziyang). Hong Kong: Wenhua jiaoyu chubanshe, 1988.

Zhao Zhichao. *Mao Zedong Shierci Nanxun* (Mao Zedong's twelve inspection tours to the south). Beijing: Zhongyang wenxian chubanshe, 2000.

Zheng Xiaofeng, and Shu Ning. *Tao Zhu Zhuan* (Biography of Tao Zhu). Beijing: Zhongguo qingnian chubanshe, 1992.

Zhonggong Dangshi Jiaoxue Cankao Ziliao (CCP History Teaching Reference Materials), xxii–xxiv. n.p.: Zhongguo renmin jiefangjun guofang daxue dangshi dangjian zhenggong jiaoyanshi, 1986.

Zhonggong Dangshi Renwuchuan (Biographies of figures from Chinese Communist History), v. Shaanxi: Renmin chubanshe, 1982.

Zhonggong Zhongyang Dangshi Yanjiushi Keyan Guanlibu (ed.). *Liu Shaoqi Fenyun Suiyue* (Liu Shaoqi and stormy times). Beijing: Zhonggong dangshi chubanshe, 1998.

Zhonggong Zhongyang Dangshi Yanjiushi Keyanju (ed.). *Mao Zedong de Zuji* (The footprints of Mao Zedong). Beijing: Zhonggong dangshi chubanshe, 1993.

Zhonggong Zhongyang Dangxiao Zhonggong Dangshi Jiaoyanshi (ed.). *Zhonggong Dangshi Zhuanti Jiangyi* (Teaching materials on special topics of CCP history). Beijing: Zhonggong zhongyang dangxiao chubanshe, 1988.

Zhonggong Zhongyang Dangxiao Zhonggong Dangshi Jiaoyanshi (ed.). *Sishiniande Huigu yu Sikao* (Reviews and reflections on forty years). Beijing: Zhonggong zhongyang dangxiao chubanshe, 1991.

Zhonggong Zhongyang Wenxian Yanjiushi. *Zhou Enlai Jingji Wenxuan* (Selected works on economics by Zhou Enlai). Beijing: Zhongyang wenxian chubanshe, 1993.

— *Jianguo Yilai Zhongyao Wenxian Xuanbian* (A selection of important documents since the founding of the state). Beijing: Zhongyang wenxian chubanshe, x (1957), 1994; xi (1958), 1995; xii (1959), 1996; xiii (1960), 1996.

— (ed). *Liu Shaoqi Nianpu, 1898–1969* (Chronicles of Liu Shaoqi, 1898–1969). 2 vols. Beijing: Zhongyang wenxian chubanshe, 1996.

— (ed.). *Zhou Enlai Nianpu, 1949–1976* (Chronicles of Zhou Enlai, 1949–1976). 3 vols. Beijing: Zhongyang wenxian chubanshe, 1997.

— Jin Chongji, and Huang Zheng (eds.). *Liu Shaoqi Zhuan* (A biography of Liu Shaoqi). Beijing: Zhongyang wenxian chubanshe, 1998.

— Zhongyang Dangan Quan, and 'Dangde Wenxian' Bianjibu (eds.). *Zhonggong Dangshi Fenyunlu* (A record of the trial and tribulations of CCP history). Beijing: Renmin chubanshe, 1990.

— — — (eds.). *Zhonggong Dangshi Zhongda Shijian Shushi* (A true account of major events in CCP history). Beijing: Renmin chubanshe, 1993.

— — — (eds.). *Gongheguo Lingxiu Yaoshi Zhenwen* (Anecdotes of the Republic's leaders and important events). Beijing: Zhongyang wenxian chubanshe, 1998.

Zhongguo Geming Bowuguan Dangshi Yanjiushi (ed.). *Gongheguo Zhongda Lishi Shijian Shushi* (A true account of the major historical events of the Republic). Beijing: Renmin chubanshe, 1999.

Zhongguo Nongye Dashiji (Major events in Chinese agriculture). Beijing: Nongye chubanshe, 1982.

Zhongguo Tongji Nianjian, 1983 (Statistical Yearbook of China, 1983). Beijing: Guojia tongjiju, 1983.

Zhonghua Renmin Gongheguo Dadian Pianweihui (ed.). *Zhonghua Renmin Gongheguo Dadian* (A major dictionary of the PRC). Beijing: Zhongguo jingji chubanshe, 1994.

Zhonghua Renmin Gongheguo Fagui Huibian (A compendium of laws and regulations of the People's Republic of China), i–xiii. Beijing: Falu chubanshe, 1981 and 1982.

Zhonghua Renmin Gongheguo Fen Sheng Dituji (Provincial atlas of the People's Republic of China). Beijing: Ditu chubanshe, 1983.

Zhonghua Renmin Gongheguo Guojia Nongye Weiyuanhui Bangongting. *Nongye Jitihua Zhongyao Wenjian Huibian (1958–1981)* (A collection of important documents on agricultural collectivization, 1958–1981). ii. Beijing: Zhonggong zhongyang dangxiao chubanshe, 1981.

Zhonghua Renmin Gongheguo Guojia Nongyebu Juece Faguisi and Guojia Tongjijiu Nongcunsi. *Zhongguo Nongcun Sishinian* (Forty years in China's countryside). Zhengzhou: Henan zhongyuan nongmin chubanshe, 1989.

Zhonghua Renmin Gongheguo Guomin Jingji Guanli Dashiji (A chronology of major events in the economic management of the PRC). Beijing: Zhongguo jinji chubanshe, 1986.

Zhonghua Renmin Gongheguo Guomin Jingji he Shehui Fazhan Jihua Dashi Jiyao, 1949–1985 (A summary of major events in the national economic and social development planning of the PRC, 1949–1985). Beijing: Hongqi chubanshe, 1987.

Zhongguo Kexueyuan Jingji Yanjiusuo Ziliao Shi (ed.). *Gangtie Shengchan Dayuejin Lunwen Xuanji* (Selected articles on the Great Leap Forward in iron and steel production). Beijing: Kexue chubanshe, 1958.

Zhongyang Renmin Zhengfu Faling Huibian (A compendium of the laws and regulations of the Central Peoples' Government), i–v. Beijing: Falu chubanshe, 1981 and 1982.

Zhongyang Wenxian Yanjiushi Diyi Bianyanbu (ed.). *Huashui Mao Zedong: Zhiqingzhe Fantanlu* (On the subject of Mao Zedong: Interviews with those in the know). Beijing: Zhongyang wenxian chubanshe, 2000.

Zhongyang Wenxian Yanjiushi Diyi Bianyanbu (ed.). *Huashui Liu Shaoqi: Zhiqingzhe Fantanlu* (On the subject of Liu Shaoqi: Interviews with those in the know). Beijing: Zhongyang wenxian chubanshe, 2000.

— and Keyan Guanlibu (ed.). *Lishi Weiren Liu Shaoqi: Jinan Liu Shaoqi Bainian Danchen Lunji* (Historical hero Liu Shaoqi: A collection of articles to commemorate the one hundredth birthday of Liu Shaoqi). Beijing: Zhonggong zhongyang dangxiao chubanshe, 1998.

Zhou Enlai. *Zhou Enlai Xuanji.* (Selected works of Zhou Enlai), ii. Beijing: Renmin chubanshe, 1984.

'Zhou Enlai Yanjiu Xueshu Taolunhui Lunwenji' Bianjizu (ed.). *Zhou Enlai Yanjiu Xueshu Taolunhui Lunwenji* (A collection of papers from research symposiums on Zhou Enlai). Beijing: Zhongyang wenxian chubanshe, 1988.

Zhou Fang. *Woguo Guogia Jigou* (The state structure of our country). Beijing: Zhongguo qingnian chubanshe, 1955.

Zhu Chengjia (ed.). *Zhonggong Dangshi Yanjiu Lunwen Xuan* (A selection of research papers on CCP history). Xia Changsha: Hunan renmin chubanshe, 1984.

Zhu Hanguo, Xie Chuntao, and Fan Tianshun. *Zhongguo Gongchandang Jianshe Shi* (A history of the construction of the CCP). Chengdu: Sichuan renmin chubanshe, 1991.

Zhu Jiamu, Liu Shukai, Chi Aiping, and Zhao Shigang (eds.). *Chen Yun he Tade Shiye: Chen Yun Shengping yu Sixiang Yantaohui Lunwenji* (Chen Yun and his career: A collection of articles from the conference on Chen Yun's life and thought). 2 vols. Beijing: Zhongyang wenxian chubanshe, 1996.

Zhu Yuncheng, Chen Haoguang, and Lu Datong (eds.). *Zhongguo Renkou:Guangdong Fence* (China's population: Guangdong volume). Beijing: Zhongguo caizheng jingji chubanshe, 1988.

Books and Monographs in English

Allison, Graham. *Essence of Decision: Explaining the Cuban Missile Crisis.* Boston: Little, Brown, 1971.

Bachman, David. *To Leap Forward: Chinese Policy-Making, 1956–1957.* Unpub. doctoral diss., Stanford University, 1984.

— *Bureaucracy, Economy, and Leadership in China: The Institutional Origins of the Great Leap Forward.* Cambridge: Cambridge University Press, 1991.

Bardach, Eugene. *The Implementation Game.* Cambridge, Mass.: MIT Press, 1977.

Barnett, A. Doak, with a contribution by Ezra Vogel. *Cadres, Bureaucracy, and Political Power in Communist China.* New York: Columbia University Press, 1967.

— *The Making of Foreign Policy in China.* Boulder, Colo.: Westview Press, 1985.

Becker, Jasper. *Hungry Ghosts: China's Secret Famine.* London: John Murray, 1996.

Bowie, Robert and Fairbank, John. *Communist China, 1955–59: Policy Documents with Analysis*. Cambridge, Mass.: Harvard University Press, 1962.

Caiden, Naomi and Wildavsky, Aaron. *Planning and Budgeting in Poor Countries*. New York: John Wiley and Sons, 1974.

The Case of Peng The-huai. Hong Kong: Union Research Institute, 1968.

Chang, Parris H., *Power and Policy in China*. 2nd and enlarged edn. University Park: Pennsylvania State University Press, 1978.

Cheek, Timothy and Saich Tony (eds.). *New Perspectives on State Socialism in China*. Armonk, NY: M. E. Sharpe, 1999.

Chung, Ching-wook. *Maoism and Development: The Politics of Industrial Management*. Seoul: Seoul National University Press, 1980.

Clark, M. Gardner. *Development of China's Steel Industry and Soviet Technical Aid*. Ithaca, NY: Cornell University Press, 1973.

Crook, David and Crook, Isabel. *The First Years of Yangyi Commune*. London: Routledge and Kegan Paul, 1966.

Dirlik, Arif, Healy, Paul, and Knight, Nick (eds.). *Critical Perspectives on Mao Zedong's Thought*. New Jersey: Humanities Press, 1997.

Domenach, Jean-Luc. *The Origins of the Great Leap Forward: The Case of One Chinese Province*. Boulder, Colo.: Westview Press, 1995.

Donnithorne, Audrey. *China's Economic System*. London: Allen & Unwin, 1967.

Downs, Anthony. *Inside Bureaucracy*. Boston: Little, Brown, 1967.

Dye, Thomas. *Understanding Public Policy,* 5th edn. Englewood cliffs, NJ: Prentice-Hall, 1984.

Franklin, Bruce (ed.). *The Essential Stalin: Major Theoretical Writings, 1905–1952*. New York: Doubleday, 1972.

Goldstein, Avery. *From Bandwagon to Balance-of-Power Politics: Structural Constraints and Politics in China, 1949–1978*. Stanford: Stanford University Press, 1991.

Goodman, David S. G. *Central–Provincial Relationship in the People's Republic of China: Sichuan and Guizhou 1955–1965*. Unpub. doctoral diss., University of London, 1981.

Grindle, Merilee (ed.). *Politics and Policy Implementation in the Third World*. Princeton: Princeton University Press, 1980.

Hamrin, Carol Lee and Suisheng, Zhao. *Decision-making in Deng's China: Perspectives From Insiders*. Armonk, NY: M. E. Sharpe, 1995.

Harding, Harry. *Organizing China*. Stanford: Stanford University Press, 1981.

Hinton, William. *Shenfan: The Continuing Revolution in a Chinese Village*. New York: Random House, 1983.

Hogwood, Brian W. and Peters, B. Guy. *The Pathology of Public Policy*. Oxford: Clarendon Press, 1985.

Jia, Hao and Zhimin, Lin. *Changing Central–Local Relations in China: Reform and State Capacity*. Boulder, Colo.: Westview Press, 1994.

Joseph, William. *The Critique of Ultra-Leftism in China, 1958–1981*. Stanford: Stanford University Press, 1984.

Klochko, Mikhail. *Soviet Scientist in China*. Montreal: International Publisher's Representatives, 1964.

Kuo, Warren. *A Comprehensive Glossary of Chinese Communist Terminology*. Taipei: Institute of International Relations, National Chengchi University, 1978.

Lampton, David. *The Politics of Medicine in China*. Boulder, Colo.: Westview Press, 1977.

— *Policy Implementation in Post-Mao China*. Berkeley: University of California Press, 1987.

Lardy, Nicholas R., and Lieberthal, Kenneth. *Chen Yun's Strategy for China's Development*. Armonk, NY: M. E. Sharpe, 1983.

Li Choh-ming. *The Statistical System of Communist China*. Berkeley: University of California Press, 1962.

Li, Zhisui, *The Private Life of Chairman Mao*. New York: Random house, 1994.

Lieberthal, Kenneth G. *A Research Guide to Central Party and Government Meetings in China, 1949–1975*. White Plains, NY: International Arts and Science Press, 1976.

— and Dickson, Bruce. *A Research Guide to Central Party and Government Meetings in China, 1949–1986*. Rev. and expanded edn. Armonk, NY: M. E. Sharpe, 1989.

— and Lampton, David M. (eds.). *Bureaucracy, Politics, and Decision-making in Post-Mao China*. Berkeley: University of California Press, 1992.

— and Oksenberg, Michel. *Policy-making in China*. Princeton: Princeton University Press, 1988.

MacFarquhar, Roderick. *The Origins of the Cultural Revolution, i. Contradiction Among the People, 1956–1957*. London: Oxford University Press, 1974.

— *The Origins of the Cultural Revolution, ii. The Great Leap Forward, 1958–1960*. New York: Columbia University Press, 1983.

— *The Origins of the Cultural Revolution, iii. The Coming of the Cataclysm, 1961–1966*. Oxford: Oxford University Press, 1997.

— and Fairbank, John (eds.). *The Cambridge History of China*, xiv. Cambridge: Cambridge University Press, 1987.

— Cheek, Timothy, and Wu, Eugene (eds.). *The Secret Speeches of Chairman Mao: From the Hundred Flowers to the Great Leap Forward*. Cambridge, Mass.: The Council on East Asian Studies, Harvard University, 1989.

Mao Zedong. *Miscellany of Mao Tse-tung Thought*. Arlington: Joint Publications Research Service, No. 61269–1–2, 20 Feb. 1974.

— *Selected Works*, v. Beijing: Foreign Language Press, 1977.

Meisner, Maurice. *Mao's China and After*. 3rd edn. New York: Free Press, 1999.

David Milton, Milton, Nancy, and Schurmann, Franz. *People's China*. New York: Vintage Books, 1974.

Nakamura, Robert and Smallwood, Frank. *The Politics of Policy Implementation*. New York: St. Martin's Press, 1980.

Nolan, Peter. *Growth Processes and Distributional Change in a South Chinese Province: The Case of Guangdong*. London: Contemporary China Institute, 1983.

Palumbo, J. Dennis (ed.). *The Politics of Program Evaluation*. Newbury Park: Sage Publications, 1987.

— and Calista, Donald J. (eds.). *Implementation and the Policy Process: Opening Up the Black Box*. New York: Greenwood Press, 1990.

— and Harder, Marvin A. (eds.). *Implementing Public Policy*. Lexington: Lexington Books, 1981.

Peters, B. Guy. *The Politics of Bureaucracy*. New York and London: Longman, 1984.

Potter, Sulamith and Potter, Jack. *China's Peasants*. Cambridge: Cambridge University Press, 1990.

Pressman, Jeffrey and Wildavsky, Aaron. *Implementation*. Berkeley: University of California Press, 1973.

Pye, Lucian. *The Dynamics of Chinese Politics*. Cambridge: Oelgeschlagar, Gunn, and Hain, Publishers, 1981.

Rourke, Francis E. *Bureaucracy, Politics, and Public Policy*, 3rd edn. Boston: Little, Brown, 1984

Schoenhals, Michael. *Saltationist Socialism: Mao Zedong and the Great Leap Forward, 1958*. Stockholm: Institutionen for Orientaliska Sprak, University of Stockholm, 1987.

— *Doing Things with Words in Chinese Politics*. Berkeley: Institute of East Asian Studies, University of California, Berkeley, 1992.

Schram, Stuart R. (ed.). *Mao Tse-tung Unrehearsed*. Harmondsworth: Penguin, 1968.

Schurmann, Franz. *Ideology and Organization in Communist China*. new, enlarged edn. Berkeley: University of California Press, 1968.

Shalom, Stephen R. *Deaths in China due to Communism*. Tempe, Ariz.: Center for Asian Studies, Arizona State University, 1984.

Shambaugh, David L. *The Making of a Premier, Zhao Ziyang's Provincial Career*. Boulder, Colo.: Westview Press, 1984.

Shue, Vivienne. *Peasant China in Transition*. Berkeley: University of California Press, 1980.

Siu, Helen. *Agents and Victims in South China*. New Haven: Yale University Press, 1989.

Smil, Vaclav. *The Bad Earth*. Armonk, NY: M. E. Sharpe, 1984.

Snow, Edgar. *The Long Revolution*. New York: Vintage Books, 1971.

Statistical Yearbook of China, 1985. Co-published by the Hong Kong Economic Information Agency and Beijing: China Statistical Information and Consulting Service Centre, 1985.

Teiwes, Frederick C. *Politics at Mao's Court*. Armonk, NY: M. E. Sharpe, 1990.

— *Politics and Purges in China*. 2nd edn. Boulder, Colo.: Westview Press, 1993.

— and Sun, Warren (eds.). *The Politics of Agricultural Cooperativization in China: Mao, Deng Zihui, and the 'High Tide' of 1955*. Armonk, NY: M. E. Sharpe, 1993.

— — *The Tragedy of Liao Biao: Riding the Tiger during the Cultural Revolution, 1966–1972*. London: Hurst, 1996.

— — *China's Road to Disaster: Mao, Central Politicians, and Provincial Leaders in the Unfolding of the Great Leap Forward, 1955–1959*. Armonk, NY: M. E. Sharpe, 1999.

Ten Great Years. Beijing: Foreign Language Press, 1960.

Vogel, Ezra. *Canton Under Communism*. New York: Harper Torchbooks, 1976.

— *One Step Ahead in China: Guangdong Under Reform*. Cambridge, Mass.: Harvard University Press, 1989.

Walker, Kenneth R. *Food Grain Procurement and Consumption in China*. Cambridge: Cambridge University Press, 1984.

Xue, Muqiao, *China's Socialist Economy*. Beijing: Foreign Languages Press, 1981.

Yang, Dali. *Calamity and Reform in China: State, Rural Society, and Institutional Change Since the Great Leap Famine*. Stanford: Stanford University Press, 1996.

Articles in English

Ashton, Basil, Hill, Kenneth, Piazza, Alan, and Zeitz, Robin. 'Famine in China, 1958–61', *Population and Development Review,* 10/4 (Dec.), 1984: 613–45.

Bachman, David. 'Response to Teiwes', *Pacific Affairs*, 66/2 (Summer), 1993.

— 'Chinese Bureaucratic Politics and the Origins of the Great Leap Forward', *Journal of Contemporary China*, 9 (Summer), 1995.

— 'Structure and Process in the Making of Chinese Foreign Policy' in Samuel Kim (ed.). *China and the World: Chinese Foreign Policy Faces the New Millennium*. Boulder, Colo.: Westview Press, 1998.

Bernstein, Thomas P. 'Starving to Death in China', *New York Review of Books* (16 June), 1983: 36–8.

— 'Stalinism, Famine, and Chinese Peasants', *Theory and Society*, 13/3 (May), 1984: 339–77.

Chan, Alfred L. 'The Campaign for Agricultural Development in the Great Leap Forward: A Study of Policy-making and Implementation in Liaoning', *China Quarterly*, 129 (Mar.), 1992.

— 'Leaders, Coalition Politics, and Policy Formulation in China: The Great Leap Forward Revisited', *Journal of Contemporary China*, 8 (Winter–Spring), 1995.

Joseph, William. 'A Tragedy of Good Intentions: Post-Mao Views of the Great Leap Forward', *Modern China*, 12/4 (October), 1986: 419–57.

Kataoka, Tetsuya. 'Political Theory of the Great Leap Forward'. *Social Research*, 36/1, 1969: 93–112.

Lampton David. 'Health Policy during the Great Leap Forward', *China Quarterly*, 60 (Oct./Dec.), 1974: 668–98.

Lieberthal, Kenneth. 'The Great Leap Forward and the Split in the Yenan Leadership', in Roderick MacFarquhar and John Fairbank (eds.), *The Cambridge History of China*, xiv (Cambridge: Cambridge University Press, 1987).

Lippit, Victor. 'The Great Leap Forward Reconsidered'. *Modern China*, 1/1 (Jan.), 1975: 92–115.

Moody, Peter. 'Policy and Power: The Career of Tao Chu, 1956–66'. *China Quarterly*, 54 (Apr./June), 1973: 267–93.

Schoenhals, Michael. 'Yang Xianzhen's Critique of the Great Leap Forward', *Modern Asian Studies*, 26/3, 1992.

Schram, Stuart. 'Mao Zedong and the Theory of Permanent Revolution, 1958–1969', *China Quarterly*, 46 (April/June), 1971: 221–44.

Shih Chih-yu. 'The Decline of a Moral Regime: China's Great Leap Forward in Retrospect', *Comparative Political Studies*, 27/2 (July), 1994.

Stavis, Ben. 'Ending Famines in China', in Rolando V. Garcia and Jose C. Escudero (eds.), *Drought and Man, The 1972 Case History, ii. The Constant Catastrophe, Malnutrition, Famine, and Drought*. Oxford: Pergamon Press, 1982: 112–39.

Teiwes, Frederick C. ' "Rules of the Game" in Chinese Politics', *Problems of Communism*, 28/5–6 (Sept./Dec.), 1979: 67–76.

— 'Mao and His Lieutenants', *Australian Journal of Chinese Affairs*, 19/20, 1988.

— 'Leaders, Institutions, and the Origins of the Great Leap Forward', *Pacific Affairs*, 66/2 (Summer), 1993.

— 'Mao Text and the Mao of the 1950s', *Australian Journal of Chinese Affairs*, 33, 1995.

Glossary

dan	a unit of weight ($= 50\,\text{kg}$)
dazibao	big-character posters
duohao kuaisheng	more, better, faster, and more economical
fanmaojin	anti-rash advance
'four bigs'	or *sida*, big blooming, big contending, big discussion, and big character posters
'four, five, eight'	projected grain output/*mu* for 1967 as specified in the NPAD: for the areas north of the Huang He, Qingling, and Bailong Jiang, the goal was 400 *jin*; for the areas north of the Huai He, 500 *jin*; and the areas south of the Huang He, Qinling, and Bailong Jiang, 800 *jin*. These targets were often called the '4, 5, and 8'
jin	a unit of weight ($= 0.5\,\text{kg}$)
maojin	rash advance
mu	a unit of area ($= 0.0667$ hectares)
'three-three system'	the division of all farmland into three parts, one for farming, one for planting trees, and one for fallowing
wuxu	use principles and ideology to guide practical work
xiafang	sent downwards, or transferred to lower level, to do manual work in the countryside or in a factory
xiang	village
xiaotuqun	*xiao* (small), *tu* (indigenous), and *qun* (mass)

Note: 'billion' used in text refers to 1,000 million.

Index